The Modern Neighbors of Tutankhamun

The Modern Neighbors of Tutankhamun

History, Life, and Work in the Villages of the Theban West Bank

Kees van der Spek

The American University in Cairo Press
Cairo New York

First published in 2011 by
The American University in Cairo Press
113 Sharia Kasr el Aini, Cairo, Egypt
420 Fifth Avenue, New York, NY 10018
www.aucpress.com

Dar el Kutub No. 2377/10
ISBN 978 977 416 403 3

Dar el Kutub Cataloging-in-Publication Data

van der Spek, Kees
        The Modern Neighbors of Tutankhamun: History, Life, and Work in the Villages of the
    Theban West Bank/ Kees van der Spek. —Cairo: The American University in Cairo Press, 2011
                p.   cm.
                ISBN 978 977 416 403 3
                1. Social Change—Luxor (Egypt)   2. Egypt—Social Conditions   I. Title
                303.49623

1 2 3 4 5 6   14 13 12 11

Designed by Adam el-Sehemy
Printed in Egypt

For Samira, Amira, Mona, and Islam who, now living away from the Mountain, may only have vague future memories of their childhood play among the tombs.

I have not considered it out of place to exhibit . . . the more salient features in the life of the present native villagers—their social position, their habits, occupations, and relation to their rulers. As the reversionary tenants of the tombs which they have converted into dwellings, as active purveyors of antiquities, and as constituting in their capacity of workmen the machinery of excavation, they and their proceedings form a kind of province on the outskirts of Egyptian archaeology. But whatever may be thought of this doubtful claim, it must be a very determined antiquarianism that, even on such a site as that of Thebes, can, under the circumstances, look so exclusively to the past as to close its eyes to the living interests of the present or the prospects of the future.

A. Henry Rhind, 1862: vii–viii

Contents

Illustrations

Tables

Foreword

Kent R. Weeks, Director, Theban Mapping Project

Tourism in Thebes dates back to dynastic times, when Egyptians, for religious and social reasons, visited archaeological sites that even then were ancient. Foreign tourists also came: visitors from the ancient Near East, Greece, and Rome often combined business with pleasure on voyages up the Nile. But it was not until the nineteenth century CE that tourism became a business, and Europeans made Thebes (modern Luxor) a popular destination. Tourist numbers remained relatively unchanged for almost a century, but in the 1960s their numbers rose, due partly to publicity generated by traveling Tutankhamun exhibits, a plethora of books and films emphasizing Egypt's so-called mysterious past, and the advent of cheap air travel.

Today, tourism accounts for over 50 percent of Egypt's foreign income, generating billions of dollars, and employing thousands of people. The two most-visited archaeological areas are Giza and Luxor. During the 2009–2010 financial year, Luxor's monuments were visited by over eight thousand persons each day, about three million a year, from over a hundred foreign countries. Most came with cheap, packaged group tours, spending a few hectic days in Luxor before moving on.

Given its economic importance, the Egyptian government works hard to encourage more tourists to visit. The Ministry of Tourism has expressed the hope that visitor numbers to Luxor's archaeological sites will double by 2015, reaching sixteen thousand a day or more. Many government agencies vie among one another for control of the money tourists leave behind and for control of how and where that money is spent. (Only a small amount is used to train antiquities staff and preserve and protect the monuments without which archaeological tourism would wither and die. It is bureaucrats, not archaeologists or conservators, who make the financial decisions.)

High priority has been given by the government to developing Luxor's infrastructure to accommodate greater numbers of tourists. Wider roads and parking areas to house tour buses, broad promenades lined with ever-larger hotels and tourist bazaars, new harbors and larger airports, are under construction. More monuments are being opened to the public. Travel itineraries, charges for tickets, and rules controlling tourist movements are constantly being re-designed to encourage more tourists to spend more money in less time.

Such schemes are not easy to implement. Over a dozen major development plans have been commissioned in the last two decades, but only the most recent, published in 1999, has been acted upon, and thanks to the active support of Luxor's governor and Egypt's prime minister, an army of workmen is currently involved in its rapid implementation. The work is based upon a "Comprehensive Development Plan for the City of Luxor, Egypt," prepared by an international consulting firm hired by Egypt's Ministry of Housing, Utilities and Urban Communities. Work on the proposal began in 2007 and is set to be completed by 2017. The plan's primary emphasis is Luxor City, on the Nile's East Bank, and whole areas of the town are being leveled and their families moved to new communities in the desert to make room for more tourists. Simultaneously, additional development plans, largely the work of the Luxor City Council with the acquiescence of the Supreme Council of Antiquities but with no outside consultation, were devised for the West Bank. The plans include new roads, parking areas, cafeterias, interpretive centers, and the removal of much of the local population.

All of these plans reflect the government's often-stated goal: to make Greater Luxor, both East Bank and West, an open-air, archaeological museum. Many believe that this is resulting in the Disneyfication of Luxor, the suppression or physical removal of its indigenous people and their culture, and the creation of an artificial Ancient Egypt Land whose appearance owes more to Hollywood than to historical veracity.

A major part of the government plan, which had first been proposed in the 1940s, was the demolition of the West Bank village of Qurna. Here, on a hillside dotted with dynastic tombs, groups of Bedouin Arabs settled several centuries ago among the remnants of an earlier Coptic Christian community. As tourism grew in the nineteenth century CE, these people supplied the antiquities trade by selling items they removed from the tombs to visiting foreigners. Ostensibly, the government's goal of demolition was to protect the ancient tombs from the modern illicit trade in antiquities. In fact, the removal of Qurna's houses in 2007–2010 did more damage to the archaeology of the place than the local villagers had ever done, and in any case, most of the damage they caused had ended decades ago. The modern, government-authorized demolition destroyed buildings that, under Egyptian law, were themselves historical monuments; it demolished walls painted with contemporary hajj pilgrimage scenes unique to the area, paintings so highly regarded they were the subject of several foreign museum exhibits; and it left behind broken tomb entrances and shattered stelae and jumbled heaps of dynastic Egyptian cultural remains. The hillside of Qurna today resembles a bombed-out war zone. It is unclear when it will be cleaned or what tourist attractions will replace Qurna's houses.

And its people? They have been moved to new villages several kilometers away, left to make new lives for themselves so that this open-air museum can be cleansed of modernity (except that which is tourist-related) and restored to its imagined past glory.

This book traces the history of Qurna and the Qurnawi who lived there. Theirs is a story as much a part of Thebes as its tombs and temples. They have been antiquities sellers, tour guides, dealers in fake scarabs and statuettes, artisans, and for a century they have worked for archaeological projects. My late wife, Susan, and I have spent over forty years living in Luxor, and we know many Qurnawi well. Scores of them have worked with us over the decades—in some cases, we've employed five generations of the same families. They have been as much a part of our lives as the monuments we worked together to clean, record, and publish, and their interest in Luxor's past is as great as our own.

What has happened to their village, their society, and their lives makes for fascinating reading. But it is depressing. Kees van der Spek's study of the Qurnawi, their close ties to Egyptology, and the effects that bureaucrats who believe theme park tourism will be the answer to Egypt's economic problems have had on their lives, offer an important lesson for anyone concerned with protecting humankind's patrimony and planning for Egypt's future. It is also an introduction to a most remarkable culture and a fascinating people who face difficult odds.

Acknowledgments
and an Invitation

This book is based on anthropological fieldwork carried out among the people of al-Qurna in the foothills and plains of the Theban Necropolis on the west bank of the Nile at Luxor between 1997 and 1999. Study of the villagers inhabiting the archaeological zone of the Theban west bank proved timely indeed: relocation plans that had been conceived as early as the mid-1940s were finally implemented with a measure of finality during 2006–07. Local villagers were removed from the Tombs of the Nobles area and their hamlets demolished, thereby severing the particular connection with the archaeological landscape that had been a defining element in their historical and social identity. This book, and the original doctoral dissertation on which it is based, represents a first and only attempt at creating a comprehensive record and wide-ranging account of life in this particular environment. Given the most recent developments, which have seen the Theban Necropolis returned to its tombs and their owners, it is also a final record, at least where contemporary life in the necropolis itself is concerned.

The networks of entangled relations which underpin and inform a study of this scope cannot but fail to be adequately expressed in a few lines of acknowledgment. Of course, the phenomenon of mostly one-sided relations of indebtedness is inherent in the position of the anthropologist, who by virtue of his or her involvement with a community during fieldwork may incur much that cannot be repaid in means both adequate and meaningful to the members of the community under study.

In the case of al-Qurna, this may not altogether apply, as the economic benefit of academic inquiry in some form or other has always been an integral part of its economic history, as this book demonstrates, and Qurnawi therefore have benefited from this particular research also. Involvement with academic fieldworkers and tourists drawn by the findings of archaeological research is an economic reality for Qurnawi on which they capitalize as best they can and according to circumstance. For Qurnawi, there are no remaining debts at the end of this, only friendly relations with foreigners that may continue through the years; but these, too, are a way of making ends meet.

Yet, as an anthropological fieldworker, I want to acknowledge my many intangible and emotional debts to Qurnawi, who offered a place within the family, extended hospitality, allowed access to their households, provided insights into their various occupational specializations, and who for the most part readily answered many questions, even if later consensus suggested that not all responses were always reliable, and that a particular slant was likely as not one of the local strategies to keep visitors 'happy,' in the hope of guaranteeing their future return. Without naming them individually, I want to here thank them all. Notwithstanding the at times economic connotations, I felt a true and accepted member of my host families with whom a real bond was forged, not least because of our shared personal experience of the dark days following the tragic event of November 17, 1997. On some deep personal level do I know that bond to be mutual. With Vivant Denon, I can say that al-Qurna was "a place where I was very well off in every respect, living in perfect harmony with the inhabitants" (1803, 3: 87) and I am content in the knowledge that for me al-Qurna is indeed *baladi*, my place in rural Upper Egypt.

As my very presence on the Theban west bank also demonstrated al-Qurna's particular connections with historically situated global processes, so my other debts extend to organizations and individuals who have accompanied me on my journey, and they, too, are global in scope. The early stages of fieldwork in Cairo during 1997 fortuitously benefited from the cultural festival *Old and New Qurna—Treasures Under Siege*, a three-month-long series of cultural events—lectures and exhibitions of photographs, paintings, artifacts—organized by Ms. Nawal Hassan of the Center for Egyptian Civilization Studies in Cairo. The various events of the festival provided opportunities to meet with people who in some capacity or other had been involved with the inhabitants of the foothills hamlets, or with aspects of the administrative and planning process associated with the design of the new settlements.

These initial contacts developed into a network of informants who at various layers of private, public, academic, and corporate involvement played a part in the range of issues particular to the Theban Necropolis and its modern-day occupants. These included, in no particular order: architects and engineers of Engineering Systems and Consultants (ESC), tasked during 1992–94 with the original design of the new settlement and its contracted urban planning and social survey consultants, both Egyptian and expatriate; the Faculty of Engineering at Helwan University, during 1997 still tasked with finalizing the ESC architectural and urban planning designs and overseeing the implementation of the various construction phases of the new settlement; the ministry of Housing, Utilities, and Urban Communities (MHUUC), responsible for the Comprehensive Development of the City of Luxor project (CDCL), partly funded by the United Nations Development Programme (UNDP); the American consulting firm Abt Associates Inc. contracted by UNDP and MHUUC for the urban planning designs of CDCL; the Luxor City Council Information Office; the Luxor City Council Engineering Department; the Egyptian firm Usman Ahmad Usman Arab Contractors working on the site preparation of the new settlement; the Egyptian Cartographic Survey offices in Luxor and Cairo; *al-Ahram* newspaper; the American Research Center in Egypt (ARCE), Cairo; the Oriental Institute of the University of Chicago and 'Chicago House,' its base in Luxor; the Theban Mapping Project of the American University in Cairo; the Department of History of the American University in Cairo; the University of Cambridge Theban Mission; the director of antiquities responsible for the Luxor west bank; the secretary general and staff of the Supreme Council of Antiquities in Cairo; United Nations Educational, Scientific and Cultural Organization (UNESCO), Cairo; UNESCO and the World Heritage Bureau, Paris; the International Council on Monuments and Sites (ICOMOS), Paris; the Bodleian Library, the University of Oxford; and the Griffith Institute, the University of Oxford.

I have previously named the many individuals associated with these bodies, and many other significant individuals who provided support during the original research, analysis, and thesis writing, both professional and personal (Van der Spek, 2004). I will not list them all here, other than to thank them collectively. There are, however, those whom I will want to mention specifically. For, as Sir John Gardner Wilkinson, Edward William Lane, Robert Hay, and Joseph Bonomi in the past, to name just a few, there are indeed other 'travelers' who have al-Qurna as their center, still. The above list of institutions and organizations will include many individual contributors for whom this holds true. In my case, and beyond those who have contributed professionally, there may be many for whom their association with the Theban foothills only extends to personal support and encouragement provided to my family during my lengthy fieldwork absences. Whether they were aware of it or not, their lives have become tied up with the concerns of one who viewed al-Qurna as a place that merited some special interest. In that sense we have all become 'travelers' and I want to mention here some of the many whom I encountered along the way, providing both professional support and encouragement of one kind or another:

Ahmad Nuzahy Abbas Ahmad, Magdi Ali, Naguib Amin, 'Madame' Amira, Yusuf Andraus, Raewyn Arthur, Asheraf Bakr, Natasha Baron, Laila Barsum, Jennifer Beattie, Muhammad al-Bialy, Joseph Norment Bell, Giovanni Boccardi, Jens Boel, André Chappot, Rachida Chih, David and Helen Cunningham, Deborah Darnell, Steve and Judy Dawson, Diaa el-Din Ibrahim Muhammad, Peter Dorman, Neil and Christine Dwyer, Francis Dzikowski, Aayko Eymaa, Sarah Flynn, Hussein Fou'ad, Gaballa Ali Gaballa, Sandrine Gamblin, Mahmud Ghander, Gayle Gibson, Lawrence Glynn, Matthew Gray, Chris Gregory, Patrick Guiness, Nilgün Gümüs, Alan and Wendy Hahn, Sherif Mahmud al-Hakim, Nicole Hansen, Colin Harris, Stuart Harris, Stephen Harvey, Nawal Hassan, Kjersti Håvardstun, Kamal Fahmy Husseen, Richard Hornsby, Lindsay and Helen Jacobs, Jennifer Jaeger, T.G.H. James, John Jarvis, Chuck Jones, Annie Koole, Karin and Ian Laird, Carol Laslett, Lori Lawson, Ines Librachi, William Logan, Sarah Loza, Søren Lund, Marcel and Monica Maessen, Toni Makkai, Jaromír Málek; Ahmad Ma'uad, Nader Matter, Abdu Menim, Lynn Meskell, Demetrios Michaelides, Lawrence Mielniczuk, Elizabeth Miles, Tim Mitchell, Magid Mosleh, Muhammad Nasr, Karen Newton, Kirill Nourzhanov, Boyo Ockinga, Wayne O'Donohoe, Pia Ohlsson, David Purcell, Abdu Rahman, Ahmad Rashed, Amin Saikal, Derk Schneemann, Kieran and Ondina Schneemann, Rudi and Sheelagh Schneemann, Caroline Simpson, David Sims, Florian Stelter, Nigel Strudwick, Ibrahim Suliman, Jan Tankiang, Ahmad Tayyeb, Shaykh Muhammad Tayyeb, Jason Thompson, Sarah Titchen, Gaby, Marieke, Sarah, Stephanie, Christopher, and Brendan van der Spek, Boutros Wadi, Kent Weeks, Michael Welbank, Terry Wilfong, Georges Zouain, Muhammad Zughayyar.

Among the above, there are several traveling companions who must rate a special mention, not least of whom is Caroline Simpson who has been a good friend, colleague and a faithful respondent for many years. In Cairo, she introduced me to many important contacts and in al-Qurna to many of her friends and acquaintances there. She offered me hospitality in London, and her support during all these years has been both encouraging and practical. Limitations imposed by the 'tyranny of distance' at times made Australia an unlikely place for a study of this kind, and Caroline has freely shared her British Library reading notes for a number of important historical sources. Importantly, she taught me how to 'read' the larger west bank necropolis landscape, imagining it as it was when early European travelers first walked there and understanding the significance of its particular topographical features and its built fabric. Her tremendous energy and perceptive insights into Qurnawi society have been a great inspiration to me. Half joking, half in earnest, we sometimes commented how we intended not to be like Robert Hay, who never worked on his al-Qurna material upon returning to England in 1834 and whose unpublished papers still await comprehensive study in the British Library. The publication of this contribution to Qurnawi studies arguably fulfils my side of that pact, but it has been equally matched by Caroline's achievements, which I want to acknowledge here also.

The founder, secretary, and driving force behind the Qurna History Project (http://www.qurna.org) and the Qurna Discovery initiative, Caroline has been a tireless advocate for Qurnawi culture and society. She lobbied UNESCO and the Supreme Council of Antiquities for the preservation of the village before it was demolished. She selected and arranged permissions from high-level government officials for a small cluster of significant properties to be preserved when the initial large-scale demolitions commenced. She organized the restoration of these dwellings with the use of local labor before these, too, following a change of heart by the same government officials, were demolished in May 2010. Additionally, Caroline continues to generate interest in al-Qurna. She has managed exhibitions in England, Cairo, al-Qurna, and at international conferences that focus on Egyptian history and vernacular earthen architecture. She has published selected articles on the history of Qurna and has arranged, in association with the British Library, displays in Qurna of copies of the Robert Hay panoramas, partly to make visiting tourists aware of the modern history of the surrounding necropolis but also with the aim of showing Qurnawi part of their own history. Through Qurna Discovery (2001–2010), its Friends of Qurna Discovery organization (2007–2010), and the Qurna History Project newsletters, Caroline advocates the need for a Qurna Studies Center and disseminates ideas for further work, including much-needed oral-historical research among Qurnawi, which is vital before its elderly people with knowledge of pre-modern ways have all passed on. The many questions she has raised and issues for consideration she has identified could drive a dedicated research program for some time to come.

Traveling closely by my side but in a different way I must make mention of Sheelagh Schneemann, who made my first visit to Qurna in 1995 possible; and to Gaby and our five children for whom, since 1995, Egypt, Qurna, and the names of several individual Qurnawi have become household names, even though their collective connotation will have been one of ambivalence for them. For Marieke, Sarah, Stephanie, Christopher, and Brendan much of their own educational career has unfolded alongside Dad's study of things Egyptian, which for them meant that he was often less than available. I acknowledge and am grateful for the sacrifices they all have made and hope that in their adult lives each of them may recognize the certain benefit for their own intellectual development that these years of research and writing have been: that intangible aspect of being a member of a family where study was actively role-modeled and where the culture of the family was one that advocated learning. There is not much I can do or say to wipe away for Gaby the memory of my lengthy absences: physical during fieldwork and mental—only separated by a closed door but in fact a world away—during the analysis and writing process; or make for these years of loneliness, the 'single' parenting, and all the hard work my preoccupations put her through. All I can say is that also through her selfless support and dedication it has finally been possible to document something of the history and life of the Theban west bank communities and that some Qurnawi who are now but children—and to whom this book is dedicated—may ever be grateful to her for that.

Other than the general fieldwork support offered by foreign archaeological missions or individual Egyptologists already acknowledged, I have previously refrained from further identifying those members of foreign archaeological missions to the Theban Necropolis who were kind enough to respond to my mailed and emailed questionnaires, and I will again do so here. I understand that their working relationship with the Supreme Council of Antiquities may at the best of times be delicate and in order to safeguard their own standing with the Egyptian authorities, I will not further reveal their identities. It is also for this reason that I have not been able to credit them for the quotations taken from their individual personal or written statements, but it is here that I do collectively acknowledge them. Those who did not respond, and those who responded—at times antagonistically so—in the briefest fashion, I thank them too, as their self-protective reluctance to participate does tell a story—here only alluded to of but largely untold—of the politics of archaeological fieldwork in contemporary Egypt.

Given the professional scope of many of the relevant individuals who have contributed information or support during the original research, and al-Qurna being what it is, the inescapable interdisciplinary perspective of my work may for many be problematic from the perspective of their individual specializations and they may question the relevance of specific facets within the totality of the 'package' presented here. For some, and in places, its final form may still be 'foreign territory,' and they may wish I had dealt with the information or advice they provided differently. In the end, what is presented here is an account of the range of historically situated cultural practices and contemporary social concerns that constitute an ethnographic portrayal and understanding of Qurnawi society. I recognize that this portrayal and understanding may well be partial, that they result both from personal interests and a consequent selection of specific foci, and that others might have opted for different choices. Suffice it to say that I have approached al-Qurna as a "province on the outskirts of Egyptian archaeology," to use Henry Rhind's 1862 turn of phrase, and for that choice, and any errors that remain, I accept all responsibility.

Should readers wish to correct any such errors they may detect, or offer any relevant materials (postcards, personally held photographs, paintings, or other graphic representations of Qurna's earthen architecture in all its forms, the identification of sources of photographs or other documentary records, or accounts of personal experiences or work they themselves have undertaken that involved interaction with Qurnawi) to add to the information database and library holdings of a future Qurna Studies Center, then you are invited to email me at kees.vanderspek@ netspeed.com.au or contact me via the publisher.

Some of the materials included in this volume have previously been published elsewhere, either as journal articles or as conference proceedings. I am grateful to the following organizations and publishers for permission to include those materials here: US ICOMOS (Prologue and other selected passages); SAGE and the Journal of Social Archaeology (Chapter 9); and the Oriental Institute of the University of Chicago (Chapter 10).

I also wish to acknowledge the permissions granted by copyright holders for materials used from other sources, including the Griffith Institute, the University of Oxford, for permission to use material from Howard Carter's notebooks; Gorgias Press for permission to use quotations from the writings of Henry Rhind; John and Elizabeth Romer for permission to quote from their 1993 *The Rape of Tutankamun*; the World Heritage Centre in Paris for permission to quote from the 2008 *Report of the Joint World Heritage Centre / ICOMOS Reactive Monitoring Mission to the World Heritage Site of Thebes and its Necropolis*; IFAO, the French Institute of Archaeology in Cairo, for permission to quote from Carla Burri's edited narrative of *The Anonymous Venetian*; the Theban Mapping Project in Cairo, and its director, Dr. Kent Weeks, for permission to use its 1979 aerial photographs, and other copyright holders as indicated. In all other instances where materials were used from other sources, all effort has been made to identify the holders of any existing copyright. Where establishing the existence of copyright or locating its current holders was unsuccessful, these materials have been referenced as appropriate and included in the bibliography, and their use is collectively acknowledged here. Where these were not already available, and where required for Dutch, French, and German quotations, the translations provided are my own. Similarly, and where sources are not otherwise acknowledged, all photographs are my own.

I am most grateful to the Australian National University (ANU) and its Centre for Arab and Islamic Studies (the Middle East and Central Asia) under whose auspices the original study was conducted. In historical terms, it is gratifying to know that the Luxor West Bank Ethnographic Research Project has been a part of the centre's ever-evolving and expanding Middle Eastern study focus and I am grateful to Professor Amin Saikal, the centre's director, for his support over the years. I also wish to acknowledge here Dr. Chris Gregory and Dr. Patrick Guinness in the School of Archaeology and Anthropology in the ANU College of Arts and Social

Sciences, and Dr. Boyo Ockinga of the Australian Centre for Egyptology in the School of History, Philosophy, and Politics, Macquarie University, Sydney, all of whom commented on early dissertation chapters.

Through the generosity of the ANU Vice-Chancellor, Professor Ian Chubb; the Dean of the ANU College of Arts and Social Sciences, Professor Toni Makkai; and the director of the Centre for Arab and Islamic Studies (the Middle East and Central Asia), Professor Amin Saikal, the Australian National University provided me with a post-doctoral grant and practical support that allowed me to take three months' leave from my daytime employment to revise and finalize the manuscript for this book. I am also grateful to the School of Cultural Inquiry in the ANU College of Arts and Social Sciences for their hospitality and for providing me with a 'room with a view,' where I could dedicate myself in all peace to the task at hand.

Finally, I am equally grateful to the American University in Cairo (AUC) and the AUC Press for having seen merit in the original dissertation and for accepting the manuscript derived from it for publication. In their own separate ways, both the Australian National University and the American University in Cairo must be commended for having recognized the intrinsic interest that exists in the interplay between the archaeological landscape and modern indigenous communities. Given the preponderance of the global academy's involvement with the archaeological character of the Theban Necropolis, both the Australian National University and the American University in Cairo occupy a unique position for having allowed illumination of its more recent social character. It is hoped that, following the demolition of the foothills hamlets and the destruction of the Theban Necropolis' social landscape, this illumination will continue to provide some insights into one small but significant facet of Egyptian cultural diversity that has now all but disappeared.

Notes on Transliteration

The system of transliteration used in this book follows the one favored by the American University in Cairo Press.

One of the additional problems that presents itself to a novice in the Arabic language is the fact that, despite now widespread primary and secondary education and literacy campaigns among adults in Upper Egypt, a community such as exists at al-Qurna is still only semiliterate. Especially when dealing with people whose occupation has required no higher levels of education—artisans, lower-level personnel employed by the Supreme Council of Antiquities, and those peddling artifacts to tourists—and whose grasp of Arabic spelling and orthography has been limited to *kuttab* religious education as a youngster, their rendition of such rarely written vernacular terms as *ghubuwa* can only be accepted for what it is. Although the lexicon by Alain Arnaudiès and Wadie Boutros (1996) proved helpful, in the midst of any remaining inconsistencies and outright errors, the ethnographer simply acknowledges his shortcomings in the recognition that in this respect, too, he is content to consider himself Qurnawi and as a (less than) semiliterate person at home among the subjects of his study.

Prologue

A Theban Sound-scape

In so many ways, the muses occupy the landscape. Musical instruments are everywhere, and although out of sight and now mute, there is a truth in suggesting that the landscape of the Theban west bank with its ancient burial grounds is imbued with melody[1]. Harps, lutes, flutes, tambourines, indeed entire orchestras figure prominently in the banquet scenes decorating the ancient Egyptian tomb chapels. The illustration of scenes from the life of a tomb's occupant is both a means to achieve, and a representation of, his aspirations for the afterlife. Essentially secular—accompanying dancing-girls or livening up a dinner party— the presence of these instruments does not suggest that the once freshly painted and newly occupied tombs themselves were cloaked in silence, nor that the rites associated with burial or the subsequent placement of offerings were performed in an atmosphere of quiet respect:[2] ancient funerary ceremonies may have included forms of religious vocal music accompanied by clapping, *sistra*, or harp, similar to temple music (Manniche, 1988: 17).[3]

It was in this City of the Dead where the Theban elite of long ago prepared their decorated tombs. It was here that those who came after them adapted the tombs in ways that suited them best: from secondary burials, to places of early Christian worship and reflection that equally focused on the hereafter, to dwellings for the living beset by the demands of everyday life at al-Qurna, the modern village built inside the necropolis. Commencing with the local villagers and spanning back across the ages, people's movements and sounds across time, both real and imagined, are one of the landscape's typifying features.

1

Sounds of a social landscape: An empty *'arabiya* water cart rattling downhill to the tapped well by the roadside.

Maybe the music never stopped, as suggested by the continuity of religious practice in today's differently interpreted Muslim Theban landscape. Indeed, the musical sounds that may accompany Muslim religious expression in the necropolis include the haunting nighttime melodies and chants of the modern devotional Sufi *dhikr* performed at the annual *mulid* of Shaykh 'Abd al-Qurna, and the other commemorative *dhikr* that regularly punctuate the Theban night sky. As audible yet seemingly timeless elements of local spiritual expression they are not too far removed from the sacred sounds that during pharaonic times similarly came wafting down the hillside from differing points at any given time.

New sounds color the landscape of the necropolis: the sounds of Qurnawi children playing, laughing, crying; the regular call to prayer from the small mosque by the roadside below the tomb of Ramose; the bouncing clatter of the empty oil barrel dancing in the metal frame of a water cart, racing downhill behind its galloping donkey, the practice a result of a heritage management induced absence of running water in the necropolis. Then there is a sound that came to be heard only these past fifty years, generated

Sounds of a social landscape: Children playing, laughing, crying.

intentionally, as if music, yet serving a simple commercial purpose that, like the water cart, resulted from a lack of infrastructure considered inappropriate in this archaeological landscape: the metallic ring of the *butagaz* merchant, audible throughout the foothills hamlets. Reaching behind him from the driver's seat of his donkey cart, or leaving the task to his young assistant sitting on top of the merchandise, he signals his approach by hitting the blue gas cylinders at regular intervals with the adjustable spanner that is the tool of his trade. Depending on proximity, their sound will range from a distant *sistra*-like chime to an ear-splitting clangor. And finally, its intensity seasonally dependent, but their intermittent passing always present, there is the drone of the air-conditioned coaches taking tourists on their way to the Valley of the Kings.

The by-products of certain kinds of activity taking place—traditional village life and international tourism with its associated economic benefits—these sounds became the structuring features that symbolized the way Qurnawi experienced the world. They act as powerful metaphors for the constraints imposed by the differing interests, worldviews, and lifestyles of others and give audible shape—like the funerary processions of old—to one of the defining features of the Theban Necropolis in the twentieth century.

Today, the foothills hamlets and the sounds that characterized the Theban Necropolis as a social and cultural landscape are gone. The yellow, white, and blue walls of the mud-brick houses have disintegrated into clouds of dust and the roaring, exhaust fume–belching bulldozers have departed from this fragile archaeological landscape, taking their insidious vibrations with them. The living have been evicted from their hillside hamlets and the City of the Dead has been returned to its ancient owners, their tomb portraits and musical sensibilities a mute witness to the sounds that were once there. Now there is only silence. . .

Introduction

Fieldwork in the Territory of Others

This book finds its origins in a crime. At least, that is if today's strict Egyptian antiquities legislation, prohibiting the illicit excavation and trade in ancient Egyptian artifacts, were applied to the rich tomb discovered around 1871 by the brothers Muhammad and Ahmad 'Abd al-Rasul in the cliffs above al-Qurna on the Theban west bank. When the discovery was made public in 1881, it became obvious that the 'Abd al-Rasul family had used their find as a 'bank account,' selling off antiquities when in need of funds. As a consequence, the question of how the 'Abd al-Rasuls and their fellow villagers make a living has been an issue of concern in Egyptological circles ever since.

Commonly known as the Theban Necropolis—Thebes' City of the Dead—the west bank cemeteries opposite modern-day Luxor are not just an ancient burial ground. The necropolis—despite its 1979 UNESCO World Heritage listing[4]—has also long been a place for the living. Unlike the archaeologists who uncovered their secret, the 'Abd al-Rasuls were not visitors, but locals. Until the recent demolition of their village and the removal of the community from the ancient cemeteries, the 'Abd al-Rasuls and their descendants inhabited the undulating stretch of foothills that makes up the lower, eastern slope of the Theban Mountain, between the so-called Tombs of the Nobles and below the ridge that on its western side gives access to Egypt's world-famed Valley of the Kings, final resting place of the boy-king Tutankhamun. Their mud-brick houses, either detached or grouped together in clusters that are often family compounds, are dispersed throughout the scattered component hamlets that make up the village of al-Qurna: these are the homes of Qurnawi, the villagers of Qurna,[5] their close proximity indeed making them Tutankhamun's modern neighbors.

Making fruitful use of that proximity by adopting a practical supply and demand labor strategy, for the past two hundred years early treasure seekers, and later professional archaeologists excavating in the necropolis, have recruited their workmen from the surrounding communities. As a consequence, many of the more recent references about Qurna and its people have come from, and are colored by, the professional reports and popularized accounts that result from archaeological fieldwork practice and the popular fiction it has inspired. In all these literary forms, and despite the necessary references to local villagers working on the excavation teams, there is mention of damage to the archaeological monuments, the theft of antiquities, and the illicit excavation and trade in antiquities. Yet, no other incident has contributed more to the common understanding that the people from Qurna are 'tomb robbers' than the 'Abd al-Rasul discovery. This attribution has at once come to define all economic activity in the foothills and represents the extent of any social analysis that might have taken place.

The question all this raises is: How could a social landscape have become subsumed by the interests of a specific academic pursuit—Egyptology—along with its accompanying technical and popular literary genres and the masses of 'Egyptophiles' and tourists following in its wake? The place of local villagers occupying this 'intellectual space' will be discussed in Chapter 1 but suffice it to say here that the scientific and popular interest in the archaeological remains at the expense of the modern village has effectively resulted in nearly everyone denying that the necropolis is also a social environment. This denial fits well with—and is further strengthening popular culture's media-induced stereotypical perceptions about—Egyptological fieldwork practice, which is traditionally assumed to take place in the desert. This perceptual 'desertification' of an essentially social landscape has also had its own impact on, and reinforced long-standing assumptions about, what people should, or rather should not, be doing amid the ancient monuments. At least at a subliminal level, such assumptions have fed into arguments that supported the removal of local communities from the necropolis.

Beyond any impact on antiquities, Egyptologists and practicing field archaeologists have generally displayed no deeper interest in the diversity of local village economics and for a simple reason: the existence of village clusters within the Theban Necropolis fell outside their archaeological focus and warranted little or no professional or even personal interest. Other than being treated as an adjunct to Egyptology, and with the exception of a few mid-nineteenth-century antiquarians (d'Athanasi, 1836; Rhind, 1862), archaeologists typically have not concerned themselves with the cultural specifics of contemporary life in this environment. Thus, the presence, history, and cultural detail of the surrounding social landscape were rendered effectively invisible through the dominance of a western academic discipline imposing its own practice and legitimacy. Consequently, and beyond cursory acknowledgments in the archaeological reports of the employment of local workmen and beyond the persistent allegations of illicit antiquities dealings in popular and fictional archaeological writings, little published information exists that focuses on Qurnawi.[6]

The absence of appropriate representation of the surrounding social landscape in both academic and popular Egyptological writing continues to perpetuate ideas about the alleged destructive impact of resident communities on the archaeological landscape and the denial of all other forms of social expression—including local economic practices—within the Theban Necropolis. The process is a circular one and assures the continuing dominance of an academic and popular archaeological understanding of al-Qurna over broader contemporary social perspectives. We may refer to this process as 'the 'Abd al-Rasul archetype.' In practical terms, this has contributed to the view that the presence of a contemporary community inside the Theban Necropolis was and is perceived as contrary to Egyptological research and conservation (and therefore tourism) objectives. As a result it also became, as we will see, an inherently political issue for Egyptologists, heritage managers, and government officials.

If the above suggests that archaeological practice and its accompanying literature hold negative views about population groups inhabiting archaeological sites, then Egyptologists themselves, both professionally and at a personal level, will question the right of residence of a community in an archaeological landscape. Arguments about their impact on surrounding antiquities will range from concerns about the stability and preservation of the monuments, to vandalism and villagers' involvement in illicit antiquities dealings—activities that are now codified in Egyptian law as illegal. Yet, Egyptologists' antiquities-focused arguments may only be valid up to a point for they ignore that, irrespective of whether an activity is legal or illegal, any individual or group action is grounded in the existence and worldview of a particular social and cultural formation. The economic and political dynamics that flow from the distinctive qualities of the surrounding archaeological landscape and the particular responses of local residents to that landscape over time will be formative elements in the crystallization of a particular cultural identity. As such, the cultural manifestations of contemporary life in an archaeological landscape are simply the most recently deposited artifacts to be found in the archaeological stratigraphy and can equally be the subject of study. There are therefore not too many differences between the objectives of the archaeologist and the social anthropologist when unraveling aspects of that cultural identity, and only relative time and trench depth keep them apart.

Obviously, this is an over-simplification of real demarcations that exist between the two disciplines. The presence of a social anthropologist in the necropolis may in fact be a contested one, as a research emphasis on contemporary social realities in that environment may go against the grain of those who believe that only the archaeological perspective has legitimacy. Indeed, Egyptologists will generally agree that contemporary village life inside the Theban Necropolis must be considered ephemeral when compared with the moral duty to preserve heritage features of 'outstanding universal value'[7] for future generations.[8]

But despite the professional demarcation that separates archaeologists and social anthropologists working in the Theban Necropolis, a study of the contemporary community living in this location is not irreconcilable because of the defining distinctions that exist between the two disciplines. On the contrary, specific social science perspectives can be identified that establish the connections and entangled relations between the two fields of inquiry, moving beyond the mutually exclusive differences otherwise inherent in the objectives to which either discipline subscribes.

For one thing, the community of al-Qurna represents a case study of the influence of a specific form of western presence on an indigenous community. West bank communities were much affected by the emergence of European antiquarian interests, and the crystallization of the community of Qurnawi was in many respects a direct outcome of this historical process. For virtually all Qurnawi, this interrelationship continues to exist, whether it be through direct involvement with archaeologists and tourists in the context of certain economic practices, through local spending power that benefits agricultural producers and other service providers without direct access to or contact with foreigners, or whether it be through those whose lifestyle is still closely defined by a personal aversion toward anything that has to do with *khawaja*, the foreigners.

Said another way, local interactions with academic archaeological practice and its attendant visitor-interest are important factors in the lives of Qurnawi, and in two of the following chapters the detail of Egyptological research-induced Qurnawi labor relations and the production of tourist art, which together underpin much of this interaction, will be discussed. However, these relations cannot be separated from the mix of formal and informal economic activities that also enable people to make a living in this environment. In articulating this mix, this book seeks to fill the gap that exists between narrow Egyptological representations and a wider social reality, and to serve as a corrective to the archaeological and fictional literary genres by providing a rather more ethnographic account of life as it existed in the Noble Tombs area of the Theban west bank.

Also, there is no doubt that Qurnawi presence has been of great importance for the archaeological history of the site, which in turn embodies much of the history of Egyptology as an academic discipline. In that sense, this book documents aspects of the social environment against the background of which archaeological research here has been and is being conducted, thus offering perspectives on Egyptological history and practice and representing a social-archaeological approach that reflects on both the Egyptological and the anthropological aspects of the surrounding landscape.

Although the story of the 'Abd al-Rasuls represents one aspect of that history, the above introduction of 'the 'Abd al-Rasul archetype' was to suggest that the treatment of their discovery in Egyptology-focused writing came at the expense of a broader understanding of the social environment in which the 'Abd al-Rasuls worked and lived, and to counter the reality that there exists little published information about the necropolis' social landscape. It is therefore appropriate to take the 'Abd al-Rasul family as a starting point here, not to focus on their role in archaeological history but to establish a balance with respect to the environment of the necropolis that also does justice to its social character.

The objective of the following chapters, and indeed the original motivation to conduct social anthropological research in the Theban

Necropolis in the first place, is to restore a degree of visibility to the local, social, historic, and contemporary landscape of the Theban Necropolis. But the intention here is not to offer a full description of life in the foothills for its own sake as if to rectify the shortcomings of other observers. Also, other ethnographic studies have already provided fine records of the detail of village life in rural Upper Egypt (Henein, 1988; Hivernel, 1996). This does not mean, however, that there is nothing that can be said about social or cultural issues that fall outside the purview of Qurnawi involvement in archaeology. Emphasizing archaeology-induced social characteristics or foci at the expense of more generic features of Upper Egyptian village life carries its own risk of mystification, and may result in the imposition of an externally conceived identity that will not be recognized or accepted by at least a segment of the community. Even so, at times it is difficult in al-Qurna to draw clear boundaries, and the inclusion or exclusion of specific analytical foci will only work up to a point: farming, spiritual perceptions and religious beliefs, other cultural manifestations, or aspects of everyday life that are seemingly distinct from the archaeological surroundings, will still in sometimes unexpected and seemingly contradictory ways connect with the specific locality that the necropolis represents. These connections enhance the distinct nature of life in this unique environment, and the ethnographic descriptions that follow will articulate some of these.

Nevertheless, the focus is on those characteristics that render al-Qurna distinct from other Upper Egyptian rural communities. Thus, life in the Theban foothills is approached from that perspective that has typically been most closely associated with it, namely its archaeological surroundings, and aims to offer insights into the history of and the web of entangled relations with the archaeological landscape in which village life takes place. As indicated by Reid (1997: 139–40), in the case of al-Qurna it can hardly be otherwise. Considering the time depth of western academic presence here and the ongoing involvement of Qurnawi in excavation work, heritage preservation, and tourism-oriented activities, in addition to the impact that the monuments in various ways and means continue to exert on the local population, al-Qurna's spatial and social archaeological context is too defining a characteristic of Qurnawi society to be ignored.[9] In balancing 'the 'Abd al-Rasul archetype,' then, the ethnographic material gathered here counters the perception that at al-Qurna there exists a singular illicit economic activity: tomb robbing. It offers in its place a plurality of subsistence practices that are, furthermore, carried out as part of the rich social tapestry that also exists in this 'City of the Dead.'

But a comprehensive study of Qurnawi society requires a focus that goes beyond both ideas about tomb robbing and the immediacy of contemporary daily economic practices and strategies. Life and work in the villages of the Theban west bank are equally informed by the intersecting trajectories of past historical circumstance and contemporary political reality: Egyptological and heritage management concerns for the preservation of the archaeological zone and their entangled and at times negative relations with a resident community, and the political and economic interests of the modern Egyptian nation-state that directly or indirectly affect the lives of Qurnawi. Despite the focus on history and ethnography, elements of all these facets are to be found in this book, for it is within the interstitial spaces of these spheres of influence that Qurnawi live their lives: their boundaries either conceptual or material, but ever present and in close proximity, both confining and defining, always effective, and always affecting resident villagers in one way or another.

To structure these themes, the book is constructed into two conceptual parts. The first part is represented by Chapters 1 to 6, where the geographical, historical, archaeological, and architectural setting of al-Qurna will be established, and its confusing and contradictory naming-conventions clarified. Accounts from a selection of early western travelers in Egypt are used to construct a historical ethnography, demonstrating the emergence of local environment-dependent economic practices that were reliant on the use of the necropolis' archaeological remains and that caused Qurnawi subsistence to at least in part differentiate itself from that of surrounding communities. This section concludes with a description of the development and specific forms of the vernacular architectural environment inside the necropolis, providing the context for and the physical spaces of Qurnawi social life to be discussed in subsequent chapters.

The second part consists of Chapters 7 to 11, which explore the social and economic realities of contemporary life in the Theban Necropolis, commencing with a broad discussion of Qurnawi social structure, including agricultural activity, conflict, and the traditional dispute settlement mechanism, followed by a discussion of the structuring feature of social cohesion. This social matrix situates those other aspects of life at al-Qurna that maintain close connections not only with much of the community's history but also with the contemporary archaeological character of the area: employment, art and craft production, and certain traditional beliefs that draw on the surrounding archaeological monuments. A final chapter documents some of the more recent developments that have resulted in the relocation of Qurnawi to several new settlements and the demolition of the built vernacular environment of the necropolis.

Collectively, and to the extent that these chapters explore particular social practices at the experiential level of a contemporary non-western community using anthropological fieldwork methodologies, this book claims to pursue anthropological objectives. However, its scope and style is not limited to strict or, following Clifford Geertz (1973), simply 'thick' ethnographic description, but is significantly interwoven with historical, archaeological, political, and economic factors. If this multiplicity of themes seems bewildering, then they are also inherent in the approach adopted by Eric Wolf, whose ideas of an historically informed anthropological political economy (Wolf, 1982) can be said to have inspired to a degree the approach taken here. In any case, the themes identified above are reflective of the 'on the ground' issues, complexities, tensions, and concerns as experienced by the villagers of the Theban foothills communities on a day-to-day basis, and in this sense, too, they provide a glimpse of modern life in the ancient cemeteries of the Theban west bank.

If this treatment indeed restores the degree of visibility of the Theban Necropolis social landscape, then there is currently a great need for that, and for several reasons. Importantly, following the relocation of Qurnawi, the demolition of their houses and the loss of much that was historically and culturally significant, a narrative that integrates both historical and social elements must be a first objective. This requires moving beyond the sparse detail of archaeological labor relations contained in technical reports and university archives, and the stereotypical references to illegal activities contained in the wider Egyptological literature. Any 'deep' visibility of community life only exists in fragmentary form and is to be found mainly in the writings of early travelers to Upper Egypt. A variety of disparate historical materials is pulled together here in order to integrate the social landscape of the necropolis into its own remnant 'ethnographic history.' In the absence of a more comprehensive history of the Theban west bank communities, this is possibly all that can be achieved, given the recent tourism development–driven destruction of the historical period's archaeological stratigraphy in and around Luxor.

Despite much of the present tense in the following narrative, it is of crucial importance that the reader keep in mind that the social life as it played itself out in the archaeological surroundings of the ancient cemetery, now—and largely due to those same tourism development plans—no longer exists. It exists to the extent that it still can in the new settlements several kilometers to the north of the Theban Mountain. But following the relocation of Qurnawi away from the foothills and the immediate environment of the tombs, something unique was lost. What that is cannot be adequately or comprehensively captured in one term, but its component elements are precisely those that made the Theban Necropolis more than the archaeological landscape with which most had come to identify it: a holistically conceived cultural landscape of value for its combined archaeological, historical, architectural, and social significance.[10]

Some of the component elements that make up these categories will be further unpacked in the following chapters. Short of offering a comprehensive list, these may be seen to relate to the place of Qurna "in the collective memory of modern Egypt" (Hassan, 1997) and include such elements as the history of adaptive reuse of an archaeological landscape; the site-specific character of human landscape use, both in terms of the ancient cemeteries and in the unique settlement pattern of more recent date; the history of the development of Egyptological practice in this environment; the distinctive quality and continuing appeal of the foothills vernacular and rural forms,[11] both architectural and social, and the cultural practices associated with them; their representation in modern Egyptian painting; the connections with the philosophy of Hassan Fathy's New Qurna concept and its place in modern global architecture (Fathy, 1963, 1973; Steele, 1997); the quality and variety of modern Qurnawi artisanal production; and the important facets of Egyptian cultural diversity that are inherent in all these historic, vernacular architectural, and social characteristics. Collectively, they stand in stark contrast to the cultural homogenization that will result from relocation to new purpose-built settlements.

Thus, and to the extent that it can, this account is akin to the sort of 'salvage archaeology' for which Egypt is also famous,[12] by offering a narrative that establishes both the history and some of the cultural specifics of a localized community before cultural homogenization resulting from government development plans and associated modernizing trends take effect. Beyond the more technical analyses of archaeological field reports and anthropological ethnographies, this is indeed one way of remembering Qurna, for Qurnawi and visitors alike.

In terms of the latter, it remains true for the most part that it is because of the *archaeological* attraction of the Theban Necropolis rather than its *people* that anyone visiting should come there in the first place. In fact, anecdotal evidence suggests that visitors in pursuit of their intellectual cravings for ancient Egypt generally had little or no knowledge of a community living inside the archaeological zone of the Theban west bank and in such close proximity to the tombs. But once accustomed to the idea, many visitors have come to take an interest and become enamored by local contemporary culture. Acquaintance of a personal nature would always have been restricted to unfettered individuals rather than to tour guide–driven and itinerary-bound groups. Such contact was primarily initiated by the villagers themselves, for whom offering hospitality fell happily within the repertoire of economic strategies, inviting foreigners into their nearby homes to drink tea and watch the women in the household bake their traditional bread. For the tourists concerned, such hospitality will have added a refreshing and memorable experience to a mostly exhausting archaeological itinerary, but in most cases would nevertheless for lack of time or training have provided little real insight beyond the literal gaze offered by such a cultural encounter. For others, these initial encounters indeed evolved into longer-term relationships of one kind or another, nurtured by periodic return visits and possibly resulting in intimate relations or business partnerships. Today, those returning visitors who had such previous exposure to the necropolis' social landscape and were charmed by it, will experience the denuded foothills with an acute sense of loss.

For future first-time visitors there will be no such thing, since most of them are unlikely to have prior knowledge of the vibrant social environment that once existed there. The naked landscape disguises that this was also the site of a village where people lived and loved, where women gave birth and people died, where some of the women's ancient mourning rituals they will soon see depicted in the tomb of Ramose were still practiced here in real life, and where daily life incorporated elements of material culture and social practice that added measurably to Egypt's surviving rural and pre-modern cultural diversity. What instead awaits visitors is a wall-enclosed open-air museum where they are greeted not by girls in colorful dresses offering for sale their homemade *'arusa* rag dolls, but by a deserted hillside moonscape only. In the absence of any interpretive signage,[13] these pages may go some small way toward filling a need for those who realize that they have arrived too late to observe the social and cultural landscape of the Theban Necropolis for themselves.

Given the certainty of ongoing social change in the new communities and of greater importance than the real or perceived needs of any future visitor, the objective here is also to document aspects of life as it used to exist in the Theban Necropolis as a way of remembering Qurna for Qurnawi themselves. Furthermore, to provide some context to their most recent history and—given the politicized environment in which Qurnawi live—to provide an honest voice for those who had neither voice nor power to affect their own destiny in significant ways, it is for this reason, and in addition to the more general discussion in the first chapter, that the concluding chapter identifies—sometimes critically so—the significant political stakeholders who direct and continue to affect Qurnawi lives. Before we eventually get to that point, we must first turn to an event that deeply affected the Theban west bank, as a point of entry into the lives of Qurnawi when they still occupied the hamlets of the Theban foothills.

1

Ancient Remains as Life's Stage: Differing Perspectives on Life in the Theban Necropolis

A glittering wrapper . . .

The gold and silver colored wrappers of the sweets offered to newly arriving visitors seemed to complement the monotone colors of the mud-brick room, the clinical blue wash of its walls combined with such wrapper-emitted sparkles as to produce a hospital-like atmosphere. Extinguished the moment the shiny paper was crushed and tossed into a corner, its short-lived effect was nevertheless only illusory, for monitoring Mahmud's condition there was no bedside state-of-the-art equipment here to reflect a ward's bright lights, and no sterile glazed tiles to cover the dust of worn adobe.[1] Creating realities out of their absence, as illusions invariably do, the infection that took hold over the next several weeks became so bad that by the end of the fourth week Mahmud had been repatriated to the intensive care ward of Maadi Military Hospital in Cairo.

Those first sparkling sweets of Arab hospitality and Mahmud's worsening condition are suggestive of a scenario that, on the surface, could have played itself out in any of the Nile Valley's mud-brick villages where a sick man was being nursed at home and attended to by his friends. What made Mahmud's case rather different was due to the location of his village, al-Qurna.

For the above scene does not simply allude to respect for a long-honored neighborly duty of visiting the sick, and the tea, sweets, and cigarettes elements of Arab hospitality bestowed upon the visitors in response. It also paints a scene in the life of a village community that is located in the middle of an ancient Egyptian cemetery famed for its priceless artworks, situated at the center of international Egyptological research, effectively the heartland of the Egyptian tourism industry, and

17

now being confronted by the excesses of militant Islam pursuing its ideals of an Islamic state, which it seeks to establish by undermining the national government's revenue base, of which international tourism forms an important part.

The trauma of having seen fifty-eight foreign tourists and four villagers gunned to death and mutilated by Islamist militants in a temple that lies at the geographical center of the village[2] had affected the entire community of Qurnawi. Mahmud's household was a showcase for a people trying to get on with their lives in the aftermath of a massacre, in some respects more so than other local families. Situated along the highest perimeter of the village and in closest proximity to the temple—visible when standing on top of the hillock behind the house—recollections of what transpired there could never be far away. Yet, for Badawi, Mahmud's older brother and head of the extended family household, preoccupations with the incident were beyond mere spatial considerations. Reduced to tears out of concern for his brother who as a temple guard was shot when confronting the assailants, Badawi confided during the occasional private moment how he had to sell or pawn the few assets he owned to finance his family's visits to Cairo as well as to finance a month's stay for himself there in order to keep his injured brother company. In addition, upon hearing the news of her husband's shooting, Mahmud's wife had gone into early labor, and was experiencing medical complications. Beyond the immediacy of these unexpected expenses, being among the poorer families of the community, there would be little prospect of economic security in the absence of any tourism for an unforeseen period of time to come.

Such was the situation in al-Qurna during mid-November 1997, at the start of anthropological fieldwork: the scenario of local and global forces behind what has become known as the 'Luxor Massacre,' the sudden collapse of the tourism industry during what otherwise would have been the year's busiest season, and the physical and emotional trauma for local villagers. Some of these were reminiscent of the elements that had historically characterized the communities of the Luxor west bank's archaeological zone: foreign interests, local economic concerns, the specifics of Qurnawi relations with the Egyptian state, the primitive living conditions, and the negative treatment meted out both in the writings of western visitors and at the hands of Mamluk and Ottoman officials. In certain respects, not much had changed, except that they had resisted leaving the foothills they considered their historical territory, despite several government initiatives seeking to relocate them, and they had come to recognize and accept the external influences for the economic betterment these could provide.

For Badawi, living in a World Heritage–listed archaeological landscape from which he could be evicted at any time, and now also targeted by Islamist extremists for its associations with hard currency–generating international tourism and the legitimacy of the incumbent regime,[3] life in this environment had always been unpredictable at best. Subsisting on a small government wage, his supplementary income came from working with tourists who were not only known to be substantially fewer in numbers during the hot summer months, but who might also stay away at the behest of global economic downturns or international political developments over which neither villager nor visitor had any control.

Badawi's concerns about the financial hardship resulting from his brother's injuries and his own loss of tourism earnings raised questions about the mechanisms Qurnawi had at their disposal to cope with both the seasonal downturn in visitor numbers and the periodic collapse of the tourism industry altogether. Community assistance could be an option and indeed, as we will see, social cohesion in the foothills is closely linked with mechanisms to provide reciprocal support in times of need. But Badawi had his pride and for him any financial support generated by the local community of believers, when asked for assistance by the mosque's imam after Friday prayers, was too embarrassing a form of charity.

The particular conditions of that 1997–98 Egyptian winter thus provided sets of circumstances that allowed ethnographic observation of not only social and economic activity in this archaeological landscape, but also of the strategies people employ to make ends meet during such episodes of adversity. The history and plurality of social and economic practices that were found to operate in the Theban foothills became a leitmotif of resilience that connected and gave meaning to much of the ethnographic material, in the process countering long-held assumptions about life and human activity in the Theban Necropolis.

The sparkle of their glittering wrappers at times of shared suffering may be seen as a metaphor for the resilience and vitality in people's lives at al-Qurna. Such Qurnawi resilience may be one of their strengths—as it may possibly be a character trait of the Egyptian farmer and rural worker more generally[4]—but in the often politicized context in which al-Qurna exists, it continues to be a psychological resource the villagers of the Theban foothills have been forced to draw on time and again.

Badawi's state of despondency at the tragic circumstances in which he found himself could only be human, but the sets of social and economic mechanisms available to him were what characterized him as Qurnawi, enabling him to get up and move forward once more. But while communal identity may be reflected in a person like Badawi, it is not constituted in the personal experiences of one individual only. Incorporating but also moving beyond the particular circumstances of Badawi, we may thus ask questions about who Qurnawi are collectively, both historically and socially. How have they come to be exposed to such events as those that so deeply affected Badawi and his family? What space can they be said to occupy intellectually in order to have become integrated into the range of both local and international dynamics at whose mercy they find themselves? What is it that characterizes their social environment, which has always found itself measured by the yard stick of foreign intellectual endeavor? We shall turn to the latter aspect first.

Shadowy practice: 'Tomb robbing' as economic specialization and its problems

The possible question "How do Qurnawi make a living?" may be assumed to have been historically answered with a simple response. The people of al-Qurna, inhabiting the cluster of hamlets built amid the ancient tombs of the Theban Necropolis on the Luxor west bank, have generally been taken to make tomb robbing and illicit dealings in antiquities their principal economic specialization. Those Qurnawi who occupy the centrally located hill of Shaykh 'Abd al-Qurna have been singled out as both the most active in this field and the exemplars for everybody else. But as straightforward as the answer seems, its implications are just as complex. Problematizing this simplistically understood economic activity and unpacking its inherent complexity make al-Qurna, and Shaykh 'Abd al-Qurna in particular, a topic of particular historic and anthropological interest.

As will be discussed later, the allegations that inform this traditional view of Qurnawi economic activity may have good reasons. Even so, historically attested and alleged incidents of illicit excavations as reported in technical, popular, and fictional archaeological writing have defined the term 'Qurna' in the public eye to the point where it has virtually become synonymous with the black-market trade in illegal antiquities, as suggested by such commonly used descriptors as "the village of the tomb robbers" (Westbrook et al., 1995), a view that continues to hold sway (Waxman, 2008: 51). Fictional representations of human presence within the necropolis range from the violent and criminal pursuit of treasure (Abdelsalam and Rossellini, 1969; Cook, 1979: passim; Schaffner, 1980) to allusions of necrophilia (Golding, 1985: 115; Rice, 1989: 249). Both genres can be seen to indicate a measure of the popular imagination's preoccupation with this form of 'otherness.'

Intended as harmless entertainment, such representations have nevertheless served a process of mystification that victimizes Qurnawi as much as it elevates their purportedly exclusive economic specialization of tomb robbing to near-mythical status, in the process obscuring everything else that is either historically relevant or economically different. By consequence, the dialogue between anthropology and Egyptology has become something of an emotive 'discourse of blame' that is out of character with the objective data gathering of modern science, its lack of objectivity fair neither to Qurnawi nor to academic Egyptology.

The mystification of Qurnawi economic practice also includes the general imprecision that characterizes common understandings about those who are allegedly involved in 'tomb-robbing' activities, and the reasons for them to be so occupied. Modern references typically view the origin and activities of the Theban villagers in one of two ways. For some, they are "the only living link with the people of ancient Egypt. They are directly descended from the embalmers, craftsmen, painters, sculptors and artists who lived here three thousand years ago" (Zakaria Goneim, quoted in Cottrell, 1950: 144, 120–21). This view also implies that Qurnawi are the descendants of the ancient tomb robbers (Breasted, 1916: 525; Carter and Mace, 1923: 70) who "have lived off the dead for millennia" (Stewart, 1997: 89), effectively making no distinction between ancient Egyptian illicit activities in the necropolis and contemporary ones (Roberts, 1993: 98). Others popularly attribute Qurnawi occupation of the Theban Necropolis to "thirteenth-century groups of medieval tomb robbers" (Golding, 1985: 116), a view that infers Qurnawi descent from Bedouin Arabs who settled here hundreds of years ago (Burckhardt, 1819: 531–33; Rhind, 1862: 279; Simpson, 1997). When overly emphasized, this latter connection imparts an unhelpful, ethnic dimension that effectively delimits objective analysis of the practice of 'tomb robbing' inside the necropolis.

The unproblematized and not further specified assumptions in these two positions are that either direct descent and cultural continuity have seen the transmission of an income-earning activity—tomb robbing—which spans the millennia, or that the Bedouin and Arab tribal psyche of those who arrived in the area more recently is particularly suited for this type of occupation. What are essentially racially stereotyped character traits of independence, non-conformity, lawlessness, courage, violence, and honor will form part of this association, but they are not rationalized and will likely result from romanticized notions of 'otherness.' The accuracy of a certain postulated psychological predisposition having sole explanatory value is in any case compromised by the time depth and 'deep' origins of Egypt's Coptic Christian communities, and the admixture of indigenous and exogenous population groups that will also have affected the Theban west bank after the Muslim conquest of Egypt in 642 CE.

Rather than infer certain economic practices inside the Theban Necropolis from ethnically situated psychological characteristics, here we seek to describe Qurnawi behavior in non-racially conceived terms, instead looking at their relationship with the surrounding archaeological landscape as a formative element in the specific characteristics of Qurnawi agency and action. However, before making that argument, it is valid to ask how we came to the point where we had to resort to the certain postulated ethnically defined psychological identity, that is 'Bedouin' and 'Arab,' of Qurnawi in describing an aspect of their subsistence base, rather than presenting their economic activities in the context of the dynamics operating between them and their physical environment.

The answer to that question is to be found in the specific ways in which the historically emerging archaeological appropriation of the landscape, the attendant gradual development of antiquities legislation, the implementation of practical protective measures, and the evolution of western heritage values more broadly in their totality have come to dominate all other forms of landscape use, including people's place within it and their relationship to it. The scientific and art historical importance of the archaeological heritage considered paramount, it was the identity and presence of indigenous people in the archaeological environment that was gradually being questioned. Understood in the context of a particular but largely postulated psychological 'Bedouin' mindset that refused to acknowledge, or act upon, the detrimental impact of their presence on the surrounding landscape, Qurnawi behavior effectively became a form of social deviance enacted against the greater cultural consciousness of the west. The psychological denigration inherent in this position and the denial of people's territorial rights have been characteristic of the treatment of Qurnawi: their presence inside the ancient necropolis has largely been ignored for the anomaly it represents or, if recognized at all, has been confined and relegated to alleged involvement in illicit antiquities dealings that could be used as a pretext for, and thereby legitimize, their removal from the cemeteries. An analysis of one influential popular archaeological account that makes reference to Qurnawi is instructive not only for what is said, and the broad context in which it is said, but also for what is left unsaid.

Maspero's legacy: Sepia tones as agents of mystification

A first glimpse obtained by mid- and late-twentieth-century readers of who or what al-Qurna is, came in a curious, even ambiguous, way. Photographed side-on, the sepia-toned black and white image presents a seated figure, hands folded in his lap, drawing the loose folds of his ankle-length *gallabiya* tight around him. His back leans against the jamb of a low doorway, his gaze focusing straight ahead, proud and impassive. The opening in which he sits—either the entrance to a tomb chapel, or alternatively the window of one of the surrounding mud-brick houses, or indeed both if his house were an ancient tomb as well—frames a background-sweep of mud-brick dwellings resting against a hillside slope. The caption describes the entire scene as: "A villager of Qurna and his village built on the necropolis of the Theban nobles" (Desroches-Noblecourt, 1963: 57).

The narrative that the photographic imagery was designed to enhance situates the account of Howard Carter's search for the tomb of Tutankhamun against a backdrop of the activities of local tomb robbers, both during ancient Egyptian and rather more recent, late nineteenth- and early twentieth-century times: "Such, then, was the setting, the atmosphere, in which the Egyptologists camping upon the west bank of Thebes lived and worked" (Desroches-Noblecourt, 1963: 57). The narrative presents the west bank area as one of "kings and brigands," (Desroches-Noblecourt, 1963: 56). where lines of social distinction have always been crossed and where both an absence of daily luxuries and a presumed existence of hidden material wealth continue to be driving motivators of human activity:

Desroches-Noblecourt's 1963 use of Gaston Maspero's 1880s but otherwise only vaguely provenanced photograph to support her stereotyping account of illicit antiquities dealings in the ancient cemeteries of the Luxor west bank. The wide distribution and the popular appeal that her book enjoyed will have been influential in portraying Qurnawi as tomb robbers in the popular imagination. © TopFoto

"sometimes the necropolis was well guarded; at others, its workmen and inhabitants regarded the old kings and their treasures as their own rightful heritage" (Desroches-Noblecourt, 1963: 56). The image we are left with is one of recalcitrance and persecution: local people throwing stones at Bonaparte's scientists; being smoked not out of their homes but out of their "lairs"; their village allegedly and until recently a "penultimate halting place for outlaws" (Desroches-Noblecourt, 1963: 57).

Prefacing her subsequent account of Howard Carter's archaeological search for the tomb of Tutankhamun by reference to the community within which and with whose members he worked, is a practice not often espoused in archaeological writing, and is therefore worthy of mention. Here, however, Desroches-Noblecourt's focus on the villagers of Qurna is doubly significant for the place her book occupies in Egyptological writing.

Desroches-Noblecourt's 1963 work about the discovery and contents of Tutankhamun's tomb, and her reconstruction of the life and death of its occupant, returned Tutankhamun and his world to the center of public as well as professional interest. Following its discovery in 1922 and the gradual removal of its spectacular furnishings during the next ten years, interest in the discovery gradually waned. After Carter's work of clearance and conservation was finally completed in 1932, a third and final volume of his popular *The Tomb of Tut.Ankh.Amen* was eventually published in 1933, but a definitive scholarly work was never produced, both because of his death in 1939 (Reeves, 1990b: 67) and, later, because of political developments in Egypt (James, 1992: 386). This void of engagement was compounded by a sense of personal disengagement: "Curiously enough, by the 1950s it was far from the tastes of many professionals. Most Egyptologists and many art historians, too, considered Tutankhamun's treasures to be overblown and rather vulgar" (Romer and Romer, 1993: 18). The commissioned work produced by Desroches-Noblecourt, with its first professional color photography of artifacts, renewed professional engagement and instilled a popular interest that has not abated since. The 1963 rebirth of Tutankhamun is now credited with generating the public interest that underpinned the success of the worldwide Tutankhamun exhibitions of the 1960s, 1970s, and early 1980s that in turn renewed interest in Egypt as a tourist destination (Romer and Romer, 1993: 18–21).[5] Coming full circle, these developments have spawned a new generation of working Egyptologists, and a consequent scholarly publication of the Tutankhamun materials is now well under way.[6]

Lifted out of obscurity alongside Tutankhamun, the villagers of al-Qurna attained new prominence, and the sepia-toned image of a Qurnawi man resting stoically against his doorjamb became a new global audience's first visual representation of the villagers inhabiting the necropolis.[7]

Were we, however, to deconstruct the use of that photograph, most certainly selected by the book's author herself, then much can be said beyond the mere visual. Although it is presented in a publication that contains many images specifically taken for the purpose, our photograph is not contemporary with Desroches-Noblecourt's writing at all. In fact, it dates closer to the years when Carter actually worked in the area, and is credited to have come from the collection of Gaston Maspero, the late-nineteenth-century director general of the Service des antiquités, the Egyptian Antiquities Organization, himself a Frenchman (Desroches-Noblecourt, 1963: 308). Although the purpose of using such older images was obviously designed to invoke something of the ambiance within which Carter had worked, and more examples of this can be found in the book, it surely also enhanced the accompanying narrative of eighteenth-, nineteenth-, and early-twentieth-century Qurnawi behavior. Combined with a possible close proximity to Maspero's records in France, such a choice could have been favored over one that would draw on the collections of the writer, who is herself personally familiar with the Luxor west bank (several other west bank photographs are her own).

In conjunction with the accompanying narrative, the associations between photograph and text will have had the arguably unintended consequence of imbuing the visual imagery with social attributes that, when transposed onto al-Qurna's contemporary inhabitants, may prove to both marginalize and culturally limit Qurnawi social behavior. Since male dress codes have changed little for those who have not adopted western style clothing since Maspero took his photograph, the association between traditional dress styles and a narrative that concentrates exclusively on one particular economic activity—tomb robbing—is likely to project a generic mental image of Qurnawi in the minds of visitors that similarly abstracts that activity to the exclusion of all other present-day economic practices. Focusing on one activity to the exclusion of all others obscures what really goes on in the lives of the villagers. Therefore, in one sense, our photograph represents a link in the long chain of half-truths, part fact and part fiction, that h:)me to typify the dealings of west bank villagers. Through the particular set of circumstances inherent in its 1963 publication, the image has served to maintain, and possibly increase, the momentum of that process of mystification.

Not unlike its subject, the photograph itself projects a deafening silence, failing to answer most questions concerning provenance, identity, or archival source. Given the vagueness of the term 'Qurna' in most publications, we might be compelled to ask: Where is the Qurna of the caption? What is this person's name and what is his relation to Gaston Maspero, both in the context of his other published or unpublished records and in personal terms? Was this photograph taken around the same time as that other one also taken by Maspero, the very same one chosen by Desroches-Noblecourt to precede her image of the male Qurnawi (number 24, "The discovery of the first royal cache at Thebes west: preparations for the removal of the mummies," Desroches-Noblecourt, 1963: 55)? That photograph was also taken by Maspero in 1881, during the clearance of the so-called Dayr al-Bahari Royal Cache, the ancient burial site discovered and exploited by the local 'Abd al-Rasul family with whom Maspero in his official position had close contact. Or was his choice of subject entirely unrelated to this episode, and simply one of the anonymous locals by whom the necropolis was "well-guarded"? What was the precise location of the photograph? Is the geometrical shape that frames his figure part of the tomb he guards, his house, or a house incorporated into the existing structure of an ancient tomb? What is the exact source of the photograph, other than "Mme. Henri Maspero–photo Maspero" (Desroches-Noblecourt, 1963: 308)? Such unanswered questions, the possible associations between the two Maspero photographs taken in 1881, and the potential for stereotyping that a crossover between possibly unrelated people and events can generate, have resulted in an image, part fact and part fiction, that is now increasingly hard to shed. Subsequently recreated through different media, the continually perpetuated image of a generic Qurnawi tomb robber is making it impossible to obtain a broader historic, social, and cultural view of who they are and what they do (see Ikram and Dodson, 1998; Piccione, 1997; Rakha, 1999; Waxman, 2008: 50–51, 95–96; and Westbrook et al., 1995, for five recent examples. For its impact on the world of literary fiction, see Cook, 1979).

Desroches-Noblecourt's portrayal of Qurnawi has further contributed to the above process in two ways. First, her use of a photograph imbued with connotations of tomb robbing, both through the immediate experience of the original photographer and through the placement of the preceding photograph taken during an actual tomb-robbing episode, can be seen to subsume the entire history of Egyptological exploration in the Theban Necropolis, where acrimonious and aggressive behavior on the part of Qurnawi often characterized relations with western travelers and early explorers. As we will see, the reports of these encounters were inevitably of western authorship, with accounts of local histories and cross-cultural relations between west bank villagers and western travelers appraised through foreign rather than through indigenous eyes.

Second, and despite references to contemporary al-Qurna, Desroches-Noblecourt's 1963 recreation of the Tutankhamun phenomenon retains the distinction inherent in professional Egyptological practice that sets the world of ancient Egypt apart from the contemporary population inhabiting the Theban west bank. *Tutankhamen: Life and Death of a Pharaoh*, and the larger literature and sphere of interest for which it (according to Romer) must claim at least some responsibility, continues to instill in present-day visitors to Egypt a degree of antiquity-focused anticipation. As a result of this tendency, many visitors arrive in Egypt ill-prepared for an encounter with not only Qurnawi of the Luxor west bank, but with modern Egypt, and contemporary Egyptians generally.

Inhabiting the Necropolis: The occupation of intellectual space

To take the above argument one step further, it is relevant to ask why Egyptologists have effectively ignored the presence of Qurnawi in the necropolis. To answer this question, some closer scrutiny is warranted of the process whereby Egyptological practice subsumes the social landscape in which it operates, and what is its theoretical basis. A more detailed account of the interaction between Egyptology and Qurnawi will follow later, but relevant here is to locate the place of Egyptology within the social sciences and how ideas about a local community inhabiting an archaeological site are conditioned by Egyptological representations. Commencing with the latter, two aspects can be identified.

The first of these has already been established by reference to the Maspero photograph, above. The generally negatively viewed trade in illegal antiquities in which communities located in close proximity to archaeological sites are allegedly implicated is not exclusive to Egypt, but the specific episode of the Qurnawi exploitation of the Dayr al-Bahari Royal Cache during the 1870s has thrown the Theban west bank communities into particularly sharp relief.

The second aspect is located at the center of the academic enterprise itself and concerns the way archaeological findings are disseminated. It has already been suggested that Desroches-Noblecourt's portrayal of Howard Carter's work in the context of the surrounding social landscape—even if conventionally and narrowly perceived—was exceptional but, while academically important, her work was also conceived as a popularizing account, and therefore distinct from archaeological field reports. The published reports that result from Egyptological field studies proper, however, often offer only passing acknowledgment of the employment of local workmen, thereby virtually disguising the fact that archaeological research is conducted with the cooperation and against the background of a vibrant local community. This practice is historically situated and can be found in the archaeological reports of most periods, and in turn can influence the popularized accounts that derive from them. Two examples will illustrate this point.

Lord Carnarvon, who financed the excavations of Howard Carter that eventually led to the discovery of Tutankhamun's tomb, simply limits himself to a brief comment about the moral character of his archaeological laborers. All of Carnarvon and Carter's workmen came from the various hamlets that make up larger al-Qurna, but it is the issue of pilfering

Qurnawi excavation team working for Howard Carter in the Valley of the Kings during his search for the tomb of Tutankhamun in 1922. Photograph by Harry Burton. © The Griffith Institute, the University of Oxford.

antiquities that predominates: "The labourers themselves were a willing and hard-working lot: but though they were no more dishonest than other Egyptian *fellahin*, inducements for them to steal were many, and we found it essential to proceed in our work with great care" (Carnarvon and Carter, 1912: 1–2). Carnarvon's tone is measured, almost diplomatic, as befits a British aristocrat, something that cannot be said for the, at times, derogatory assessments of Egyptologists seemingly steeped in the world-view of British colonialism. Even so, Carnarvon's level of social analysis remains shallow.

Three decades later, Herbert Winlock, field director for the Metropolitan Museum of Art Egyptian Expedition, in his account of work at Dayr al-Bahari improves slightly on Carnarvon. In a wittily crafted passage, Winlock makes reference to his workmen "from Kurneh village" who take turns to invoke a locally revered Saint ("Sheikh 'Abd elKurneh") and a powerful "rival holy man . . . Sheikh Tay'a." Winlock illustrates how local workmen lifted a particularly heavy load by drawing on local beliefs, yet his point is not to describe religious practice but an aspect of archaeological fieldwork method. When the operation proves unsuccessful and the scaffold supporting the lifting gear collapses, Winlock in fact makes light of local custom, insisting "on a return to Sheikh 'Abd elKurneh, who was evidently less powerful than Sheikh Tay'a, but more conservative" (Winlock, 1942: 41). The episode maintains a close focus on Egyptological practice and objectives, as distinct from representations that conjoin that practice through relations of interdependence to the local community of archaeological workmen.

Inherent in these two archaeological fieldwork vignettes is the theoretical question that asks why the discipline of Egyptology itself has not been able to contribute constructively to a discussion of the social aspects of the archaeological landscape in which it conducts its investigations. Conversely, and from a local perspective, the place of Qurnawi in the archaeological landscape is also one of intellectual space, where the presence and recognition of a contemporary community is confronted by archaeological inquiry, heritage preservation, and the associated value that the west has come to place on ancient Egyptian art.

As a consequence, the social characteristics of the landscape have lost most definition under the dominance of the archaeological and art historical focus. Thus, the silence that surrounds the cultural specificity of west bank villagers stands in sharp contrast with the epigraphic and archaeological activities of Egyptologists whose many annual research projects seek to shed light on all aspects of life and death in ancient Egypt. The issue is one of academic specialization and the demarcation between distinct areas of research. Egyptological objectives—the study of ancient Egyptian history and culture by means of archaeological fieldwork methodologies, through the translation of texts, and the linguistic analysis of its ancient languages—by definition are not concerned with contemporary populations, making such professional demarcations understandable.[8]

Yet, the lack of interest in the social landscape within which Egyptological research takes place is surprising. In the United States of America, academic archaeology is a subset of a broader anthropology that distinguishes less between past and present human behavior. By contrast, European and British social anthropology are self-contained in their focus on the present and for the most part distinct from archaeological inquiry. By the sheer weight of numbers that members of the American academy represent within any given intellectual endeavor, some interest in the broader, social qualities of the archaeological landscape could have been expected within the wider anthropological discipline.

That such, at least with respect to the Theban west bank but probably for the whole of Egypt, has not been the case, is inherent in the nature and history of Egyptology itself, which has mostly seen itself as being more closely aligned with literary studies and the classics than the social sciences proper. Because of this, American Egyptology occupies a place somewhat removed from engagement with the broader social sciences than would be the case for American archaeological anthropology. Yet, the art historical and philological characteristics of Egyptology's classical leanings are global in nature and not exclusive to American Egyptology. Given the dominance of American Egyptology compared to the relative worldwide distribution of Egyptologists, it remains remarkable that the few extant examples of west bank ethnographic writing have come from German Egyptologists (Eigner, 1984; Stelter, 1991).

Admittedly, to allow Egyptology to generate questions about its own impact on the surrounding social landscape, be this from a historical or a social anthropological perspective, falls outside the boundaries of its own intellectual objectives. That this should be so is understandable, but for those who are less concerned with the archaeological past, the possibility of an exchange between Egyptology and anthropology in the very social landscape where the former is conducting its excavations could be equally interesting. That is to say, grass roots–level ethnographic inquiry generated by political and economic questions resulting from the presence of archaeological activity in the surrounding social landscape seems entirely legitimate. This should be especially so for Egyptology, which has shown itself to be sufficiently interested in its own history and practice to warrant such considerations (for examples see: Bierbrier, 1995; Clayton, 1982; Dodson, 1999; Wilson, 1964). It is indeed a promising sign that in recent years there have begun to emerge interdisciplinary analyses of the socio-political world that has surrounded the practice of archaeology in Egypt (Colla, 2007; Meskell, 2000; Reid, 1985; 1997; 2002). It may thus represent no great leap of the imagination to reflect on Egyptological practice in ethnographic terms as well.

There is indeed a story to be told about the broader political economy of Egyptological research-induced local labor relations. Such may not necessarily only apply to Qurnawi of the Luxor west bank. Through the sheer density of archaeological sites, archaeologists have worked and are continuing to work the length of the Nile Valley, with labor provided by local communities. Among these communities, several (Quft, al-Qurna) have developed a specialist status, with the *ra'is*, the name given to the foreman in charge of excavation teams, often recruited from these two communities. Within the history of Egyptological practice, their contribution has attracted little consideration and the sociological implications of the interaction between western academics and local workmen (or the competitive, sometimes even acrimonious, nature of relations between Qufti and Qurnawi, for that matter) have largely gone unrecognized as issues worthy of academic consideration. An anthropological account of such relations will complement the discipline of Egyptology by providing its practice with the social context within which its field operations exist. Egyptologists may come to acknowledge that, even with most of the precious tomb furnishings now no longer in situ, a glittering wrapper may still provide evidence of a wealth of social relations meriting interest in their own right.

Wider implications: Heritage tourism and the dismissal of contemporary Egypt

In their totality, and as a consequence of the lack of more appropriate social representation, archaeological reports give the impression that the field research on which they are based is conducted in a social vacuum, an intellectually sanitized and imagined desert landscape cleansed of the social life and cultural surroundings against the background of which archaeological data is obtained. This archaeological 'desertification' of contemporary social life in the Egyptological literature has given rise to a disjunction of wider social implications. First-time visitors to Egypt, many of them lured there by an Egyptological interest based in large part on the popularized syntheses of these rather more technical and specialist reports, are often unprepared for an encounter with contemporary Egypt. The un- or under-anticipated aspects of such visits are first encountered in the Egyptian Museum in Cairo and the Giza pyramids on its outskirts, that is, the two most immediate and obvious locations likely to be inspected by an archaeologically or art historically motivated first-time visitor to Egypt.

For such a visitor, the Egyptian Museum in Cairo is a sobering experience. Conditioned to decontextualized and sanitized photographic images of ancient Egyptian art and artifacts, lifted from dark and solitary confinement at the opening of a book, a visit to their real-time repository in the heart of a city that bristles with life may come as something of a shock to the uninitiated. The artifacts have not changed from how they are remembered, nor is there any reduction in the collective knowledge that their survival supports. Except, of course, the exhibits would have benefited from the sort of photographic lighting that made the detail and definition of the two-dimensional published representation possible. Notwithstanding the vivid memories those published representations of the artifacts have left on the mind's eye, the density of artifacts on display and the obvious absence of modern museum technology can make it difficult to locate and identify any looked-for items, especially among the ground floor exhibits where light fails rapidly once the winter sun has passed its zenith. The exceptions are the main Tutankhamun exhibit and the Gold Room, which have been upgraded to internationally acceptable standards.

Yet, such impressions are based on visual criteria alone. The real shock of misrecognition is one that comes from the audible component of the viewing experience, resulting from noise invading the mental image and scrambling the process of identification between cerebrally recorded and real-time artifact. The once sacred and ritual paraphernalia of Tutankhamun's funerary equipment are not exempt here either. In the end, what remains are the ancient objects, but the initial mental imagery that on some level will have been responsible for a person visiting Egypt in the first place has receded into the mind's subconscious. Indelibly altered, Egyptian art will now be remembered as artifacts surrounded by and existing within the context of a megacity. The sounds of central Cairo, punctuated by the incessant honking of car horns characteristic of Cairo traffic, freely enter the museum's open windows, mingling with the objects on display, and contributing to an experience that can no longer be adequately considered or described as a process of 'viewing.'

To be sure, for a first-time visitor who discounted or underestimated the social realities of contemporary Egypt, the realization that the anticipated Egyptological experience does not exist in a social vacuum, but may in fact be one of confrontation and negotiation, can come quickly. With a visit to the Giza pyramid plateau often first on the itinerary, the expectation to reflect on the grandeur of the monuments and the passing of time is soon found to be made impossible by the constant overtures of camel drivers offering their services and other merchants peddling their wares. What was expected to be a monumental experience soon turns into an irritating lack of privacy and denial of personal space. Anecdotal evidence suggests that the ability to confront such entrepreneurial intrusion on the part of camel drivers, perfume sellers, papyrus vendors, and artifact peddlers may make or break a tourist's appetite for all things Egyptian.

Experiences of this type indicate that, despite the glossy coffee-table books containing images of present-day Egypt (for example, Caselli and Rossi, 1992), an emphasis on the culture and monuments of ancient Egypt and a seemingly ever-increasing popular interest in Egyptology has resulted in what amounts to a denial of modern Egypt. In this sense, academic Egyptology has fostered its own particular brand of 'coevalness denial,' that is, refusing the "sharing of present Time" as identified by Johannes Fabian (1983: 33–34). Or, as one writer succinctly put it, "I had come to a simple truth; that Egypt is a complex country of more-or-less Arab culture and it is outrageous for the uninformed visitor to confine himself to dead Egyptians while the strange life of the valley and the desert goes on all around him" (Golding, 1985: 11). Dauber's representation of al-Qurna, a pictorial illustration of exactly that sentiment, is exceptional among popular Egyptologically focused publications (Dauber, 1994).

Heritage selection, local communities, and the national interest

However, beyond a more immediate and superficial level of what pleases or displeases tourists, these observations point to and raise larger questions about the relationship between archaeological and heritage management practice in Egypt, and the contemporary social environment within which Egyptological research, conservation, and presentation takes place. Archaeological practice and heritage management in Egypt do not exist in isolation, but neither are the social relations of which they are a part limited to the social environment of specific local communities. Rather than remaining "enmeshed in the intricacies of social life at the local level," to use Joel Migdal's phrase (1988: xvi), a study of social relations characteristic of the west bank archaeological landscape must also be considered in the sphere of nation-state politics and the perceived national interest it pursues.

It is important to acknowledge here that 'refusal to share time' is not restricted to under-informed tourists only, but is also being practiced by policy makers at the national level who appropriate the discipline of Egyptology toward a specific, ideologically situated purpose. While first-time visitors to Egypt may arrive with expectations predominantly framed by their particular knowledge of Egyptology, what we find in Egypt is that archaeological practice and Egyptology have been called upon to serve political objectives that center on the construction of a national identity and its associated tourism-industry revenue base.

But while the Egyptology-inspired international identification of modern Egypt with that of pharaonic times has immediate economic benefit, so the construction on which it rests is maintained only at the expense of other histories, including that of Qurnawi. Furthermore, due to Egypt's international responsibilities with respect to its cultural heritage, the archaeological past and its management in their totality have become subsumed in the rights and responsibilities of the modern Egyptian nation-state. In part through Egypt's signatory membership of such supra-national and inter-governmental frameworks as UNESCO's World Heritage Convention, issues relative to its national cultural heritage have emerged as important political factors in economic, social, political, and legal considerations, and international relations.

It is against this larger socio-political background that the interests of local communities such as those of the Luxor west bank are being evaluated and decided. The marginalization that this implies is not new, and can historically be traced throughout the Egyptological literature, encompassing both British colonial interests and post-independence objectives. Academic Egyptology cannot necessarily be blamed for the ideological and politicized use being made of the archaeological past. However, the general tone of Egyptological discourse that can now be found in statements made by Egyptian antiquities officials[9] has meant that a 'denial of coevalness' is also evident in Egyptian government circles. Supported by such discourse, archaeological objectives of preservation feed comfortably into government policy objectives that view the past as serving larger national political purposes, their specific forms of heritage management designed to help realize economic objectives that in the process marginalize local communities.[10]

If previously the west bank was tacitly recognized as being of interest only to academics and tourists, during the 1990s the economic benefits inherent in the Luxor west bank archaeological zone became directly linked with the national interest. National economic objectives facilitated by political decisions, directed through the marketing apparatus of the tourism industry, supported by Egyptological discourse, and given international status through World Heritage listing, now aim at constructing a 'Theban Mountain' that emphasizes a particular interpretation of ancient landscape use, rather than the broader social geography of past and present human activity in this environment. Practical heritage management strategies combine archaeological exploration and conservation with an officially sanctioned 'open-air museum' interpretation of the archaeological landscape. This form of presentation requires the eviction of local villagers from the necropolis with a view to returning the cemeteries to some imagined original, deserted state, in the hope of attracting tourists seeking to experience the authenticity of ancient Egypt.

For government officials and Egyptologists, eviction and resettlement initiatives have become effective heritage management strategies, purportedly benefiting the long-term preservation of the ancient monuments, but also serving associated ideological objectives. Here, the practice of heritage selection not only includes immediate politically motivated economic objectives, but also, as Timothy Mitchell has argued, the political process through which the nation "makes" itself (Mitchell, 1998b; 2001).

For Qurnawi, these measures amount to a practical disinheritance, favored by objectives of external political and economic concerns. In its unfolding, such disinheritance may also be a part of something rather more sinister. Timothy Mitchell (1995) has argued that open-air museum concepts constrain the experience of visitors to archaeological criteria alone, consciously segregating them from contemporary social ones and effectively seeking to separate tourists from local residents. Strategies toward such an evolving "enclave tourism" may indeed be seen to represent instances of 'heritage cleansing,' whereby nearby communities are moved away from tourist sites. Despite government discourse of development and sanitization, this is arguably done to protect villagers from corrupting western influences, as much as it is to prevent foreigners from writing about social conditions they observe in their encounters with local people.

Ultimately, such policies may fail, or at least be less successful in some places than others, for contact with locals cannot altogether be eradicated. Situated at the very heart of the Egyptian tourism industry, the site of the Egyptian Museum in Cairo continues to be ethnographically fruitful. Here, too, contact between foreign visitors and local Egyptians may throw into stark relief the certain disparity that exists everywhere—even in the center of the national capital—between the legacy of western intellectual endeavor and indigenous practice. Here, the late afternoon conservation-conscious visitor may be surprised to find cleaning staff mopping the tiled museum floors underneath raised display cabinets containing artistic and intellectually priceless artifacts. The characteristic rapid flicking of the hand to scoop soapy water from the bucket across the tiles probably reflects some ancient method that can still be observed in domestic contexts all around the country where concerns about humidity control are rightfully absent. In the near-sacrosanct museum environment, however, this unexpected observation embodies the obvious clash of two worlds, the sensory experience revealing and reinforcing the juxtaposition of ancient and modern Egypt as one of real-time process: time-honored indigenous practice versus the humidity-sensitive requirements of western-inspired, modern museum technology and conservation practice.

Rather than isolated and localized instances, such Cairo-based observations are neither exclusive to it nor exceptional. In al-Qurna and until recently, everyday life was comprehensively superimposed over a protected archaeological landscape where similar social realities, seemingly in contradiction to conservation objectives, were made manifest on a daily basis. The certain tension inherent in this inescapably layered, physically ancient, yet contemporary cultural and social stratigraphy, is one that invites observation and analysis. The next chapter will consider the physical basis of the community by reviewing its village setting on the Theban west bank.

2

The Natural and Social Setting of the Theban West Bank Communities

Separating the Western Desert from the Nile River, the natural landscape of the Libyan Plateau's terminal escarpment reminds one of a breaking wave, the rising crest of its Theban Mountain attempting one final crescendo before rolling ashore. Despite the imagery, the Western Desert's Theban Mountain and its foothills have generally been construed during recorded history more in terms of their cultural qualities than their natural characteristics. Yet, it was the mountain peak's natural features that most likely reminded ancient Egyptians of their ancestors' pyramidal mortuary architecture, inspiring royalty and public dignitaries to have their funeral chapels and chambers cut into the shadows at its foot. Travelers who visited these tombs during the last two millennia, both in the Valleys of the Kings and Queens and in the larger west bank necropolis, have for the most part lost this connection with the natural surroundings of the place, being drawn there more specifically by the site's cultural qualities. Today, if at all recognized or experienced, an appreciation of the natural setting is an unintended consequence of travel agents' selling epithets, which may stress the location's 'romantic' and 'mysterious' qualities, but which, unless encapsulated in the cultural experience, would not attract visitors for its natural beauty alone.

Yet, to frame the location of al-Qurna in such terms as 'cultural' or 'natural' landscapes is to invoke a terminology that itself is culturally constructed. Lived culture in the form of enacted and experienced sociality does not make the distinction. The ancient Egyptians may have chosen the mountain and its foothills for a culturally perceived association between architectural convention and a natural landscape form. Similarly, more recent population groups will have been drawn to the area not only

Tony Binder's 1926 aquarelle of the Theban Mountain. A postcard from the 1920s–1930s, with title on reverse "A golden view of the Theban Hills opposite Luxor." From the author's private collection. © Gaddis and Co., Luxor, used by permission.

for the agricultural opportunities provided by the Nile flood plain, but also by the presence of caves offering opportunities for spiritual retreat, refuge against outside aggression, or respite from the summer heat. The decorated walls will have alerted later occupants to the man-made nature of such 'caves,' but their earlier human history will have played no role in the decision to adapt their use. First and foremost, people's choice of location will have stemmed from immediate survival needs and/or those dictated by lifestyle, both physical and metaphysical, thus effectively merging natural and cultural landscape characteristics into one of purposeful pragmatics based on criteria of suitability.

Today, such considerations about origins or rationale are not uppermost in people's minds. Qurnawi emotional attachment to their village is essentially community based. When asked how they feel about the government's plans to move them away from the archaeological area, the most frequent response is that this is "my village." While cognizant of the unique economic opportunities of the area, and despite broadly held views about Qurnawi resistance to moving, their answer is premised entirely on the collective social history of the community. People see it as their village because it was their father's and their grandfather's village. Significantly, many reject any suggestion of relocating unless such a move is in the company of neighbors, and the spatial patterning of neighborly and wider social relations is replicated in the architectural and urban planning designs of the new settlement.

If such socially motivated responses indicate that any new settlement with time should take root, this is not to say that the village's physical qualities are not recognized or valued. The "good air," that is, the cooling breezes noticeable at higher elevation, the absence of mosquitoes suffered by those living closer to the agricultural fields, and the insulating qualities of the mud-brick architecture are cited by those who contemplate the anticipated changes in personal comfort upon relocation. Yet, such individual considerations are secondary to the sense of community that typifies life in the foothills. The spatial arrangement of the houses is, as Stewart astutely observed, often linked with the disparate patterning of tomb entrances across the face of the foothills, but less so for the clandestine activities implied by him (Stewart, 1997: 90). Instead, this scattered quality, and the use of the tombs' forecourts to serve as external domestic space, has given rise to much of the open or 'courtyard' lifestyle, which is one of the characteristic features of necropolis' sociality.

For unsuspecting tourists who come anticipating to find only tombs and temples, discovering the vernacular architecture of the hillside hamlets and its glimpses of village life both surprise and delight: the sounds of the village and the coming and going of children leading their donkey cart to and from the roadside taps. In visual terms, the spectacle can be stunning: looking across the verdant fields toward the desolate desert, the pastel colored façades of the hamlets' vernacular architecture break the monotony of the hillside's blinding limestone, a stark blue sky, and the shaded reds of the escarpment's crags and recesses framing the background.

Charmed by the scenery and the encounter, visitors may simply be told by their guide that this is "Qurna" or the guide may even whisper the popular ascription that this is "the village of the tomb robbers." For those familiar with the history of Egyptology, the name Qurna may indeed conjure up all the romantic notions associated with the ever-increasing popularity of that discipline. Yet, and as manifested over and over again in the writings of an ongoing procession of popular and professional commentators (for example, Golding, 1985: 115–20; Roberts, 1993: 92–110; Stewart, 1997: 90–91), its mere sound implicates an entire community in the search for treasure and the illicit excavations of a discredited economic activity. Taken collectively, they effectively emphasize as factual the historical, social, and cultural particulars of a population group to the point where any meaningful distinction is either obscured or rendered impossible.

A central feature in this process is the name of al-Qurna itself, which is not always used in unambiguously understood terms. The following discussion seeks to locate al-Qurna within the intellectual space of academic concerns that has given rise to this ambiguity, to reevaluate al-Qurna toponymically, and to situate al-Qurna both geographically and in real time. The aim here is to clarify and to place on record the spatially dispersed nature of the al-Qurna community. Geographical precision establishes a baseline against which the historical development of larger al-Qurna and the dispersal of smaller community units across the foothills can be charted, and is necessary to identify the various loci of sociality in the narrative that follows.

Glimpses of village life both surprise and delight: Hannan's recalcitrant donkey.

A historically informed conception of the foothills communities leans heavily on a topographical and toponymical understanding of the Theban west bank's geographic and social landscape, and its representation in the assortment of literary sources that make reference to it. This is because the name al-Qurna is generically applied to the scattered hamlets lining the Theban foothills, and cannot be allocated to one singular geographic locality or topographic feature. This follows the practice already observed by one of the nineteenth-century travelers, where "the name of the district and the name of the principal village are generally the same" (Richardson, 1822, 2: 70). That 'principal village' was understood to be the village built in and around the temple of Seti I, at the time known locally as 'Qasr al-Rubayq'[1] but now more commonly referred to as the 'Temple of Qurna.' The village was possibly already deserted at the time of most nineteenth-century observers, and is still often referred to as 'Old Qurna.'

Beginning with the evacuation of Old Qurna some time around 1811, leading up to today's population pressures and government-sponsored relocation projects, al-Qurna now not only extends west and south into the Theban Mountain, and east into the agricultural lands, but also north into recently reclaimed desert areas. The resulting difficulty in identifying precisely where al-Qurna is located is further hindered by the existence of one centrally located hill whose composite name does indeed include al-Qurna—Shaykh 'Abd al-Qurna. Given the archaeological importance of the hill of Shaykh 'Abd al-Qurna, the practice has become established among academic Egyptologists to equate the name al-Qurna either with Shaykh 'Abd al-Qurna specifically (for an example see Kampp, 1996, Plates III–VII), or with the foothills more generally.

The Theban Necropolis as a 'typical landscape'

This practice may stem from confusion about local toponymy as much as from a lack of interest in west bank contemporary social geography, but antecedents can be found in the accounts of early travelers who either unwittingly or intentionally collapsed locationally demarcated experiences into a single geographical frame for which the foothills came to serve as backdrop.

Simpson (2001: 2–3) has convincingly argued this to be the case with Vivant Denon, who visited the necropolis on several occasions in 1799 as part of the Napoleonic army's incursions into Upper Egypt. Denon

illustrates his account with a sketch of one of the large *saff* tombs characteristic of the northern al-Tarif region, but still includes tomb openings
reminiscent of the Shaykh 'Abd al-Qurna area in the background of his
rendering, even though such tombs do not exist in the hills behind al-
Tarif, and those of Shaykh 'Abd al-Qurna would not have been visible
from Denon's particular perspective (Denon, 1803, 2: 190, Plate XXI,
Fig. 2). Similarly, Richard Pococke's 1743 street-like portrayal of the
Valley of the Kings was likely influenced by the *saff* tombs at al-Tarif
he had visited only hours earlier (Pococke, 1743: 97; Simpson, 2001: 4).
Other than resulting from faulty recall on the part of the observer when
committing memories to paper at a later stage, or liberties taken by subsequent engravers, such conflation of different perspectives may rather
be inherent in certain philosophical preoccupations characteristic of the
time, and their impact on specific ideas about landscape art.

A discussion of landscape art may draw on a variety of analytical
approaches, as demonstrated by Hirsch and O'Hanlon (1995). Here,
Michel Foucault's observations about the dominance of "opinion" during
the eighteenth century seem valid. According to Foucault, Gothic novels
written during the second half of the eighteenth century "develop a whole
fantasy-world of stone walls, darkness, hideouts and dungeons" where,
among others, "brigands and traitors" hide (Foucault, 1980: 153–54).
Deriving from a "fear of darkened spaces, of the pall of gloom which
prevents the full visibility of things, men and truths" (Foucault, 1980:
153), the imaginary representations provided in literature and graphic arts
served as the inversed image, the 'negative,' of the visibility they sought to
reveal. The ensuing knowledge, "opinion," thus became a form of power
which refused "to tolerate areas of darkness," at once illuminating and
eliminating "the shadowy areas of society" (Foucault, 1980: 154, 153).

Whether it concerns the worldview of the original observer or the later
engraver is difficult to argue without a deeper investigation into the lives
and the worldviews of the individuals concerned, but either way the above
Enlightenment notions, which sought to dispel darkness, easily merged
with such artistic conventions of the Romantic era as the representation of non-western cultures through "picturesque" framing techniques,
where landscape depiction came to act as a form of early ethnographic
description (Hirsch, 1995: 11). This merging of ethnological information
with conventions of artistic depiction resulted in the emergence of "typical landscapes" that evoked the sense of people and place characteristic of

the area, and which demonstrated the type of landscape perceived to be peculiar to each country (Hirsch, 1995: 11, summarizing Bernard Smith, 1985: 112). Stereotypical perceptions of Qurnawi as 'brigands' and 'outlaws' may quite easily have become symbolized by and condensed in a representational emphasis on the 'typical landscape'–specific character of their 'hideouts and dungeons,' an emphasis that concentrated or exaggerated the placement of the tombs inside one artistic frame.

Whatever the social and art historical rationale behind such apparent geographical and topographical distortions, these early graphic representations have either "been thought a little quaint and full of artistic licence," or considered as problematic by archaeologists (Simpson, 2001: 3, 4). In both cases, they have contributed to a certain confusion surrounding issues of perspective, identification, and location in the necropolis.

Akin to the process of graphically isolating a 'typical landscape' out of a variety of topographically distinct locations, the generic usage of 'Qurna'—which is also the name of the larger administrative district—to describe the toponymic diversity of the west bank settlements has led to a similar collapse in specificity, and resulted in the imprecision now found in academic writing on the Luxor west bank generally and the Theban Necropolis specifically. Before correcting this imprecision and realigning the locally used nomenclature with the various settlements of the Theban west bank, it is first necessary to understand locally operative toponymy.

What's in a name: Academic convention versus indigenous practice

The name of al-Qurna proper derives from *al-Qurn* ('The Horn'), the highest peak of the Theban Mountain, and the west bank's single most dominant geographical feature.[2] In its shadow, and lining the easterly facing foothills, are located from south to north Qurnat Mara'i, Shaykh 'Abd al-Qurna, al-Khukha, al-'Asasif, and Dra 'Abu al-Naga. These names derive from locally remembered legendary holy men (Qurnat Mara'i, Shaykh 'Abd al-Qurna), once-named geographically distinguishing features (al-Khukha, 'the Peach'; al-'Asasif, 'the Labyrinth'), or a mixture of the two (Dra' Abu al-Naga, 'the Arm of Abu al-Naga,' another local saint). Whatever topographic, social, or religious associations may have given rise to such names now may or may no longer be remembered,[3] and without exception they are recognized as geographical locations only. Thus, Shaykh 'Abd al-Qurna may still be a revered local shaykh, and his simple commemorative shrine on the ridge above the village continues to play an important function both in the life of the community and its residents, but the pronounced hillock that carries his name is signified by it as a geographical feature only.

By contrast, those who took up residence in that central part of the foothills on and around the hill of Shaykh 'Abd al-Qurna know the surrounding physical and social community by reference to a kinship-based nomenclature—Hurubat—rather than a geographically or geomorphologically inspired toponymy.[4] Similarly, Qurnat Mara'i, al-Khukha, and al-'Asasif are understood as those parts of al-Qurna that are likewise largely occupied by descendants of Harb, and are therefore identified with the community of Hurubat over and above any geographical significance invested in their names. Indeed, anecdotal evidence suggests that younger Qurnawi now no longer even recognize the name of Dra' Abu al-Naga, instead they exclusively refer to the communities inhabiting that part of the foothills as those of al-Hasasna, al-'Atyat, and al-Ghabat.

Egyptological sources, both academic and popular, may refer to the site of Egyptological fieldwork, or to the location of ancient Egyptian monuments inside the Theban Necropolis, simply as 'Qurna.' Many may also refer to Dra' Abu al-Naga and Shaykh 'Abd al-Qurna as a rough but suitable way to reflect the spatial division that exists in the foothills or Noble Tombs area of the necropolis, north and south of Hatshepsut's Temple at Dayr al-Bahari respectively. But, as has been suggested, the composite nature of the name Shaykh 'Abd al-Qurna has also mistakenly been understood to simply mean 'Qurna,' or has been equated with the foothills generally. In excavation and epigraphic reports, more precise renderings may also be used to locate the tomb or site under discussion: Qurnat Mara'i, (al-) Khukha, (al-) 'Asasif. However, it will be noted that in these examples their application is essentially Egyptological, with the use of such local toponymy always belonging to the geographical and geomorphological categories identified above. A selection of examples from the extensive body of Egyptological literature includes renowned Egyptologist Labib Habachi who exclusively limits his use of the name "Gourna" to the locality of Shaykh 'Abd al-Qurna (Habachi and Anus, 1977: 3–6) but, somewhat curiously, uses "Qurna" to signify the entire west bank archaeological zone (Habachi and Anus, 1977: 4n4), seemingly referring to the larger administrative district of that same name. John Romer does the opposite, referring to "the private tombs of Gurna" and "the hill of Gurna," in both instances referring to Shaykh 'Abd al-Qurna as understood by Egyptologists and thus minimizing the geographical extent of al-Qurna by a considerable margin (Romer, 1981: 130). Kurt Lange, in a rare account of the foothills artisans, likewise locates their village by reference to the Egyptological nomenclature he knows best: "Dirâ Aboe 'n-Naga" (Lange, 1952: 145). Finally, and more recently, Darnell and Darnell locate the area of their archaeological survey work as "North of Qurna" (Darnell and Darnell, 1997: 241). Their stated intention is to keep the location deliberately vague, in part for fear of vandalism and in part until full publication of the material. However, their reference to other Egyptologists who "suggested that [ancient Thebes'] northern boundary on the west bank ran just to the north of Qurna" (Darnell and Darnell, 1997: 247) indicates that Egyptological naming conventions concerning al-Qurna are both deep-seated and widespread.

Local toponymy and the construction of archaeological type-sites

The practice of identifying and naming archaeological zones by reference to contemporary regional toponymy is well attested. Especially when dealing with extinct prehistoric or preliterate societies where received linguistic markers are absent, the practice of naming locally present archaeological remains by reference to contemporary geography seems obvious and reasonable. Adopting such names as type-sites became, furthermore, instrumental in the creation of typologies that also identify geographically dispersed cultural assemblages and entire networks of cultural exchange. Such concepts as Oldowan or Acheulian lithic technologies and the Lapita Cultural Complex may serve as suitable examples of cultural assemblages based on geographically derived type-sites (Olduvai Gorge in Tanzania, St. Acheul in northern France, and Lapita on New Caledonia Island respectively).

Apart from historical precedent, it is largely because of such archaeological naming conventions that a topographically derived nomenclature has become enshrined in the literature concerning the Theban west bank. Effectively, present-day literary concerns with the area are largely confined to the writings of academic Egyptology and its attendant art historical, popularized archaeological, and travelogue genres, while locally operative and rather more socially derived names have remained essentially unknown to outsiders. Relevant specialists and their readers will readily recognize Qurnat Mara'i, Shaykh 'Abd al-Qurna, al-Khukha, al-'Asasif, and Dra' Abu al-Naga as important west bank archaeological sites, but the kinship-based nomenclature obtaining from the social landscape that overlays these sites has gone unrecognized. Thus, a prominent Egyptologist describing the west bank villages can write that "The name [Qurna] is now loosely applied to the entire stretch of land between the cliffs and the fields, but the conglomerations of houses have their individual names. To the north . . . is Dra 'Abû el-Naga', . . . to the south . . . is the 'Asâsîf . . . Khôkha . . . Shaykh 'Abd al-Qurna . . . Qurnet Mura'i . . . " (Manniche, 1987: 2). These names may reflect their archaeological and geographical understanding, but they have nothing in common with the socially constructed naming conventions used by those who inhabit the relevant "conglomerations of houses." As a consequence, and in combination with the essentially and increasingly fragmented topography of larger al-Qurna, the use of the name 'al-Qurna' in past and contemporary writings has remained unspecific at best and is in need of clearer definition.

Locating al-Qurna: Settlement patterns of the Luxor west bank communities[5]

Larger al-Qurna comprises a number of hamlets and named populated areas. One count has put the total number of hamlets of the Luxor west bank as high as twenty (Mitchell, 1995: 9).[6] The majority of these, and excluding the hamlets associated with the district of al-Ba'irat, belong to larger al-Qurna. In 1999, the population will have been in excess of the twenty thousand reported by ADL (1981b: 82). Moving in clockwise direction from the agricultural zone closest to the Nile, the following west bank named populated areas can be identified:

Al-Gezira (Gezirat al-Qurna), 'the Island,' takes its name from the island located here before nineteenth-century changes in the Nile's course and state irrigation works brought about major changes in local hydrography. The shape of the original island is still roughly defined by the course of the Nile proper and the 1887 al-Fadliya irrigation canal. The village is not indicated on the Survey of Egypt map (1922), and its relatively recent development must be linked with eastward expansions during the post–High Dam era, when the absence of the annual inundation made year-round habitation in the low-lying agricultural areas possible.[7] Surrounded by sugarcane fields, the growth of al-Gezira must also be linked with its strategic location in close proximity to the nearby tourist ferry constructed during the 1980s, a position it lost when a bridge linking the east and west banks was opened in 1997 several kilometers further south. Not totally divorced from involvement with the tourism industry, its rustic agricultural setting and its vernacular rural appearance make al-Gezira popular with tour operators, several of whom include a camel ride through the village in their itinerary. Just south of al-Gezira is Gezirat al-Ba'irat, its presence explained by the nearby ferry terminal used by locals crossing between Luxor and the west bank.

Al-Qarya, 'the Village,' also known as al-Qarya Hassan Fathy, is situated west of Gezirat al-Qurna, its southern boundary formed by the road that links the local ferry and the necropolis, its eastern boundary by the al-Fadliya irrigation canal. The village was built by renowned Egyptian architect Hassan Fathy during the 1940s in a state-sponsored attempt to relocate the foothills inhabitants away from the archaeological areas. Guidebooks and tourists may refer to the village by the name of 'New Qurna,' a name that is not used locally.[8]

The approach road to the necropolis, which passes al-Qarya Hassan Fathy, is at the same time the southernmost boundary of larger al-Qurna. The more exclusively agricultural villages and hamlets located to its south, including Gezirat al-Ba'irat, Nag' Kom Lula, Nag' al-Qatr, Nag' Madinat Habu, and the southern part of Qurnat Mara'i, all form part of the district known as al-Ba'irat. The demarcation derives from historically situated differences between the two communities, but has recently become important with the community of southern Qurnat Mara'i rejecting relocation initiatives in a northerly direction as inappropriate.

The hill of Qurnat Mara'i is located where the westerly approach road to the necropolis veers northeast to follow the general direction of the foothills. The foothills to the left of the road have already been identified by their historically situated geographical names: Qurnat Mara'i, Shaykh 'Abd al-Qurna, al-Khukha, al-'Asasif, and Dra' Abu al-Naga. Although other clan names have become established in their midst, the northern part of Qurnat Mara'i, Shaykh 'Abd al-Qurna, al-Khukha, and al-'Asasif are locally known as al-Hurubat, that is, the community descending from Harb. Similarly, the region of Dra' Abu al-Naga comprises the communities claiming descent from Hassan (al-Hasasna), Ghaba (al-Ghabat) and 'Atya (al-'Atyat).

Located in the plain between the hills of Qurnat Mara'i and Shaykh 'Abd al-Qurna is Nag' al-Rasayla, the hamlet of the descendants of

'Abd al-Rasul, a name that figures prominently in Egyptological history and which, largely inspired by economic initiatives based on that history, still represents something of a separate identity in the social geography of the foothills.

To the east of the road and bordering the agricultural fields are located a number of initially scattered dwellings, their linear settlement pattern growing increasingly dense toward the road's northern extremity. Nag' al-Ramesseum (also known as al-Sahal al-Sharqi) comprises the houses built in the vicinity of the Ramesseum, the memorial temple of Ramesses II. Inhabitants here generally consider themselves part of Shaykh 'Abd al-Qurna's al-Hurubat community. Indeed, most of these roadside settlements represent population overflows from the foothills proper. Thus, facing Dra' Abu al-Naga, the communities of 'Izbit al-Ward and al-Sualim are generally comprised of those who align themselves with al-Hasasna, al-Ghabat, and al-'Atyat. Toward this northern end of the road, these communities also in economic terms represent a continuation of Dra' Abu al-Naga's artisanal and commercial practices, the painted façades of the numerous 'alabaster factories' designed to attract the business of tourists passing on their way to the Valley of the Kings.

The road that lines the foothills reconfigures at the intersection at the northern end of Dra' Abu al-Naga, sending off branches north to the new communities of al-Qubbawi, Qurna al-Gedida, and al-Suyul located in the desert west of al-Tarif; in a northwesterly direction to the Valley of the Kings; and in a southeasterly direction back to the al-Fadliya irrigation canal. This southeasterly branch passes between the Seti I Temple, site of eighteenth-century Old Qurna village, and the modern Muslim cemetery, with the adjoining, extensive, and densely built but largely post-1920s urban area known as al-Tarif. Replacing the original access track to the necropolis used by eighteenth- and nineteenth-century travelers, the modern road leads to the community of al-Genina, built over the landing place used by early European travelers when disembarking on the west bank. The original river course is now incorporated in the al-Fadliya irrigation canal, the road along its embankment forming a main link with the west bank cities north and south of Luxor. The agricultural settlement of al-Madali opposite al-Tarif on the east bank of the al-Fadliya canal, and accessible via the Abu Shau Bridge at al-Genina, for reasons of social interaction may be considered part of al-Qurna. The canal's west bank and its road constitute the eastern boundary of al-Genina and al-Tarif, but they have in the northerly direction continued to attract urban developments that must constitute the northern boundary of larger al-Qurna: al-Rawageh and al-'Ababda.

The naming of the areas beyond the foothills hamlets follows a historically evolved geographical toponymy, but, as has been observed for the linear roadside settlements, in large part their social identity continues to be aligned with the established clans of the historically populated foothills areas. Thus, within the al-Tarif area, it is said, there also exists 'Hurubat.'

The historicity of such social groupings and alignments is difficult to trace. The foothills communities who assign their ancestry back to specific founding fathers state that the al-Qsasiya clan from al-Tarif represent late arrivals, which at least in part may explain ongoing tensions between the two areas. Contemporary tensions among members of the 'Abd al-Rasul family may have a similar background, at least if the account of one of the dissenting family members is accepted.[9] Yet, the social crystallization of these kinship groups, other than through historical arrivals, may indeed also have resulted from natural increase, with Qurnawi moving over time and gradually into less densely populated areas.

It is this very reason of a rather more recent population increase that may help to explain the absence in early western records of a clearly acknowledged and identified west bank human geography. Population numbers are likely to have been very low, with the foothills communities amounting to no more than a few hundred individuals who, furthermore, often remained out of sight due to their underground habitation. Caroline Simpson has highlighted the treatment that the eighteenth-century French expeditionary force meted out to west bank villagers, offering ample explanation for the persistent reticence on the part of locals to come forward and initiate outsiders in the detail of existing sociality (Simpson, 2001: 2–3). In turn, the lack of significant numbers of visible people in certain areas may have given rise among western travelers to the use of a geographically inspired local toponymy rather than a social one. Be this as it may, once these travelers—for their individual geographical and mapping purposes—had established the name of al-Qurna as a locally operative nomenclature for a specific part of the west bank region, further concerns about locally named social configurations evidently fell outside the scope of their interest, which concerned itself largely with the landscape's archaeological remains.

3

Early European Travelers and the Emergence of the Theban Communities in the Consciousness of the West

M uch of what characterizes the people of al-Qurna today is not only inherent in the physical aspects of the surrounding landscape, but also the historical process of archaeological recognition and interpretation that has resulted in the culturally constructed characterization of the Theban foothills. This perspective immediately directs the attention to the historically situated development of western academic involvement with the Theban west bank, necessitating a global perspective in explanation of the particular cultural constructions that resulted from the contact with foreign interests. In this sense, a study of al-Qurna fits the trend identified by Dale Eickelman, where anthropological studies of village life increasingly incorporate a global-local dichotomy, as distinct from "an earlier era of describing villages as self-contained and slow to react to wider economic and political currents" (Eickelman, 2002: 62).

This emerging importance of historically situated globalizing processes in the evolution of cultural formations is in large part due to the work of Eric Wolf, who has been seminal in introducing a historical perspective to anthropological interpretation. In his *Europe and the People without History*, Wolf takes issue with the tendency in the social sciences to treat human activity throughout history as a series of disconnected processes. He criticizes academic inquiry for its failure to reassemble these separate entities into an interconnected and unified whole, thereby effectively arriving at "misleading inferences" that "falsify reality" (Wolf, 1982: 3). Arguing that "it is conceivable that things might have been different," (Wolf, 1982: 6) Wolf suggests a process of "myth-making" is taking place if human endeavor is "celebrated" as the "unfolding of a timeless essence" that ignores the "orchestration of antagonistic forces" (Wolf, 1982: 5).

Wolf cites, among others, the "schoolbook versions of the history of the United States," where a westward colonization, culminating in the occupation of the Pacific seaboard, is represented as historically inevitable rather than the result of the "contested outcome of many contradictory relationships" (Wolf, 1982: 5–6). The role played by native Americans, African slaves, Haitian slaves, French plantation owners in the Caribbean, Hispanic landowners, and the opposing parties of the Civil War and its ensuing regional alignments, according to Wolf, indicates that "the republic was neither indivisible nor endowed with God-given boundaries," the United States was never "a thing propelled toward its unfolding goal by some immanent driving spring, but rather a temporally and spatially changing and changeable set of relationships, or relationships among sets of relationships" (Wolf, 1982: 6).

Wolf's project, then, is to restore the identity of those common people who "were as much agents in the historical process as they were its victims and silent witnesses" (Wolf, 1982: x). Rather than historiography concerning itself exclusively with the history of "victorious elites" or the subjugated ethnic groups dominated by them (Wolf, 1982: x), an account of "the people without history" should focus on the activities and influence of such groups as "peasantries, laborers, immigrants, and besieged minorities" (Wolf, 1982: x).

Wolf does not introduce here the concept of subaltern studies, and resistance as an expression of contested relationships is not his project. But there is a manifest resilience present in those groups who are denied their own historical 'voice,' who are the victims and silent witnesses in often externally imposed events that run counter to their interests, but who nevertheless survive to act as agents in unfolding historical processes.

The methodology of Wolf is one that takes account of external processes that go beyond individual cases, but that nevertheless affect and transform them. In the treatment of several such processes, Wolf demonstrates how essentially external and in some sense overarching processes like the fur trade in North America and the slave trade in Africa, among others, impacted on, and in distinct ways transformed, local communities. Wolf suggests that these cases "exemplify spatially and temporarily shifting relationships, prompted in all instances by the effects of European expansion," and considers "that this expansion has for nearly 500 years affected case after case" (Wolf, 1982: 18).

Following this broader theoretical and analytical approach, it is argued here that the communities of the Luxor west bank represent one such case, that the emergence of the originally western academic practice of Egyptology acted as one of those external formational processes, and that it is in this light that the al-Qurna material, at least in part, must be presented and understood. The published literature on both town and rural communities in Egypt already includes in-depth historical studies (Garcin, 1976) and solid ethnographic accounts (Henein, 1988; Hivernel, 1996), which may indeed provide both historical background and recent transformations resulting from economic and political developments (Fakhouri, 1987). But other than the people from Quft and its surrounding villages, where archaeological practice has likewise crystallized into a distinct vocational orientation, and such examples as Mit Rahina, Saqqara, and Nazlat al-Samman quoted by Reid (1997: 139–40), few communities in Egypt have been caught up in historical processes and external developments to the obvious and particular extent that al-Qurna has.

Following the broad course charted by Eric Wolf, we may contemplate a number of issues that demonstrate the range of historical and global interdependencies that fit his model. Some of these themes will be further developed and unpacked later, but for now we may simply posit them as likely historical processes or events that have a basis in fact. First, the early interaction between Qurnawi and western travelers eventually evolved into a supply and demand relationship that centered on Egyptian antiquities. Second, nineteenth-century European nations, competing with one another for national prestige through the acquisition of collections of antiquities, placed local agents in al-Qurna in charge of the collecting process. Third, the introduction of constructed dwellings inside the necropolis by these agents offered local populations a blueprint for accommodation other than the occupation of tombs. Fourth, early western antiquarian collecting and dwindling supplies of antiquities evolved into the manufacture of tourist art. Fifth, the use of local labor—from collecting to excavating—came to represent an early specialization that has since evolved to include more scientifically based archaeological excavation and conservation. Sixth, alongside these activities, allegations of illicit excavation and involvement in a black-market antiquities trade have continued to persist. Seventh, the very history of these allegations has contributed to the development and maintenance of a certain mystique that has become an essential ingredient in the marketing practices

of locally manufactured arts and crafts, at the same time as they demar-
cate economic and social relations between segments of the community.
Eighth, the impacts of contemporary archaeological practice and global
tourism not only define artistic production, but also typify many of
al-Qurna's socioeconomic characteristics. Ninth, allegations of tomb
robbing, combined with national economic objectives aimed at developing the tourism industry, have been used as arguments for the relocation
of the villagers away from the archaeological areas. Tenth, the associated
political and economic discourse and decision-making processes, in part
legitimized through Egypt's membership in the UNESCO World Heritage Convention and the World Heritage–listed status of the necropolis,
serve national and international rather than local interests.

The accounts left by early European travelers offer an oblique if meager glimpse of indigenous west bank occupation, and it is their records
that have come to constitute what we may tentatively call Qurnawi history.
It is a liberty we can take largely because of the absence of local historical
records and the dearth of analyses of more recent archaeological deposits.
The lack of such records indicates that the people of al-Qurna are no
less a manifestation of Wolf's "people without history." This is not the
same as saying that the community concerned has no history. Unimagi-
nable in practical terms, and in summary of the above, the reference to
Wolf applies when considering the Egyptological appropriation of the
foothills landscape through the construction of a certain Qurnawi image
by antiquities-focused travelers, archaeological exploitation by European
collectors, which gradually evolves into contemporary archaeological
practice, and recent politically motivated attempts to return the necropolis to what the tourism industry could recognize as a deserted and sacred
pharaonic burial ground. All have involved the denial of the overlying
social landscape, effectively viewing the archaeological areas as *terra nullius*, uninhabited land, where contemporary communities not only should
not be and do not belong, but where also notions of historical use rights
over the area go unrecognized or are deemed invalid.

Other than scientific preoccupation and political expedience, one of
the reasons that such notions have been allowed to come to the fore is
that the historical passage of communities of humans in search of food
and shelter through this landscape is difficult to reconstruct. Treatment of the archaeological record has typically been biased in favor
of the ancient Egyptian remains, while detailed historical analyses of

administrative, legal, cadastral, and oral records relevant to the area remain to be undertaken. It is in the context of such analytical constraints that the Wolfian notion of al-Qurna as a community without history appears. The dominance of a western literary record that documents the encounter between Europeans and al-Qurna, and the subsequent incorporation of the west bank community in the Egyptological project, suggests that here we have a people whose emergence and identification from surrounding population groups closely relates to the arrival of western travelers, and whose distinctive identity crystallizes into its presently distinguishable form under the influence of European presence.

Yet, human occupation of the Luxor west bank was not coincidental with the arrival of the first Europeans, nor has the use of the necropolis for domestic purposes been limited to Qurnawi. Before concerning ourselves with this more recent history, it is worthwhile to review what can be said about the period before European records began.

Earlier times: Demographic and cultural substrata

Given the geographic characteristics and inherent agricultural potential of the Nile Valley between Qus and Armant (Garcin, 1976: 6–7), it may be assumed that the Luxor west bank at no time was devoid of human occupation. During Late Antiquity, that is, the Byzantine period between the collapse of the Roman Empire and the Arab conquest, the largest west bank community was the Coptic town of Jeme built on the site of Madinat Habu, the Nineteenth Dynasty Ramesside temple at the southern end of the Theban Necropolis (Wilfong, 1998: 181; Wilfong, 2002; Winlock and Crum, 1926: 4, 108). Linked by name with the dynastic District of Jamat, Jeme is thought to have developed out of a nearby ancient Egyptian village that existed from the Eighteenth Dynasty to Roman times.

During the Byzantine era, the occupants of the site extended the community's boundaries inside and over the temple precinct (Winlock and Crum, 1926: 4). These developments may have been gradual and under the influence of demographic pressures, but are also likely to have resulted from religious motivations. The banning of paganism by Byzantine Emperor Theodosius I in 391 CE resulted in a period of Coptic iconoclast fervor that eventually gave way to a church hierarchy–sanctioned practice of establishing centers of worship in ancient temples, with intrusive churches and monastic settlements making adaptive reuse of temple and burial complexes throughout Egypt (Ritner, 1998: 29–30).

Jeme seventh- and eighth-century documents establish that the town was occupied well into the Arab era, serving as a regional center for the monastic communities located in and around the ancient tombs of the nearby Holy Mountain of Jeme, that is, the Theban Mountain,[1] between the sixth and eighth centuries (Wilfong, 2002: 1, 4 n8, 145).

The demise of Jeme as a regional center of importance was likely an outcome of political rather than demographic circumstances. Godlewski

Hurubati Coptic weaver at his loom.

(1986: 77–78) postulates a connection between the abandonment of one of the Jeme monasteries, the Monastery of Phoibammon at Dayr al-Bahari, and the uprising of Dihya ibn-Musab in 782 CE in Upper Egypt. The subsequent countermeasures against him and his followers could account for the lack of any written documents from Jeme after 785 CE.

The sequence of events involving the various west bank settlements is far from clear. The archaeological record suggests that the inhabitants of Jeme thought they were leaving temporarily, blocking up doors and hiding valuables as they left, but it remains difficult to establish if the reasons for their departure indeed applied to all sites. The Monasteries of Dayr al-Bahari, Qurnat Mara'i and Dayr al-Bakhit (above Dra' Abu al-Naga) appear to have been abandoned around the same time as Jeme, but the Monastery of Epiphanius (the tomb of Daga at Shaykh 'Abd al-Qurna) had already been disbanded before that time, as had many other desert-based monastic sites (Winlock and Crum, 1926: passim).

It is likewise unclear what happened to the Christians after their departure from Jeme and the dissolution of the monastic communities in the adjoining hills. If political suppression was a factor, some wholesale enforced evacuation may have been conceivable. Accounts of an exodus to Esna at the time of the Muslim conquest figure in the writings of nineteenth-century travelers, and may reflect survivals of an eighth-century southerly departure from Jeme (Wilfong, 2002: 153).[2]

The permanent scattering of Jeme Christians across the countryside in front of a military advance may be ruled out. It seems unlikely that onetime town dwellers would readily opt for a rather more rural existence in favor of evacuating to another large town. At least one other nearby settlement that could have absorbed Jeme inhabitants not only failed to show any evidence of an increasing population concentration, but in effect ceased to exist about the same time. Pottery analysis has established that the area of the Seti I Temple at the northern end of the necropolis was continually occupied during the Byzantine period (Myśliwiec, 1987: 119), its Christian community, like Jeme, established in accordance with the church-sanctioned reuse of ancient sites. Excavated remains of sixth-, seventh-, and eighth-century pottery kilns (Myśliwiec, 1987: 119, 192) suggest the community may have been of some economic or utilitarian importance for nearby Jeme, as it was for the nearby Monastery of Epiphanius (Myśliwiec, 1987: 192). Despite the disturbed archaeological contexts for early Islamic ceramics found in the Seti I Temple (Myśliwiec,

1987: 167), an upper eighth-century age for Coptic wares may be taken to represent a break in the archaeological record that coincides with the demise of Jeme. It is here postulated that this northerly Seti I Temple community likewise became dissolved and dispersed against a background of contemporary and linked circumstances.

These developments may not have meant a total evacuation of the Theban west bank, with desert-based solitary monastic practitioners and scattered farming settlements remaining. Possibly their continuing activities provided some remembered or familial link, for at the end of the ninth century there is evidence for people returning to the area. Such may not necessarily have involved the rehabitation of the earlier sites, at least not until much later when earlier connections with the specific sociality of these locations would have been long lost, and possibly only after Muslim settlements had become established there in the meantime.

But, as Henein has demonstrated (Henein, 1988), even small Coptic communities can survive and thrive in relative social and demographic isolation, provided access to a local or regional church or monastery ensures continuity of religious practice. Dayr al-Muharab, place of worship for today's decentralized west bank community of Coptic Christians and located just west of the ruins of Jeme, eventually took the place of the institutional facilities once offered by the Jeme-focused community. Winlock postulates that the church has functioned in that location "since medieval times and possibly occupies the site of one of the still earlier establishments of Jême" (Winlock and Crum, 1926: 5, 177), although others claim the structure to be modern (Coquin and Martin, 1991: 717).[3]

Shifting sociopolitical circumstances or independent demographic factors, which saw the return of Christians to the Theban west bank, did not lead to a reconstruction of the former Jeme. But neither did it result in the permanent evacuation of the site: the Madinat Habu temple complex, until the time of its archaeological clearance, remained one of the settlements inhabited by dispersed Coptic Christians, linked by a common place of worship, and evidencing a decentralized settlement pattern that came to characterize the west bank Coptic community. Some of its members may again have chosen to occupy the tomb habitations of the earlier hermits in the Holy Mountain of Jeme, or again settled around other prominent sites offering both shelter and potential for ecclesiastical worship such as offered by the temple of Seti I at the northern end of the necropolis. Winlock postulates here a pre-Mamluk (that is, before 1250)

Coptic village of "some size" (Winlock and Crum, 1926: 23) as a precursor to the Arab village of Old Qurna in this same location, although it is not clear whether he here refers to the community contemporaneous with Jeme or one that existed at a later date. It is no longer possible to obtain a full occupation history of the site. The area of the Seti I Temple has been archaeologically cleared on several occasions, most recently by the German Archaeological Institute, with an emphasis on pharaonic remains. Although seventh- and eighth-century Coptic materials have (at least in part) been published (Myśliwiec, 1987: 98–179), no archaeological record of more recent periods has survived, therefore rendering it impossible to reconstruct a reliable history of the site.[4]

However, archaeological excavation of one of the hillside monasteries in the necropolis established strong similarities between the material culture of seventh-century monks and twentieth-century 'peasants' (Winlock and Crum, 1926: 96). The fact that Qurnawi excavators recognized some of this Coptic material as their own does not unambiguously prove that occupation of the hillside locations has been continuous since the seventh century. It does, nevertheless, establish that the matrix of material culture used during the Byzantine era did not essentially change in the face of significant demographic and sociopolitical developments brought about by the Arab conquest, but was adopted wholesale by population groups newly settling in the area (Winlock and Crum, 1926: 96). Given the overlap of the Christian and Muslim periods during the seventh and eighth centuries, local knowledge regarding the types of shelter available to the communities who occupied the tombs and temples at the foot of the Theban escarpment during the monastic period will have represented a cultural substratum capable of influencing the choices available, initially to Muslim newcomers, but also in turn to Coptic Christians returning to the area at later dates.[5]

Arab arrivals and Qurnawi origins

It remains far from clear where the origin and history of contemporary Qurnawi connect with the 'Muslim newcomers,' and the details of their arrival remain conjecture. Although continuity of human occupation of the Theban west bank in varying degrees since pharaonic times cannot be ruled out, as has been suggested, it is nevertheless now difficult to locate the biological origins of Qurnawi. It remains speculative to pinpoint a particular moment in time when their community crystallized out of the ethnic flux of indigenous and exogenous influences that followed in the wake of the Arab conquest of Egypt in 642 CE. In the future, definitive answers may be provided by new genetic technologies and Human Genome Diversity Projects.[6] Until such time, those who attribute Qurnawi occupation of the Theban Necropolis to thirteenth-century Bedouin Arab groups of medieval tomb robbers will continue to do so, as will those who make no distinction between illicit activities in the necropolis that have taken place in ancient and more recent times.

Despite such general imprecision disguising most historical specificity of composition and cultural affiliation, it cannot be disputed that Qurnawi origins derive at least in part from ancestral clans of itinerant desert dwellers. These clans must be assumed to have had their roots in the Arabian Peninsula, migrating across North Africa as part of the Islamic expansion and following the Arab conquest of Egypt. Records of such migrations across North Africa survive encoded in the epic narratives of the Banu Hilal Bedouin tribe, which date to the tenth and eleventh centuries (Reynolds, 1995: xiii).

These Bedouin incursions became politically important during the periods of social instability that characterized the Mamluk era of modern Egyptian history (1250–1516). The Mamluks, who originally emerged from a regiment conscripted from Turkic slaves, created a clear demarcation between Egypt's indigenous population and its foreign leaders. Political unrest within Mamluk ranks created periods of internal upheaval that often resulted in open country-wide revolt, the social fabric further undermined by the periodic twin scourge of plague and famine. The sociopolitical climate enabled Bedouin infiltration of the cultivated lands, causing peasant farmers (fellahin) to flee, and weakening the state's economic position with the disruption of trade links through fellahin and Bedouin acts of brigandage (al-Sayyid Marsot, 1985: 33–34). Such historically documented brigandage has been described as diagnostic of the so-called *badu-hadar* division, that is, the tense and conflict-prone opposition between Bedouin and sedentary population groups that runs through Arab society and culture (Barakat, 1993: 48).

Yet, in reality, the history of Egypt's Bedouin population groups is far more complex than the above would suggest. Even a close reading of the detailed archaeological and historical study by Jean-Claude Garcin of the medieval regional center of Qus, which includes the macro-historical background that will also have informed social and political events in

Luxor, located thirty kilometers upstream, can barely begin to unravel the population movements and patterns of sedentarization taking place across Egypt during Mamluk and Ottoman rule (Garcin, 1976). The dispersal of groups of Bedouin across the Sa'id—that is, Upper Egypt—and their resulting territorial claims is not simply a history of incursions into new areas, but also of forced transmigration, economic expansion, internal dissension among factions, tribal enmity, political alliances among tribes as well as with Mamluk or Ottoman rulers, and a complex network of kinship affiliations. Although a review of this history falls well beyond the scope of this chapter, some small detail relevant to Qurnawi history may be penciled in.

Johann Ludwig Burckhardt, who traveled extensively in Egypt between 1812 and 1817, provides an insight into existing tribally defined territorial demarcations. According to Burckhardt the Hawwara tribe occupied the west bank between "[al]Siout up to Farshiout" (Burckhardt, 1819: 531). South of the Hawwara were "the tribe of Kaszas [Qasas] who people the country on the west banks from Thebes to near Esne, and to whom belong the inhabitants of Gourne, Orment, and Reheygat (all celebrated for their bold plundering enterprises), [and who] were their determined enemies; although both these and the Howara report that they have the same origin from Barbary" (Burckhardt, 1819: 532).[7]

Garcin, drawing on Arab-language sources, further identifies Qasas as belonging to a group called "Labid of the Sulaym" who originate in the "Desert of Barqa," but confesses he has lost their trail and does not know when they settled at Thebes: "since when . . . are they settled there?" (Garcin, 1976: 500–501).[8] During the early Mamluk era, around 1380, the Sulaym were among several groups either migrating from the Delta to Upper Egypt, or ordered to settle there, as in the case of the Hawwara (Garcin, 1976: 469). Both the Sulaym and the Hawwara thus have in common a northern origin, although such may not extend to 'Barbary,' as claimed by Burckhardt. Garcin equates the Sulaym with Arabian Peninsular origins, while his persistent use of the term 'Berber' for the Hawwara indeed suggests North African connections.[9]

Burckhardt's reference to "bold plundering enterprises"—and its identification with a particular form of sociocultural behavior—provides a reference point marking the interaction between western travelers and Qurnawi. It does so in two ways. Many early European commentators have remarked in their diaries on the seemingly antisocial behavior experienced by them when visiting the Theban west bank. This behavior may be explained at least in part by the sort of brigandage associated with the sixteenth-century episodes of sociopolitical and economic instability referred to earlier. But the very presence of these Europeans will have stimulated both interaction and reaction too, and must therefore be considered as a factor impacting on local forms of behavior.

The Anonymous Venetian reconsidered

Early western—primarily European—travelers have visited Egypt during the past five centuries at least. As we will see, such early visits to Egypt may have been undertaken for professional reasons, but many also included it as a destination on a rather more culturally focused 'Grand Tour.' The underlying motivation for either category of traveler will have been different and may have included an Enlightenment-inspired quest for knowledge, a personal search—possibly also inspired by a dawning humanist worldview—to establish the veracity of the Old Testament biblical narrative, or the perceived need to advance nationalist views of material and intellectual expansion. In this latter sense, the term 'traveler' does not simply denote those who undertook a journey, but also longer-term expatriates, such as diplomats and those locally employed in private enterprise or practicing some professional expertise, and who, in the course of their duties, visited various localities in and gained knowledge of Egypt. Many have left written records in the form of personal papers preserved in western manuscript collections, representing an ongoing source for further research and publication, or they have published written accounts of their experiences.[10]

The earliest narrative relating a sojourn in Upper Egypt was written in 1589 by the so-called 'Anonymous Venetian' who, for the most part we will simply call 'the Venetian.' The Venetian, possibly an engineer tasked with researching early Venetian plans for a canal across the Isthmus of Suez (Burri, 1971: 25–26), was the first European traveler to venture beyond Cairo and explore Upper Egypt, or at least the first to have left a written account of such a journey. The surviving codex manuscript, preserved in Florence, evidences a process of editing and copying, but its precise history is unclear: "one cannot say, if the hand which has written the codex is that of the author himself" (Burri, 1971: 7). The Venetian does not mention the villages of the Luxor west bank by name, but nevertheless, a first reading immediately and emphatically evokes what is known about al-Qurna through later authors, namely evidence of Qurnawi behavior that is based on the safety offered by the nearby tombs.

The passage in question concerns observations made by the Venetian while traveling upstream in a place called "El Chosas," which is between the villages of Dendera and Gebelein, a two-days' sailing distance.[11] He makes reference to the unruly character of local west bank Arab tribes and recounts how boat captains, in fear of attack, prefer to disembark on the east bank.[12] He describes the violent relations and the taxation arrangements that exist between the Arabs and the Turks, and he relates how the Arabs hide in the mountain when attacked by the Turks (Burri, 1971: 79–81). Immediately following these observations, he continues to describe the ancient monuments of the Luxor west bank, visible only from a distance due to the yearly inundation (Burri, 1971: 81–83), before describing in some detail the archaeological sites of Luxor proper (Burri, 1971: 83–105).

While the section covered by pages seventy-nine through eighty-one may refer to Arab opposition to Ottoman rule along the Nile south of Qena, the specific location used as the background for this argument is not the immediate environs of Qena, as interpreted by Burri, but rather Luxor further to the south, and more specifically the Luxor west bank. This assessment is not only inevitable, but also crucial, as the entire passage makes little sense without it. Several issues of note come to us from Burri's annotated transcription which must lead to this conclusion.

The Venetian's use of the name 'El Chosas' requires clarification. The question arises how he could have identified 'El Chosas' as "that place" in an area representing a two-days' sailing distance. His account condenses this distance into just two paragraphs and he may have understood the name of 'El Chosas' to refer to the Nile's entire 'Qena Bend,' that is, the distance from "Dendale à Giebelen." Alternatively, he may have mistaken an earlier name for a later locality when writing his account for the preceding days, or a juxtaposition of names occurred during the manuscript's history of subsequent copying. But this remains conjecture.

Carla Burri, the manuscript's editor, firmly identifies ("without doubt") the Venetian's "El Chosas" as the village of "El Khassas" (or "Naga el Ekhsas"), which she locates nine kilometers southeast of Qena. This location matches that of the village of "el Qasas" in Garcin (1976, Plate III), but other than through changes in the course of the Nile, is

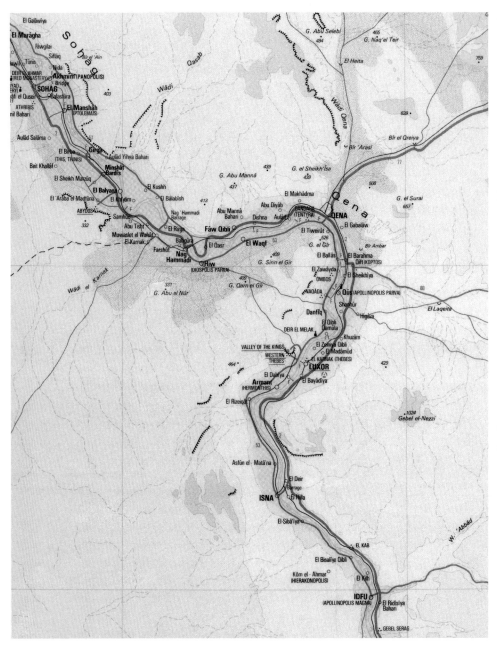

The course of the Nile between Edfu and Sohag, including the 'Qena Bend' with Qus, Luxor, and Western Thebes. Detail of the 1994 Bartholomew 1:1,000,000 map 'Egypt.' Grid lines indicate 25° and 26° north, 32° and 33° east. © Collins Bartholomew, 1994. Reproduced by kind permission of HarperCollins Publishers. www.bartholomewmaps.com.

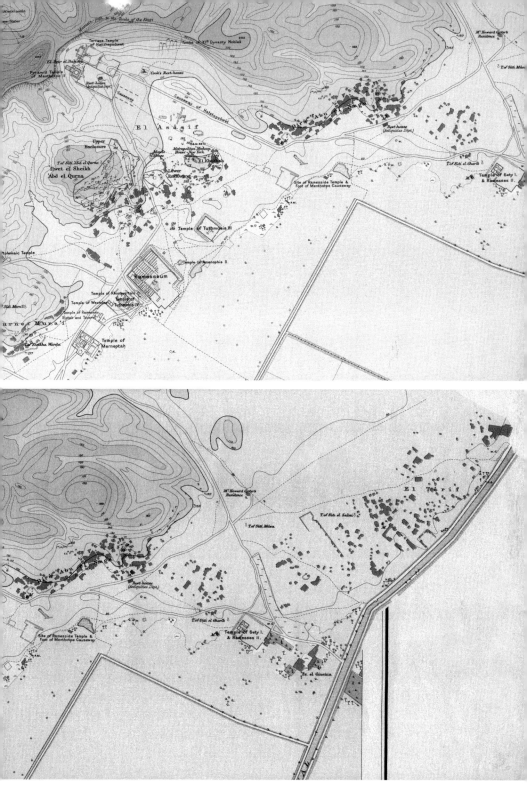

Details from the 1922 Survey of Egypt 1:10,000 map of the Theban west bank. From the author's private collection. © Survey of Egypt.

difficult to reconcile with a discussion about the west bank (Burri, 1971: 81n96). Because of the disjunction between Burri's location and that of the narrative itself, it seems more probable that the Anonymous Venetian never intended his 'place' to refer to a single village or physical locality, as in Burri's interpretation. In fact, Burri's very annotation of *"ce lieu"* ("that place") as "district" indeed seems to preclude this option, making her identification of the Venetian's 'place' with the specific location of "El Khassas" (el Qasas) village all the more curious.

Yet, following Richardson's observation that regional names may follow the name of the principal village, Burri's "El Khassas" (el Qasas) may indeed constitute a "district," possibly even the distance from "Dandale à Giebelen," if that is what the narrative implies. However, the linkage between named village and district is not simply geographic, but forms part of an environment that is first and foremost social, and we may conclude that the name of "El Chosas" provided by the Venetian is less that of a specific place or district than it is the name of the dominant tribe, "Kaszas" (Qasas), who inhabited the larger west bank area south of Farshut, as recorded by Burckhardt (1819: 352).[13] The correlation between the demonstrated anxiety of the Venetian's captain and Burckhardt's description of "their bold plundering enterprises" supports this interpretation of a wider social rather than a simply geographical context.

However, if it is also accepted that the tribal name of Qasas is synonymous with the territory they occupy, located by Burckhardt between Thebes and Esna, then it follows that the Venetian's description of this central part of the Sa'id, with references to the distance between the mountains and the river, and the visual appeal of the countryside, is therefore not something that is specific to the immediate region of Qena, but applies to what Garcin has called "the great Theban Plain" formed by "the relative width of the valley" between Armant in the south and Qena in the north, a distance of about sixty kilometers (Garcin, 1976: 6–7). The point here is that the Venetian's "place," therefore, applies equally well to any location between Qena and Armant, or indeed any location inside Qasas territory, and is not specifically exclusive to the immediate surroundings of Qena. That the narrative indeed is not confined to a location in the direct vicinity of Qena, but is in fact concentrated on the Luxor west bank, can be concluded from several textual markers that indicate specific topographic and social features peculiar to that area.

First, a certain concentration of villages appears to have stood out as remarkable for European travelers acquainted with the intermittent procession of rural settlements observed while sailing upstream, and several make reference to what may have been the contrasting density of the villages in the Luxor area.[14] Claude Sicard, the Jesuit missionary responsible for the first modern map of Egypt, listed these villages by name in 1722: "Habou, Corna, Beairat, Luxor, Carnaq" (Martin, 1982b: 228; Sauneron and Martin, 1982: 155, 169). Likewise, Pierre Pincia, Sicard's 1721 traveling companion, reports on the "miserable villages" that are all that is left of ancient Thebes (Martin, 1982a: 138). Pincia's inadvertent linking of ancient Thebes with the modern villages is important for, significantly, the location of four of these villages directly results from the presence of the ancient Theban monuments and the shelter offered by them. In 1721, Habu, Qurna, Luxor and Karnak villages were located in and over the unexcavated remains of Madinat Habu, Seti I, Luxor, and Karnak temples respectively. If such a concentration of villages was sufficiently significant also to be mentioned by the Venetian, then it seems probable that they concern the same cluster of settlements scattered throughout the Theban area.

Second, the use of "the mountain, which is their fortress" (Burri, 1971: 81; and note the appropriate use of the singular) can only refer to the Theban Mountain opposite Luxor. The use of the tombs for refuge there constituted the very element of resilient social behavior that was later identified as characteristic of the local community's response to times of stress, and was noted by such European observers as Bruce (1790: 125), Denon (1803, 2: 86–87; 3: 30–32, 47–51, 177–78), Norden (1757: 83), and St. John (1845: 381, 384). Such use of the mountain was quite singular, and did not refer to any other area, be it closer to Qena, or in the Theban plain generally. Apart from the absence of other suitable locations serving a similar purpose, this can be concluded from the fact that, in addition to local population groups, the tombs of the Theban Necropolis were also used by those seeking refuge from the east bank at Luxor, as well as by those coming from other dispersed areas throughout the Theban plain. Knowledge of the potential for refuge in the necropolis thus seemed widespread throughout the area, turning the Theban Mountain indeed into a focal point during times of armed unrest, as demonstrated at the time of the Arab Rebellion of 1822–23: "Next day the disastrous result of the battle was known over the whole Plain of Thebes, and parties of the insurgents began to drop into Gournou, and get ready to fly to the excavations on the first appearance of the soldiers. . . . Many of the inhabitants of Luxor passed over to Gournou and took up their abode in the tombs" (St. John, 1845: 383).[15]

Third, and decisive for identifying the area about which the Venetian writes, is his immediate reference to the Colossi of Memnon, which he locates "in this countryside, which belongs to them, opposite Luxor," thereby linking ownership of the surrounding fields to the very Arabs who take refuge in the mountain mentioned in the preceding paragraph. By association, that mountain can only be the Theban Mountain. Both the flow of the narrative and the text's internal evidence thus point to the Theban west bank, and local communities taking refuge in the Theban Necropolis during times of political unrest.

To link the above evidence to a specific west bank locality, Caroline Simpson (2001: 2) has suggested that 'the place' about which the Venetian writes refers to al-Qsasiya, one of the large *saff* tombs and tribal quarters in what is now the northern Qurna area of al-Tarif and which is located close to the west bank landing place used by Europeans when making the crossing from Karnak village on the east bank. Viewing the names of Qasas and al-Qsasiya as related and—following Richardson—representing both a distinct locality and a larger region, as well as the dominant tribe inhabiting that area, then the certain social and historical context also appears entirely compatible with this identification, providing further proof that the Anonymous Venetian's 'place' was in fact the Theban west bank. Yet, according to his text, no west bank landing was ever made here. Closer inspection of the Colossi was made impossible because of the inundation, and although al-Tarif lies on higher ground and may have been accessible, the text nevertheless makes no mention of a visit there. In fact, the Venetian observes that boat captains refused to go to the west bank and he was likely told the name, location, and relevant social particulars of its inhabitants by his own captain in explanation of why he similarly refused to disembark there. Indeed, in later accounts that same west bank area is described as "the resort of the most formidable banditti . . . the meanest, the most frightful, and most miserable place in appearance I ever beheld" (Sonnini, 1800: 650).

Whichever was the reason why the Venetian never set foot on the west bank, a clear articulation of the Theban west bank communities by European travelers was not to take place for another 130 years. It was not until 1722 that the Theban villages finally received their first mention by a European when identified by name on Sicard's map: "Habou, Corna, Beairat, Luxor, Carnaq" (Martin, 1982b: 228; Saunéron and Martin, 1982: 155, 169). For the first time in modern history, al-Qurna was being lifted out of obscurity to become inscribed in the west's emerging Egyptological consciousness, and to become increasingly located at the center of western academic preoccupation. In all respects it was a noteworthy development, but one only made possible by the Anonymous Venetian defaulting on a much earlier claim.

The emergence of Qurnawi communal identity

If the above interpretation of the 1589 Anonymous Venetian is advanced as the correct reading, then attributing a much earlier date to our first observations of west bank sociality has important consequences for a historical reconstruction of the Theban west bank villages, in particular al-Qurna. The existence of this earliest European literary reference to the west bank communities enables us to assign a measure of visibility to what can tentatively be called a community of Qurnawi, with a high degree of probability, and at the very least, to the early part of the sixteenth century.

The significance of this observation lies not only in the recognition that here we have a first account of the villages of the Luxor west bank, nor in the fact that this early literary record confirms its inhabitants as exhibiting the sociopolitical practice of using the Theban Mountain and its ancient funerary architectural spaces for refuge during Ottoman attacks, a practice commented on in much later accounts. Importantly, if such early historically documented behavior is in evidence of a culturally situated resilient predisposition and a more general resistance to the imposition of Ottoman rule, and if we postulate that this behavior was already established in some recognizable form by 1517, that is, at the time of the Ottoman conquest of Egypt, then we may rightly question whether Qurnawi society evidencing these characteristics may not have been present earlier still.

From the Venetian's description, it appears that west bank tribal aggression was specifically directed at the Turks, that is, the members and armed representatives of the Ottoman ruling elite. The levying of taxes, despite the somewhat benign execution claimed by the Venetian (Burri, 1971: 81), would have been a constant reminder of the imposition of foreign rule, and further perpetuated the violence. Ultimately, this situation was not very dissimilar to the foreign presence of the Mamluks, and the demarcation that their presence created in society, referred to earlier. Based on this commonality, the inference is that, if the reaction to Ottoman domination, with its attacks on Turks and the subsequent withdrawal to the mountain for refuge during times of reprisals, was in some ways a direct outcome of the imposition of foreign governance, then similar practices may also have characterized west bank tribal and Mamluk relations, and therefore possibly date back to as early as 1250, when Mamluk influence first became established. This would indeed situate the presence of resilient west bank social behavior predicated on the presence of nearby tombs right inside the timeframe when political unrest was rife and when Bedouin incursions contributed to a weakening of the state's economic position. Rather than requiring forms of social behavior postulated in terms of Arab or Bedouin tribal ethnicities, we may argue the strong relationship between a cognitive awareness of the existence of safe refuge in the form of nearby tombs, and an emerging measure of resilient behavior that became culturally constituted and transmitted to successive generations of Qurnawi, and recognized and described by local observers.

What prompted the need for such shelter will be addressed in the next chapter. Here, it is worthwhile recognizing that the use of the tombs for refuge was only one aspect of western observers' commentary. The other aspect concerned the alleged particularly antisocial behavior of the Theban west bank inhabitants that colored relations with western travelers for centuries. Here too, and instead of resorting to ethnic categories, the archaeological qualities of the Qurnawi social landscape and its connections with early global dynamics may provide clues.

Badu blood lines, *mumiya* supply lines

The use of the necropolis' architectural landscape in explanation of social behavior does not intend to deny the reality of thirteenth-century west bank Bedouin *(Badu)* and Arab tribal groups settling on the edge of the cultivation at Thebes. The point has already been made that identifying the surrounding archaeological landscape as a crucial factor in emerging local social forms excludes an emphasis on real or implied ethnic behavioral characteristics. Whether intended as a romanticized, Orientalist representation of the 'noble savage' or even plain racial stereotyping, such imagery will likely subvert an analysis of other sociocultural factors that could explain specific forms of west bank human behavior and adaptation. The presence of ancient funerary architecture and its connection with a form of communal resistance may be understood as one such explanatory factor.

Nevertheless, when Garcin, drawing on the experiences of both the Anonymous Venetian and Ludwig Burckhardt, refers to the reputation of the Theban tribes as "sinister," "dangerous," (Garcin, 1976: 501), and "hostile" (Garcin, 1976: 524), he thereby acknowledges them to be different from surrounding Bedouin tribes. Going by these travelers' reports, the behavior of the Qasas at Thebes indeed appears atypical and uncharacteristic even for groups already in conflict with the state and rife with internal dissension.[16] This difference cannot be explained in terms of perceived west bank Bedouin behavioral characteristics alone, and the question may legitimately be asked what other factors can have impacted on the behavior of the Theban Qasas.

Rather than accepting west bank tribal aggression as predisposed by virtue of a postulated *Badu* gene pool, it has already been suggested that sociopolitical and economic factors must also be brought to bear. But Mamluk and Ottoman rule and their particular taxation regimes represent only one aspect of this. Local tribal behavior was also affected by the impact of external western influences: the gradual emergence of a specific European pattern of consumption, and the arrival of western agents seeking to organize and maintain the necessary relations of production. These external factors warrant equal consideration.

Although issues concerning the collection of antiquities are not featured in the Venetian's account, and were in fact not among the preoccupations of Renaissance travelers in Egypt (Dannenfeldt, 1959: 16), this is not to say that the involvement of the west bank in a trade centering on ancient remains did not exist or did not play a possible role in the observed behavior of west bank indigenous communities. More historical work is required on the origins and extent of this early trade, or the nature of European control of, or involvement in, its organization, extraction, and transport. But there are several observations we can make at this point to further demonstrate that an emphasis on some ethnically constituted psychological or genetic predisposition in explanation of west bank tribal behavior is too simplistic, and that such ignores the particular archaeological aspects of the west bank landscape, and a specific form of early European demand that was directed at it.

The fear of boat owners and captains to disembark on the west bank between Dendera and Gebelein is linked by the Anonymous Venetian with the rebellious nature of its inhabitants, but the Venetian's account nevertheless sounds uncannily familiar when compared with that of Frederick Norden's 1737 visit to the Theban west bank. Here, too, the captain of Norden's vessel has extreme reservations about disembarking his passengers on the west bank: "though he had navigated more than twenty years upon the Nile, he should never have ventured to land in this place; the inhabitants had such a character of being villains" (Norden, 1757: 83). When Norden chooses not to heed his advice, the captain swears not to wait for the travelers' return and to depart in their absence. Being threatened in kind that he would be made to "pay dearly for his insolence" the captain backs down, but he continues to plead that the traveling party should not land there, if only out of respect to him:

> he began to pray and beg of us not to go for his sake; for, said he, if you are so happy as to escape, you will however expose me to the utmost danger, for if I am ever forced to land here again, I shall certainly be murder'd for having brought you hither, from whence the inhabitants will be assiur'd you have carried off the hidden treasures. I had before heard so much of this sort of stuff, as to be very little moved by it. (Norden, 1741: 9; 1757: 67–68)

The captain's final statement is indeed surprising, for his main concern, that the inhabitants of the west bank are murderers and villains, now takes on an extra dimension. Assuming that any materials of value associated with 'hidden' objects indeed constitute 'treasure,' he seems to suggest that local inhabitants' behavior is at least in part tied up with claims of ownership over locally found antiquities. Richard Pococke, who visited the Theban west bank within days of Frederick Norden's visit, confirms reigning eighteenth-century local sentiments about Europeans and antiquities:

> The people had come rudely to the boat when I was absent, and had said that they would see whether this stranger would dare come out another day, having taken great umbrage at my copying the inscriptions; and they had dropt some expression as if they could assault the boat by night, if I staid, which, without doubt they said, that they might make me go away,

for they seemed desirous that I should leave the place; as strongly possessed with a notion of a power that Europeans have of finding treasures,
and conveying them away by magic art. (Pococke, 1743: 105)

It thus appears that antiquities did indeed constitute a factor in west
bank communities' relations with visitors during the 1730s, and the question may fruitfully be asked if the same motivations were also an ingredient in the Venetian's account of boat captains' reticence to disembark on
the west bank 148 years earlier. If so, this would not simply strengthen
the view that the Venetian's account of west bank tribal behavior indeed
concerned the archaeological landscape of the Theban west bank and not
the northern end of the 'Qena Bend.' Additional questions must also be
asked in order to clarify why the communities of the Theban west bank
had made a reputation for themselves in this manner. For example, what
were the circumstances and organizational dynamics that gave rise to this
situation? Assuming that locally held notions of treasures being conveyed
away "by magic art" reflects a mythical representation of reality, what were
the structuring features that caused antiquities to become central in the
relations between local people and west bank visitors at this early stage?

Although it is not evident in the visits of Norden and Pococke, during
the late eighteenth century, visitors' interests became strongly focused
on the acquisition of antiquity collections: "I thus made a pretty ample
collection of fragments of antiquity" (Sonnini, 1800: 650). During the
nineteenth century, the collecting of antiquities indeed took on wholesale
proportions. But by contrast, interest in ancient Egypt between the eleventh and the seventeenth centuries had largely been confined to *mumiya*,
ground and powdered mummy that served as a raw material in medicines
and artists' paints.[17] Although the extraction of this resource will surely
have resulted in the discovery and pilfering of ancient artifacts, it may be
too early to speak of an existing focus on antiquities collecting during the
life of the Anonymous Venetian: "Few of the travelers to Egypt brought
back with them objects found in the tombs and sands or, at least, this fact
has not been recorded" (Dannenfeldt, 1959: 16).

Dannenfeldt's observation is important in view of longstanding local
beliefs that the tombs of the Theban Mountain were cut as repositories
for treasure in the event of flood. By consequence, as Garcin puts it,
"The search for pharaonic treasures has, without doubt, never ceased,"
and is mentioned in the records of Arab geographers from the tenth

century onward (Garcin, 1976: 11).[18] Despite Pococke's statement that local beliefs in 1737 held Europeans capable of finding treasures and spiriting them away either by means of magic or otherwise, as also reflected in the statement by Norden's captain, Dannenfeldt suggests that 148 years earlier there was as yet no, or very little, interest in the acquisition of antiquities. Consequently, the wholesale European extraction of ancient artifacts characteristic of later centuries will not have been an issue, and indigenous sensibilities involved with the loss of such 'treasure' will therefore not have materially impacted on relations between west bank communities and such early visiting Europeans as the Anonymous Venetian. Yet, negative relations appear to have been in place well before the era of large-scale antiquities collecting commenced. To explain this circumstance we must look more closely at the place of *mumiya*, the other local resource that could simultaneously have represented 'wealth,' the extraction of which may have left indigenous west bank communities vulnerable to exploitation.

Arab geographers provide early references for the use of *mumiya*. According to the eleventh-century al-Bakri, in the area between Qus and Aswan "there are caves cut into the mountains of that region that contain the tombs of the dead from where they obtain fragrant *mumiya*: they find it in the bones and the shrouds of the dead."[19] In an attempt to more precisely locate the source of this "fragrant *mumiya*," it seems reasonable to suggest that among eleventh-century Arab or Egyptian writers what is now known as the Theban Necropolis could not be identified in any meaningful manner. The prominence accorded to western Thebes by such Greek and Roman authors as Diodorus Siculus and Strabo formed no part of Arab or indigenous Egyptian consciousness, nor did any locally remembered historical information survive until recovered through post-Renaissance western scientific inquiry. It stands to reason, therefore, to assume that the mountains of that region as referred to by al-Bakri are synonymous with the Theban Mountain and its necropolis. Additionally, Thebes' close proximity to Qus, if that city indeed acted as a *mumiya* trading center, as suggested by Garcin (1976: 12n3), would have greatly facilitated the supply of raw material. Alternatively, and in the very least, supply options must have included the Theban Necropolis as one among other ancient burial grounds, although one would be hard pressed to find such a site between Qus and Aswan that would potentially have yielded more *mumiya* than the cemeteries opposite Luxor.

The Theban Necropolis, therefore, is likely not to have been simply one of the locations in the supply network of the *mumiya* trade, but was rather situated at its very center, at least in Upper Egypt, as confirmed in 1799 by Vivant Denon: "the situation of their village had given them almost an exclusive trade in this singular article of commerce" (Denon, 1803, 3: 82). Not much detail of its operations is known. Garcin suggests that the city of Qus may have been a trading center, and that its business was not practiced openly (Garcin, 1976: 12n3). Dannenfeldt reports that the export of a large shipment of *mumiya* was "accomplished by bribery" (Dannenfeldt, 1959: 20). According to 'Abd al-Latif, writing at the end of the twelfth century, "the inhabitants of the countryside transport [the mummies] to the city, where they sell them for very little: I have purchased for half an Egyptian *dirhem* three heads filled with this substance" ('Abd al-Latif, quoted in Garcin, 1976: 12n2).

The information available from scattered Arab sources, complemented by the extant observations of western travelers, is in many respects akin to the fossil record in palaeontology, where fragmentary finds are the only source of available information to reconstruct the most likely trajectory of human evolution. Similarly, the written records that have survived from early western travelers may represent only a sample of the number of westerners who have actually ventured into Upper Egypt, most of whom will not have left any evidence of their activities there. Furthermore, Carla Burri has suggested that the Anonymous Venetian may have been an engineer living in Egypt, one of a contingent of late-sixteenth-century expatriate Venetians in Egypt who, significantly, also counted among their number "many" involved in commerce (Burri, 1971: 26).

It may be hypothesized, in an effort to fill in one of the 'missing links' in this 'fossil record,' that this community of European traders in Egypt also included those who managed the supply side of the European demand for *mumiya*. Again, the mechanics of their practical control over local labor are not known, but it seems reasonable to expect that Europeans, operating alongside Egyptian agents, may have visited the Theban burial grounds to oversee the extraction of *mumiya* long before the Anonymous Venetian first documented the behavioral characteristics of west bank tribes, and long before the search for ancient artifacts resulted in similar operations during the nineteenth century. John Sanderson, a late-sixteenth-century English merchant who arranged the export of a large shipment of *mumiya* from Egypt, documented visiting a tomb and described his part in the recovery of mummified remains (Dannenfeldt, 1959: 20–21). His direct involvement suggests that European merchants may not simply have controlled a long-distance trade between Cairo and Upper Egypt, but themselves participated in the exploration of ancient cemeteries. It is postulated here, then, that the Theban Necropolis' place in the *mumiya* trade, the controls exercised over local communities by Europeans managing its supply, and the possibly exploitative relations inherent in this process, were contributing factors in the early formation of the negative attitudes toward Europeans as first described by the Anonymous Venetian, but which had become sufficiently entrenched so as to surface time and again in the interaction between the Theban west bank communities and European visitors.[20] It is to the subsequent representations of Qurnawi in the accounts of these visitors that we shall now turn.

4

"In Justice to the Inhabitants of Gournei": European Presence and Its Literary Record

The yet to be fully documented mummy trade discussed in the previous chapter demonstrates that historically the overriding preoccupation with Egypt on the part of Europeans concerned its ancient past. Ignore ideas about Venetian engineering works and generalist Enlightenment travelers in search of whatever was different, unknown, or of biblical interest. The demand for *mumiya*-derived products back in Europe, and the quest for ancient artifacts by individual and institutional collectors, at different times represented forms of consumption that mined ancient Egypt as its source.

As part of this process, the emergence of al-Qurna as a location of significance in the consciousness of the west, as evidenced in its academic corpus as well as in its use of archaeological naming conventions, in the first instance resulted from the accounts and observations made by early European visitors. But to trace the western identification of 'Qurna' with an essentially archaeological area through travelers' accounts is also to trace aspects of the Theban west bank's social geography. Initially, the documentary process occurred almost inadvertently, with ill-defined figures moving through the background of an unintended social landscape, read between the lines in travelers' pages, from where they gradually emerge both in text and in graphics. It is by the identification of individual monuments, descriptions of roads traveled, or other specific textual markers, and illustrations of identifiable sites that, in association with references to nearby population groups, a measure of social geography and its possible extent can be established within the physical landscape of the necropolis. In this way, geographically demarcated experiences, while documented under the blanket name of al-Qurna, may nevertheless contain indicators of regionally present population groups and offer clues about their relationships or movements across the foothills and the larger al-Qurna area.

At first, the European experience of Qurnawi appears very much influenced by the general legacy of west bank Qasas behavior, anchoring European assessments of local history and culture. By July 1778, when Charles Sonnini's visit took place,[1] the notoriety of west bank inhabitants had been firmly established in the travelogues of western visitors. Their reports narrate personal experiences and secondhand accounts, but do not reflect analytically on the factors that may have contributed to this situation. Norden's dismissive comment about having "heard so much of this sort of stuff" (Norden, 1741: 9) evidently made any deeper consideration superfluous.

Yet, the marginal engagement with Qurnawi on the part of obviously differently focused, often fearful, early travelers, is not all bleak, and the records of their apprehension, local appraisals, and actual experiences do offer snippets of historical and ethnographic information that document aspects of everyday indigenous west bank existence. Later accounts even document specific aspects of European interaction with the west bank communities. But in their totality, they have resulted in a scattered and at times contradictory narrative. In the following section, an overview will be given of the social space accorded to west bank villagers as represented in the records of European travelers. The intention here is not to provide a detailed overview of individual travelers themselves, but to paint a relevant if not necessarily comprehensive picture of real and perceived Qurnawi sociality as it emerges from their notebooks and published accounts. The structure advanced here will synthesize, as much as is possible, selected travelers' observations that were often separated by many years, their dispersed comments on individual topics combined into a representation of what it is that can be distilled from their records about Qurnawi sociality. Although travelers' presence was strongly focused on the ancient monuments, an ethnological account is nevertheless hidden within the corpus of their records. The purpose here is to make that account explicit, in order to create a set of historically located reference points capable of offering a context for the contemporary ethnographic continuities to be discussed in subsequent chapters.[2]

The historiography of Qurnawi society

Something must be said, first of all, about the way in which this ethnographic material has come to be represented in the literature. As will be evident from the dates and incidents reflected in the accounts of European travelers, the historiography of Qurnawi society can be divided into four phases. These phases can only be very roughly equated with distinct periods of time, as individual writers, depending on their sensitivity and powers of observation, may be seen to go against the trend of a respective period.

Phase one includes the accounts from the Anonymous Venetian (1589) to the visits by Vivant Denon (1799, published 1803), in which the characterization of Qurnawi remains firmly located in perceptions of unruly tribal behavior, and visits to the Theban west bank were often represented from the perspective of the danger inherent in such an enterprise. In the case of Denon, the earlier accounts will have received further emphasis from the hostile reaction of local communities against French military aggression but, as we will see, European perceptions of negative Qurnawi behavior were also rooted in their own misrecognition and misunderstanding of local sociopolitical and cultural sensibilities.

The second phase appears marked by the demise of Old Qurna, the village built in and around the Seti I Temple and from where a certain dispersion across the foothills, real or imagined, appears to have originated. We will comment further below on the possible background to this, but here it is important to note the fact that the event appears to have brought about a degree of pacification, as a result of which visitors apparently no longer had to fear for their personal safety, and an evident working relationship seems to have become established between Qurnawi and the increasing number of antiquities collectors who have come to frequent the scene. The extent to which the arrival of these collectors and the associated economic benefits were a factor in this pacification must be left open at this point, as such economic benefit may not always have been existent within the political environment of the day. What we may notice is an overlap between phase one and phase two, where western attitudes toward Qurnawi involvement in the excavation of antiquities are colored by the disparaging and negative perceptions characteristic of the earlier phase, as is evident in the writing of Belzoni and, later, also Rhind. At the same time, the increasing focus on the archaeological surroundings resulted in writers remaining silent on Qurnawi, except in the context of antiquities. Other than in the panoramas by Robert Hay, writers during the 1820s expended little effort on giving an account of the social environment in which they operated, despite several of them—Wilkinson, Lane, Hay, Bonomi—having spent considerable time there. Robert Richardson's 1822 account, offering brief but accurate observations on the community at al-Tarif and life on the west bank generally, is a noteworthy exception in this context (Richardson, 1822, 2: 8, 74, 112). In at least one case, that of Joseph Bonomi, whatever ethnographic observations were made, these were, somewhat inexplicably, expurgated from his personal papers along with any other references to al-Qurna.[3]

The prominent exception to this group of long-time residents of al-Qurna is Giovanni d'Athanasi, also known as 'Yanni,' the collecting agent working for Henry Salt, the British Consul (Manley and Rée, 2001), who lived in Shaykh 'Abd al-Qurna for eighteen years. His 1836 account of that period marks the third period, where some greater degree of emphasis is beginning to be placed on the life of the people among whom he lived. The practice continues to some extent in the work of Henry Rhind (1862), the title of whose work is full of promise, although his actual treatment is disappointing both for the lack of development and his personal negative attitude toward Qurnawi. In terms of literary genre, the trend of ethnographic reflection appears limited to the work of these two writers, although certain social practices continue from time to time to receive attention in the form of short treatises on antiquities, fakes, illegal excavations, and so on (Edwards, 1877: 409–17; Engelbach, 1924; Gardiner and Weigall, 1913; MacKay, 1916: 125). In virtually all of these latter cases the practices cited invariably relate to archaeological concerns, much influenced by incidents of illegal antiquities dealings during the 1880s.

As a result, the ethnographic focus of the third phase is largely forgotten and replaced by a fourth phase where the general literary emphasis is one that links antiquities with the unruly characterization of the earliest phase. Incorporating the first three of these four phases, the following paragraphs will review both the geographical recognition and the emerging cultural representation of al-Qurna and its people in the literature of the west between the late sixteenth and the late nineteenth century.

The landing place

Marked by a waterwheel and a large, "fine, spreading" *gemaze* (sycomore) tree (Lane, 2000: 324), this location was where the township of Genina is now located, most likely in the area of the modern hospital. As a mooring place, the site appears to have been used almost exclusively by European travelers, who favored it for the shade the tree cast over their boats. John Madox, visiting on September 30, 1823, describes the tree as "immense," and "affording excellent shade to four or five oxen feeding under it upon chopped straw" (Madox, 1834: 276). Qurnawi frequented the area when attending the waterwheel, or crossing the river from there to Karnak village, if circumstances required this. Crossings to Luxor village traditionally took place from a location further south, in the area of today's ferry service to Luxor, although at least one historically recorded incident suggests a local practice of downstream crossings from Luxor to Old Qurna (Bruce 1790: 138). Descriptions of western Thebes, and indeed the roads traveled, invariably commenced at the sycamore tree (Lane, 2000: 324).

If such was the preferred location for nineteenth-century visitors, it is not clear if this was also the case during the eighteenth century. In one version of his account, Norden states "we had fastened our barque on the western shore of the Nile, opposite to Carnac" (Norden, 1757: 66), a change from his earlier account in which he states "over-against Luxorene" (Norden, 1741: 9).[4] He makes no mention of either a shaded area, a nearby village, or paths providing easy access to the two Memnon Colossi that "were not above a league off, if we could have gone directly to them; but we found the grounds so divided by channels, and so covered with Turkish corn, and were forced to take so many turns, that three hours were spent, before I got near enough to the statues to take my first Drawing of them" (Norden, 1741: 9–10). Following some tense moments in a confrontation with locals there, his party moved north to the Ramesseum; they visit "several grottos" (tombs) in the foothills while traveling south to Madinat Habu, where Norden concludes his west bank sojourn. His narrative thus suggests that he only visited the southern part of the necropolis, and not the northern al-Tarif area or Qurna village in the Seti I Temple. It would appear Norden and his party walked a cross-country and possibly diagonal course to the Colossi, through the agricultural fields and bypassing the regular path leading to al-Tarif and Qurna village. Evidently, his frightened captain chose a mooring spot somewhat further south at a point east-northeast of the Colossi and at some safe distance from the immediate vicinity of a village.

Although similarly making no reference to a sycamore, Richard Pococke arrived within days, and judging by his itinerary of west bank sites (Pococke, 1743: 97–106), *did* avail himself of a landing place in the general area used by later travelers, just east of al-Tarif. The most plausible explanation for the difference between the two travelers—other than a captain's paranoia—may be that there was then no sycomore tree to draw their attention and that several localities may have presented themselves as suitable mooring places, with Norden simply selecting a site a little further upstream than did Pococke.

Village locations: 'Old Gourna,' al-Tarif, and their foothills' extensions

Half a mile from the sycomore landing place, after ten or twelve minutes and passing through a narrow stretch of agricultural land, a ruined village was reached. Situated left of the track and built against an ancient temple, this is the village identified by Lane as "El-Choor'neh," built inside and around the temple of Seti I, and uninhabited. Lane reports that the village was deserted and destroyed when government troops came through the area in pursuit of Mamluks (Lane, 2000: 325–26). Wilkinson reports in 1824–25 that this occurred some fifty years earlier (Wilkinson, MSS c.5 fol. 91ᵛ). Denon's illustrations indicate that the village in 1799 was not quite so ruined, although his inclusion of humans could simply serve purposes of scale or result from artistic license. Alternatively, and as argued by Caroline Simpson (2001: 3), the village may simply have been temporarily deserted following rumors about the advancing French army. The village was possibly permanently deserted some time around 1811, the year government forces traversed the region in pursuit of, and finally defeated, remnant Mamluk insurgents. It is uncertain what happened to the population. Wilkinson states that they "took refuge in the catacombs in the mountains which they finally fixed upon as a permanent abode & where they still live" (Wilkinson, 1835: 3).

Nevertheless, Robert Richardson provides a different account. He visited Qurna in January 1818 and, although the village was deserted, he believed it to be only temporarily so:[5]

> [Gornou] stands in a grove of palm-trees, where the cultivated soil joins the rocky flat, exactly at the spot where the road turns off to the right to go to the tombs of the kings. It consists of a number of houses of unburnt brick, generally small, but some of them much larger and of superior workmanship to the average of ruined houses in this country. At the time

when we visited it, it was quite uninhabited. The natives had abandoned it, and retired to the caves in the adjoining rocky flat; because from the low situation, and the filling up of the canals, the village is liable to be overflowed during the time of the inundation. However, when the river subsides, and the ground becomes dry, they quit their rocky tenements and return to their mansions of clay, which are more conveniently situated for water, grazing and agriculture. (Richardson, 1822, 2: 8)

According to Edward Lane, following the demise of Old Qurna, "the inhabitants fled to the neighbouring grottoes" (Lane, 2000: 325–26), where "the inhabitants of this district live not in houses or huts, but in ancient tombs, excavated in the rock" (Lane, 2000: 324). He clearly observed two inhabited areas, the plain of al-Tarif, and the foothills, most likely the nearer area of Dra' Abu al-Naga, but possibly also Shaykh 'Abd al-Qurna: "Many of the grottoes in the tract adjacent to the mountains, and many of those which are in the sides of the mountains, but not too high to be easily accessible, are now inhabited; the whole population of El-Ckoor'neh . . . residing in them" (Lane, 2000: 327).

It is indeed in the al-Tarif area where European visitors first encountered local people, but how early this occurred remains speculative. Richard Pococke, passing through al-Tarif on his way to the Valley of the Kings in 1737,

went about a mile to the north, in a sort of a street, on each side of which the rocky ground . . . has rooms cut into it, some of them being supported with pillars; and as there is not the least sign in the plain of private buildings, I thought that these in the very earliest times might serve as houses, and be the first invention after tents, and continued as a better shelter from wind, and the cold of the nights. It is a sort of gravelly stone, and the doors are cut regularly to the street. (Pococke, 1743: 97)

Pococke's use of the word 'continued' is not precise enough to suggest they were inhabited at the time of his visit, especially when upon arrival the shaykh "conducted me to his house at the village of Gournou," (Pococke, 1743: 97) marked on his map in the general area of the Seti I Temple, by which he must have intended to indicate the principal west bank settlement in the area (Pococke, 1743: 96, Plate XXIX). Since many years later Lane himself only saw "inhabited grottoes . . . here and there"

(Lane, 2000: 328), it remains possible that Pococke may not have sighted contemporary occupants of the *saff* tombs, and that both "Gournou" and the tombs of al-Tarif were occupied simultaneously. Nevertheless, the large "street"-like *saff* tombs that Pococke describes were inhabited at least at the time of Denon's visit in 1799 and will possibly have coincided with the occupation of Old Qurna village, depending on the precise date of its demise between 1778 and 1811. Be this as it may, upon the destruction of Old Qurna village, the emphasis of occupation will have shifted to the foothills at the same time as it may have further expanded across al-Tarif, with people possibly also settling among the community already encountered there by Denon.

Caroline Simpson postulates that the al-Tarif area may have been inhabited by settled nomads who are distinct from the community in and around the Seti I Temple, which consisted of indigenous "fellahiin descended from and intermarried with the earlier Coptic community" (Simpson, 2001: 4, 5). She further argues that these fellahin ultimately settled in Shaykh 'Abd al-Qurna, with today's inhabitants of al-Tarif being "long standing residents" (Simpson, 2001: 5). Yet, the modern Muslim foothills communities see themselves as descendants of the brothers Harb, 'Atya, and Ghaba who previously inhabited the Seti I Temple village, thereby suggesting that this area was also inhabited by settled nomads. The descendants of these three brothers, furthermore, view the Qsasiya of al-Tarif as relative newcomers. If the Qsasiya are indeed associated with the west bank Qasas mentioned by the Venetian and Burckhardt, as suggested by Simpson, and if such ancestral characters as Harb and his brothers are more than the mythical remnants of legendary founding narratives, then their presence, that is, the presence of other, rival, nomads in the Seti I Temple area, seems to argue against a homogenous Qasas population. This is not to say that sociopolitical divisions along clan lines may not have given rise to intraregional conflict or tension, or that no admixture may have occurred with locally present pre-Arab Coptic Christians and fellahin. We will return to the issue of tribal relations and the likelihood of factionalism below.

The relative relationship of 'Gourna' and al-Tarif may be clarified by the placement of the modern cemetery and the type of its graves, but only very tentatively so. Applying Blackman's distinction between graves in the lower desert and those in or at the edge of the cultivation (Blackman, 1927: 116), the Qurna cemetery located to the northeast of the Seti I

Richard Pococke's 1737 representation of the Theban Necropolis, showing clockwise from top: I) the peak of the Theban Mountain, the *Qurn*; G) the escarpment behind Shaykh 'Abd al-Qurna; E) Dayr al-Bahari; D) the Ramesseum; C and B) tomb entrances in the foothills; Q) the road to the Valley of the Kings; A) 'Old Qurna' village near the landing place; M and N) the Memnon Colossi; L) al-Ba'irat village; and K) Madinat Habu (Pococke, 1743: 96). Used by permission of the National Library of Australia.

Temple is not altogether conclusive. Using Henry Rhind's map (Rhind, 1862: 7), the cemetery is located in the lower desert, but equally near the edge of the cultivated area. Yet, tombs here are prepared in advance, as they are, following Blackman, in cultivated areas. If this were suggestive of connections with the agricultural area bordering Old Qurna, then the cemetery nevertheless traditionally also serviced the funerary needs of the al-Tarif community and this may also explain its desert location. Linking the cemetery with Old Qurna and the agricultural area to the south and west of the Seti I Temple may suggest that al-Tarif is a northerly expansion of Old Qurna, but to state so with some degree of confidence, we need to know more about the early settlement history of al-Tarif and its particular funerary practices, the oral history surrounding the modern cemetery, and the specifics of tomb construction there.

It is possible that attempting to make these distinctions between inhabited areas and their individual trajectories through time is unnecessary. Historical realities may in fact have been of such fluidity as to make the drawing of boundaries along spatial and ethnic categories superfluous: a western mindset seeking to create order where there was none, other than people simply moving through the landscape in search of the most appropriate form of vernacular shelter when and as driven by circumstance. In this context, it is worthy to note here that contemporary local accounts link the destruction of Old Qurna with the annual inundation, which may have been a factor before the completion of late-nineteenth-century state-sponsored irrigation projects. Clearly linking Old Qurna with al-Tarif, Richardson confirms the practice of moving "to the caves in the adjoining rocky flat," although he suggests that this would be seasonal rather than permanent: "when the river subsides, and the ground becomes dry, they quit their rocky tenements and return to their mansions of clay, which are more conveniently situated for water, grazing, and agriculture" (Richardson, 1822, 2: 8). What possibly characterized the two geographical areas more than anything else, therefore, was the seasonal migration of at least some of its occupants as directed by the agricultural and inundation cycle. For the western mindset, such might seem a logistical nightmare; however, given people's minimal possessions, vacating and reinhabiting occupation sites could be achieved quickly and with relative ease (Simpson, 1999: 7; 2000: 4; 2001: 3; 2003: 245).

Richardson not only credits this seasonal migration to the "low situation" of the village, but also to "the fillings up of the canals," which could indicate that community organization may have broken down, especially during such times of social upheaval as experienced during the period of Mamluk insurgence between 1778 (the year of Sonnini's visit, who comments on war breaking out in Upper Egypt) and 1811 (the year of the Mamluks' final defeat), causing maintenance of the irrigation channels to deteriorate, resulting in general hydrological difficulties after the inundation, and prompting a gradual shift to higher ground. Such 'hydrological difficulties' may also be inherent in the course of the Nile itself, which both Lane (2000: 295) and Bonomi (Bonomi MSS for June, 1830) comment on as continually changing.

Irrespective of the reasons for the abandonment of Old Qurna, be they military or environmental, the relationship between Old Qurna, al-Tarif, and the foothills communities remains ambiguous, the reason being that there is evidence of human occupation in the central foothills at a time when Old Qurna must still have been in existence. As early as 1737, the shaykh accompanying Pococke to the Valley of the Kings is afraid of an attack on his party by people using the mountain path that leads to Shaykh 'Abd al-Qurna (Pococke, 1743: 99). During his 1737 visit, Norden mentions the "villains" who "lodged so high" in the mountains, although he does not claim to have actually encountered them himself. The narrative suggests his knowledge stems from hearsay, and likely comes from his captain (Norden, 1757: 83), but it nevertheless indicates human habitation in the hill of Shaykh 'Abd al-Qurna, facing the Ramesseum, the northernmost point on his itinerary. James Bruce records in 1769 that people live "in the holes of the mountains above Thebes," by which he could mean both Shaykh 'Abd al-Qurna and Dra' Abu al-Naga (Bruce, 1790: 125). It may be that the accounts by Norden and Bruce refer to the practice of using the tombs for temporary refuge, rather than permanent habitation. Yet, in 1799, Denon gives evidence of danger in the area of the Ramesseum that prevents him from conducting survey work there: "It would have taken some time and examination to have made out the plan of this temple, but the cavalry were galloping on and I was obliged to follow them closely, not to be stopped for ever in my researches" (Denon, 1803, 2: 92).

In the absence of further precise information, then, we may postulate that population groups were present in what James Bruce called "the mountains above Thebes" long before Old Qurna was deserted, and that these foothills communities were part of a west bank settlement pattern that was much more decentralized than the generally accepted population concentrations in Old Qurna and al-Tarif suggest. The independent existence of communities in the foothills may be linked with workers involved with the long-standing mummy trade, as well as agricultural workers who wished to stay in close proximity to their fields and who increasingly made the nearby tombs their home. In this sense, the foothills population came to act as a core community ready to absorb the subsequent migration out of Old Qurna. With time, population numbers in the foothills increased as a result of all factors combined: military campaigns that prompted the evacuation of Old Qurna in favor of safer accommodation, both in al-Tarif and the foothills; inundation and irrigation-related environmental developments in and around the Seti I Temple area; and the intensification of the European demand for antiquities from the early nineteenth century onward, drawing Qurnawi away not only from al-Tarif, but likely also from Old Qurna before it was totally abandoned.

Which of these factors came first or proved most significant is difficult to argue. The precise nature of the fate that caused the demise of Old Qurna remains unclear. Maybe it fell victim to the sort of punitive action of which Bruce heard in 1769. Maybe it was destroyed at the hands of armies in pursuit of Mamluk insurgents between 1778 and 1811. Maybe the town simply fell into disuse when its occupants favored the safety of the tombs during times of ongoing and long-term political unrest. This process may have been gradual, and may have taken place in combination with a breakdown of the irrigation system and increasingly frequent inundation-related seasonal migration. The gradually declining infrastructure may account for the vague dates associated with the demise of Old Qurna.[6] To this extent, accounts of a single military destruction of the Seti I Temple village, while not necessarily untrue, may in some ways also be a mythical representation of complex sets of historical, political, and environmental circumstances and developments of some duration. Likely, Qurnawi themselves will have contributed to the destruction of Old Qurna by salvaging any usable parts from their deserted dwellings, a practice that could recently still be observed when people were evicted from the foothills.

Following centuries of mummy exploitation and the academic interests that emerged during the eighteenth century, the advent of the most intensive phase of antiquities collecting may be dated from 1811 onward, when Muhammad Ali's victory over the Mamluks marked the beginning of a period of renewed stability. It was at this time that Bernardino Drovetti was among the first of many to become active in the area, and Old Qurna and al-Tarif Qurnawi became increasingly drawn to the excavations among the Noble To   s. After 1827, when Wilkinson occupied his tomb house at Shaykh 'Abd al-Qurna, he considered Qurnawi as his neighbors (Thompson, 1992: 105): a multilocal settlement pattern had become firmly established, on the ground as well as in the pages of western manuscripts and published accounts.

First contact
In 1769, James Bruce viewed Qurnawi as "robbers who resemble our Gypsies," and "wretches," many of whom had already been exterminated by "Osman Bey, an ancient governor of Girgé" (Bruce, 1790: 125). By July 1778, first impressions had not changed much. According to Sonnini, the village around the Seti I Temple "was the resort of the most formidable

banditti" and "the meanest, the most frightful, and most miserable place in appearance I ever beheld . . . a truly detestable place" (Sonnini, 1800: 650). Apart from being "banditti," never had Sonnini seen such

> ill looking wretches. They were half black, and almost entirely naked, part only of their body being covered with miserable rags, while their dark and haggard countenance was fully expressive of their ferocious disposition. Following no trade, having no taste for agriculture, and, like the savage animals of the barren mountains near which they live, appearing to employ themselves solely in rapine, their aspect was not a little terrific. (Sonnini, 1800: 650)

Several years later, Denon, having on numerous occasions been received with volleys of stones and spears, refers to the inhabitants of al-Tarif as "incorrigible," and "the only place in Upper Egypt which held out against our government," a dubious honor awarded with a telling commendation: "Strong in their sepulchral retreats, they came out like spectres, only to alarm men: culpable by their many other crimes, they concealed their remorse, and fortified their disobedience in the obscurity of these excavations" (Denon, 1803, 3: 30–32). That news of the French expeditionary force may well have reached these "sepulchral retreats" ahead of Denon does not enter the equation. As Caroline Simpson has observed, "there was nothing nice about the invading army" (Simpson, 2001: 3), and Qurnawi self-defense rather than innate hostility appears to be at issue here. By contrast, during the 1820s Qurnawi appear to have lost their sharp edges. The legacy of the 1811 defeat of Mamluk insurgents by government troops in Upper Egypt, and the further crushing of the Arab Rebellion in 1823, may be key factors here, although the pacifying influence of gainful employment fostered by ever-increasing western antiquarian interests will have contributed a stabilizing focus as well. Even so, John Madox in 1823 observes that Giuseppe Passalacqua, an Italian excavator living at Dra' Abu al-Naga, carried a saber and pistols, "though he says he is under no kind of apprehension from the natives" (Madox, 1834: 280).

Population size
Arriving at a population number for al-Qurna during the time of the early European accounts is problematic in view of the scattered locations seemingly occupied by the west bank communities. Vivant Denon,

commenting on the al-Tarif area, states that the "excavations"[7] there are "innumerable" and provide "lodging to the inhabitants of the village of Kurnu and their numerous flocks," these being "a considerable number of people" (Denon, 1803, 3: 177–78; 2: 86–87). He gives no indication of population numbers for Old Qurna, which, his illustration suggests, may still be inhabited (Denon, 1803, 3: 179–80, Plate XXII Fig. 2). According to Belzoni,

> I do not know whether it is because they are so few in number that the government takes so little notice of what they do; but it is certain, that they are the most unruly people in Egypt. At various times many of them have been destroyed, so that they are reduced from three thousand, the number they formerly reckoned, to three hundred, which form the population of the present day. (Belzoni, 1820: 158–59)

Belzoni's account is vaguely reminiscent of such reprisals against west bank inhabitants as relayed to James Bruce in 1769, but he provides no further supporting details of actual events.

As we have noted, Lane distinguishes between two inhabited areas, the plain of al-Tarif and the foothills, most likely the nearby area of Dra' Abu al-Naga. The population numbers he offers amount to about a thousand people, but it remains unclear whether this is for both areas: "The number of inhabited grottoes in this place is between 130 and 150; and few of these are occupied by less than five or six inmates" (Lane, 2000: 327). A figure of around a thousand inhabitants concurs with the 320 men, 350 women and 350 children estimated by Bonomi in May–June 1830, although he—like many after him—fails to specify what he means by "the village of Gurna" (Bonomi MSS). If he meant the administrative district of Qurna, then his numbers should have included al-Tarif also, and his numbers may have been on the conservative side. If he only meant the vicinity of Wilkinson's house at Shaykh 'Abd al-Qurna, near where he lived, then the figure appears high for that area alone. John Madox, in his reference to one of the European collectors living in Dra' Abu al-Naga, reports that some five or six hundred "natives" are living in that area (Madox, 1834, entry for October 2, 1823), possibly suggesting a fifty–fifty distribution for Bonomi's figure for the northern and central foothills settlements only, and excluding al-Tarif. Confirming Madox's observation, and based on the number of people represented in the hillside drawings of Robert Hay, Caroline

Simpson arrives at an estimate also of around a thousand people "for the people on the hillside only," that is, Shaykh 'Abd al-Qurna, al-Khukha, al-'Asasif, and Dra' Abu al-Naga, but excluding Qurnat Mara'i (possibly then still uninhabited) and al-Tarif (Simpson, 2000: 9).

Organization of domestic space

Travelers' observations of the tomb dwellings include a variety of geography-dependent perspectives. The Venetian, Norden, and Bruce simply view them in the context of refuge, in doing so seemingly referring to the tombs located in the upper foothills. Writers like Belzoni, Denon, Lane, Pococke, Rhind, Richardson, Sonnini, and Wilkinson comment on those used for long-term habitation purposes, mainly those in the area of Shaykh 'Abd al-Qurna or al-Tarif. Descriptions range from Pococke and Richardson's erroneous scientific speculations about their possibly original domestic rather than funerary purpose, even leading Richardson to compute that a total population of twenty thousand could have been feasible (Pococke, 1743: 97; Richardson, 1822, 2: 74), to reflections about their perceived squalid nature by European standards. Interspersed among all these are the more architecturally focused comments.

Referring to al-Tarif, Denon reports that many of the inhabited "retreats" were interconnected, thereby suggesting they had multiple entrances (Denon, 1803, 3:50). Repeating Richardson's earlier observations (Richardson, 1822, 2: 74, 77), Lane judges the tombs to be very comfortable habitations, providing shelter from the summer heat and from the winter cold better than any other village houses do. Some of the dwellings could barely be observed due to the undulating landscape and lower areas in which they were often situated, their precise location indicated by the barking of guard dogs upon approach (Lane, 2000: 328). By contrast, Sonnini, recognizing only the enclosures in front of the tombs, calls them "badly built mud huts, [which] are no higher than a man, and have no other covering than a few leaves of the palm-tree" (Sonnini, 1800: 650). Although writing somewhat later, Henry Rhind gives a comprehensive overview of the physical appearance of the late-1850s Qurnawi social unit as it existed in the central foothills:

> The mode of living is simplicity itself, their dwellings, their dress, and their food being of the most primitive kind. The outer rock-cut chambers of the tombs, in conjunction with mud erections in front, serve them as abodes;

and these they share with the few cattle which the richer of them possess, the sheep, goats, dogs, fowls, and pigeons, which always go to constitute the household. A heap or two of thick dhoora straw, some earthen pots, and cupboards of sun-baked clay, would complete the inventory of the furnishings of an ordinary habitation. The luxury of raised beds formed of a framework of palm branches is a rare occurrence. (Rhind, 1862: 290)

Other than offering respite from climatic extremes, Robert Richardson's description suggests that the tomb dwellings primarily served the purpose of sleeping space, and that daily life was generally spent outside:

The mistress and daughters of the family sit round the door, and retire into the cell on the approach of a stranger, who is received by the master of the family, and sits down in the open air, among the dry sand, or on a mat, if there happens to be such a luxury at hand. He is generally presented with bread and milk, coffee and tobacco. The dogs being entrusted with the defence of the settlement, occupy the heights above, and furiously assail every stranger who ventures to approach. (Richardson, 1822, 2: 74)

This picture of the 'courtyard lifestyle' is consistent both with various extant artistic renderings, and with Henry Rhind's account of Shaykh Lazim's four wives:

The house of the sheikh was a square rock-area with the doorways of tombs on three sides and a brick wall on the fourth. In these inner dens each wife had her separate abode; but during the day they were all together in the court, spinning or oftener chattering childishly (as they were very young girls), amicably for the most part. (Rhind, 1862: 297)

Rhind's spatial and social characterizations nevertheless gloss over some of the architectural specifics, for which we need to turn to the observations of Richardson:

The modern inhabitants, on taking possession, are too indolent to clear out the rocky cave, and to avail themselves of the whole of the accommodation formed by the ancient settlers. Instead of this they merely scratch a hole, by which to crawl in, and clear out a little of the rubbish from the first chamber, in which they deposit their sleeping mats, and any trifling furniture which they possess. Here they repose during the night, and retire from the heat of the sun during the day. All the shaft, and all the excavations, and inner chambers remain blocked up with rubbish and sand that have drifted in from the surrounding flat. It is no uncommon thing to find a family residing in the outer chamber, and the master of it sleeping in the bottom of an ancient sarcophagus, by way of being in the state bed; while at the same time the shaft and interior niches continue to possess the sarcophagus and mummy cases, filled with the bones and bodies of the former tenants of the soil, that had been lodged there between two and three thousand years ago. (Richardson, 1822, 2: 74)

Richardson's account reflects the conditions in al-Tarif, while Rhind's observations were made in Shaykh 'Abd al-Qurna at a time when external wall enclosures had become more common. Of the early European commentators, Richardson is the only one to describe in some detail the unique vernacular features generally typical of Upper Egyptian rural communities, the various types of thin-walled mud bins, used for the storage of grain and personal belongings:

To supply in part the accommodation that the whole of this subterranean abode would afford them, if restored to its pristine condition, they generally build near the door a round hollow tower . . . of unburnt brick, or stone plastered over with mud, with openings in its side, in different places, to serve for presses and other conveniences. It is closed at the top, and shaped like a funnel or open bowl, from which the camel eats his grass, cut straw, beans or other provender. The asses, the goats, and the sheep take their station near the same place, and eat their repast off the ground. (Richardson, 1822, 2: 74)

Apart from Belzoni's reference to the clay and straw "wedding box" used to store prized possessions (Belzoni, 1820: 183), and Rhind's brief mention of "cupboards of sun-baked clay" (Rhind, 1862: 290), it seems peculiar that Richardson is the only one to have described these structures. It is possible that, because of their ubiquitous presence throughout Upper Egypt, travelers viewed them with no particular interest worthy of comment, as suggested by Rhind, who simply states that their presence is in "the manner of the country" (Rhind, 1862: 80). Their indifference is unwarranted, especially since in combination with the tomb openings,

Glimpses of village life both surprise and delight: the vernacular forms of the foothills' Upper Egyptian mud storage structures are a "sculpture gallery waiting to be appreciated" (Simpson, 2003: 248). Photograph courtesy of Caroline Simpson and Elina Paulin-Grothe.

the mud-walled extensions, and the open courtyards, these mud storage structures form an integral part of the striking vernacular assemblage characteristic of the architectural landscape in the necropolis. Indeed, they could not be ignored in the graphic representations of that landscape by artists and draftsmen, and the various mud features stand out in Denon's illustration of the Seti I Temple (Denon, 1803, 3: 179–80, Plate XXII, Fig. 2), the Hay panoramas (Hay MSS), the 1842 William Prinsep painting (Conner, 1984: 46; Manniche, 1987: 3; Simpson, 2003: Plate 138), and they were eventually of sufficient visitor interest to be circulated in postcard form (Binder, 1914). Later ethnographic reference to these mud storage bins can be found in Winlock (Winlock and Crum, 1926: 51–53) and Eigner (1984: passim).

Richardson's description of their use as feeding troughs has not been ethnographically attested. Camels, however, were apparently not uncommon. Belzoni includes them in his list of tomb-dwelling occupants (Belzoni, 1820: 158) and James Webster (1830, 2: 145) makes reference to camels being stabled in inner-tomb chambers. Mud bins, therefore, may at times well have been used in relation to them. However, the specific bowl-shaped function of this particular type (called *manama*) served to provide scorpion-proof sleeping spaces (Eigner, 1984: 42–43; Winlock and Crum, 1926: 52).

Agriculture and animal husbandry

One of the issues on which opinion is divided in the travelers' records is the extent to which agricultural pursuits provided an economic base and a livelihood for the people of the Theban west bank. The accounts of Charles Sonnini and James Bruce offer a neat summary of the opposing positions. Sonnini in 1778 found them to be "following no trade, having no taste for agriculture, and, . . . appearing to employ themselves solely in rapine" (Sonnini, 1800: 650). Yet, Bruce in January 1769 "had seen limes and lemons in great perfection at Thebes" and went to considerable length to obtain some:

> We were resolved to refresh ourselves with some punch, in remembrance of Old England. But, after what had happened the night before, none of our people chose to run the risk of meeting the Troglodytes. We therefore procured a servant of the governor's of the town, to mount upon his goat-skin filled with wind, and float down the stream from Luxor to El Gournie, to bring us a supply of these, which he soon after did. (Bruce, 1790: 138)

Vivant Denon in his account, while not commenting on agricultural practices as such, nevertheless mentions the ownership of animals by the al-Tarif community. Three hundred "cattle" were taken during the attack on the tombs, people were reported as fleeing with their "flocks" (Denon, 1803, 3: 50), and Denon himself at one point lived in fear of being taken hostage in exchange for their "sheep" (thereby possibly suggesting that the figure of "three hundred" did not involve cattle at all).

Giovanni Belzoni in 1815 was fully aware of his agricultural surroundings and observes their "cows, camels, buffaloes, sheep, goats, dogs, &c" (Belzoni, 1820: 158). He even comments on how "the labourer comes home in the evening, seats himself near his cave, smokes his pipe with his companions, and talks of the last inundation of the Nile, its products, and what the ensuing season is likely to be" (Belzoni, 1820: 182), but nevertheless downplays the economic and subsistence importance of agricultural activity in favor of the extraction of antiquities behind which, ironically, he himself is one of the driving forces:

> They are forced to cultivate a small tract of land, extending from the rocks to the Nile, about a mile in breadth, and two and a half in length; and even this is in part neglected; for if left to their own will, they would never take a spade in their hands, except when they go to dig for mummies; which they find to be more profitable employment than agriculture. This is the fault of the travelers, who are so pleased the moment they are presented with any piece of antiquity, that, without thinking of the injury resulting from the example to their successors, they give a great deal more than the people really expect. (Belzoni, 1820: 159)

Belzoni's views have been influential and continue to color the views of those who feel a need to say something about the Theban foothills communities (Waxman, 2008: 50–51). Yet, Belzoni's effective denial of the importance of agriculture here is contradicted by Madox in September of 1823, when he not only notes the waterwheel at the landing place, but also the "four or five oxen feeding upon chopped straw" (Madox, 1834: 276). Not only is the observation a confirmation of a technically functioning irrigation system, but inherent in the reference to straw—in the very least a by-product of some cereal crop—is an indication that the irrigation system was also productive.

Edward Lane is aware of these agricultural activities. He notes the same waterwheel, the narrow width of the cultivable lands north of the landing place, and its "wide expanse of fertile land" to the southwest. He lists the types of produce: "dor'ah sha'mee, door'ah sey'fee, wheat, beans, cotton, indigo, &c," and he remarks how in order to reach the old village from the sycamore, "we first cross the narrow strip of cultivated land" (Lane, 2000: 325). Despite these observations, Lane is compelled to conclude that "the occupation of excavating they prefer to agricultural labour; as it is more profitable," even though they dress the same as the peasants, and even though they look as poor, which Lane suggests is to prevent having to pay higher taxes (Lane, 2000: 328). In his assessment of village life Lane can therefore conclude that "the men were generally absent, engaged in their usual occupation of excavating" (Lane, 2000:

A tomb chamber for a stable: "The people of Gournou live in the entrance of such caves as have already been opened, and, by making partitions with earthen walls, they form habitations for themselves, as well as for their cows, camels, buffaloes, sheep, dogs, &c" (Belzoni, 1820: 158).

329), seemingly leaving the fields to tend themselves. Although Lane is not an excavating collector, his time on the west bank was spent in the company of those who were; his mapping activities were in many respects archaeological in nature; and his focus was thus constrained by the European view of the west bank, which was sufficiently dominant to overrule and obscure all other economic activity, despite his references to the "fertile land," his listing of crops, and "their cows, goats, and sheep" (Lane, 2000: 328).

In addition to this European focus on antiquities, the similarities with respect to the denial of agriculture that exist in the travelogues of different observers may in large part also be due to later travelers being influenced by earlier accounts. In a pre-copyright world, the practice is taken to extremes by James St. John, whose account almost entirely exists of passages written by earlier travelers (St. John, 1845, passim). It is because of such practices that we must not look at the consensus of opinion as expressed in these accounts, but rather at the exceptions represented by the contrary accounts of travelers who are apparently not influenced by others and who, furthermore, manifest a certain individuality in the additional information their accounts contain. Richardson and Bonomi are two such observers and we will here advance their descriptions as most likely reflecting the true state of affairs.

Richardson confirms the presence of local agricultural pursuits in his reference to the practice of moving "to the caves in the adjoining rocky flat," suggesting that this would be seasonal rather than permanent: "when the river subsides, and the ground becomes dry, they quit their rocky tenements and return to their mansions of clay, which are more conveniently situated for water, grazing, and agriculture" (Richardson, 1822, 2: 8). However, Richardson not only credits this seasonal migration to the "low situation" of the village, but also to "the fillings up of the canals" that confirms the existence of an irrigation infrastructure, even if it indicates that its upkeep and the necessary community organization may have broken down during recent periods of social upheaval.

Joseph Bonomi in 1830 records that 224 Qurnawi cultivators pay land tax, adding that this is out of a total of some 320 men, including twenty west bank Christians who are "carpenters, scribes, fishermen and vendors of drugs" (Bonomi MSS, May–June 1830). Despite the alleged Qurnawi preoccupation with antiquities, Bonomi's figures suggest an essentially agricultural community. His account concurs with the assessment of Richardson, who paints a balanced picture of west bank inundation-affected agricultural subsistence and locally operative seasonal market forces: "In this season of the year, the Egyptians, having little occasion to employ their time in the labours of the field, devote themselves to opening and plundering the tombs of their ancient countrymen, of every article that can tempt the European traveler to make his own" (Richardson, 1822, 2: 112).

A number of other writers confirm the observations of Richardson and Bonomi. John Gardner Wilkinson was a long-term west bank resident and a potential ethnographic observer of some substance if only he had expended his considerable energies in that direction. The founding father of British Egyptology, his essentially epigraphic work did not, for the most part, concern itself with a search for antiquities, the absence of this all-consuming preoccupation therefore leaving some room to observe aspects of his social surroundings. Sadly, Wilkinson's powers of observation were not focused on the social structure or daily activities of

Jerbakh, brush made from the fruit-bearing stalks of the date palm, is still widely used in the dusty mud-brick vernacular environment of the Theban west bank. When the woman of the house sweeps its floors, ascending dust particles look like silver clouds when caught in the sunlight penetrating through an open door or window. Sir John Gardner Wilkinson painted a similar brush during his years in al-Hurubat (Wilkinson MSS a.21, a volume of illustrations dating *c.* 1825–1837).

his Qurnawi neighbors, but he does allude to their agricultural economic base when calculating "the produce of a piece of land I measured at El Byrát, near Thebes" (Wilkinson, 1843: 274). In his computations, Wilkinson indicates that he has "calculated the taxes as at Qoorneh" (1843: 274), that is, at 40.5 piasters per feddan (Wilkinson, 1843: 275). This equates with the amount of tax payable "at Thebes . . . for the best land" (1843: 268), this being land that yields the maximum of eight *ardeb* of wheat per feddan (Wilkinson, 1843: 268).[8] Even though the land measured by Wilkinson at al-Ba'irat was only "of mean quality" (Wilkinson, 1843: 273), giving a yield of just under three *ardeb* per feddan (Wilkinson, 1843: 273), Wilkinson used the productive capacity of al-Qurna as his benchmark.

Giovanni d'Athanasi, who lived at al-Qurna for some eighteen years, unequivocally states that sowing the fields "contributes [to] the pecuniary necessities of the village" (d'Athanasi, 1836: 130–31). Henry Rhind, writing a little later, confirms this picture when observing that "nearly all of them own livestock . . . and they all have a portion of land . . . which now yields them so good a return . . . that the more active are supposed to have small hoards of coin" (Rhind, 1862: 296). He adds that only "some" are supplementing their income from the discovery of antiquities "which they have been so fortunate to make" (Rhind, 1862: 296), suggesting a less than systematic pursuit of, or overriding dependence on them.

These more reliable accounts indicate that the agricultural identity that many of today's Qurnawi subscribe to has a long history. It must be concluded that, especially in the portrayal of agricultural activity, much of the western record appears flawed, imposing on the local community an identity that was far from representative. Despite d'Athanasi's comment that "Mr. Belzoni . . . was strangely mistaken in them—he did not observe them properly" (d'Athanasi, 1836: 132), the detail in the work of a person of Lane's stature indicates that Europeans in general were not poor observers, but that their focus was nevertheless clouded by antiquarian preoccupations and the quest for ancient artifacts. Like gold fever, the quest for antiquities not only masked a sense of reality when characterizing local population groups, but also infected the language in which those characterizations were being written. Not only was it alleged that the men had abandoned agriculture and were away excavating for antiquities, Lane furthermore reports—using language rich in archaeological imagery—that the women they left behind were "dark-complexioned and wrinkled . . . like resuscitated mummies" (Lane, 2000: 328–29). Some fifty years later, Amelia Edwards invokes the ancient Egyptian pantheon when describing cows driving one of the west bank waterwheels as having "mild Hathor-like faces" (Edwards, 1877: 439). Thus, by and large, the reality of the Qurnawi preference for antiquities over agricultural work is one of western representation and portrayal, and a product of European single-minded antiquarian pursuit, as future archival studies of taxation and cadastral records, and the records of legal proceedings involving land disputes, should attest.

Mining the past as local subsistence strategy

This being the case, what was the reality of Qurnawi archaeological activity, what were its driving forces, and what were the characteristic features of its organization and practice that it took on over time? As we have argued, involvement in the ancient remains of the archaeological landscape will have been ongoing for centuries, but was primarily focused on the procurement of mummies to satisfy the European demand for *mumiya*. Because the trade was both illegal and incompatible with religious beliefs (Dannenfeldt, 1959: 19–20),[9] Europeans themselves will have been instrumental in setting up lines of communication, supply routes, and the organization and oversight of local suppliers. The Theban Necropolis will have been an important source, and continued in this role until at least the end of the eighteenth century: "they sell at Cairo the resin which they find in the belly and skull of these mummies, and there is no preventing them from committing this violence to them" (Denon, 1803, 3: 63). The intensity of these operations can still be recognized in the so-called 'mummy pits,' the circular depressions visible especially in the lower foothills of Dra' Abu al-Naga, their workings described by Irby and Mangles (1823: 142–43; also see Appendix 2, Plates 8 and 9).[10]

As a result, local communities will have been intimately familiar with the tombs, and the maze of passages and subterranean chambers that honeycomb the mountain, so graphically described by Belzoni (1820: 155–58). It is through expert knowledge thus acquired that the additional use of this underground network presented itself, and that its potential for safe refuge became obvious. Any interest in antiquities would have been limited to those containing precious materials, but otherwise ancient artifacts will not have figured prominently in the search for, and extraction of, mummified remains. As already observed, at least during the sixteenth century, few travelers brought back objects to Europe (Dannenfeldt, 1959: 16).

Travelers' records for the mid-seventeenth century indicate an increasing interest in Egyptian artifacts (Thevenot, in Rhind, 1862: 243), a continuing trend we may see reflected in incidental sales to intermittently arriving visitors such as Sonnini, who described his negotiations over antiquities. It was not until the French military and scientific expedition to Egypt in 1798 that we can begin to speak of any organized collecting activities, the larger mandate of the Commission in some small fashion represented by Denon's Qurnawi-assisted search for antiquities. It was this scientific expedition and its subsequent lavishly illustrated publication (Commission, 1802) that created the European interest in Egypt, which explains the increase in activity during the early nineteenth century: "A few years later the pursuit was in full progress on an extensive scale; and from that time to this, although in various degrees, it has never ceased" (Rhind, 1862: 243–44).

The resulting search for antique artifacts proper may be dated tentatively to around the early nineteenth century, when some of the big names—Bernardino Drovetti and Giovanni Belzoni, who were eventually responsible for acquiring major collections—arrived on the Theban west bank. Belzoni makes reference to an antiquities collector in Alexandria who had been obtaining antiquities from 'Gournou' "for many years" (Belzoni, 1820: 42), a date that we will consider to fall around 1811, which is also the year Drovetti first began acquiring antiquities in Upper Egypt and which, following victories by the troops of Muhammad Ali over the Mamluks between Qus and Qena, brought a degree of government influence to Upper Egypt (Garcin, 1976: 530). It is during these early years that Richardson in 1818 can still comment that "the surface of Thebes is hardly scratched, its mine of diamonds remains unexplored" (Richardson, 1822, 2: 78).

During the next several decades this situation was to change dramatically when the necropolis was extensively excavated by European collectors and their agents, who were seeking to advance both the interests of their respective countries in an age of nationalist point scoring, as well as their own purses (Ridley, 1998: 248–82). It was during this time that Europeans erected the first modern above-ground structures in the necropolis, the Shaykh 'Abd al-Qurna house of Henry Salt used by his agent Giovanni d'Athanasi ('Yanni'), and the house of the Italian Piccinini at Dra' Abu al-Naga. Ongoing economic opportunities through independent collecting or more formal employment arrangements will have provided Qurnawi with an incentive to settle here and among those already present.

Although her assessment was premature in view of later finds, the intensity of the work was such that Isabella Romer, a British 'tourist' in 1846, could remark that "there is scarcely an entire mummy to be obtained for love or money at Thebes" (Romer, 1846: 291). Caroline Simpson has rightly pointed out the sad irony of this situation: while Europeans were responsible for this pillage, it was in fact Qurnawi who ended up with the reputation of tomb robbers and "mummy-snatchers" (Simpson, 2010: 204). These views continue to hold currency, with people like Belzoni, through a curious process of inversion, now portrayed as the great savior of ancient Egyptian art, while those who did the work for him, the villagers from Qurna, "long ago destroyed what was worth saving in the tombs. They stole anything that could be stolen"

(Waxman, 2008: 95–96). But to elide European agency in the whole collecting process amounts to so much mystification, which victimizes Qurnawi as much as it elevates their reputation as tomb robbers to one of myth. Whatever damage was inflicted, and much was, Europeans were equally culpable by initiating a collecting frenzy, the reflections of which can still be seen in the ongoing demand for antiquities by western private collectors; by not limiting themselves to portable artifacts but also physically removing sections of decorated wall panels (Romer, 1981: 123–25); and thereby acting both as role model and teacher to local villagers. Clearly understood in 1862, Henry Rhind could correctly allude to the driving mechanism of the pillage: "Not many [extracted antiquities] were, as might be supposed from their nature and size, the subject of native traffic. Most have owed their removal to the more organised procedure instituted by respective Governments, or by bodies charged with administering the resources of national museums" (Rhind, 1862: 256).[11] This nationalist perspective shifted to blaming the west bank communities especially after the 1881 incident involving the 'Abd al-Rasul family, an issue to which we will return later.

But if such was the scale of things, how may we then view the role of Qurnawi in this process, at least during this period of intense activity, bracketed by the 1818 observations of Robert Richardson, the 1846 assessment of Isabella Romer, and the account of Henry Rhind, himself an excavator in the necropolis during the 1850s and one who referred to the period of indiscriminate collecting as "those times" (Rhind, 1862: 244)? The recurring theme of local villagers excavating in the panoramas of Robert Hay (Hay MSS) seemingly establishes this activity as a common daily practice, and is further attested by the circular depressions of a pockmarked landscape, as has been mentioned. We may reasonably identify three different processes: 1) where people like Belzoni marshalled a group of locals to do a certain task for him; 2) where local villagers appear to have worked independently from collecting agents, excavating on their own accord or in groups formed as per certain community-based rules, in order to sell the items thus uncovered to local collecting agents like Yanni and Piccinini; and 3) the involvement of middlemen dealing in antiquities. In practice, and where this involves European collectors themselves excavating in the necropolis, the overall process may have been a mixture of the first two approaches, as evidenced also in Belzoni's operations.

During the early collecting years, it seems both the will and the local organization on the part of Qurnawi may have been lacking to readily volunteer their services to the excavating Europeans. British Consul Henry Salt, Belzoni's employer, made arrangements in his instructions to Belzoni for a soldier "to go up with him, for the purpose of engaging the Fellahs to work whenever he may require their assistance, as otherwise they are not likely to attend Mr. Belzoni's orders" (Belzoni, 1820: 27). In turn, Belzoni did not think highly of his workmen: they had no faith in their own ability, believing it to be the devil when they were successful in moving a heavy statue, and regarding his note-taking as the writing of a charm that had made it happen (Belzoni, 1820: 43). For his part, Belzoni considered their skills no better than those of beasts, and only sufficient to pull on a rope or to act as a counterweight, while believing that payment received for moving a stone probably meant that it had gold inside it and should therefore be prevented (Belzoni, 1820: 45, 44).

Yet, their lacking aptitude for organized teamwork of an essentially engineering nature did not suggest that no other qualities were evident, and Belzoni himself noted their "scheme . . . to show me the sarcophagus, without letting me see the way by which it might be taken out, and then to stipulate a price for the secret" (Belzoni, 1820: 53–54). Later, he alleges that such practices nevertheless paid off and allowed them to turn down organized paid labor, "having become opulent by the trade in antiquities, and tricking travelers, [Qurnawi] were not so anxious to gain thirty paras a day" (Belzoni, 1820: 116). Although Belzoni's difficulties appear to have come from Turkish officials and the scheming of his European competitors rather than from Qurnawi, he nevertheless has little that is positive to say about them:

> Could it but be accurately known, with what a wretched set of people in these tribes travelers have to deal, their mean and rapacious dispositions and the various occurrences that render the collection of antiquities difficult, whatever came from thence would be the more prized, from the consideration of these circumstances. (Belzoni, 1820: 155)

Belzoni's dislike seems to stem from their unruly nature, largely premised in the experiences of Denon, and the inflated prices they now charge for antiquities: "Some of them have accumulated a considerable sum of money, and are become so belligerent, that they remain idle, unless whatever price they demand be given them" (Belzoni, 1820: 159). His comments and experiences contrast with those of Giovanni d'Athanasi, recorded a few years later, who has issues with his workers on the east bank but who thinks highly of Qurnawi:

> They are very ready and useful at such work; they understand antiquities as well as a European antiquary, and whenever they find a rare morsel of antiquity, recollecting that a similar piece had never been found in the course of the excavations, they ask no trifling price for it from any one who may want to have it. (d'Athanasi, 1836: 135)

It is within his framework of general discontent that Belzoni offers some insights into the local organization involved with the search for antiquities. He observes how they are divided into different parties, or "companies," each supervised by a chief, with the proceeds of any items sold divided among them all (Belzoni, 1820: 159). In this way, "They are apparently very true to each other, and particularly in cheating strangers; but when they can find a good opportunity, they do not scruple to cheat each other also" (Belzoni, 1820: 159). Yet, Belzoni also reports on lengthy negotiations with an individual who, amid a great pretense of secrecy, was discovered to have conducted the sale on behalf of the company after all, the feigned secrecy simply serving to ingratiate himself and thus obtain something extra for himself, "in which he had succeeded" (Belzoni, 1820: 161).

Although Henry Rhind may have been influenced by Belzoni's narrative, his excavations in the necropolis constitute credible confirmation of such attempts at secrecy also during the 1850s when, in order to secretly view antiquities, "I have often, when living at Thebes, gone covertly with the owners to their strange abodes":

> When a piece of good fortune of this kind falls to their lot, they know well how to adopt the precautions necessary, in their view, to make the most of it. Secrecy and mystification are the great points. . . . In the innermost recesses of their tomb-dwellings they usually hide the larger or more important of such relics; and a likely purchaser is conveyed secretly to look at them there. . . . As those precautions are in reality prudent with regard to the more important objects, it is only in accordance with the cunning of the local character that the necessity for them should also be

frequently simulated, to give a sort of prestige to the relics to be disposed of. It was no unusual circumstance to find quite inferior specimens hedged round by the most mysterious preliminaries; or a fellah might imply that it was of the greatest consequence his possession of some article should be unknown to others, who were in reality his partners in the transaction. There are, in fact, few such tricks which their ingenuity has not turned to account. (Rhind, 1862: 250–51)

Belzoni's operations evidently included laborers who were paid a regular daily wage, as well as those who searched independently, although the latter eventually allowed themselves to become formally employed also, thus offsetting any losses suffered whenever their searches were fruitless:

The men were divided into two classes. The most knowing were making researches on their own account, employing eight or ten to assist them. . . . I met with some difficulty at first in persuading these people to work in search of tombs, and receive a regular daily payment; for they conceived it to be against their interest, supposing I might obtain the antiquities at too cheap a rate: but when they saw, that sometimes they received their pay regularly, and I had nothing for it, they found it was rather in their favour, to secure twenty paras (three pence) a day, than run the risk of having nothing for their labour, which often happened to those who worked at adventure. (Belzoni, 1820: 165)

Even so, it was not uncommon for Belzoni when staying overnight as a guest in the inhabited tombs to be offered items discovered independent of his own operations, suggesting that such other activity was regularly going on, the waste product of their searches given domestic usage:

Various articles were brought to sell to me, and sometimes I had reason to rejoice at having stayed there. I was sure of a supper of milk and bread served in a wooden bowl; but whenever they supposed I should stay at night, they always killed a couple of fowls for me, which were baked in a small oven heated with pieces of mummy cases, and sometimes with the bones and rags of the mummies themselves. (Belzoni, 1820: 181)

Incidents of mummy cases used for fuel are later repeated by Lane (2000: 328) and Stephens (1837: 109–110) and may have been inspired by Belzoni's account. As a common fuel source for Qurnawi themselves, such widespread use seems unlikely in view of their access to cakes of dried cow dung, as described by Rhind (1862: 295) and indeed still common today. As seems evident from Lane's account, the households of the European excavators in the necropolis will have been devoid of this energy source, and it remains possible that their servants did use such wood for fuel, thereby very likely rendering the practice one that was exclusively European (Lane, 2000: 328; Thompson, 2010: 206).

For Belzoni to be offered antiquities in the seclusion of private homes may seem unusual, as such private dealings might be seen to work against the interest of other company members. This may have been one of the reasons behind the use of a distinct trading location, which was located in the 'Asasif in one of the large Twenty-sixth Dynasty mud-walled tombs and where visiting Europeans and possibly also Luxor-based antiquities dealers came to make their purchases. Lane refers to it as "the Ghoo'ree'yeh," which is "the name of one of the principal soo'cks (or ba'za'rs) of the modern Egyptian metropolis," and derived from the "great quantity and variety of antiques found in its excavated chambers" (Lane, 2000: 333). This market will have been the same location used by Belzoni when addressing his workmen: "we assembled in the grotto, that usually serves as a public place for strangers, and a sort of exchange for buying and selling antiques" (Belzoni, 1820: 197). The history of this trading location may indeed have resulted from an initial amount of antiquities found there, as suggested by Lane. Also, and especially at times of intermittent visits, when something of a stockpile had been gathered in the quiet interlude, the place may have acted as a gathering point for the different companies to present their wares to newly arrived visitors or middlemen in order to prevent any unfair dealings between groups of excavators and to level competition between different companies. The location seems a little distant from Shaykh 'Abd al-Qurna where Lane lived, but is centrally located when considering the foothills as a whole. The area of al-'Asasif will have been an intensive area of operations and it was conveniently situated between the foothills areas north and south of Dayr al-Bahari.

The existence of this antiquities market nevertheless did not prevent the transfer of antiquities between individuals, which is what can be expected if such transactions were on behalf of a company and other companies got equal opportunity to dispose of their wares. Indeed, the case related by Rhind (above) indicates that such dealings in the privacy of people's homes represented no danger to the interests of the company, as these were surreptitiously involved anyway. Even when Belzoni no longer actively organized his own search parties, because of difficulties with officials and competing collectors, it was in this manner that he continued to build his collections:

> As I could not dig on the grounds I wished, I contented myself with collecting what the peasants of Gournou used to bring me; and I must say, that in consequence of having so many acquaintances among these mummy plunderers, I have been able to make a little collection of my own, in which I can boast of having a few good articles, particularly in manuscripts, &c. (Belzoni, 1820: 294–95)

Apart from working for foreign collectors or conducting independent excavations for private sale, Qurnawi had a third avenue to dispose of any antiquities found by them for financial gain; namely, through antiquities dealers who acted as middlemen between them and prospective buyers. Most of these middlemen will have resided in Luxor, which had long been a center for the trade in antiquities, and before more recent legal restrictions reduced its importance. In the time of Henry Rhind, these middlemen often were Coptic Christians for their "having some command of money and experience in the business," with Qurnawi using their services "particularly in the summer months, when there are no strangers on the river to offer chances of a ready market" (Rhind, 1862: 247–48).

Yanni left it to Qurnawi to conduct their own independent searches. It is his account that offers a picture of the destructive working methods employed by Qurnawi when encountering a find that now would have been considered highly significant:

> During the researches made by the Arabs in the year 1827, at Gourna, they discovered in the mountain, now called by the Arabs, Il-Dra-Abool-Naggia, a small and separate tomb, containing only one chamber, in the centre of which was placed a sarcophagus, hewn out of the same rock, and formed evidently at the same time as the chamber itself; its base not having been detached. In this sarcophagus was found . . . the body as originally deposited. The moment the Arabs saw that the case was highly ornamented and gilt, they immediately, from their experience in such matters, knew that it belonged to a person of rank. They forthwith proceeded to

satisfy their curiosity by opening it, when they discovered, placed around the head of the mummy, but over the linen, a diadem, composed of silver and beautiful mosaic work, its centre being formed of gold, representing an asp, the emblem of royalty. Inside the case, alongside the body, were deposited two bows, with six arrows, the heads of which were tipped with flint. The Arabs on discovering their rich prize, immediately proceeded to break up the mummy, as was their usual custom, for the treasures it might contain. (d'Athanasi, 1836: xi–xii)

The crude working methods are deplorable, but Yanni is unlikely to have demanded particular standards from those Qurnawi excavating for him as his own practices were equally damaging (Manniche, 1987: 103–104). Such was simply the nature of an earlier, and more primitive, archaeology. Yet, some of Yanni's ideas about archaeological practice were generally sound, as evidenced in his critique of Belzoni's operating methods (d'Athanasi, 1836: 14–15).

Yanni is also critical of the local practice to split up an assemblage of artifacts and to sell individual items separately. There is no evidence he attempted to change this habit, but he does comment on the reasons behind it:

The custom which prevails among the Arabs, of their selling separately, and to different persons, objects of antiquity found together, is really to be lamented. It arises from their wish to conceal from the chief of their village the riches they possess, which they effectively do, by selling those objects at long intervals. (d'Athanasi, 1836: xii–xiii)

We will return to the issue of taxation later, but it appears to be only one reason for the practice:

We should not even have found what we did to purchase, but for the custom of the Arabs of not choosing to sell at one time and to the same person, all the collection of antiquities which they happen to have; preferring rather to sell them from time to time, and to different travelers, in order that they may demand a higher price for them. (d'A·hanasi, 1836: 10)

It is not certain that the influence of collectors and their agents will always have benefited local community members, either economically or in terms of their personal well-being. Amelia Edwards reports for the mid-1870s that archaeological excavation had achieved an official and permanent presence in the necropolis, where "the Bulaq authorities keep a small gang of trained excavators always at work" (Edwards, 1877: 412). Bulaq is the Cairo district where one of the predecessors of the Egyptian Museum was located, indicating that this was government sponsored, Service des antiquités–initiated and thus, it may be assumed, properly paid work. Fifty years earlier, the receipt of payment was up to the terms set by individual operators such as Belzoni, but even his account indicates that a fourth set of excavating circumstances may have existed beyond the three income-generating arrangements already mentioned.

There is some evidence that forced unpaid labor may at times have applied to the excavation of antiquities. If the extraction of unpaid labor was a fact of life, with village shaykhs periodically requested to supply labor for military purposes or irrigation works, then there is evidence that local government representatives extracted forced labor in relation to antiquities as well. The incident described by Belzoni, where the village shaykh was lashed to near-death for not being able to procure within the hour an unopened mummy coffin for the Luxor governor, and Belzoni's inaction during the entire episode, do evidence the certain impunity with which local rulers could also control archaeological labor. Where such occurred, the reasons were not out of interests over antiquities per se. The Belzoni case stemmed from the personal opposition between Belzoni and Drovetti, and the obvious promise of "presents" made to the governor by Drovetti for obstructing Belzoni's operations (Belzoni, 1820: 185–98). In practice and beyond such self-serving motivations, the abuse of local labor resources was also linked with the political domain. During the nineteenth century, the firman, the permission to travel and excavate, in the first instance was issued in the context of Egypt seeking closer ties with Europe, but may also have served as a tool for local officials seeking to ingratiate themselves with Cairo in a political environment where nepotism-induced reciprocity will have favored certain travelers and their Cairo-based government protectors over others. In other instances, discriminatory practices toward travelers on the part of Upper Egyptian Mamluk rulers will have been a manifestation of their effective independence, with Ottoman influence being increasingly weak the greater its distance from the center.

The opposition between Bristish and French excavators, the formation of excavation teams along nationalist lines, and the 'commission' payments in the form of 'presents' to local officials are described by Irby and Mangles:

About a dozen of the leading characters of Gourna, or rather the greatest rogues, have constantly headed their comrades, and formed themselves into two distinct digging parties, or resurrection men, designating themselves the French and the English party; these people are constantly occupied in searching for new tombs, stripping the mummies, and discovering antiquities. The directors have about three-fourths of the money, and the rest is given to the inferior labourers. They dread lest strangers should see these tombs, which to them are so many mines of wealth, and should commence digging speculations of their own—hence the care of the Gourna people in concealing them. It would be endless to describe to you all the intrigues which are carried on by the opposite parties to augment their collection; or the presents given to the Defterdar Bey, the Agus, and the Cashiefs, to attach them to either party. Lately Mr. Drovetti obtained an order from the Defterdar Bey, that the natives should neither sell nor work for the English party, and a cashief was most severely bastinadoed by the bey's orders, and in his presence at Gourna, for assisting the English. (Irby and Mangles, 1823: 139–40)

'Spurious antiquities'

Despite, or maybe because of, the personal rivalry that existed between several early-nineteenth-century collectors—and their ability to manipulate the local political landscape in order to gain access to archaeological labor, as documented by Irby and Mangles—antiquities operations became increasingly intense, resulting during the 1820s and 1830s in an ever-decreasing availability of antiquities. Gardner Wilkinson, who himself was for the most part not in the business of collecting, instead concerning himself with epigraphic work and the general study of the royal and Noble Tombs' wall paintings, noted its impact:

Those who expect to find abundance of good antiquities for sale at Thebes will be disappointed. Occasionally they are found, and brought to travelers: and those who understand them and know how to make a judicious choice, not giving a high price for the bad, but paying well for objects of real value, may occasionally obtain some interesting objects. The dealers soon discover whether the purchaser understands their value; and if he is ignorant they will sell the worst to him for a high price, and fake ones, rather than the best they have. (Wilkinson, 1847: 324)

During the 1850s, the apparent lack of local antiquities even caused Qurnawi to travel to distant villages to purchase "stray ornaments and such like" and to go over sites previously explored in the hope of acquiring some lesser finds (Rhind, 1862: 249).

The continuing demand for antiquities, and the probable gullibility of many a visitor not sufficiently expert in the recognition of authentic antiquities, generated a new industry at which Qurnawi quickly became skilled, the "concoction of spurious antiquities," to use Henry Rhind's turn of phrase (Rhind, 1862: 251). The carving of limestone wall panels and assorted statuary appears to be of more modern introduction (Lange, 1952), reflecting both the shifting tastes of visitors and the adaptive artistic skills of Qurnawi craftsmen. But during the nineteenth century there was much interest both in papyrus documents and in carved scarabs,[12] the production of which, according to Wilkinson, achieved high levels of proficiency:

Indeed a great portion of those sold by dealers are forgeries; and some are so cleverly imitated, that it requires a practised eye to detect them; particularly scarabaei. Papyri are made up very cleverly, on a stick, enveloped in fragments, or leaves; the outer covering of a piece of real papyrus, and the whole sealed with clay. Good papyri are broken up to obtain these outer coatings to false ones; and unless a papyrus can be at least partly unrolled, it is scarcely worth while for a novice in antiquities to purchase it. (Wilkinson, 1847: 325)

Rhind, writing several decades later, is less complimentary and observes that local artistic ability "can rarely be accomplished more cleverly than to impose only on the quite inexperienced" (Rhind, 1862: 251). As in Wilkinson's time, scarabs and papyrus are apparently still popular, although the former are "unwieldy imitations" and form part of only a very limited repertoire of "small rogueries [which are] within the limits of their slight artistic ability" (Rhind, 1862: 252).

The production of fake antiquities was not limited to the west bank. Rhind simply refers to "Thebes" and it is not always clear if the protagonists he names reside on the east or the west bank (Rhind, 1862: 253–56). Amelia Edwards' account indicates that nearby Luxor was a center of production (Edwards, 1877: 411–12), if not in scale then certainly in quality, with some scarab specimens even purchased by the Egyptian Museum in Cairo "as instructive examples of the best forgeries" (Wilson, 1964: 77).[13] Despite such tantalizing snippets as offered by Wilson (1964: 76–77), and apart from the scattered glimpses contained in the writings of Edwards (1877), Lange (1952), and Rhind (1862), a historical study of this industry—detailing the external forces that generated the demand; its development in the context of depleting authentic supplies; the interrelationship between east and west bank in the supply both of examples and ancient raw materials; shifting customers' tastes, methods of production, and sales strategies; its evolving artistic qualities; its prominent historical characters, including the intermittent role of Egyptological specialists—remains to be undertaken (Budge, 1920: 323–26; Rhind, 1862: 254–55; Wilson, 1964: 76–77).

Religious observance

Despite Sonnini's observation that Qurnawi "displayed as much integrity and fairness in these little bargains, which employed us a great part of the day, as if they had been the most honest people in the world" in their antiquities dealings with him (Sonnini, 1800: 650–51), several Europeans have sought to question the moral fortitude of the west bank villagers. Reasons for this may have been earlier negative reports, particular experiences involving antiquities, or simply a sense of perceived European superiority. The denial of a legitimate, that is, agricultural, occupation forms part of this, as do allusions to the lack of religious observance. The characterization offered by Giovanni Belzoni has been influential, and is still being repeated by modern writers (Thompson, 1992: 106): "They have no mosque, nor do they care for one; for though they have at their disposal a great quantity of all sorts of bricks, which abound in every part of Gournou, from the surrounding tombs, they have never built a single house" (Belzoni, 1820: 159).

The notion is repeated by Rhind, although he remains curiously ambivalent:

The ordinary outward observance they seem to completely neglect, never, so far as I could perceive, visiting the mosk in the neighbouring town of

Luxor; and I have no recollection of ever seeing one of them engaged in the prescribed formality of daily prayer, which in many parts of the country is so commonly attended to. (Rhind, 1862: 279)

Rhind attributes this situation to Qurnawi being "Arabs of the desert, who are often not very strict in their devotions" (Rhind, 1862: 279). Yet, and despite their negligence, Rhind continues, they nevertheless do take pride in being Muslim, there are several who have made the pilgrimage to Mecca, and they frequent religious festivals as far away as Cairo (Rhind, 1862: 279–80).

Although Rhind did not observe public worship, Lane in his 1825–28 map of Thebes clearly indicates a mosque at Dra 'Abu al-Naga, just a little to the north of where the al-Hasasna mosque was located. In the modern cemetery Lane also identifies four shaykh tombs, domed buildings erected over the tomb of a holy man (Lane, 2000, Plate 74; 325), the same tombs as are also drawn in the panoramas of Robert Hay (Hay MSS). The presence of these structures confirms the Qurnawi identification with respected figures who are associated with spiritual gifts and a capacity to bestow blessings, that is, *baraka*. Although part of the Sufi tradition rather than orthodox Islam, these shaykh tombs especially are witness to a level of spiritual depth and practice that is centered on the veneration of holy men. The existence of these tombs, the presence of the mosque on Lane's map, and such ethnographic snippets as the circumcision ceremony described by Robert Hay (Hay MSS, diary entry July 17, 1826: 141), indicate that local spiritual expression at the time evidently manifested the same mixture of popular, formal, and traditional religious practices that also characterize the west bank communities today.

It must be argued, therefore, that some of the Europeans who worked in al-Qurna were either poor observers, as Belzoni apparently was, or they had their own particular agenda for misrepresenting local religious expression. It is suggested here that such misrepresentation was very much informed by the widespread public perceptions of west bank tribal behavior with which European travelers had been made familiar since 1589, the year of the Venetian's visit to Thebes, and through the reported subsequent negative experiences of Norden, Pococke, and Denon.

While religious observance, or rather the alleged lack of it, was seemingly one of the legitimating factors marshalled by Europeans in explanation of perceived antisocial Qurnawi behavior, there is some indication that religion may also have been an issue in west bank inter-tribal relations. Lane observes that their religious negligence is due to their particular occupational specialization, that their "rifling of mum-mies" in search of antiquities is something "which a strict Moos'lim would regard with the utmost abhorrence, as subjecting the person to constant defilement, and altogether impious and sacrilegious" (Lane, 2000: 328). It has already been argued that the Theban Necropolis in all probability played a significant role in the medieval *mumiya* trade. Qurnawi "rifling of mummies" is therefore not something that only became fashionable upon the arrival of European antiquities collectors, but the specific focus on the procurement of dead human bodies will have been a practice of long standing. This greater time depth of "constant defilement" will have had both regional and local implications for Qurnawi.

European commentaries remain vague about the negative attributes commonly ascribed to Qurnawi. The Venetian refers to them as "cursed tribes of insubordinate Arabs" (Burri, 1971: 81), James Bruce calls them "robbers who resemble our gypsies" and "out-laws" (Bruce, 1790: 125), for Sonnini they were "the most formidable banditti" (Sonnini, 1800: 650), while Denon "learnt that . . . they were almost always in rebellion against authority, and had become the terror of the vicinity" (Denon, 1803, 2: 87). Most of these opinions result from hearsay and can be traced to such individuals as travelers' respective boat owner or cap-tain, or in Sonnini's case, the shaykh of Luxor and a Turkish officer in Qus. As such, these secondary opinions will have been inflected by personal bias, antipathy, or fear on the part of local informants and will in most instances have been removed from the personal experience of the European travelers. It is remarkable that in spite of these subjective and negative opinions, almost all visitors to the west bank did arrive at amicable working relations with the villagers, to the point of being commended by Sonnini for their "integrity and fairness." Even Denon, whose regiment was attacked on several occasions, albeit probably not without reason, speaks of "my friends from Kurnu [who] had come to me privately when I was at a distance from our camp, and attended me with great fidelity" (Denon, 1803, 2: 81, 56).

This picture contrasts significantly with the warnings foreigners received against visiting the west bank. We may, therefore, assume that something else is at issue here, which causes local informants such as boat captains and military officials met along the way to continually and consistently portray the villagers of the Luxor west bank in a negative light. Accusations of violent and antisocial behavior may serve to impose conditions of spatial segregation prompted by derogatory and discriminatory attitudes located in perceptions of social difference, where religious beliefs may constitute one such area of difference. Such segregation is not necessarily imposed by accepted common perceptions and attitudes only, as inherent in the advice of a Luxor shaykh, a Turkish officer, or Cairene boat owners, but can also be seen to operate between neighboring communities. As we will discuss below, relations characterized by rivalry and enmity also existed between the inhabitants of the necropolis and those who belong to the area of al-Ba'irat just south of the ancient cemeteries. Since al-Ba'irat is exclusively agricultural and not involved with antiquities, the essential difference between legitimate agricultural pursuits and involvement in the *mumiya* trade or the collecting of antiquities, is the "impious," "sacrilegious," and spiritually defiling aspect of these latter activities. In the absence of knowledge about the nature and cause of factional rivalry within the west bank Qasas tribe or other relevant historical factors, it is postulated here that both the wider regional reputation of Qurnawi and their neighborly relations with al-Ba'irat are located within notions of spiritual purity, and the lack thereof, inherent in their respective 'mainstream' agricultural and cemetery-dependent economic specializations.

Local politics and tribal tensions

The Venetian and Burckhardt's identification of the Luxor west bank with Qasas territory does suggest a homogeneous population, although little is known of the surely considerable degree of admixture with earlier Coptic and traditional fellahin population groups, or indeed the extent of Qasas independence. Whichever the case, this is not to suggest that no intertribal rivalries or factional divisions between clans existed. The early travelers' records indeed indicate that a measure of enmity existed between different groups, although the exact nature of these differences can only be speculated upon.

Hostilities appear to have been ongoing for close to a century. For Edward Lane, reporting in the mid-1820s, "They now behave with all possible civility" (Lane, 2000: 328), but as early as Norden and Pococke's visits in 1737 there are clear indications of simmering tension. By the time Sonnini arrives in July 1778, there exists open conflict:

I could have wished much to visit some spacious excavations, hewn out in the rock, at a league to the westward of Gournei, which were the tombs of the ancient monarchs of Thebes; but I could find nobody that would undertake to conduct me thither; the sheick himself assured me that the inhabitants of Gournei being at war with those of the neighbouring villages, some of whom they had recently killed, it would be highly imprudent to expose myself with guides taken from among them, and who, far from affording me any sort of protection, would infallibly draw upon me the revenge of their implacable opponents. (Sonnini, 1800: 652)

Denon recounts, likewise, how during the French army's assault on one of the *saff* tombs in the al-Tarif area, a group of its occupants escaped into the desert, where they "were without provisions, and could obtain none from the neighbouring villages, with whom they were at war" (Denon, 1803, 3: 51).

Which are these "neighboring villages," and what are the reasons for their inhabitants' discontent? Sonnini identifies one of them as "Kamoulé, a village half way to Néguadé," but this is north of Qurna and should not have deterred him from visiting the Valley of the Kings (Sonnini, 1800: 654). For the area south of Qurna, none of these villages are clearly identified, and it is only by an analysis of certain textual markers that the geography of west bank discord can be traced. One of these 'villages' could concern the occupants of the central foothills of Shaykh 'Abd al-Qurna, in accordance with the accounts of Norden and Bruce, already referred to. The anxiety of the shaykh accompanying Pococke to the Valley of the Kings in 1737 indicates that a population indeed resided in its vicinity:

The Sheik also was in haste to go, being afraid, as I imagined, lest the people should have opportunity to gather together if we staid out long. From Gournou to this place there is a very difficult foot way over the mountains, by which the people might have paid us an unwelcome visit, tho' we were under the protection of the Sheik. (Pococke, 1743: 99)

It would seem inconceivable that the shaykh feared an attack from his own villagers, and the episode rather suggests the presence of a community at the other end of the mountain path leading to the Valley of the Kings, that is, in the area of Shaykh 'Abd al-Qurna, with whom they were evidently not on friendly terms. In 1799, Vivant Denon appears likewise to have had fears for his personal safety in the area of the Ramesseum, indeed suggesting the presence of a community at Shaykh 'Abd al-Qurna (Denon, 1803, 2: 92).

The other likely player in these relations is the village of al-Ba'irat, south of the necropolis. When approaching the temple of Madinat Habu on his way to the Memnon Colossi, Pococke was hurried away from there by his accompanying shaykh, who "was near his enemy" (Pococke, 1743: 101). Pococke returned the next day, seemingly without the shaykh, and was accosted while drawing the Colossi, likely by the same people who confronted Norden just a few days earlier and who were evidently in conflict with the shaykh of al-Qurna/al-Tarif. Pococke initially appears not to have made the connection: "The common people have the weakness to imagine that inscriptions discover treasures" (Pococke, 1743: 102), despite the demonstrated anxiety of his shaykh guide the day before. Returning to the boat, Pococke learns that the same group paid a rude visit there, "having taken great umbrage at my copying the inscriptions" and hinting at a nighttime assault (Pococke, 1743: 105). This Ba'irati visit seems an audacious move, if the boat was indeed moored at what was to become the regular landing place, that is, in the territory of the shaykh of al-Qurna. Pococke thinks that their aggravation has to do with beliefs about Europeans having the power to magically remove treasure, although he acknowledges that "they might also be envious of the Sheik, imagining that I made him great presents" (Pococke, 1743: 105). Still planning to stay in order to visit the temple of Madinat Habu the next day, Pococke finally "found these two governors of the neighbouring villages were not friends" (Pococke, 1743: 105) and was persuaded by his shaykh to leave. If there is any significance in this, then it would be that relations between the two leaders were sufficiently strained for Pococke's shaykh to see the risk his guest could be exposed to if staying any longer.

One can only speculate about the reasons for this animosity and the underpinning demographics. If a rival group did indeed inhabit the tombs in the central foothills, then these may have derived from settled nomads who arrived there independent from such other groups as the Qasas. This is indicated by Qurnawi from Hurubat who trace their ancestry to Harb and his two brothers who, according to legend, initially settled at Old Qurna, the Seti I Temple village. If this area was also part of Qasas territory, then acceptance of any settled nomads—Harb and his brothers included—inside Qasas territory would seem problematic. Legendary accounts that the Qasas are recent arrivals and that Harb and his brothers were the first to settle there, may be the narrative remnants that reflect episodes of tribal conflict or, at its most benign, a history of clan rivalry. Similarly, if the Seti I Temple area of Old Qurna was outside Qasas jurisdiction but, assuming clear demarcations, adjoining its territory at al-Tarif, then such close proximity may equally have provided ground for intermittent skirmishes and possibly prompting the move to the tombs in the foothills. But such would nevertheless seem contrary to Richardson's account, which provides evidence for seasonal migration between the two areas, while the placement of the cemetery also possibly suggests close links between the two areas. Caroline Simpson views the occupants of Old Qurna village as mainly "fellahiin descended from and intermarried with the earlier Coptic community" (Simpson, 2001: 4, 5). She sees these as eventually inhabiting the tombs in the central foothills, although one might question how and why they acquired the status of a seemingly independent group, simply beyond anybody's reach, safely ensconced in their hideouts, for government officials and opposed Bedouin groups alike, as suggested by Bruce and Norden. Irrespective of these dynamics, the question remains how they came to be integrated with later arrivals in the foothills when Old Qurna was abandoned, and what the facilitating incentive was for this process of seeming pacification. Paid employment from antiquities collectors? In the face of these uncertainties, and leaving the legend of Harb aside for the moment, we may simply postulate in the area of Shaykh 'Abd al-Qurna a rival Qasas faction with remembered links to the Old Qurna and Tarif areas, for whom integration with later arrivals from there was not impossible.

In the case of al-Ba'irat, two main reasons for the differences may tentatively be identified. Beyond underlying tribal factionalism, disagreement may have existed over religious conviction and practice. As rather more traditional agriculturalists, the Ba'irati will also have been conventional adherents to Islam, and may have judged the involvement with the mummy trade and the desecration of tombs on the part of their neighbors reprehensible, consequently treating them with the contempt they evidently deserved. Beyond what has already been said about Qurnawi religious practice, oral-historical research among Ba'irati may reveal the nature of the discord between the two communities, but the possibility of past religious differences must not be ruled out.

Beyond differing notions of spiritual purity, existing rivalries over the allocation of resources and a perceived differential distribution of wealth may have offered further grounds for discontent. In addition to agricultural pursuits, Qurnawi subsistence included a range of informal economic activities, from initial involvement in the mummy trade, to that of providing guidance, food, and horses to visiting parties in return for 'presents,' to later still the trade in antiquities and modern-day tourism. By contrast, al-Ba'irat was largely, if not exclusively, agricultural, and the extra, if meager, income available to Qurnawi may have evolved into a history of jealousy of considerable time depth, and which to some extent continues to this day. The requests for "*backsich*" made of Norden's party, and Pococke's perceptive comment about their envy of the shaykh's imagined presents, are clear indicators in this respect.

Taxing the peasant: Issues of national, regional, and local governance

The known history of the west bank communities as it comes to us through the observations of European travelers is one of severely strained village-state relations. The imputed rebellious nature and the negative behavioral characteristics of the west bank tribes did not only involve possible issues relevant to antiquities, but also, and invariably, their interaction with agents of government. The Anonymous Venetian records in 1589 the mortal enmity that exists between west bank inhabitants and the Turks, in which the levying of taxes plays some part (Burri, 1971: 81). James Bruce in 1769 calls them "robbers . . . out-laws, punished with death if elsewhere found" and recounts how:

> Osman Bey, an ancient governor of Girgé, unable to suffer any longer the disorders committed by these people . . . took possession of the face of the mountain, where the greatest number of these wretches were: He then ordered all their caves to be filled with this dry brushwood, to which he set fire, so that most of them were destroyed. (Bruce, 1790: 125)

In a similar vein, and in order to attest the veracity of "their ferocious disposition," Charles Sonnini in 1778 draws on the pronouncements of a Turkish officer, the "*kiaschef* of Kous," who "would not venture to travel there, even with his little party of Mamalûk soldiers" (Sonnini, 1800: 649). Wilkinson and Lane report that the original village near the Seti I

Temple was destroyed by government troops. Yanni (Giovanni d'Athanasi) reports that "there were at Gourna more than eighteen hundred houses," the number having been reduced to "about two hundred and sixteen by the war of extermination which the Mamelukes so long waged against them, in order to deliver the country from the horrible system of pillage which they practiced" (d'Athanasi, 1836: 131).

How may we interpret these strained relations and what factor may have been at issue without us having to rely again on certain postulated Bedouin behavioral characteristics? The instance referred to by Lane and Wilkinson may be readily enough explained in the context of regional political and economic instability. After 1769, Upper Egypt had become a refuge for political dissidents seeking to conquer Cairo (Garcin, 1976: 528), while "the country had been ruined by the excesses of fugitive Mamluk rulers and the coming-and-going of armies" (Garcin, 1976: 530). Political instability with open war between Mamluk factions cut short Sonnini's visit to Thebes, caught as he was "between two parties of combatants, equally undisciplined and ungovernable, and alike inclined to commit the greatest excesses" (Sonnini, 1800: 648–49).[14] Muhammad Ali's victory over Mamluk insurgents between Qus and Qena in February 1811 (Garcin, 1976: 530) will plausibly have involved military activity on the Luxor west bank, if only for the purpose of 'mopping up' Mamluk troops fleeing south. Thus, the destruction of Old Qurna by transiting armies between 1778 (the year of Sonnini's visit) and 1811 may be linked with possible complicity on the part of west bank villagers who may have assisted the rebels in making use of the mountain retreats for refuge.

As such, the safety of the mountain will have attracted all sorts of people in conflict with the state and seeking local assistance, thereby causing government wrath to also fall on the Theban west bank communities. Whether there was any benefit for Qurnawi to be had in such altruism—especially toward Mamluks—is now impossible to say, beyond observing that certain rules of social obligation toward distant but affiliated groups, or commitments in possible political alliances with other tribal groups, will likely have involved some form of reciprocal arrangement. Even so, a propensity for Qurnawi to assist others in trouble with officialdom may be part of a larger picture in which they are likewise implicated.

The relative history and position of the Hawwara tribe may be of importance here. Their installation in Upper Egypt in 1380–81 resulted from a Mamluk-initiated episode of transmigration (Garcin, 1976: 450) which, in the eyes of surrounding tribes, may have blurred any boundaries between their perceived independence and the interests of the state. Similarly, the initial alliance between Turks and Hawwara against the Mamluks resulted in a degree of cooperation, which resulted in the free movement of Ottoman troops throughout the region (Garcin, 1976: 517, his argument in part based on the Anonymous Venetian's 1589 account). This working arrangement with Hawwara was especially important for the Turks, as Ottoman control over Upper Egypt at the time of Norden's 1737 visit in practical terms did not reach further south than Girga (Garcin, 1976: 525), and such control by proxy through an alliance with Hawwara possibly also helped cement the power base of Turkic Cairo at times when its place in the larger Ottoman Empire was perceived to be weak (Garcin, 1976: 517). The inference could be that Hawwara were seen to act first as Mamluk and later as Ottoman agents and exploited tribal rivalries for state purposes. Such state opposition mediated through relations of enmity with certain tribes will have reinforced political alliances with others, and it is in this context of interdependence that the people inhabiting the Theban Mountain will have commanded a degree of importance for the measure of safety they were able to provide, even if they themselves were not directly implicated in actions directed against the interests of the state.

At least during the eighteenth century, such 'actions against the interests of the state' involved attacks on trade routes, which channeled products from the south of Egypt to Qus, from where transportation through the wadis of the Eastern Desert was possible to al-Qusayr on the Red Sea, a port crucial in the trade with the Hijaz and the Arabian Peninsula, and supporting both the requirements of the annual hajj and the long-distance trade with India. Different tribes (including the Hawwara and 'Ababda) collaborated with Ottoman troops in the protection of these trade routes, escorting caravans and defending them from attacks by other tribes (Garcin, 1976: 527). During the mid-eighteenth century, this network of trade routes also included the town of Farshut located northwest of Luxor at the opposite end of the 'Qena Bend,' receiving Sudanese trade goods relayed by way of the town of Esna via a camel track through the Western Desert (Garcin, 1976: 527–28). The Western Desert between Luxor and Farshut constitutes a network of tracks that has been used since antiquity (Darnell and Darnell, 1996). Assuming their continued use in modern times, the lure of trade goods was thus brought in relatively close proximity to the communities of the Theban foothills. Although the desert trails themselves may have been a little too distant for Qurnawi to be readily involved in raiding parties, tribal affiliations or intertribal political alliances will have required them to offer safe keeping in the tombs of the Theban Mountain to those who were thus involved. The existence of these alliances at the end of the eighteenth century may have resulted in what Henry Rhind called "local hereditary jurisdictions, yielding then a fitful and uncertain allegiance," and existing in opposition to a distant central government whose "controlling power . . . was hardly felt at all in those and other portions of the Upper country" (Rhind, 1862: 309).

Yet, localized confrontation—or a fear thereof—inherent in a center–periphery opposition will nevertheless have persisted, as evidenced in the accounts of Bruce and Sonnini. Yanni states, rather melodramatically, that "not one of their ancestors had ever died in his bed, nor even suddenly carried off by disease—they had all died sword in hand; and the terror which their ferocity inspired was felt as far as Berdis, so named on account of the plunder they committed there" (d'Athanasi, 1836: 131–32). Elsewhere, Yanni contradicts himself when saying that smallpox every three years "decimates" the population but that otherwise "both sexes live very commonly to the age of hundred" (d'Athanasi, 1836: 131). We may conclude that his account reflects the preconceptions current among travelers, and typical of the day. Even so, direct complicity in attacks on trade routes cannot be ruled out, even if the distance covered in such raids as indicated by Yanni's "Berdis" (that is, Bardis, some thirty-five kilometers northwest of Farshut and measured in a direct line at about ninety kilometers distance from the Theban west bank) suggests involvement of other tribal groups (d'Athanasi, 1836: 132).

It may be inferred that it is against this background of involvement in activities contrary to the interests of the state that Qurnawi acquired a reputation of real or imputed fierceness which, in combination with the ostracizing un-Islamic practices referred to earlier, will have effectively marginalized them in the eyes of such state representatives as "an ancient governor of Girgé" in Bruce's 1790 account, and the Turkish officer in Qus described by Sonnini in 1799. Reprisals and punitive expeditions will have blurred the distinction between recovery of state property and the levying of taxes proper, thus explaining the ongoing violence surrounding the mutually understood taxation regime alluded to by the Anonymous Venetian in 1589 (Burri, 1971: 81).

In the midst of these blurred political and economic relations, the levying of taxes and the extraction of human labor for the purposes of either military conscription or public works corvée duty are, nevertheless, recurring themes in the history of the west bank communities. Lane describes local strategies adopted to evade taxes during the 1820s, and their repercussions for the village shaykh (Lane, 2000: 328). Wilkinson remarks that "the numerous exactions of the provincial governors have the invariable effect of leaving the peasant *always in arrears*" (Wilkinson, 1843: 276, original emphasis). Belzoni describes the beating of the village shaykh and the forced recruitment of Qurnawi by a regional official to procure antiquities (Belzoni, 1820: 185–98). The "secrecy and mystification" surrounding the finding of antiquities also reported by Rhind at least in part—and in addition to the pricing motivations identified by Belzoni (1820: 161)—concerned motivations of taxation, serving their disguise from "some local functionary" who would visit "with tolerable certainty" if knowledge of significant finds became public, and resulting in the loss of "no trifling share of the find" (Rhind, 1862: 249–50). Likewise, Rhind offers a description of nineteenth-century conscription practices also affecting Qurnawi and their impact on the relations between local villagers and their village shaykh charged with gathering the required number of men (Rhind, 1862: 311–20). The studies by Lawson (1981; 1992: 92–102, 119–29) on the Arab Rebellion of 1822–23 have identified the centrality of economic issues over and above the religious motivations suggested by St. John (1845: 378, based on Madox, 1834).

Central in many of these travelers' accounts of taxation and forced conscription or corvée incidents is the issue of local governance, and the role of the *shaykh al-balad*, the village shaykh, in particular. A manifestation of the old 'divide and rule' adage, the *shaykh al-balad* was essentially the government agent at the local level. A senior villager, his position was at once one of prestige and the object of hatred on the part of his community. Charged with the levying of taxes and the rounding up of either military conscripts or corvée laborers to be assigned to public works programs, his position was at all times sensitive, both in relation to the government—as demonstrated by the lashing episode reported by Belzoni—and in relation to his fellow villagers, as described by Rhind (1862: 313–20). Wilkinson indicates that in addition to his levying of taxes, the village shaykh was also a link in the chain of extortions and injustices practiced by regional officials far removed from the center of government (Wilkinson, 1843: 278–82). Listed under items that "increase the loss of the peasant," the "claims of the Shekh" included "presents of different kinds according to the means or fears of the donor" (Wilkinson, 1843: 274, 277, 278). Henry Rhind adds that the shaykh "will take care to have a considerable picking for himself" at any opportunity, as a result of which they are "universally detested and detestable" (Rhind, 1862: 308). Rhind's strong wording and lengthy treatment demonstrates his indignation about the injustices perpetrated under a system corrupted by extortion at all levels of regional officialdom (Rhind, 1862: 305–29), but he chooses "not [to] interfere in the matter at all" for lack of proper authorization (Rhind, 1862: 319–20). As previously with Belzoni (1820: 188–90), and reminiscent of the reticence of later Egyptologists to speak out in favor of Qurnawi, there is a sense that Rhind's inaction may have served to preserve the authorization that mattered to him most, namely the permission to excavate.

Under British rule, the title of *shaykh al-balad* was converted into that of *'umda*, but the position essentially continued to be one which, both by means of benevolent social compulsion and overt force, married the taxation and labor potential of the local community to the objectives of the state.

Living among the dead: The social life of 'troglodytes'[15]

Having remained beyond the purview of most early western observers, it may be recognized that Qurnawi social and cultural practices were either not consciously observed or did not feed into travelers' understanding of the incidents they experienced. Indeed, travelers' silence surrounding issues of indigenous custom is endemic to most accounts. The reasons for this are various, ranging from lack of access due to aggressive behavior on the part of the visitors, as in the case of Denon's military party in 1799, to travelers' singular focus on antiquities, and to being preconditioned by the many negative accounts of west bank behavior evidently extant as much among travelers as among Cairene captains and local officials.

Even so, some travelers could be struck by certain human characteristics they could identify with, resulting in a degree of ambivalence in their reports, where the sedimentation of many years of negative reporting became juxtaposed with the sudden recognition of a rather more positive trait. Such was the case with Sonnini who, despite the fear and protestations of his fellow travelers, seated himself upon the sand in the middle of a dozen of these rascally fellahs, pulling out my purse every moment, and paying their own price to all those who brought me idols or antique medals. I thus made a pretty ample collection of fragments of antiquity; and I must say, in justice to the inhabitants of Gournei, that they displayed as much integrity and fairness in these little bargains, which employed us a great part of the day, as if they had been the most honest people in the world. (Sonnini, 1800: 650–51)

While the impression of such proper business-like conduct may have assuaged any fear and softened the perceived qualities of "this truly detestable place" (Sonnini, 1800: 650–51), ambivalence between "these rascally fellahs" and their "integrity and fairness" also precluded any further interest into why such dealings in antiquities could be entered into in such seemingly customary and natural fashion. This lack of inquiry into local custom not only concerned such astute business dealings surrounding "fragments of antiquity," but insensitivity toward indigenous cultural practices covered the range from a dismissal of locally held notions of hidden treasure and other folk beliefs, to ignorance of local hospitality rules and the appropriateness of giving a little "*backsich*" in return for the right to draw the monuments undisturbed, as in the case of Norden.

The lack of an inquisitive western response to the surrounding communities is largely grounded in travelers' preoccupation with their immediate personal experiences, but there are nevertheless considerations in their reports that transcend these. For the most part these serve to situate and establish the legitimacy of travelers' negative preconceptions about the west bank and are largely obtained from seemingly independent observers sharing similar sentiments, or historical accounts they encountered along the way. James Bruce in 1769 did not consider issues of political difference or resistance, but anchored his appreciation of west bank inhabitants in an earlier incident, that of the punitive expedition mounted by "Osman Bey, an ancient governor of Girgé," and connecting with the present by commenting that "they have since recruited their numbers, without changing their manners" (Bruce, 1790: 125).

This is not to say that such secondary accounts supporting the legitimacy of travelers' observations and preconceptions were necessarily always effective. The fearful warnings expressed by Norden's Egyptian captain rather contrast with Norden's actual experience. The fracas with the local shaykh that occurred while visiting the west bank was largely due to some of the people in Norden's own party being "as insolent" when confronted with "noisy and insolent" requests for "*backsich*." The fifty Arabs who had gathered while Norden was drawing the Colossi "at first only saluted us, and seemed under some surprise; but were most of all troublesome to me with their curiosity to find what I was doing," but their behavior can hardly be said to have represented a life-threatening form of aggression (Norden, 1741: 10).

The above incident goes to the core of some of the negative experiences encountered by early western visitors. For beyond ignorance of tribal origins, local political affiliations and endemic tribal conflict, travelers' knowledge about the history of exploitation by western mummy dealers, or local notions of magic associated with the ancient monuments, the obvious disinterest in, and misrecognition of, locally operative rules of social behavior must be taken to represent one of the main reasons why tension in the relations between European visitors and members of west bank communities often came to the fore. In many cases, including the Norden incident, above, and as also experienced by Pococke and Denon, such tension arose as a result of ignorance about local rules of hospitality. They were briefly alluded to by d'Athanasi (1836: 132), but have only recently been recognized as a factor in the often strained relations between visitors and west bank villagers (Simpson, 2001: 4–5). These rules involve obligation of protection toward strangers; they are strongly territorially based, pertaining to physical spaces controlled by particular families or under the authority of a village shaykh; and they often comprise a form of allegiance that is also and increasingly economically motivated. Language barriers will have inhibited understanding of these rules and their geographical extent. As a result, visitors wishing to see monuments located in different territories failed to recognize that relations of mutual allegiance and some associated gift giving needed to be continually reestablished with local families and rulers when moving through geographical space. Relations of animosity ensued when locals were denied the mutual arrangements of allegiance with visitors to which they felt rightfully entitled within their territory. Additionally, these poor relations were often further compounded by the differing tribal affiliations and degrees of prior enmity existing across the territories involved, especially where visitors' allegiance was perceived as remaining with an opposing shaykh, as exemplified in Pococke's movements across the territories of al-Qurna and al-Ba'irat. With time, such negative encounters crystallized into accounts of overt west bank hostility toward visitors in the publications of western travelers. As Caroline Simpson perceptively observes, "With a few simple courtesies it could have been so different" (Simpson, 2001: 5).

Against this background of unrecognized and violated local custom, and apart from the more socially focused snippets contained in travelers' works we have already reviewed, the accounts by Henry Rhind (1862: 242–329) and Yanni (Giovanni d'Athanasi, 1836) stand out for their treatment of the socio-cultural characteristics of the community in whose midst they lived and worked, in Yanni's case for a period of eighteen years. Yanni's comments are contained in a curious work, which is both catalogue and polemic: an inventory of the antiquities collection he acquired for Henry Salt, the British Consul in Egypt, and a defense of Salt against the writings of Belzoni. Rhind's work is essentially Egyptological, offering an account of his explorations in the necropolis and his interpretation of archaeological data. His language is of interest for the sense of cultural superiority that shines through, a precursor to the colonialist flavor that runs through the narrative of later British Egyptologists. Although both accounts are not comprehensive, and both are at times ambiguous in their references to communities or places other than al-Qurna, Rhind's and Yanni's commentaries nevertheless provide the historical context for contemporary ethnographic considerations of Qurnawi sociality.

Going against the gradually evolving convention of confusing locally understood social categories with a geographically based toponymy, Yanni was the only western commentator who demonstrated familiarity with local tribal names. He offers a social structure of locally present population groups that comprises six 'families' or 'tribes,' organized in 'classes' of two united tribes each, with each such class constituting a third of the village (d'Athanasi, 1836: 130). Despite his phonetic transcription, four of the six can still be equated with current toponymy. "Ilhouroubat," aligned with the smaller family of "Karsir-Ildigagat," and "Ilgabat-Oullatiat" constitute al-Hurubat, al-Ghabat, and al-'Atyat respectively. "Karsir-Ildigagat" equates with Lane's *Ckusr Ed-Dacka'ckee,* the "Palace of Ed-Dacka'ckee," or the Ramesseum, the memorial temple of Ramesses II in the plains below Shaykh 'Abd al-Qurna which, according to Lane, took its name from "a person possessing great flocks and herds, and who, coming to El-Ckoor'neh, took up his abode in this ancient building, and kept up but little intercourse with the other inhabitants of this district"

(Lane, 2000: 342). According to Yanni, this smaller family was under the protection of the al-Hurubat tribe. The name of al-Daqaqi is no longer used, and the area is effectively considered as al-Hurubat, even if local toponymy refers to it as al-Sahal al-Sharqi. The two component families of a third class identified by Yanni, "Ilmassaah Oullovassa," have left no immediately recognizable successors, as possibly foreshadowed by Yanni himself: "it has very small power and scarcely any consequence in the village" (d'Anasthasi, 1836: 131). It is of interest that there was no group as yet that could be identified with present-day al-Hasasna in the northern foothills, possibly confirming the late arrival of Shaykh Tayyeb's ancestors here, and there is no clear reference to the al-Tarif area.

It must also be noted that Yanni looks at these population groups as social entities, rather than as groups that equate with physically recognizable locations, which is one of the reasons why the identification of al-Tarif as a community is problematic. He does not further specify the particular families by their locations in the foothills—in fact he names the one identifiable location, that of the Ramesseum, in social terms and by reference to the family name that had become, according to Lane, associated with it—and there is thus no reason to believe that families' respective territories indicated by him will have been different from today. Yanni simply refers to "the village," qualifying that "the lands are also divided into three portions, for the occupancy of which the three classes draw lots, in order to avoid all complaint and dissension on the subject. Gourna is the name given to the three lots of territory." The division of agricultural lands is linked with families' respective tribal territories: "Each class sows the fields which fall to its lot, and contributes its portion to the pecuniary necessities of the village" (d'Anasthasi, 1836: 131).

Yanni's account of the system of drawing lots remains ambiguous, since it seems impractical for tribes to periodically exchange entire territories. It possibly reflects a received tradition of how land issues were settled initially among the first Arab arrivals or, alternatively, it may allude to an impartial ballot-based system of allocating tomb dwellings and associated use of agricultural lands among families within each of the tribal areas, something not mentioned by Belzoni in his discussion of household matters (Belzoni, 1820: 183), but an issue that future historical research may choose to investigate further. Altogether, with its emphasis on social entity rather than location, Yanni's account reflects an earlier phase in the eventual urbanization of the foothills, where occupation by extended and

Glimpses of village life both surprise and delight: In the midst of history and framed by their vernacular surroundings, the smiling faces of a new generation of Qurnawi.

related families gradually became equated with the specific location that constituted their territory, as understood today: al-Hurubat, al-Ghabat, and al-'Atyat.

Other than people migrating into the foothills for the purpose of being in proximity to the provision of archaeological labor, the main mechanism driving that eventual urbanization would be natural population increase resulting from marriage. D'Athanasi devotes much of his commentary to it, but his references to other communities leave their relevance to the foothills at times open to question, although they may well have been generic to Upper Egypt. Of value for our present purposes are his references to the practice of first-cousin marriages (even if he does not specify its frequency, the broader social context, or the particular kinship patterns involved); the financial requirements on the part of the groom; and the rules of restitution in case of divorce. Other wedding arrangements included men exchanging their respective sisters, or men obtaining a bride from the village of al-Karnak on the east bank. However, Qurnawi did not permit their daughters to marry men from al-Karnak, considering them "an ignoble race" (d'Athanasi, 1836: 134). Importantly, Yanni also makes reference to the sharing of the expenses involved with wedding celebrations, thereby alluding to, although not elaborating on, the extensive practice of *wajib*, duty, and its rules of social obligation toward the wider kinship group.

Henry Rhind provides complementary insights in his description of family composition, the multiple wives of the village shaykh and its associated domestic discontent, the observed lack of "conjugal affections" and the evident segregation of the sexes, and habits of dress and personal adornment (Rhind, 1862: 290–98). In the context of the latter, he identifies the use of stone beads in necklaces, "handed down as invaluable talismanic aids" and serving fertility-associated purposes (Rhind, 1862: 291).

Other than these marriage rules, at least in part intended to consolidate harmonious community relations, Yanni makes reference to rules of asylum and conciliatory practices designed to resolve blood feuds (d'Anasthasi, 1836: 138–40), festivals that include displays of horsemanship, serving in part to keep alive "hereditary animosities" in the absence of open inter-tribal warfare (d'Anasthasi, 1836: 135–36), and funerary customs.

Despite the paucity of much specific detail in these two accounts, because of their emphasis on the local population and their social institutions, they provide an important matrix into which other travelers' isolated ethnographic observations can be slotted: Richardson's reference to marriageable age and women's activities (Richardson, 1822, 2: 121–22), the logistics of establishing a household upon marriage described by Belzoni (1820: 183), and Hay's account of circumcision practices (Hay MSS, diary entry July 17, 1826: 141). Other observations, such as the arrangement of domestic space and the use of clay cupboards, discussed by Richardson (1822, 2: 74) and Belzoni (1820: 183), provide the architectural environment within which, and against the background of which social life conducted itself. In their totality, these representations, crystallized from the pages of European observers, provide the communal and still mostly subterranean urban-environmental context within which the economic and political perspectives discussed earlier, as well as the social and vernacular-architectural emergence of the contemporary foothills communities, took place.

5

Protected Space as Domestic Place: Human Presence and the Emergence of the Built Environment in the Theban Necropolis

Qurnawi and their remembered past

Beyond the comments already made about west bank population movements throughout history and the possible detail of Qurnawi presence there as seen through the eyes of western observers, what is the sense of history that Qurnawi have of their own presence in the region? How may we view the genealogical history of the modern community, if at all possible? Establishing a sequence for the time depth of occupation of the Theban foothills based on a Qurnawi remembered past is problematic, if only for the practice on the part of some to trace local ancestries back to the time of the Muslim conquest of Egypt.[1] The inclusion of such names as 'Amr Ibn al-'As and Abu Sufyan in local genealogies proves less than helpful and, while similar ancestry may arguably be claimed by all Egyptians of Arab descent to some degree, the time spans involved may be assumed to be beyond Qurnawi ability for accurate genealogical recall. Others, by contrast, assert that the distance to Abu Sufyan is indeed "very far."

The three foothills communities of al-Hurubat, al-Ghabat, and al-'Atyat claim descent from three founding fathers, Harb, Ghaba, and 'Atya respectively. They allegedly were three brothers whose father, Adman, according to some, is said to have settled upon arrival at the site of the Seti I Temple, the area often referred to as Old Qurna. Some claim to have heard of the name Adman, but do not know his place in the scheme of things. Others' accounts end up in confused sequences that include several individuals named Harb of differing importance (for example, Harb al-Kabir, Harb al-Zughayyar). The fact of the matter seems to be that those questioned simply did not know the detail, or were incapable of giving an accurate account of the local genealogical sequence. In this sense, and recognizing nevertheless that in all these accounts there may be an element of some residual received wisdom, the significance of these founding fathers and any associated genealogical construct derived from them may simply be seen in terms of some legendary and mythical importance, but may no longer be taken to reflect verifiable truths.

However, male Qurnawi personal names incorporate the names of their immediate ancestors in the male line, and informants were generally able to provide a time depth going back some eight generations. In this manner, Badawi claimed descent from a person nicknamed Barur who was indicated as the founder of a Hurubati clan that is at times in jocular fashion still referred to by that same name. For our purposes, the name of Barur is significant, as the name "Baroor" is also mentioned by Henry Rhind and, if indeed the same person, locates Badawi's family in al-Hurubat during the early to mid-nineteenth century at a time when Old Qurna will have been vacated, when archaeological activity in the foothills had become intensive, and when a measure of population increase may be expected to have taken place (Rhind, 1862: 316). Barur may thus constitute a marker of recognizable identity at the same time as he comes to represent the point at which any prior ancestry becomes speculative or even mythical: Barur is also identified with the family of Abu Zayd, who was allegedly a son of Harb. But by then the trail has become so vague that to substantiate any connections beyond reasonable doubt has become impossible.[2]

The best that can be said at this stage is that Adman and his sons arrived on the scene relatively late, or that they are separated by many generations that can now no longer be accounted for. As for Badawi and his family, the part he has played in the present research and his connections to Henry Rhind's "Baroor" provide a satisfying link between the historical and ethnographic parts of this study and bring full circle the interdependence and continuities that exist between Qurnawi of old and those of today, and those *khawaja* who have been so inextricably involved in their journey.

From adaptive reuse to vernacular expansion

The urban landscape of the Qurnawi foothills, as observed by some of those early *khawaja* travelers, presented a picture rather different from the settlement pattern characteristic of the foothills during the late twentieth century. Rhind's lithograph of Shaykh 'Abd al-Qurna (Rhind, 1862, Plate II) and William Prinsep's 1842 painting of roughly the same area (Conner, 1984: 46; Manniche, 1987: 3; Simpson, 2003: Plate 138) show a landscape in which the houses of both Giovanni d'Athanasi (Yanni) and John Gardner Wilkinson are prominent. The living spaces of their Qurnawi neighbors are indicated by low enclosure walls in front of tomb openings, their spatial functionality enhanced by mud grain silos, storage columns, assorted mud vessels and cupboards, and sleeping platforms. Roofed structures are rare, and appear limited to the dwelling of the village shaykh neighboring Yanni's house.

Yanni's house, built by him in 1817 as a base for the collecting of antiquities on Henry Salt's behalf, is likely to have been the first free-standing, above-ground, roofed domestic dwelling in that part (al-Hurubat) of the foothills.[3] The drawings made by Robert Hay during his stay in the nearby Wilkinson house between 1829 and 1834 suggest that occupation of tomb chambers then was the common practice (Hay MSS).

As a collection point for amassed antiquities, Yanni's house clearly differentiates from the house Gardner Wilkinson had established for himself some time between 1824 and 1827.[4] The Wilkinson house was an elaborate version of the tomb dwellings he saw Qurnawi use around him (Thompson, 1992: 102; Thompson, 1996) and not a custom-made free-standing structure like Yanni's house. Neither was the Wilkinson house a staging post for shipments of antiquities, for such was not his business.[5]

Apart from previously resident families or tribal groups, it may be assumed that the employment opportunities offered by European antiquities collectors such as Yanni will have resulted in an increasing population density in the foothills, especially during the 1820s and 1830s, when foreign antiquities collectors appeared to have been at their busiest.[6] Both the accounts of Belzoni (1820: 158) and Lane (2000: 327–29) indeed indicate that there may have been a considerable number of people living in the Theban foothills, where Qurnawi life essentially conducted itself in the enclosed and at least partly subterranean spaces of their tomb dwellings.

However, amid the demographic changes affecting the foothills, it must be accepted as plausible that Yanni's house eventually came to serve as an additional incentive for Qurnawi to adopt or upgrade their dwellings to enclosed and roofed structures that were at least in part of European inspiration, an emerging practice we can begin to observe in the 1842

Prinsep painting and the 1862 Rhind lithograph. This subsequently expanding practice came to represent the new norm, in part explaining the twentieth-century appearance of the southern foothills hamlets, and establishing the historical importance of Yanni's house.[7]

Grounded in these early developments, the eventual wholesale transition from subsurface living spaces to above-ground vernacular architecture is one which represents one of the major historical and visible changes in the modern occupation of the necropolis, and one which, also post-Yanni, is still closely connected with archaeological issues. An important consideration in this transition is the fact that the presence of people in this environment was a decisive factor in early attempts to pursue suitable forms of heritage management for the area. The history of these protective measures forms a relevant chapter in Qurnawi social history that remains largely untold.[8]

Heritage management concerns were not simply in response to the pressures associated with the domestic presence of people in this sensitive environment. The history of protection of the Theban Necropolis also is one in which the perceived destructive quality of Qurnawi economic relations and their impact on the surrounding antiquities were often central, eventually making these heritage management measures inevitable. As a consequence and collectively, the imposition of the various measures and restrictions employed came to underpin the subsequent transition from adaptive reuse of largely invisible tomb dwellings to above-ground vernacular structures, demonstrating the reciprocal impact of protective heritage management measures on the urban landscape and the web of entangled relations between people and their environment.[9] In view of the impending changes that can be expected to affect Qurnawi society, it becomes of increasing historical importance to chart the impact of these early archaeological heritage management initiatives on Qurnawi society and their connections with the formation of the foothills' late-twentieth-century vernacular settlements.

To give context to the changes affecting the urban development of the foothills, and before discussing contemporary ways of making a living in this environment, it is necessary to develop a picture both of the archaeological characteristics of the foothills landscape generally, and of one particularly formative episode that has affected perceptions about Qurnawi habitation of the necropolis ever since. It is not the intention here to enter into the realm that Egyptologists rightly view as theirs. The subject is in any case well covered by publications too numerous to mention, with the citations listed here offering less than a representative sample of both scholarly and more popular works. Yet, a very general reference to the ancient cemeteries themselves, and one particular local response to them, will assist to place the economic practices of Qurnawi who allegedly draw on them in their proper context.

The Necropolis of Western Thebes

It is important to note that the entire Luxor west bank constitutes one vast necropolis. Although emphasis tends to be placed on the royal tombs in the Valley of the Kings, the Valley of the Queens, and the decorated Eighteenth and Nineteenth Dynasty foothills tombs, the larger west bank area contains burials of most periods of Egyptian dynastic history. The northern Qurna area of al-Tarif contained Fourth Dynasty (2575–2467 BC) Old Kingdom burials,[10] but was itself superimposed on predynastic strata (Ginter et al., 1979), including a burial ground.[11] The same area was used during the First Intermediate Period Eleventh Dynasty and included the royal burials of Intef I, II, and III (2134–2061 BC) (Arnold, 1976; Dorner, 1976; Manniche, 1987: 17).

Royal burials commenced in the foothills at Dayr al-Bahari just west of al-'Asasif during the later Middle Kingdom period of that same dynasty, under the Mentuhoteps (2061–1991 BC). The foothills area, too, had previously been used for burials, with Sixth Dynasty tombs located in al-Khukha. The Valley of the Kings became the favored location for the royal tombs during the Eighteenth Dynasty, under Thutmose I (1504–1492 BC) (Reeves, 1990a: 13, 17–18; Reeves and Wilkinson, 1996: 15). Although secondary and commoner interments occurred frequently, especially during the late period (Kákosy, 1995; Vandorpe, 1995; Van Landuyt, 1995; Vleeming, 1995), the proximity of the Eighteenth and Nineteenth Dynasty royal tombs in the Valley of the Kings is a crucial factor in the placement of non-royal decorated private tombs and the expansion of the foothills Noble Tombs areas.

During Old Kingdom times, apart from the royal tomb itself, pyramid funerary complexes included the memorial temple and allocated areas for the burial of high-ranking government officials. For topographical reasons, the New Kingdom burial complexes in the Valley of the Kings did not allow for the inclusion of memorial temples. Instead, these were constructed in the plains below the foothills. Because the Valley of the

Kings itself was limited to royals and members of their immediate family only (Reeves, 1990a: 271), government officials built their tombs in the foothills, often in some direct spatial relationship with the memorial temple of their ruling monarch. Concentrations of tombs pertaining to a particular ruler or period thus became characteristic for specific foothills localities. Exceptions to this general rule included instances where the quality of the rock or crowding in the area of choice necessitated alternative locations (Habachi and Anus, 1977: 1–7; Habachi's analysis is based on the inventory of Theban tombs in Porter and Moss, 1927). In this sense, the Theban Necropolis nevertheless came to resemble an Old Kingdom burial assemblage, with royal tombs, memorial temples, and the private tombs of priests and high-ranking officials located in a delimited area that had the natural pyramid of the Qurn as its visibly most dominant feature.

The lure of hidden wealth: Past

The concentration of so many royal and private tombs in a relatively small area, and the veritable industry associated with their construction and maintenance, meant that knowledge of hidden wealth and the location of specific items within entombed funerary assemblages were not only difficult to keep secret, but probably circulated widely within the community of tomb builders. Court proceedings of caught tomb robbers contained in Nineteenth Dynasty legal papyri, and an analysis of the several ancient intrusions into the tomb of Tutankhamun, indeed suggest that the location of desired valuable artifacts was known to the intruders (Reeves and Wilkinson, 1996: 190). Consequently, during the Nineteenth Dynasty, the village community of tomb builders at Dayr al-Madina, situated behind the hill of Qurnat Mar'ai (Appendix 2, Plate 5b), was reorganized in an attempt to prevent thefts from the royal tombs. Even then, incidents of pilfering continued to occur at the hands of necropolis personnel, in at least one instance assisted by high-ranking officials (Reeves and Wilkinson, 1996: 193). Following Bedouin raids during the Twenty-first Dynasty, the community was moved to the safety of the nearby Madinat Habu temple complex, its history there too "characterized by reports of many years of thieving in the tombs where their forefathers had been working" (Borghouts, 1994: 119–20).

Reeves characterizes tomb robbing as Egypt's "second-oldest profession," dating back to predynastic times (Reeves and Wilkinson, 1996:

190). He distinguishes four distinct categories: rare incidents of systematic and large-scale activity during times of weak central and local administration; the common occurrence of petty pilfering by tomb builders and/or members of the funeral party shortly after interment; the common occurrence of accidentally discovered old tombs during new tomb construction work; and the state-sanctioned dismantling of the royal tombs during the Twenty-first Dynasty for the purpose of safeguarding the royal mummies and to extract the buried funereal wealth for objectives of economic or political expediency (Reeves, 1990a: 271–78). A fifth category may be found in episodes of outright poverty, with additional and life-sustaining income derived from illegal tomb entry necessitated by periods of economic hardship, as suggested by Borghouts (1994: 120).

The lure of hidden wealth: Ahmad and Muhammad 'Abd al-Rasul

The above discussion has relevance for a consideration of Qurnawi economic practice, since the link between past episodes of tomb robbing and those that have taken place more recently is frequently made. James Henry Breasted, one of the founding fathers of American Egyptology, alluding to one of the 'tomb-robbery papyri' mentioned above, referred to Qurnawi as "the descendants of those same tomb-robbers whose prosecution under Ramesses IX we can still read" (Breasted, 1916: 525). Howard Carter observed: "It was in the thirteenth century BC that the inhabitants of this village first adopted the trade of tomb-robbing, and it is a trade that they have adhered to steadfastly ever since" (Carter, 1923: 70). Similar sentiments shine through more recent travelogues: "[Qurnawi] have lived off the dead for millennia, first as tomb robbers and then as tomb guardians" (Stewart, 1997: 89); and: "For over three thousand years the Qurnawis have made their living . . . among the ancient burial grounds. . . . the Qurnawis have been in business as long as the source of their supply has existed" (Roberts, 1993: 93, 94).

This stereotypical understanding of Qurnawi economics obtained its essential definition from what has become the archetypal episode of Qurnawi tomb-robbing activity. Probably around the year 1871, the brothers Ahmad and Muhammad 'Abd al-Rasul discovered what Egyptologists now know as cache DB320 in the cliffs above the temple of Queen Hatshepsut at Dayr al-Bahari. They visited the tomb over a ten-year period on a number of occasions, selling smaller items from

Nag' al-Rasayla, the hamlet of the 'Abd al-Rasuls in the central foothills of al-Hurubat. The house with the arched doorway and windows to the left of the white house in the center belongs to Ahmad and Muhammad 'Abd al-Rasul (also see Romer, 1981: 132).

the Twenty-first Dynasty burial assemblage of members of the Pinudjem royal family to Mustafa Aga Ayat, vice-consular agent for Britain, Belgium, and Russia, whose black-market antiquities dealings were protected by diplomatic immunity.

Then a rarity, the acquisition by European collectors of Twenty-first Dynasty funerary equipment raised the suspicion of Gaston Maspero, director of the French School of Archaeology in Cairo and later the director of the Service des antiquités. Following an undercover operation by Charles Wilbour, a student of Maspero, the source of the antiquities was revealed, with the tomb found not just to contain the anticipated Twenty-first Dynasty funerary equipment, but also some forty other royal mummies that had been moved there when the Valley of the Kings was dismantled as a royal burial place during the Twenty-first Dynasty. Significantly, the tomb's occupants were found to include such prominent rulers as Thutmose III, Seti I, Ramesses II, and Ramesses III. These 'restorations,' as Egyptologists call them, have been understood as a measure to safeguard the royal dead from further sacrilege at the hands of tomb robbers, although Reeves has argued that the real reason may have been to retrieve their buried funerary wealth for state purposes (Reeves, 1990a: 277–78). The process was carried out over a period of time and involved several other caches and differing routes for each mummy (Reeves, 1990a: 244–57). Once there, the cliff tomb became their final repository, until the 'Abd al-Rasul brothers found them some three thousand years later.

The discovery was celebrated at the time, and the history leading up to its discovery and its aftermath enshrined in the annals of Egyptology, without reference to which no treatise on the subject is complete. First recounted by Maspero himself (1881 [Reprinted in Ceram, 1966: 149–153]; 1889), the episode continues to be a focus of scholarly analysis (Graefe, 2004; Reeves, 1990a: 183–99); popular syntheses of specific Egyptological topics (Romer, 1981: 129–38; Wilson, 1964: 81–85); travelogues (Roberts, 1993: 92–101, in large part based on Wilson); films (Abd al-Salam and Rossellini, 1969; Schaffner, 1980); and fictional representations (Cook, 1979).

If a Qurnawi reputation of tomb robbers can in part be traced back to the 'Abd al-Rasuls, the question can rightfully be asked to what extent their actions have been detrimental both to the archaeological record and the surviving artifacts of DB320. There are some observations that need to be made to place the entire episode in context. It being the nature of the black market, evidently the pieces purchased by collectors have been preserved for posterity. In terms of archaeological value, their provenance is known, which is better than can be claimed for most items that have entered collections as a result of illicit excavations. Although a certain amount of damage was inflicted by the brothers on some of the royal mummies in their search for jewelry, the extent of the damage remains a topic for scholarly discussion. Reeves argues that there is "no certainty that all the damage apparent" is due to their actions, and that some of it will date to antiquity (Reeves, 1990a: 186). The jumbled state of the tomb's contents, in part due to the activities of the modern intruders, furthermore, only affected the smaller items rather than the heavy mummy coffins, and it would thus "appear unlikely that any radical alteration could have been effected in the basic sequence" (Reeves, 1990a: 186).[12] The recent reclearance of the tomb has confirmed that such was indeed the case (Graefe, 2004). John Romer has put these archaeological observations in rather more social terms: "the objects and the mummies that they had left behind were not smashed in the normal manner of tomb robbers. . . . the brothers handled their discovery in a calm, collected way" (Romer, 1981: 139–41).

Of course, their discovery of the tomb did involve the disturbance of an intact Twenty-first Dynasty royal burial, and the removal and repositioning of funerary equipment will have involved the loss of archaeological data necessary for an understanding of an undisturbed and complete royal burial of that period. It appears, though, that the greatest damage to the integrity of the assemblage and the knowledge that still lay embedded in it was inflicted at the hands of the archaeologists charged with the clearance of the tomb. Their manner was everything but "in a calm, collected way." In the absence of Maspero, the responsibility fell predominantly to Émile Brugsch, his German assistant who, for fear of further pilfering, undertook to clear the tomb within two days. No photographs were taken, no plans were drawn up, and there is only speculation of an official report, its existence inferred from a "critical analysis of Maspero's writings on the subject" (Reeves, 1990a: 184).

This is not to say that the brothers Ahmad and Muhammad 'Abd al-Rasul are to be absolved. Despite the fact that Muhammad was offered a reward of £500 for showing Brugsch the location of the tomb, and was given the position of foreman for the Theban excavations conducted by the Antiquities Service (Romer, 1981: 141), in November 1901 both brothers were again implicated in the rifling of a royal mummy in the Valley of the Kings, that of Amenophis II, discovered only in 1898. It may have been naïve to think that their illicit activities would stop upon receipt of a reward payment. Evidently, that money had long since been distributed among the extended family (Romer, 1981: 141), and in the scheme of things was in any case not very different from income received from the sale of antiquities. If there was any prestige attached to it, then it was also money received in exchange for a tomb and was thus payment for antiquities-related work, rather than an incentive to discontinue the sort of work that had earned the money in the first place. Howard Carter, who was then chief inspector for Upper Egypt, subsequently established their culpability by using a tracker who followed the trail to Ahmad's house, while Carter himself matched photographs of Muhammad's footprints taken in the royal tomb with those obtained elsewhere. Despite all this, Carter could still comment in his official report that even though the bandages of the royal mummy had been ripped open, the body had not been broken and only those places were searched where usually jewelry was hidden, the work having "evidently been done by an expert" (Carter, 1902: 117).

Antiquities as a means of economic resilience during times of hardship

There is some merit in placing the activities of the 'Abd al-Rasuls in the framework of tomb robberies identified by Reeves (1990a: 277–78) and Borghouts (1994: 120), mentioned above, as some of these defining motivations can also be found in the 1881 scenario. "Common pilfering" (Reeves' second category) may be linked with his notion of "systematic" (Reeves' first category) in that Qurnawi in-depth knowledge of the landscape surrounding them will have alerted them to the possibility of hidden tombs in the crags and chimneys of the escarpment. If the search for hidden antiquities was not always systematic (some of the Robert Hay panoramas suggest that it was during the 1820s), and the discovery of antiquities was probably often fortuitous, there is a *systemic* quality in the way local landscape knowledge constitutes the 'cultural capital' that informs, at least in part, the identity and worldview of Qurnawi. This worldview predisposes them to, and is used by them to good effect in, their dealings with foreigners interested in antiquities.[13] This point is entirely overlooked by Wilson (1964: 81) and in his wake, Roberts (1993: 95), who seem to accept as credible a discovery narrative based on the 'lost goat' motif. Not only is tending goats the work of women and children rather than adult males, the detail is also too reminiscent of the discovery in 1947 of the Dead Sea Scrolls at Khirbet Qumran in Palestine for it to be credible.

The second part of Reeves' first category, "large-scale activity during times of weak central and local administration," may be linked with Borghouts' identification of poverty and economic hardship that plagued the ancient community of Dayr al-Madina during its latter years. Such motivations of human survival cannot be considered in isolation. Representing an important adaptive strategy of resilience during episodes of economic hardship, times of decline may form an important context for nineteenth- and twentieth-century damage inflicted upon the tombs in the necropolis. For Romer, they form a part of the 'Abd al-Rasul story, and he rightly links the bankrupt state of the Egyptian economy in the years just prior to British intervention in 1888, and the burden of the taxation regime that was causing starvation among the fellahin of Upper Egypt, with the local interest in antiquities:

For the villagers of Thebes, the tomb represented an extraordinary source of wealth during this terrible period, for in the strong extended family units in Egyptian village life the money from the sale of the illicit antiquities ensured that the entire family, about a fifth of the village, would never, like so many of their contemporaries, suffer or starve for lack of money. (Romer, 1981: 132)

It was for this reason, Romer argues, that Brugsch acted as hastily as he did, possibly fearing repercussions from the villagers who saw themselves being deprived by foreigners of the one source of economic stability they knew: "it was a microcosm of the Egyptian situation at that time and in the end, sadly, archaeology suffered and a part of ancient history was lost to us all" (Romer, 1981: 138).

The Theban Necropolis during times of decline

Episodes of social and political instability resulting in economic hardship as postulated by Reeves and Borghouts, and their correlation with encroachment on and damage inflicted upon ancient monuments, appears valid for the necropolis. In turn these events, commencing with the 1881 incident, are feeding continuing allegations of tomb robbing and persistent characterizations of Qurnawi as tomb robbers. These allegations and characterizations largely ignore and thereby mystify the socioeconomic and political conditions that drive such episodes.

The period of the First World War, when few antiquities inspectors or excavators were available to maintain supervision, was characterized by encroachments, although actual damage appears to have been limited.[14] In due course the onset of the Second World War would again dry up regular forms of income provided by visiting tourists and foreign archaeological missions. It was at the conclusion of that war, when assessments of damage inflicted upon the monuments were made (Fakhry, 1947a), that wholesale relocation was first contemplated as a means to deal with the necropolis' villagers (Fakhry, 1947b). The justification of those initiatives is again linked with the absence of watchful archaeologists during the war years (Manniche, 1987: 126), but it can only be part of the story. Probably closer to reality is that the entire two decades leading up to the end of the Second World War were exceedingly difficult and destabilizing periods, both in the history of the necropolis and in the lives of its villagers.

The widespread impact that Egypt felt as a result of the Great Depression will also have had its repercussions in Upper Egypt. Designed to supply raw material for the English textile industry, Egypt under British rule had converted its agricultural production into one which was largely monocultural in orientation—that is, cotton—a structural change that left the Egyptian economy vulnerable to international economic fluctuations. The collapse of the international financial market in 1929 impacted heavily on the international demand for cotton, with decimated prices for cotton triggering a downward spiral in the price of all other agricultural products (Vatikiotis, 1969: 283–84). As a result, between 1929 and 1933 the national average rural wage fell to pre–First World War levels, inflicting severe economic hardship on Egypt's large fellahin population (al-Sayyid-Marsot, 1985: 86–87). It must be assumed that reduced income levels will also have affected the foothills communities, with the economic realities of the day necessarily, and negatively, impacting on the surrounding decorated tombs. Recent damage to wall paintings in the necropolis, therefore, must not only be associated with a lack of archaeological supervision during the war, but indeed, and probably more so, be linked to the collapse of the international financial system.

The impact of the worldwide recession on the international art market would require further in-depth analysis to assess if a wholesale collapse of the demand for antiquities did in fact occur. At first glance, the evidence is that it did not. Preceding the Wall Street crash, Howard Carter, who—himself a connoisseur and intimately familiar with the dealer shops of Luxor and Cairo (James, 1992: 74, 97, 197)—at various stages in his life dealt in Egyptian antiquities, during July 1929 had entered into an agreement with the Detroit Institute of Arts to act as their agent in the acquisition of Egyptian antiquities. His first purchases were concluded in Cairo during the spring of 1930 (James, 1992: 372–73). The arrangement was terminated shortly after, "because of the state of the Detroit city finances" (James, 1992: 373). Although not specified by Carter's biographer, it seems likely that the cause may ultimately have been linked with the general financial crisis at the time. Other instances document Carter's activities of this type (James, 1992: 388, 390–91; Reeves and Taylor, 1992: 175), with an occasional sale indeed concluded, even if at "a price reflecting the financial problems of the time" (James, 1992: 391).

Such a snapshot of the years during which Egypt was experiencing the worst effects of the depression suggests that an international art market nevertheless existed, even if artifacts were traded at reduced prices and despite the possibly diminished chances of concluding a sale. Carter's activities were legitimate to the extent that his acquisitions came from (then) legal antiquities shops, and concerned pieces that could not be provenanced.[15] Yet the very existence of such shops and the clientele they represented would have offered an obvious incentive for local operators to maintain the supply of art works they knew the market demanded, in the process providing households with ready access to increased expendable income, even if such an increase is now impossible to quantify.

Egypt's economic position did not necessarily improve when from 1934 onward the effects of the international recession gradually dissipated. The effects of the British monocultural agriculture policy, and a declining land-population ratio under the influence of rapid population growth, resulted in diminishing standards of living (Vatikiotis, 1969: 310). Consequent food shortages and rising prices for food and clothing, declining per capita income, and deteriorating health standards during the 1940s (Vatikiotis, 1969: 323) will have created further pressures for breadwinners to access alternative forms of income. Under the circumstances, it could hardly be expected that Egypt's monuments would escape unscathed.

"A state of shock . . ."

The extent of the damage is difficult to assess. It is likely to be considerable, and in any case must be a contributing factor to current assessments made of the necropolis generally:

> Large parts of the Theban pictorial material have been lost since their rediscovery in the 19th Century, and all observers agree that the rapid decay of the necropolis advances. The Tomb of Sobekhotep offers a sad illustration of both the truth of this claim and the urgent need for documentary work in Thebes. (Dziobek and Abdel Raziq, 1990: 16)

The recent study by Dziobek and Abdel Raziq (1990) of tomb TT63,[16] from which the above assessment comes, revealed considerable damage when comparing its present condition with photographic records dating back to the 1930s, leaving Dziobek reportedly "in something of a state of shock . . . after discovering these photographs" (Strudwick, 1995: 264). To be sure, Dziobek's enumeration of defaced decorated wall panels reads like a litany of loss (Dziobek, 1990: 74–80). The photographs in question were made by Harry Burton, photographer for the Metropolitan Museum of Art in New York's Egyptian Expedition. Burton not only documented the discovery and clearance of Tutankhamun's tomb, but in addition left some 3,200 negatives of the Theban tombs (Bierbrier, 1995: 75–76). Their systematic comparison with present conditions should indicate the extent to which the times of decline from 1929 onward can be seen to have contributed to the deterioration of the monuments, even if some damage may well be of more recent dates, as suggested by Strudwick (1995).

Although the loss of history and works of art is deplorable, and the irreparable damage inflicted on the monuments is tragic indeed, it is essential that we also pay heed to the twentieth-century realities. Specifically, communities at a local level have become increasingly affected by global political and economic developments in such a way that these developments, seemingly removed from immediate local concerns—and indeed the concerns of specific interest spheres such as Egyptology—will nevertheless, ultimately, make themselves felt in some way or another. The social formations that find themselves embedded in a matrix of these external factors, compounded by demographic changes and the legacies of an earlier colonial era, will be constrained by them as much as they are their product. Such is the case at al-Qurna. It is simplistic in the extreme to discount—as evidenced by the dominant discourse—the sociopolitical and economic realities that have fostered particular cultural practices and that have forced the foothills communities into a particular relationship with the surrounding landscape, and by implication with the 'surrounding' Egyptological community. To content oneself with a characterization of tomb robbing may have represented acceptable social analysis at a time when imperialist motivations still inspired a certain worldview among western academics working in Egypt; today it will no longer suffice. The contrasting account that should take its place emphasizes the impact of external national, international, and market relations, the outworkings of colonialist-motivated changes to agricultural production, and local demographic conditions, in explanation of particular indigenous economic strategies.

The 'Abd al-Rasul legacy: Indigenous and foreign fieldwork practice as motivating factors in early-twentieth-century heritage protection

When practical measures of protection were first instituted they sought to deal with the negative impact of domestic usage on the tombs. Those measures also sought to curtail further encroachment across the necropolis, and to prevent damage caused by the illicit excavation and the extraction of antiquities. Howard Carter, an energetic, practical, and meticulous field archaeologist, had been appointed in 1899 as chief inspector of antiquities for Upper Egypt (James, 1992: 65–96). Although the terms of reference for the new position were vague (James, 1992: 71; Maspero, 1912: 10), Carter's first assignment was to report on the state of preservation of the Theban Necropolis with a view to instituting new measures of protection (James, 1992: 71), which under his direction at first came in the form of wooden doors (Maspero, 1912: 58) and later in the form of iron gates (Maspero, 1912: 120).

Although the output of Carter's initiative is now recognized as having been rather limited (only eight tombs had been protected in this manner during his watch as chief inspector of antiquities for Upper Egypt—see Hankey, 2001: 76, 134), it is significant that Carter's first Theban measures of protection were of an entirely practical type and distinct from viceregal instructions that were typically issued to local governors during the mid-nineteenth century. Carter's protective measures set a course that was to lead to the later expropriations and eventual relocations, and must therefore be understood as the introduction of ongoing heritage management practices that were to typify Qurnawi spatial relations for the remainder of the twentieth century.

The perceived need for that work to be done at that time requires elaboration to explain the intensity and emphasis with which that task was invested during the first two decades of the twentieth century. The explanation on the one hand lies in the natural progression of Egyptological work being undertaken at that point in time of the discipline's history. Following the frenzied collecting activities of a not-too-distant past, and following the first legal frameworks and institutional mechanisms regulating antiquities and heritage issues, the time was simply ripe for practical, on-the-ground measures. The availability of certain funding sources as exemplified in the person of Robert Mond and others (Hankey, 2001: 78) certainly played a major factor, as did the 'accidents of history'

represented in the presence of such particularly competent field archaeologists as Howard Carter and Percy Newberry and—importantly—Arthur
Weigall, who in 1905 took up the post of chief inspector of antiquities
for Upper Egypt and who vigorously continued the work of protection
commenced by his predecessor.[17]

There is another reason, however, and it is that, through the accumu-
lative action of Egyptological engagement with the Theban Necropolis,
a body of knowledge surrounding the local Qurnawi population had gathered, which in the minds of western academics made the protective method
in archaeological fieldwork practice both inevitable and paramount. By
then, the encounter with European ..avelers and collectors had crystallized knowledge of the economic activity generated by that encounter
into an imposed, unquestioned, and assumed identity of Qurnawi society. The ʿAbd al-Rasul incident and its subsequent legacy—acquiring for
itself archetypal proportions—will have reinforced those assumptions. For
many, they would have found confirmation in the less dramatic but often
more damaging episodes which were nevertheless numerous. References
to them in the Egyptological literature constitute what one scholar has
called "heartbreaking reading" (Manniche, 1987: 127).

It is understandable, in this context, that published sources of the time
came to represent a pinnacle of anti-Qurnawi sentiment, giving release
to a hundred years of vexation with the observed reality of local practices
so contrary to expected western academic standards. Yet, Egyptology's
historical role in the evolution of damaging local practices that were at
least in part responsible, and the imposition of its own academic standards at the expense of all other cultural considerations, formed no part
of the analysis but are subsumed in the unquestioned superiority of the
western approach. Indeed, the tone of Egyptological writing during the
early twentieth century betrays the worldview of those for whom the British imperialist ideal in those days was both self-evident and considered
beneficial, their derogatory assessments of Qurnawi[18] contributing to the
subsequent distorted appraisals of local villagers' economic practice.[19]

Keeping the past, changing the future: Expropriations

Carter's operations of conservation and protection at Shaykh ʿAbd al-
Qurna did not involve the expropriation of occupied tombs, but his
work of protecting decorated tombs was continued by his successor,
Arthur Weigall, from late 1905 onward. Significantly, during his term,

conservation practice also came to include expropriations, with families evicted from decorated tombs used as domestic dwellings or for stabling animals. During 1909 alone, eleven tombs were expropriated, "cleaned, repaired, closed with iron gates or wooden doors, all at the expense of Mr. Robert Mond, whose generosity has not failed one single moment for four years" (Maspero, 1912: 289). In the absence of applicable laws until 1912,[20] the operation appears to have involved case-by-case negotiation, the financial terms settled from the personal wealth of Robert Mond.[21] Expropriation in exchange for money ceased with the appointment of Reginald Engelbach as chief inspector for Upper Egypt between 1920 and 1924 (Bierbrier, 1995: 142). Implementing Antiquities Law No. 14 of 1912, on one occasion four tombs were "being expropriated immediately" (Engelbach, 1924: 8–9). That no amenable financial arrangement was in place this time is implicit in Engelbach's reference to the earlier practice of, most obviously, the Robert Mond operations: "The excavators, during the past, have been more than generous, sometimes protecting the tombs they have rescued at their own expense, often buying out the natives and presenting the tombs to the Government" (Engelbach, 1924: 10).

With this interpretation and application of the 1912 Antiquities Law, the Antiquities Service was effectively claiming ownership of the Theban Necropolis, and identifying contemporary occupants as squatters. By consequence, Engelbach's concern was largely with the encroachments inherent in clandestine occupation resulting from the First World War (Engelbach, 1924: 6).

Engelbach's understanding of the reasons for these encroachments remains shallow. The wartime years represent too confined a period for natural population increase to have played a significant role, and it seems rather more likely that people took to formalizing their permanent occupancy, in the form of visible architectural arrangements, predominantly in response to the very expropriations that had started in the years prior to the outbreak of war. Expecting that evictions from the tombs might continue upon the return of Antiquities Service personnel and archaeological missions after the war, it seems plausible that an increase of aboveground structures and demarcated areas was to offset any anticipated losses in subsurface domestic space, a sociopolitical factor lost on, or at least not articulated by, Engelbach. This seems likely, since Qurnawi families themselves will not necessarily have been in a position to assess correctly whether their particular tomb dwelling was of sufficient merit to either warrant or escape expropriation: "the others, with about half a dozen exceptions, contain so few inscriptions or scenes that their acquisition by the Antiquities Department may be deferred indefinitely" (Engelbach, 1924: 6).

It would appear that Qurnawi families were not informed of this flexibility and it must be assumed also that people inhabiting such exempted tombs will have thought it prudent to proceed staking surface claims, just in case. In either event, Engelbach chose to ignore the fact that most people would already have lived in the necropolis and that the encroachments primarily were not the result of new people moving in, but of long-time residents 'moving out' under the impact—real or anticipated—of Antiquities Service–instigated expropriations.

Mond's legacy: Vernacular architectural expansion among the tombs

Alan Gardiner's allusion to Sir Robert Mond and other benefactors who "contributed generously to the heavy expense" involved in the "expropriation, restoration and protection of inhabited tombs" (Gardiner and Weigall, 1913: 8), and his reference to Mahmud Effendi Rushdy, Weigall's Egyptian inspector, "whose services have proved particularly valuable in conducting the delicate negotiations for the purchase of tombs used as dwelling places" (Gardiner and Weigall, 1913), is suggestive of an aspect of the history of the foothills hamlets that still requires appropriate historical investigation. This will be essential to fully understand the driving mechanism behind the transition from subterranean dwelling spaces to above-surface vernacular architecture, and the subsequent expansion across the foothills that it generated. Beyond what has been documented about the involvement of Mahmud Effendi Rushdy (Hankey, 2001:133), the archives of the Supreme Council of Antiquities in Cairo and the relevant personal papers of Sir Robert Mond and other benefactors may reveal the detail of the transactions involved in this purchasing strategy, the finer aspects of their "delicate negotiations," and the existence or otherwise of any attached conditions with regard to the further limiting of residential use of the necropolis by individuals and families so expropriated.

As has been suggested, the encroachments observed by Engelbach were, for the most part, not the result of new residents moving into the necropolis, but of longtime occupants vacating their tomb dwellings either as a direct result of expropriation, or in the expectation of its likely occurrence. It is in this process where the link between heritage management initiatives and ongoing architectural and socio-demographic change is at its most obvious, and where relevant antiquities legislation and practical conservation measures meet with and impact on the local population.

As the most pragmatic of methods, the purchasing of tombs for the purpose of effecting heritage protection will have had a number of associated issues and repercussions that are relevant to a consideration of the foothills' architectural development. On the evidence of it, it would seem that expropriation in exchange for money did not involve any attached conditions that aimed at limiting the further occupation of the foothills. Families are thus likely to have accepted the payment in exchange for vacating their tomb dwellings, only to use those funds to erect a dwelling in close proximity to their former home. In this way, expropriation did not require departure from the necropolis, and leaving the tombs simply meant establishing an above-ground dwelling nearby. The emergence of above-surface accommodation was not new, but will have added significantly to those dwellings already extant and which found their inspiration in the existing nineteenth-century European houses.

In the absence of information to the contrary, it must be argued that the concept of expropriation as a heritage management tool was in many respects ill-considered, with the voluntary and charitable initiative of such philanthropic excavators as Robert Mond initially gratefully accepted by antiquities officials, before being instituted by them as a form of enforced heritage management policy. The evident archaeological and conservation benefits will have been primary motivations, and any local social i ications were either not recognized or ignored. Unanticipated by antiquities officials and hence described by them as encroachments, the very process of expropriation thus laid the foundation for the urban developments that eventually resulted in the contemporary foothills hamlets.

Antiquities officials will similarly have been unprepared for additional unintended consequences. Possibly due to a lack of communication about which tombs were to be expropriated, the increasingly urbanized character of the necropolis will at once have also encouraged the occupants of tombs that were not expropriated to extend their living quarters in a similar fashion. Furthermore, a sudden increase in building activity will have signaled to the surrounding areas that the Luxor west bank foothills

The central area of the Theban foothills, with the hill of Shaykh 'Abd al-Qurna (showing the tomb of Daga/the Late Antique Coptic Monastery of Epiphanius) on the right, and the houses of al-Hurubat at its foot. The shrine of Shaykh 'Abd al-Qurna is on top of the hill at the far right. The houses to the left are those at al-Khukha. The Ramesseum and the Memnon Colossi are visible in the center.

were evidently open for development, with the resulting likelihood of true encroachment.

Oral-historical research will have to further establish the extent of any associated influx. That it took place can hardly be doubted, and could in 1999 still be seen reflected in the presence in al-Hurubat of at least three families who have their origins in towns and villages at considerable distance from Luxor. Their particular arrival postdates the early-twentieth-century evictions and is linked with the completion of the Aswan High Dam during the 1960s, when those who had contributed to its construction were entitled to settle anywhere they liked in Egypt. A number of those who recognized the tourism-associated income potential of Luxor established themselves on the Theban west bank. Although their neighbors still recognize them as newcomers, which may at times involve some discriminatory conduct,[22] the fact that people were nevertheless allowed to settle in their midst is reminiscent of a settlement history that included non-locals.

Before we turn to the modern environment of the necropolis that emerged from these historical developments, one further consideration needs to be made. That is, a final consequence of the expropriations will have been the sudden need for building materials to construct above-ground dwellings. Engelbach reports, almost with a sense of indignation, the use of permanent and therefore undesirable "red brick" (Engelbach, 1924: 9), possibly suggesting that there were no prior instructions regarding the sort of building materials considered appropriate to replace the tomb dwellings, and thereby indicating that no planning was considered to mitigate both the infrastructural and the social consequences involved. Early architectural forms of that period included small pieces of limestone, many of which can be found lying around the foothills and which primarily will have been the debris resulting from tomb construction during ancient times. Other pieces were decorated and obtained from collapsed or damaged tombs, a practice about which Auguste Mariette had already expressed concern as early as 1862: "The inhabitants of Gournah, Luxor and Karnak continually search for antiquities and build walls etc. with stones from the ancient monuments" (Marriette, quoted in Khater, 1960: 66).

It is likely not only that this practice will have continued, but also that the need for raw material to build mud-brick houses may have been resolved in the way that the eighth-century Coptic monks did when constructing their cells and monasteries, by using or recycling ready-made brick from ancient mud-brick monuments still present in the foothills and the plains of the 'Asasif. Following in their footsteps, the practice was almost certainly adopted by Yanni when building the house for Henry Salt, and definitely used by John Gardner Wilkinson when building his tomb house at Shaykh 'Abd al-Qurna (Thompson, 1992: 103; 1996: 56). Varying with the antiquities inspection regime of the day, the 'Asasif structures and the nearby remains of the Thutmose III memorial temple may have similarly provided mud bricks during the early twentieth century. There is as yet no clear evidence that this occurred, but the possibility must be raised as one of the unforeseen and unintended consequences of expropriation.

6

Qurnawi Foothills Architecture: Footprint, Form, and Function

The urbanizing process initiated by the protective measures of expropriation and eviction discussed in the previous chapter not only accelerated the expansion of contemporary vernacular forms, but also resulted in a particular architectural assemblage typical of the Theban Necropolis. The evolving domestic floor plan eventually came to comprise a footprint which still included the ancient funerary spaces, the new above-ground architectural forms, and the traditional mud structures characteristic of Upper Egypt. As a rule, the following individual components can be recognized: the main dwelling proper, but often still abutting an ancient funerary space, which no longer supported any artwork in need of protection and upon which no prohibitions limiting domestic use were evidently placed (and suggestive of confusion about which tombs were to be expropriated); the tomb forecourt, serving as exterior living space; the *hush*, the enclosure for the family donkey, where often also the *furn*, the domed oven, was located; and the array of thin, mud-walled storage bins, now rarely used and any remnant specimen increasingly under threat of destruction. In the following, each of these component elements will be reviewed more closely.

The house

Upon expropriation, the location of the new house could never be entirely divorced from the essential funerary character of its surroundings, and tombs will always have been present in the immediate vicinity of the house. This could mean in practice that the house was built directly above the tomb, or alongside it. In either case, funerary architecture could still

Village in the Desert
UPPER EGYPT

Period postcard roughly contemporaneous with the years of expropriation. Although the tomb door (behind the donkey's head) is closed with the sort of domestic lock typically built by the village carpenter (also see Henein, 1988: 45), thereby suggesting that the tomb is still in use and not closed off by antiquities officials, the spatial arrangement of walled structures, enclosed thatched rooms, and mud storage bins was essentially similar to the increasingly common domestic architectural assemblages of the early half of the twentieth century (Binder, 1914). From the author's private collection.

be incorporated into the floor plan of the house, often through the use of any adjoining tomb courtyard or through access to undecorated rooms of nearby tombs.

Early construction methods involved the cementing of small lime-stone blocks and chips—*hajar jir*—into a mud matrix, as well as building up walled structures from loose mud with limited increases in height over a period of time. In the latter case, and in order to make wet mud 'stand,' thirty-centimeter–thick wall sections were raised to a height of about fifty centimeters, allowed to dry, and then raised a further section. These techniques predated the use of mud bricks and are consistent with the sort of wall constructions already in use during times when the tomb was still the principal dwelling place (for examples see the descriptions by Sonnini, 1800: 650; and Rhind, 1862: 290). These earli-est dwellings were simply enclosed spaces of sufficient height to be able

Small limestone blocks and chips—*hajar jir*—were cemented into a mud matrix to form early period walls.

to stand upright and furnished with beams to support a thatched roof of sorts, called *bus* and consisting of a cover of Nile reeds or cereal stems (Binder, 1914).

Apart from construction method, and their more modest size, the form of these earliest houses differs significantly from the predominantly rectangular impression that the modern often two-storied façades—when in their prime, pastel-colored, and decorated with hajj paintings—evoke. Consensus among several middle-aged informants was that the grandfathers of the present (1999) adult generation still lived in the tombs, before moving out and building the first house from 'stones.' Their sons, fathers of those same informants, were credited with building the first mud-brick house, which was to be rebuilt and extended again by the present generation. Depending on the respective ages of the individuals concerned, the assumed span of each generation, and the particular point in their childhood at which their fathers acted in the way indicated, the grandfathers' actions would have taken place during the first two or at most three decades of the twentieth century. Therefore, we can infer an approximate time frame for phases of reconstruction and extension of individual dwellings. The particular point in time will again differ for each generation and depends on family composition and ages, but on the basis of the above we may postulate generational episodes of renewal to have taken place during the 1940s–1950s and the 1970s. The latter episode can be linked with the financial benefits associated with the increase in tourism numbers under president Anwar al-Sadat (Lippman, 1989: 89, 99). This episode of renewal occurred before the antiquities-related building prohibitions, imposed by al-Sadat's Presidential Decree No. 267 of 1981, took effect. The decree prohibited new construction and the extension of existing buildings in archaeological areas.

This history of tomb-based occupation, its subsequent expansion into the immediately adjoining areas, and its distinct phases of renewal have provided the foothills with its recognizable settlement pattern and the evident stability in its cartographic appearance. Close comparison of the modern village layout with the Survey of Egypt scale 1:10,000 map (Survey of Egypt, 1922) and with the scale 1:1,000 maps (Survey of Egypt, 1924) indicates that the general 'footprint' of the hamlets largely corresponds with that earlier record. This is not to say that the population has not increased or that no greater number of dwellings existed in 1999 than was the case in 1922. While a degree of fill-in construction has occurred, for the most part such will have taken place within the delineation already marked in 1922 as pertaining to a particular dwelling or family, thereby not greatly altering the previously mapped footprint of villagers' claimed domestic space. Mostly, however, the increase in living space will have been achieved by converting from single- to two-story households, often prompted by sons continuing to reside in the parental home upon marriage. Examples of such ongoing upward expansion were still in evidence during the early 1990s despite Presidential Decree No. 267 (Caselli and Rossi, 1992: 266–67). Additionally, the massive expansion of al-Tarif will have absorbed many in cases where the parental residence was too small to accommodate all married children.

The development of two-story dwellings inside the necropolis has had obvious implications for their internal layout. Internal spatial arrangements in contemporary Qurnawi homes differ considerably, with some families possessing as many as sixteen rooms. The term 'room'—*uda*—admittedly is a loose concept, and has been used to convey a variety of use spaces that include tomb chambers, internal and external spaces for animals, storage rooms for agricultural produce, and reception areas for visitors. However, for the most part, numbers toward the higher end of the scale reflect extended kin groups, with several brothers and their respective families inhabiting what is a compound of conjoined but distinct family spaces, rather than an individual dwelling.

Apart from this variation in number inherent in family composition and size, there is a basic configuration in the use allocation of different domestic spaces that applies to all Qurnawi homes. Other than the tomb chambers that may still be in use as domestic spaces, the following may be distinguished: *mandara*, entrance hall, or its alternative meaning, a downstairs sitting room; *zegiffa*, the reception room for visitors, which for reasons of privacy is often in close proximity to the main entrance. The *zegiffa* is often decked out with carpets and cushioned *deqa*, that is, wooden couches. When this space is located upstairs, the term *sala*—also used to denote a sitting room—may be used. The terms *mandara*, *sala*, and *zegiffa* may be used interchangeably. Similarly, the term *zawiya*, used for the extended kinship house, can also denote a family's visitors' room and be used interchangeably with *mandara*, *sala*, and *zegiffa*. Literally, the *udat gulus* denotes the sitting room, but is also used for a small *zawiya* with inside and outside access. Sleeping spaces tend to be flexible. While married couples will have their *udat num*, at least among poorer families, children and their grandparents may choose to sleep on any of the available *deqa*s or, during the summer heat, on a mat, a palm-frond couch, or a *deqa* placed outside.

Two methods of human-waste disposal are employed in the Theban foothills. Children and adult males will relieve themselves *fil gebel*, that is, 'in the mountain.' Toilets are used by women, older girls, and visitors. Three latrine systems are used, with waste deposited in a buried, perforated, and eventually corroding oil drum known as *bermil*; a red brick-lined excavated septic pit; or a *dowlat meia*, the more conventional WC, its outlet going down a tomb shaft.

Food preparation takes place indoors in a regular kitchen space by means of a contemporary kitchen range fueled by *butagaz*, that is, liquid petroleum gas, although poor families may still use the *babur*, a small kerosene burner. For the weekly supply of the rural *'aish-shamsi* bread, the clay oven, the *furn*, is used, generally located in the courtyard. Most recently, modern *butagaz*-fired ovens have started to replace the clay *furn*. *Beniya*, nesting spaces for pigeons, may be found in indoor storage rooms, involving mud structures that incorporate ceramic jars (*ballas* or *qadus*).

The tomb

Local terms for a tomb—*bab al-hajar*, stone door, and *bayt al-hajar*, stone house—are used largely interchangeably, although the latter may more accurately reflect the original and historical use made of them by Qurnawi. Despite the certain closure that the relocation initiatives commencing in 1945 represent, the earlier process of expropriation was at no stage complete. Indeed, tombs have continued to be an integral part of the foothills' domestic space and for the most part where any decorations are either altogether absent, too damaged to warrant protection, or are already bricked up and out of reach. Even so, in the instances observed, such use does occur in tandem with a nearby mud-brick house as well, and may be restricted to the hot summer months. In at least one Hurubati case, the adjoining house was built by the occupant, indicating that the tomb was still fully occupied until quite recently. At the time the fieldwork for this book was undertaken, the occupant continued to use the tomb for sleeping purposes, the shaft leading to lower burial chambers located beneath his bed, a door post still supporting the remains of a heavily damaged carved standing figure, hieroglyphs visible on the lintel of a doorway, and the clip-clopping of a trotting donkey to be heard overhead.

Tomb chambers that form a part of the internal house plan may serve a variety of purposes, largely dictated by size, accessibility, and relative distance from the surface. If they are sufficiently spacious and cut deep enough into the rock they will be used as sleeping places during the heat of summer. Additionally, they can serve as storage spaces. In other instances, where the space is too small and too close to the surface for it to be sufficiently cool, these chambers, at times little more than a cave, will be used to house cattle, goats, and poultry, fodder, or the season's share of onions. Often, and where such tomb chambers are either not present or already used for animals or the storage of fodder, occupants may retire to a nearby suitable tomb that is available and not associated with any house to take an afternoon nap. In all such cases, only the men avail themselves of this opportunity: since they come from different households to a particular nearby tomb of their choice, it would be inappropriate for women to share that same sleeping space with them. In any event, sleeping in tombs at some distance away from the house was not practiced as frequently in 1999 as it was in earlier times—a development in large part due to the availability of electric fans and the occasional air-conditioning unit.

The tomb courtyard as *hush*: Multi-functionality as a strategy of resistance

The term *hush* is used to signify the courtyard of a rural Egyptian house, which in its most general sense comprises an open-air extension of the enclosed domestic space. In the Theban Necropolis, these modern courtyards incorporate the courtyard that was traditionally a part of the Eighteenth Dynasty tombs. Although this is not the place for a discussion of Theban funerary architecture, the variety of courtyards that are typically associated with the tombs in the foothills (Kampp, 1996, 1: 58–81) have traditionally also been a part of the assemblage of Qurnawi domestic architectural features. Situated in front of the inhabited tomb chapel

Fully occupied until quite recently, this *bayt al-hajar* continued to be used for sleeping and other domestic purposes during the summer of 1999. The sound of a passing donkey indicated that the outside world was not all that far away, raising serious concerns for any tombs subjected to the vibrations of bulldozers working overhead during the large-scale demolitions commencing in 2006.

proper, the observations by Rhind (1862: 297) and Richardson (1822, 2: 74) demonstrate how the courtyard provided the outdoor living area and thereby constituted the other half of a household's domestic space.

Today, where this ancient funerary space still exists and has not been encroached upon by the mud-brick house itself, these tomb courtyards continue to play an important part in communal relations, as do the vacant spaces between the scattered groups of adjoining houses. Used as thoroughfares by all and passing the family courtyards along the way, they provide the porous and permeable boundaries between public and private spaces, offering scope for physical as much as social contact.

Contrary to Stewart (1997: 90), who interprets the foothills' settlement pattern in the context of a search for antiquities conducted from within individual houses, and who fails to connect its urban plan with the original tomb-based occupational history of the community, the placement of the houses is in close association with the spaces that are left vacant. Largely due to the location of the tombs and the cluster of houses dictated by the group of tombs with which they are associated, it is this very dispersed nature of the settlement pattern, the open spaces it creates, and the open access to the tomb courtyards that has resulted in the uniquely public 'courtyard lifestyle' that typifies life in the foothills. Allowing life to be lived mainly outdoors, especially during the summer evenings when mud-brick interior spaces cool more slowly than the outside temperature, the practice invites a fluid movement of people into and out of the domestic space, both in manifestation of, and continually contributing to, the close social relations of the individual hamlets. As in the past, one of the older men telling stories becomes a focal point for arrivals from adjoining or nearby houses, in the same way as that practice now is increasingly superseded by a television set being placed on the mud *diwan* that lines the front wall of the house, providing a natural stage for the innumerable 'soap operas' produced for Egyptian television and attracting a veritable audience of neighbors and relations using a tomb courtyard for their theater.

Beyond this social function, the courtyard also serves a variety of practical and interrelated domestic purposes, signaled most visibly by the presence of the ubiquitous *'arabiya*, the donkey-powered water cart invariably parked in the courtyard and pointing to the presence of animals. The term *hush* indeed carries agricultural associations and is also used to indicate a low-lying, permanently dry field, surrounded by

Working the *furn*.

dykes and used for the cultivation of sugarcane (Fathy, 1973: 17). The meaning is also reflected in the occasional use of *ard*, soil, with which it may be used interchangeably. The domestic *hush* maintains associations with soil and agriculture by incorporating along one of its sides the *qasab* (sugarcane) straw-covered pen that stables the donkey and other large animals. This general area may also contain the latrine or water closet. For practical reasons, it is in close proximity to the animals where the *furn*, the traditional dome-shaped clay oven, is located. The *furn*'s firing process is in part dependent on *saffir*, that is, *qasab* trampled and mixed with animal dung. It is probably in part because of the location of the oven that Henein describes the courtyard as "the personal domain of the woman" (Henein, 1988: 13), although, as we have seen, that designation is too limiting in the Theban context.

In terms of its recent history, the *hush* has been of considerable strategic importance. As was noted above, the footprint of individual houses in 1999 differed little from the spaces allocated to individual families as recorded in the 1922 and 1924 Survey of Egypt maps. With large-scale structures in the early 1920s only rudimentarily present or still absent altogether, families projected sizable *hush* areas as a means of securing sufficient room for any future expansion. Negotiations with Engelbach and the Commission of Delimitation charged with "ascertaining the true limits of occupation" (Engelbach, 1924: 9) inside the necropolis during November 1921 often centered on the extent of this space, and Engelbach's account is instructive for the strategies employed by Qurnawi to secure the maximum area possible.[1]

The importance of mapping domestic boundaries was not lost on Qurnawi who attempted to secure for themselves their projected requirements for future family needs. Importantly, it also demonstrates a measure of premeditated resilience where such a strategy could be used to some effect in any future dealings with antiquities officials. Alongside their practical use, these one-time politically-motivated projections continued to have value during the late twentieth century. During the 1990s, families in the foothills strategically exchanged with Luxor City Council and antiquities officials part of their *hush* for a number of flats in one of the new communities. Sacrificing a part of their outdoor domestic space, the exchange returned some of the necropolis area to the Supreme Council of Antiquities, with Qurnawi acquiring property in one of the new communities without needing to vacate their adjoining house.

Creating space: Form and function of vernacular storage

It was during the 1970s renewal phase that many of the traditional storage features that had been typical of the foothills' vernacular architectural landscape for so long fell into disuse. During 1999, several informants remembered the last usage of mud storage structures in their respective homes as having taken place some thirty years ago, their function replaced by increasingly accessible consumer goods, a process that continues to this day and that most recently has seen families replacing their *furn* by a large stainless steel *butagaz* oven. Eigner (1984: 84) has associated the demise of especially the mud granaries with the agricultural shift from wheat to sugarcane production.

The larger mud bins and sleeping platforms were previously often located in the courtyard. Depending on the available space, they were also built in varying sizes inside the mud-brick homes and inside the tomb chambers. In the latter instance, this is where they may still be found, providing the last vestige of a lifestyle and an architectural adaptation that has now all but disappeared from the Theban Necropolis. Once Qurnawi families were forced to leave the foothills, antiquities officials reclaimed ownership of the tombs, but it cannot be expected that these structures will be preserved in evidence of the tombs' onetime domestic function.

Even in al-Tarif, surviving mud structures, although now largely dysfunctional but nevertheless meriting heritage status, are increasingly being removed from the domestic space, their disappearance, there too, adding to the loss of indigenous history and cultural diversity characteristic of the necropolis' vernacular and social landscape.

Variations in names and shapes as reflected in both Henein (1988: 49–53) and Winlock (Winlock and Crum, 1926: 51–53) suggest a certain fluidity of form and associated terminology, features inherent in their vernacular quality. At al-Qurna several names and types may be recognized. The square-topped *safat* is a granary, while the conically-roofed *suma'/ suwama'* is the storage vessel for flour. The *sanduq* is a rectangular mud cupboard closed with a small wooden door and latch, and often placed as a separate unit on top of a *safat*. The *sanduq* is the "wedding-box" about which Belzoni reported (Belzoni, 1820: 183), and was previously built by a young wife for her new husband's belongings. The *dulab* or cupboard was initially little different from the *sanduq*, although it was integral with

Suma' mud storage bin built by the girl's great-grandmother during the late 1940s. Decorations include a geometrical design and two *'arusa* bridal dolls. Note the mud *dulab* and shelf in the background, the reused remains of an earlier *manama* incorporated into a wall.

Creating space: Form and function of vernacular storage   167

Beyond the use of mud bricks, the annual production of *magaris* is a remnant manifestation of a culture that populated its physical surroundings with a multitude of forms shaped out of wet earth, straw, and buffalo dung.

safat rather than a separate superimposed structure. Today, *dulab* is also identified with modern storage devices. *Manama* is the mud sleeping platform, its supporting column also serving as a storage space. As was observed earlier, added functionality may have included that of a feeding trough for animals. Part-decorative, part-functional designs include repetitive geometric patterns, hand stencils to ward off evil influences, and *'arusa* bridal dolls for good luck. The latter were traditionally applied as decoration by a bride when constructing storage bins, part of establishing a household at the beginning of her married life.

The functional disappearance of most of these vernacular mud forms[2] from the Theban Necropolis is now all but complete, and a brief discussion of the material composition and construction of this component of the necropolis' architectural assemblage, beyond what has been recorded by Eigner (1984: 84) and Winlock and Crum (1926: 52), is warranted.

Raw mud or *tin* is mixed with *dahs*, trampled *qasab* leaves mixed with animal excrement obtained from the *hush*. *Dahs* is a finer version of the *saffir* used to fire the *furn* and may be obtained from the family donkey or buffalo, or bought from others who keep animals, for LE12.50 per large bag. To produce *dabs*, *saffir* is first dried for four or five days, then pulverized and mixed with water and mud. Left standing for a week and stirred daily, the mixture slowly integrates, with further *dabs* and water to be added every day, "because the mud eats it." As the plant fibers rot and the substance becomes glutinous, the increasing strength of the smell serves as an indication that what is now called *tuf* is ready for use. When dry, the resulting material is extremely hard and durable, and has a smooth surface *(tara)* that is resistant to cracking. Built in situ, the thin walls of these storage structures are built up in sections—as is the case with the domed *furn*—each section left to dry before being extended upward, the completed structure strong enough to support its own weight and to withstand the outward pressure of its contents. For all these reasons, the use of *tuf* is also one of the techniques in Badawi's tool kit during his restoration work of the painted mud-coated walls in the Dayr al-Madina tombs.

The bread-boards *(magrassa/magaris)* produced every year from a 1.5:1 ratio of buffalo dung *(zibn gamusa)* and mud are still in common use. A small quantity of *dabs* is also added. Small heaps of the mixture are flattened to one inch in thickness, smoothed, and left to dry. As will previously have been the case with the construction of the grain and flour mud bins, the hot summer months are preferred for this domestic task because of the favorable drying time—no more than a few days—which during the winter months would take two weeks. These bread-boards are not used in the oven, but serve as a base—coated in flour to prevent sticking—while the *'aish-shamsi* bread-mixture is rising in the sun.

It is in the midst of this vernacular necropolis' environment that Qurnawi lived and worked. It is to the broader social and economic aspects of Qurnawi foothills sociality that we shall now turn.

7

Agriculture, Conflict, and the Maintenance of Stable Social Relations

The agricultural matrix of Egyptology-induced labor relations

Despite the archaeological context in which Qurnawi labor has generally been considered, the account of Qurnawi archaeological work practices offered in the next chapter cannot be divorced from the variety of ways in which members of the foothills communities make a living. Since archaeological work for the Supreme Council of Antiquities (SCA) is government employment, the nature of Qurnawi economics for those so employed is one that combines formal with informal money-earning activities. Even where such formal government work is not related to archaeology, informal aspects may still be present: in the house of a local teacher who is also an elected representative on the Luxor City Council, soapstone carvings at various stages of completion and intended for sale to tourists may be seen lying around the family room. Similarly, a guard employed by the SCA will also peddle artifacts at the nearby tomb of Ramose, or gain supplementary income from his various agricultural activities. Significantly, many such persons who count some form of agricultural involvement among their economic pursuits consider themselves *muzari'in*, farmers, first and foremost, and view, when pressed, their tourist activities or government work as secondary.

Yet, for Qurnawi to impose any distinction on local economic practice, and to separate formal from informal, or primary from supplementary income-earning activities, is both artificial and immaterial. Qurnawi simply respond to the various opportunities at their disposal in order to broaden their economic base and to reduce the impact of any seasonally experienced economic downturn. However, for many Qurnawi to identify themselves in the first instance as farmers, confirms that which escaped most of the early European visitors, namely the inherently agricultural quality of west bank subsistence. In order not to make the same mistake, or to see local archaeological practice in isolation, a discussion of Qurnawi agricultural practice must be offered before considering Qurnawi involvement in archaeology. It is not the intention here to provide an in-depth study of land ownership and agricultural production: here we simply wish to establish the variety of ways in which agricultural pursuits continue to form part of the range of economic practices to which Qurnawi in the Theban foothills have access.

Ownership of agricultural lands at al-Hurubat

Before a more general discussion of some of the agricultural practices involved, responses about ownership of land and domestic animals obtained during fieldwork household interviews in the foothills area of al-Hurubat are revealing. With respect to ownership of agricultural land, in responses from sixty-six completed household interviews and informal visits to fifteen additional households, thirty-three respondents, or 40.7 percent of the total number of respondents (n = 81), indicated that they own land.[1] Among these, and apart from extended families already accounted for with individual holdings among the thirty-three respondents, there were six respondents whose land ownership also benefited the wider family. Of households for which only demographic information was collected, twelve respondents indicated that they own land, ranging in size from unspecified to "much land." These twelve responses included two cases where the ownership of land benefited a further six related families, again suggesting that the collective ownership of land by extended families impacts on a greater number of families than is indicated by the number of responses alone.

Land owned by respondents ranged in size from three *qirat* to eight feddan, with the largest parcel owned by extended families measuring twenty feddan. In the latter case, individual responsibility for respective plots was distributed among family members in a range of two, three, three, three, seven and two feddan. Before the 1952 Revolution, most land was in the hands of large operators. While small holdings were allowed to be retained, many of the larger estates were expropriated by President Nasser, and their holdings redistributed. Land owned among Qurnawi is a combination of such smaller parcels that have been held in ownership by individual families for a long time, and allocations resulting from redistribution. No clear distinction was made in respondents' answers between private ownership and government-leased land, and in practice such a distinction seems negligible.[2] Although listed in government records under the name of its original owner, these parcels can be inherited and sold. If sold, a contract documents the change of ownership between the parties involved and specifies any taxation arrangements that now fall due to the new owner. Landowners may also choose to rent their holdings or part thereof to a third person who will pay LE700 rent per year per feddan,[3] with all further expenses and profits to go to the tenant.

The above ownership arrangements only represent an indication of the intensity of agricultural pursuits at al-Qurna. The use of agricultural resources is not limited to the benefit inherent in owning land only, but may also involve sharecropping where a part of the produce falls to landless coworkers, thus adding to household resources. As will be discussed, a somewhat similar arrangement exists with animal husbandry.

Land Ownership at al-Hurubat*	
Category	**Total**
Respondents owning land from total sample of 66 completed household interviews and 15 social visits $n = 81$	33
Ownership by 33 respondents as percent of sample $n = 81$	40.7 %
Total land owned by 33 respondents as measured in *qirat*	1,806
Total land owned by 33 respondents as measured in feddan	75.3
Average land owned by 33 respondents	54.7 *qirat* = 2.3 feddan
Range of parcel size across all 33 respondents	3–192 *qirat*
* Rural Egyptian land measurements are as follows: 1 feddan = 24 *qirat* = 1.038 acres or 0.42 hectares or 4200.834 square meters 1 *qirat* = 24 *sahms* = 175.035 square meters 1 *qasaba* (surveyor's measuring rod) = 3.55 meters 1 feddan = 333.33 square *qasaba*[4]	

Ownership of agricultural land at al-Hurubat.

Agricultural practice at al-Hurubat

Ahmad Muhammad Ahmad, brother-in-law of Badawi, was a tired man. A guard with the Supreme Council of Antiquities, his area of duty concerned the Noble Tombs of al-'Asasif, between Hatshepsut's Temple and the northernmost part of al-Hurubat. Possible shifts are either one day on, one day off, or between six in the evening to six in the morning. Ahmad's shift was always of the latter type and was evidently the more demanding of the two. Having collected his large-gauge shotgun from the *taftish* antiquities inspectorate near Madinat Habu, his late-afternoon walk to work would take him past Badawi's house. Shotgun slung over his shoulder and the linen bag with ammunition rattling as he walked, his arrival could cause some unease among the female members of the household. Since Ahmad's two brothers were also guards, with each of them allocated different shifts, this meant in theory that among the three brothers there would always be time to attend to the half feddan of jointly owned sugarcane land. The reality was that during crucial stages of the sugarcane cycle Ahmad's combined multiple jobs—agricultural work, peddling artifacts at the tomb of Ramose near his house, and his night-time guard duties—were clearly too demanding. Found asleep one night while on duty, he was given a one-month jail sentence without pay to be served in the town of Armant, south of Luxor.

Ahmad and his family live in a greater degree of poverty than other observed households and their lifestyle invokes the imagery of an earlier period when housing was less developed here. The single-storied mud-room enclosure has the usual palm roof beams, and is covered with an assortment of items: remnants of palm-frond beds and crates, over which *qasab* leaves were thrown that seemingly have not been replaced since the room was built seven or eight years ago. The leaves are brown and blackened from dust, with strands of gray-black cobwebs hanging down from the roof. Ahmad's furniture consists of a small cupboard with padlock, which is kept by his wife for food and kitchen supplies; two *deqa*s, one used to stack bags of poultry cereal; and a refrigerator. Such is Ahmad's furniture. The kitchen is a *babur* kerosene cooker on the dirt floor in a corner, and there is no *butagaz*. Other than on the one available *deqa*, people sleep on the floor or outside, depending on the weather. The general atmosphere is one of squalor, the only color provided by pieces cut from cardboard soap-powder boxes tied to the blades of a ceiling fan that provide red and yellow streaks when rotating.

The fan sucks down dust out of the ceiling in a continuous fashion when rotating, diffusing the incoming sunlight through its fine mist. Plastic bags hang from the mud wall, holding paper and other items, while the top of the refrigerator and the space underneath the *deqa*s serve as general storage areas, including items for sale to tourists, wrapped in scraps of newspaper.

The evident need of Ahmad's government salary and the resulting hardship imposed on his family by its temporary absence evoked both a response coordinated largely by Badawi to support his wife's sister and her children, and the social games played—the telling of little lies and half-truths—to prevent embarrassment on her part for having received assistance. Upon his release Ahmad could not display any knowledge of the help offered to his family: communal support was to be expected and not further commented upon, with reciprocal *wajib*, duty, eventually to be offered by him when called for. The episode demonstrated the close interplay between economic practice and the safety inherent in this specific form of foothills sociality that may mitigate the risks of at times conflicting income-earning strategies. The merging of formal government work with tourism and agricultural activity is common especially among such small holdings as that of Ahmad and his brothers,

Supreme Council of Antiquities *ghaffir* on duty at the tomb of Sennefer.

and typical of the smaller parcels of land owned in al-Hurubat, where in thirty-four out of forty sampled cases agricultural activity formed part of a wider household revenue base.

Other than renting land to a tenant, a range of labor options is available to distribute the work involved with land ownership, freeing up time for other economic activity. In Ahmad's case, his two brothers facilitated some of this distribution, although Ahmad's range of work commitments, including his own agricultural labor offered to others, and seasonal work for foreign archaeological missions during his annual leave, did not necessarily gave him the respite he needed to do his formal job effectively.

Mixed economic activity involving agricultural work at al-Hurubat*		
Type	Total	Percent
Supreme Council of Antiquities (SCA) work	16	40
Seasonal or full-time employment with foreign archaeological missions	3†	7.5
Luxor City Council (LCC) government work	3	7.5
Government work other than SCA or LCC	3	7.5
Tourism-related work	7	17.5
Self-employed other than tourism-related work (various)	2	5
Government pension only—no other sources of income	1	2.5
Farming exclusively—no other sources of income	5	12.5
Total = n	40	100
* Number of responses sample n = 40 (including the 33 visited households from sample n = 81; and 7 households for which only demographic data was collected). † For the sake of simplicity, seasonal employment for foreign archaeological missions by SCA personnel during their annual leave has not been reflected here.		

Distribution of mixed economic activity by employment type involving agricultural work at al-Hurubat.

The use of different labor resources is roughly dependent on the crop grown. Women generally do not work the land unless they are unmarried, although they may be seen gleaning wheat or cutting *bersim* and *mulukhiya*. The latter two activities suggest that female labor may be used where it concerns the routine gathering for domestic use of fodder and food produce. The more physically demanding onion and wheat harvests fall to the men, and sharecropping arrangements whereby labor is offered in exchange for payment in produce may be entered into by men who do not own land. After the onion harvest, domestic tomb chambers serve as ready storage for the fruits of such labor.

Qasab or sugarcane is also a crop of importance for Qurnawi, both for its leaves, which serve as fodder, and for the cash it provides. Timothy Mitchell has demonstrated the importance of sugarcane as a source of hard currency necessary to pay for all other expenses involved with domestic agricultural production: seeds, fertilizer, fuel for irrigation pumps, and so on, and has argued that commercial sugarcane production survives because it serves the cash requirements of such "self-provisioning" (Mitchell, 1998a: 25).

Based on an admittedly small sample ($n = 28$) obtained from interview responses where sufficient definition was provided to enable this interpretation, the situation at al-Hurubat diverges from this model. A significant number of small- to medium-sized holdings produce sugarcane in combination with income sources other than agriculture ($n = 16$). Where it may reasonably be expected that exclusive sugarcane production combines with some undeclared small-scale production for domestic consumption, there is still a reduced dependence on sugarcane due to the presence of other income sources to cover costs.

Other holdings produce fodder and food crops for mixed domestic and commercial use only ($n = 8$). In the latter instance, the term 'commercial' must not be overstated, and is suggestive of some additional income from sold produce rather than one of scales of production. Thus, a Luxor City Council worker who also owns a half feddan may typically produce twenty-five large bags of wheat for his own consumption and twenty bags of beans, ten of which he sells for a total of LE700. But rather than representing a clear increase in expendable household income (other than savings made on bread and beans), such revenue merely recovers the cost of production for their own consumption and any applicable tax. However, what is important is that such is done in the absence of sugarcane production.

Importance of crops in relation to other sources of income at al-Hurubat		
Crops	**Total holdings**	**Other income sources**
Sugarcane only	965 *qirat* = 40.2 feddan *n* = 16	Tourism (3); SCA or work for foreign archaeological missions (7); LCC (1); other government (1); self-employed (2); farmer (1); unspecified (1)
Sugarcane combined with wheat* and other food crops grown for domestic production	506 *qirat* = 21.1 feddan *n* = 4	Tourism (2); farmer (2)
Mixed domestic and/ or part commercial production of food crops only	107 *qirat* = 4.5 feddan *n* = 8	SCA or other archaeological work (5); LCC (2); farmer (1)

* There is evidence of some increase in the production of wheat at the expense of sugarcane as a result of a prohibition against sugarcane cultivation within two hundred meters of roads in some areas. In the past, sugarcane fields have been used as cover by armed extremists when staging attacks. At al-Qurna, the prohibition was introduced to secure the safety of concert audiences at the time of the west bank's first *Aida* performance in 1994.

Distribution of the relative importance of crops in relation to other sources of income.

Instances in which sugarcane coexists with other agricultural activity represent a minority (*n* = 4). In all these cases the additional crops were for domestic consumption. Because of the commercial cultivation of sugarcane, such operations may still involve sizeable holdings, totalling 506 *qirat*. Of the four producers in this sample, two conducted their agricultural activities alongside other tourism-related employment. In these cases Mitchell's dependence of domestic production on *qasab* will therefore be less obvious. The remaining two agricultural producers in this sample claimed farming as their single economic activity. One of these uses six feddan to grow sugarcane, and uses his remaining two feddan for wheat, producing twenty seventy-five-kilogram bags for domestic consumption. The other farmer uses one and a half of his four feddan for sugar, the remainder to grow domestic crops such as *bersim*, *mulukhiya*, and onions. Comprising 50 percent of the sample ($n = 4$), these farmers also represent the only two instances in the total sample ($n = 28$) where we find evidence of Mitchell's stated interdependence between sugarcane and production for domestic consumption.

Thus, it may be postulated that the presence of sugarcane holdings insufficiently large to guarantee financial security, and the presence of holdings producing for domestic consumption but financially entirely independent from sugarcane cultivation, is explained by the availability of other income sources, mainly in the form of archaeological, other government-related, and tourism-related work. Conversely, medium-sized sugarcane holdings, which, depending on extended family participation, could provide financial stability, may still be found in combination with government-derived income, largely for the retirement benefits that such employment guarantees.

Mitchell's analysis is of interest in that his observations pertain to al-Ba'irat, the neighboring village which for many centuries has had strained relations with the people of al-Qurna. In a previous chapter it has been argued that the discord between the two communities may at least in part have resulted from diverging economic specializations. Indications that there is indeed a reduced financial dependence on cash crops in the presence of other income sources at al-Hurubat suggests that there is, still, a practical basis for that difference.

Today, these differences are still located in the greater access to a variety of economic resources at al-Qurna compared with the rather more exclusively agricultural identity of al-Ba'irat, although archaeological workers now may also be Ba'irati. In certain respects these differences are indeed nominal, as foothills households benefit from both wage-earning opportunities that the sugarcane harvest and planting cycles provide to those who are landless, from the fodder that its leaves supply to those who keep animals, and from the degree of production for their own consumption. But in virtually all cases, such activity is complementary to other income-earning strategies. For most of those who own land, and especially where such land is owned by extended families, the cultivation of sugarcane is neither a singular economic specialization nor a means toward financial independence, but only one component in a range of options—including the securing of a government pension—which maximize income and reduce risk.

Ahmad and his brothers utilize their half feddan to grow sugarcane only, achieving yields of twenty metric tons and sharing the proceeds between them and their one sister, while choosing to buy all other produce required for domestic consumption. The growing season for sugarcane runs from May to December, but may also extend into January or February. Newly planted cane continues to produce in five-year cycles, but with each successive year grows increasingly *ta'ban*, tired. In the absence of an annual inundation, soils become impoverished under the influence of salinization (*ghalawiya*), rendering yields that vary well below those of Ahmad's and averaging from thirty, thirty-five, thirty, twenty-five, to twenty metric tons per feddan across the five-year cycle, and requiring increased use of fertilizer. For large-scale producers such as the Shenuda family from Luxor, who operate seventy-one feddan on the west bank, at twenty tons returns become uneconomical and a new cycle is planted. After burning the stubble left from the previous cycle—its distant orange glow at night and acrid smoke during the day noticeable from the necropolis—a new cycle is commenced by placing lengths of mature cane, nurtured from the cycle's final crop, head-to-toe in parallel shallow grooves, covered, and watered twice a month for the next eight months. Even in reasonable soils, the use of fertilizer is now as much a part of cultivation as the revitalizing force of the Nile's annual inundation was in centuries past. The larger Luxor-based producers would use fifteen fifty kilogram bags of *nitrokima*—nitrogen fertiliser—per feddan, but Ahmad and his brothers may only afford six for their half feddan. In addition to *nitrokima*, a pesticide called *sobar* may still be necessary, despite claims that "the government" adds it to the irrigation water. The process is time intensive, with both *nitrokima* and *sobar* applied manually, Ahmad scooping amounts from the bags into his *gallabiya*, from where he throws handfuls around the stems, walking between the rows of sugarcane, half hidden as by a forest, washing his *gallabiya* in the irrigation canal and hanging it to dry across the cane stalks when he is finished.

The 1.2-meter-wide irrigation channel that waters Ahmad's land is filled by pump from the main canal. None of these pumping stations are now government owned but all are privately operated and paid for in hourly sessions costing LE5 each, with watering booked in advance from session to session. The pump takes three hours to supply enough water for Ahmad's half feddan, with the water released onto the land by breaking small clay and rock seals in the elevated embankment of the irrigation channel.

Farmer Ahmad.

Come harvest time, Ahmad invites people to cut the cane for free. They can keep the leaves for their animals, with each person knowing how much he has cut and what his portion is. This is the cheapest way for Ahmad to clear his crop quickly and before its quality deteriorates, with ten to twenty people taking four or five days to harvest his half feddan. His animals need more fodder than his own cutter's share provides, but he will similarly make his labor available on other people's land once his crop has gone to market and after finishing his guard duties at six in the morning, working an additional four-hour shift from seven to eleven in the morning for LE7 per day. The large estates operated by Coptic families from Luxor are labor-intensive by virtue of their size. They provide casual employment during harvesting and planting time for people like Ahmad's brother who, during his day off, is free for extra work, which he arranges via an agent *(ra'is)* in al-Tarif who coordinates labor for medium-sized holdings and the larger estates. Such estates will employ fifteen to twenty men working in two shifts, from five in the morning to seven-thirty in the morning and from eight in the morning to ten-thirty in the morning, each shift completing one feddan, also at a daily rate of LE7 per person.

Getting the sugarcane to market is not without its worries for the smaller producers who may face competition from the larger operators for available transport resources. Before cutting the cane, Ahmad has to go to the office in Qariya Hassan Fathy, to book the wagons necessary to transport the sugarcane to the government factory in Armant, south of Luxor. Once the officer has recorded Ahmad's booking for rail equipment, one wagon will be made available on each successive harvesting day, which equates with the volume that can physically be cut during the early morning shift. Any time lag between the cutting and transport to Armant will cause the cane to dry out, reducing its weight and thus its market value. As it stands, the number of rail wagons required at the siding will vary, with volume depending not only on the freshness and sap content of the cane, but also on its general quality, which in turn relates to the particular year in the five-year cycle a harvest occurs and consequently the amount of *nitrokima* applied, for which Ahmad and his brothers will have had no money to buy more than they could afford. Thus, the number of rail carriages needed may range between seasons from three to five. The fact that Ahmad's transport requirements were recorded at the office will nevertheless not guarantee that his equipment needs will be met on the day of the harvest. The train from Armant may not have come in, or the officer may have released Ahmad's allocated wagon to someone else. At the time of booking, therefore, a customary bribe of LE20 is paid to the officer to ensure his cooperation. Once cut, the sugarcane is moved to the rail siding by a tractor-pulled flatbed trailer at a cost of LE35 per trailer load. Ahmad's twenty metric tons will be purchased by the government sugar factory for LE100 per ton. Production costs, including fertilizer, watering, tractor hire, and bribes at the rail siding, were claimed by Ahmad to amount to LE500. With LE300 set aside to be claimed by the tax collector who will visit Ahmad's house any time soon, the net return on the sugarcane crop will be in the order of LE1,200. When distributed, the brothers receive LE325 and their sister LE225. This division is a generous one toward the sister, as the traditional distribution ratio between men and women is two to one (or in this case LE343: LE171).

However, the costs indicated by Ahmad appear conservative when compared to the breakdown of actual expenses given by him for individual items, amounting not to LE500 but LE650. Farmers like Ahmad operate within the funds available to them, and obtaining credit from the

Farmer Ahmad's projected expenditure and revenue before cost-cutting			
Cultivar	Sugarcane 0.5 feddan (12 *qirat*)		
Yield	20 tons at LE100 per ton		LE2,000
Costs	6 x 50kg bags *nitrokima* at LE25	LE150	
	2 x 50kg bags *sobar* at LE20	LE40	
	Plow hire 1 hour	LE25	
	Water 3 hours twice for 8 months at LE5 per hour	LE240	
	Tractor/trailer hire at LF˥˥ each x 5	LE175	
	Bribe to rail equipment booking officer	LE20	-LE650
	Tax applicable to .5 feddan	LE300	-LE300
	Total all expenses before any realized cost-cutting		-LE950
Profit	Total profit after all projected expenses		LE1,050
Earnings	Individual earnings per brother at LE1,050: 7 x 2 =		LE300
	Individual earnings for one sister at LE1,050: 7 x 1 =		LE150

Farmer Ahmad: Typical sugarcane expenditure and revenue breakdown for a small-sized 12-*qirat* land holding of good quality soil with all possible costs included and before cost-cutting.

agricultural bank in Luxor, to be repaid upon sale of the crop, is generally not considered an option.[5] Since there are no available household savings and all expenses will have to be paid for from other income, it may be concluded that expenditure is reduced by cutting back on the cost of fertilizer, pesticides, and possibly even the frequency of watering. Ahmad's land looked healthy when compared with other parcels seriously affected by salinity, and he may thus rightly feel that his cost-cutting in some of these areas will not carry significant risk. When applying the real cost of LE650, his individual earnings would achieve outcomes exactly in line with the traditional two to one payment ratio for men and women, indicating that these costs are indeed correct, and inadvertently revealing that Ahmad has maximized profits—largely benefiting his sister—by realizing expenditure reduction through cost-cutting.

Farmer Ahmad's three scenarios of projected and realized individual earnings		
Earnings 1	Individual earnings per brother at LE1,050: 7 x 2 =	LE300
	Individual earnings for sister at LE1,050: 7 x 1 =	LE150
Earnings 2	Individual earnings per brother at LE1,200: 7 x 2 =	LE343
	Individual earnings for sister at LE1,200: 7 x 1 =	LE171
Earnings 3	Realized earnings per brother at LE1,200: 4 x Y =	LE325
	Realized earnings for sister at LE1,200: 4 x Y =	LE225

Farmer Ahmad: Projected and realized individual earnings as reflected in scenario (1) where all necessary expenses would have been met; scenario (2) actual earnings after cost-cutting on basis of two to one male/female payment ratio; and scenario (3) actual payments received by three brothers and one sister, including non-standard male/female payment ratio, where Y represents the siblings' agreed distribution formula.

The relative benefit for Ahmad's contribution in the cultivation of sugarcane is an indication that these small holdings may represent annually predictable income, but they hardly create wealth or offer financial independence in their own right. In fact, finances dictate that cost-saving measures be applied, as the above analysis suggests. Compared with Ahmad's monthly antiquities guard wage of LE150, his time and energy expended on sugarcane production only provides him with some two months' additional income. But it is in this marginal improvement on his government wage that the importance of involvement in agricultural production becomes apparent. In combination with his other activities—raising animals for profit, hiring himself out as day laborer on other people's holdings, and peddling artifacts to tourists—the supplementary income that all these investments in time and energy provide do offer him and his family the resilience not only to make ends meet, but also the ability to cope if and when any of these strategies fail to offer financial returns. While antiquities work provides a regular salary and additional retirement entitlements, tourist work is seasonal and its revenue, even if periodically lucrative, is nevertheless at the best of times unpredictable. It is, therefore, not difficult to see why Ahmad describes himself in the first instance as a farmer. Not only do his preoccupations fall three out of five times in the agricultural sphere, but his agricultural work also provides him with the ability to manage—and manipulate—financially where a singular dependence on either government or tourist work would leave him vulnerable.

Ownership of animals at al-Hurubat

Not all financial aspects of agricultural practice at al-Hurubat are, or can be, quantified. Goats, pigeons, chicken, and geese are raised by women either for domestic consumption or to be sold at market, in both instances contributing to household resources, as do the consumption and sale of milk, eggs, and butter. Likewise, the production of fodder and food crops for domestic use will reduce household costs and, in the case of fodder, contribute to the cost-benefit objectives of raising animals. The known replacement cost of fodder or foodstuffs will not be factored in but expected as predictable returns from known assets. Similarly, labor invested to obtain sugarcane leaves for fodder will eventually find its reward in any profit made on the sale of animals so raised rather than being included in any projected wages.

Ownership of especially cows and buffalos is significant for their income-earning potential. The phenomenon is a distinct one in that in many cases it is not true ownership and in that it also goes beyond simply keeping domestic animals for dairy products or a future meat supply. For Badawi's SCA colleague, Mahmud Ahmad Muhammad Yusuf, who like Badawi is landless, his animals provide him with the limited supplementary income he needs. Even if his government salary at LE180 per month is a little higher than Badawi's by virtue of longer service, Mahmud conducts no business with tourists like Badawi does to help him make ends meet. Instead, Mahmud spends all his free time caring for his animals. There is a type of charity in these practices, with those who can afford to buy animals arranging for them to be raised by those who cannot, a share of the eventual profit its reward. Informants were reluctant to reveal the identity of the actual owner, stating this was "secret," either because such would disclose—and possibly place at risk from unwanted competition—their certain dependence on a known benefactor, or because it would make public and thus limit the owner's charitable intentions. A young animal may be bought by its true owner for LE1,000, raised by Mahmud, and in due course be sold for LE2,000. Any milk and cheese produced from the animal is used by Mahmud for domestic consumption, although others may decide to sell such products. After repaying the owner his initial investment of LE1,000, Mahmud is entitled to a three-quarter share of the profit, which, in the above case, will earn him LE750. Values and proceeds will vary depending on the respective ages of the purchased and sold animal, while for others the profit share may be less generous and in

Animal Ownership at al-Hurubat*	
Category	Total
Respondents owning animals in sample completed household interviews *n* = 66	62
Animal ownership all species as % of completed household interviews *n* = 66	93.9%
Ownership of (8**) buffalos by 6 respondents as % of 62 respondents	9.7%
Ownership of (15†) cows by 7 respondents as % of 62 respondents	11.3%
Ownership of (66††) donkeys by 57 respondents as % of 62 respondents	91.9%
Ownership of (64) sheep by 13 respondents as % of 62 respondents	21%
Ownership of (67) goats by 17 respondents as % of 62 respondents	27.4%
Ownership of poultry✤ by 48 respondents as % of 62 respondents	77.4%

* Animal ownership as reflected in the total sample is not inclusive of one horse, two domestic cats and two counts of rabbits. Dogs are ubiquitous, their presence one of premeditated security or condoned adoption of a household by the dog. They figure throughout travelers' records, and are regarded as ferocious by non-locals. Numbers are controlled by throwing unwanted litters down a tomb shaft. Desiccated adults visible in tomb shafts may be bitches who went searching for their young.

** Includes one calf

† Includes two calves

†† Includes two foals. The high number reflects the donkey's main use in the *'arabiya* transport of water from the roadside taps to the hillside houses.

✤ 'Poultry' here includes: chic┐ ducks, geese, pigeons, turkeys. Often informants responded with ┕ ┌nter when asked for numbers for certain species as no clear count is kept, also because of regular menu requirements. Named subspecies recognized within some of the species have not been further differentiated here.

Ownership of domestic animals at al-Hurubat.

the order of 50 percent. To raise the animal, during the summer months Mahmud uses LE120 worth of *tebn*, hay, and buys one *qirat* of *bersim* from a landowner, which from one seeding will grow five or six recurring crops, at a cost of LE125. During the winter months, Mahmud takes part in the sugarcane harvest to obtain the waste foliage for fodder that will last him for the next four to five months. However, both Mahmud and Ahmad, who raise animals in this manner, are adept at converting the process into one of continuous production by having their cow inseminated, with the resulting offspring either sold or used for further breeding. Mahmud now keeps a five-year-old buffalo cow, her three-year-old son, and their calf. With successful breeding and force-feeding the animal by hand on a mixture of bread and beans, he may sell a forty-five-day-old calf every year for LE500-LE600, with half of its proceeds to go to the owner of the adult animal. Before either of the two adult cows grows too old, he will sell them, and keep his calf to start a new cycle all over again. Since Mahmud will not sell an adult animal every year, and his proceeds differ from year to year depending on the stage of the respective breeding cycle, he only budgets the proceeds of the annual sale of a calf, which averages an extra LE20 per month on top of his monthly government wage. His time investment explains why Mahmud, too, considers himself primarily a farmer. But the process is not a lucrative one: there are no savings, and Mahmud looks forward to the day when his son Mustafa is released from the army to work with him or find an independent job, enabling Mahmud to save money for his son's wedding. Neither of these arrangements are totally dependable, the owner of Ahmad's now pregnant cow having indicated that he wants to sell his animal, leaving Ahmad in a considerable state of anxiety over the untimely demise of his breeding program.

Land, feuds, and the traditional settlement of disputes at al-Hurubat

Beyond such instances of land redistribution as took place under President Nasser and the confiscation of parts of Ahmad's grandfather's land under King Farouk as initiated by antiquities officials because his holdings were near the Memnon Colossi and therefore on 'temple land,' the vested economic interests inherent in the ownership of land suggest that conflict over access to and ownership of agricultural resources is likely to have been also a common occurrence throughout Qurnawi history, as indeed it was throughout Egypt. (For examples see Fakhouri, 1987: 111–12; Hopkins, 1987: 165–69; Nielsen, 1998: 367.) A historical study surrounding land issues at al-Qurna based on cadastral and legal records is a worthwhile project that remains to be undertaken.

At the conclusion of fieldwork carried out in 1999, two particular disputes affecting al-Hurubat remained unresolved. One case involved a widow owning her late husband's five *qirat*. She uses the land to grow

Farmer Mahmud.

vegetables, which her children sell door-to-door in the village, as a means to complement her small monthly government pension of LE70. She also raises animals, and may periodically sell two small geese for LE17, or one large one for LE27. The family has no business with tourists such as selling homemade cloth *'arusa* dolls by the girls, nor does she allow her children to ask for baksheesh, because she considers the practice offensive. She has even instructed her children to refuse tourists' requests for photographs when they encounter the children walking with a basket of vegetables on their heads. She considers such behavior improper for fear that "President Mubarak may see the picture and think the village is poor."[6] Despite her dependence on her land, her late husband's brother now wants it for his own son, with the claim to be arbitrated by Shaykh Tayyeb, who would be expected to rule that either the son pronounce the land as hers, or buy her out. In both cases a record of the decision will be signed by all parties as proof of ownership should there be any future disagreement.[7]

Of greater complexity was the case that made many in al-Hurubat angry, largely because of the stubbornness of the main protagonist. Badawi's sister-in-law Samira and her husband Mansur, who live on the other side of the agricultural land opposite al-Hurubat near the al-Fadliya irrigation canal, had stayed inside their house for several weeks, Mansur unable to drive his tourist coach for fear that something might happen to his family in his absence. A five-*qirat* parcel of land next to his house belongs to his elderly father Muhammad, which he says he bought from his brother many years ago. No papers were signed and there were no witnesses, as it was thought this was unnecessary between brothers. Muhammad's brother had since died, but the brother's son is now claiming the land as his, with his headstrong and difficult uncle Muhammad, Mansur's father, in disagreement and refusing to have Shaykh Tayyeb or any other third party settle the issue. Enraged by his uncle's intransigence, the nephew went to his uncle's house and fired three shots in the air, reason for Mansur to fear for his own family, and staying indoors for several weeks, before eventually taking his wife and infant son to Samira's parents in al-Tarif. Now free to mediate, and despite his anger because of his cousin's use of a gun near his father, Mansur suggested to let the issue rest until after his father had died, when he can have the land. His cousin, who himself is already elderly, declined the proposed solution, because he does not trust Mansur, even though Mansur is prepared to draw up a contract to that effect, and notwithstanding the fact that the cousin's sons are in agreement with Mansur.

The general feeling was that a ruling by Shaykh Tayyeb would be in favor of Muhammad's nephew, since without any documents the claimed transaction between Muhammad and his brother would be seen as nonexistent. The entire episode was in some respects remarkable, as Muhammad was himself a *dallal*, a land surveyor, and in the past had contributed to land-dispute settlements by maintaining a map indicating land divisions. The function of local cadastres in these dealings remains indistinct. In Muhammad's case the land involved remained in the family, and no formal records may have required adjustment. But even in case of a contract of sale having been signed and witnessed, there would apparently have been no obligation to formally register the transfer, although to do so "would have been better."

To make matters worse, during recent plowing of a seven-feddan parcel of land owned by Muhammad and adjoining his nephew's land, the tractor had obliterated the boundary line, with Muhammad claiming his land one or two feet further out, thereby gaining at least a *qirat* difference, which, according to Mansur with justification, was again being disputed by Muhammad's nephew. The total land under dispute was now six *qirat*, with a possible solution for Shaykh Tayyeb, upon having had the land re-measured by a *dallal*, to suggest a division of three *qirat* each, although neither party might agree to that.

In the meantime, Mansur, afraid of further violence that could lead to five or six people being killed, had asked Shaykh Tayyeb to notify the police, who upon his request sent a car to arrest both Muhammad and his nephew. Shaykh Tayyeb told the police to "not even believe his phone call, should he ring," but to wait until his arrival to set them free. Taking his time to do so, he effectively made them serve a cooling-off period. In the end, the two protagonists only spent one night in jail, but especially the position of Muhammad had hardened further, who was still refusing to mediate through Shaykh Tayyeb. Even so, Shaykh Tayyeb had already initiated the *majlis al-'arab* (Arab council), the traditional dispute settlement mechanism or *majlis 'urfi* over which he presides,[8] by calling in a delegation of impartial elders from some five or six other towns, ranging from Armant and al-Ba'irat to the more distant Ballas and Nagada.

If no earlier means of settlement can be reached, such a traditional dispute settlement involves payment by each party of LE10,000, LE15,000, LE20,000, or LE50,000 to Shaykh Tayyeb, the money to be paid beforehand. In disputes where there is no money, as occurred in a case between al-Ba'irat and Nagalta over which Shaykh Tayyeb's father once presided, so many feddan of land may be taken. The protagonists then make their case before Shaykh Tayyeb and a panel of impartial elders from other towns and villages who act as jury. When making their individual case, each party must listen to the other and is not allowed to interrupt or speak without permission. Should they do so, a penalty of LE200 or LE500 will be imposed, the money to be placed on a table in front of them. As a consequence, people will be careful not to speak out of turn for fear of losing this money, which may be allocated by Shaykh Tayyeb to charitable purposes or be given to the party ultimately deemed to be in the right and similarly distributed.

Before speaking, they swear on the Qur'an that they will speak the truth: *"wallahi al-'azim akul al-haq."* After each party has spoken in his defense, the jury withdraws to deliberate, with a spokesman pronouncing the verdict. The party judged to be in the wrong will lose their money and must settle the offending issue, in this case return the misappropriated land. The party judged to be in the right will receive the money back, as well as receive the money paid by the opponent. Shaykh Tayyeb can be appointed to distribute this money to nominated charitable causes (a mosque, school, hospital, or a sick person), the recipient can distribute the funds, or he can keep the money for himself, although this is frowned upon. The recipient party must state before the gathered onlookers after the trial how he will administer the money. Women who have an issue between them can have their dispute settled likewise, using their gold as payment. If the other woman does not like the gold she can decide to return it, or sell it and distribute the funds similarly. The payments involved are less of a punishment than they are didactic, and said to "keep people polite," meaning that through the payment of fines it is hoped they will learn not to commit the same offense again. Proceedings conclude with the signing of a peace contract and the communal reciting of *al-Fatiha*, the Qur'anic exordium.

Even so, both parties must agree to this kind of dispute settlement, and Shaykh Tayyeb cannot force Mansur's father to have the case adjudicated in this way if he does not want to cooperate. Despite the impartiality of the panel, Muhammad indeed did not want to participate, essentially because of the incident with the gun, preventing the case being settled in this manner. As a result of Muhammad's intransigence, a "very angry" Shaykh Tayyeb adjourned the case until the following week, the panel of elders returned to their towns for Friday prayers, and many in al-Hurubat expressed their dismay with Muhammad, accusing him of "locking his children out of his house." One way to break the deadlock would be for the police to arrest the entire two families until such time that the unfairly imprisoned members put sufficient pressure on the opposing parties to make them come to their senses. Despite his evident frustration, Shaykh Tayyeb favored a more conciliatory course, one in which he with family elders and other influential Qurnawi mediated low-key negotiations between the parties, thereby defusing any escalation in tension and its attendant possibility for violence, and raising expectations that the dispute could be resolved. But at the conclusion of fieldwork, relations remained strained and a peace contract was yet to be signed.

Old enmity: al-Hurubat versus al-Qsasiya

Such unresolved conflict over access to and ownership of economic resources in the past will have given rise to many of the bloody family feuds, *tha'r*, which, driven by kinship alliances and revenge killings, were historically endemic to Upper Egypt and which do occasionally still make headlines (BBC, 2002; Nafie, 2004). Revenge killings are included among the observations Yanni made while residing at al-Hurubat (d'Athanasi, 1836: 138–40). During 1999, two episodes of feuding erupted. Although access to economic resources was only overtly present in the second instance, the first conflagration was but the latest in periodically recurring episodes of conflict between two different tribal groupings and was evidently rooted in historical circumstance, which may well have included competition over agricultural resources.

This latter and longest episode of intertribal conflict, between members of the Qsasiya in al-Tarif and the people of al-Hurubat, through kinship ties eventually came to involve much of al-Hurubat, while also generating tensions within families who had intermarried with Qsasiya members. There is a perceived sense of superiority among Hurubati families who, especially in relation to Qsasiya, view themselves as one of the founding communities: "al-Hurubat was here first"; "al-Hurubat is the largest kinship group"; "al-Hurubat is the most important because it has all the money and all the fields"; and "it was always from al-Hurubat that the *'umda* for al-Qurna came." To support such arguments, Hurubati will readily recount how some fifty years ago people would still dismount from their donkey when passing al-Hurubat out of respect for the *'umda*. By contrast, Qsasiya is being looked down upon as a family of latecomers who came here as beggars, shaving and cutting people's hair to make a living. Even today, they are still referred to as "the family of the haircutters," that very activity also associated with vulture-like behavior by some.

News of a fight at one of the al-Tarif Saturday morning markets between Hassan Ali Hassan Ahmad, son of Badawi's maternal parallel cousin, and a boy from Qsasiya, quickly set tempers flaring for the perceived injustice of the attack and the revisiting of long-standing tensions between the two groups. First pushed and taunted by the Qsasiya boy, Hassan landed some punches before being set upon by six others, fighting them off with his just-purchased *babur* kerosene fuel. By nightfall, rumors were circulating that the next day a two-hundred-strong force would be gathering at the roadside coffee shop to retaliate. A flurry of activity ensued, with Qsasiya family elders not turning to Hassan's father Ali, who was as yet in no mood to make peace, but descending on the house of Sayyed Muhammad, Hassan's mother's brother, a successful artist and businessman, and a prominent member in the community.

Saturday morning market at al-Tarif, the peak of the Theban Mountain, the Qurn, in the background.

The previous major conflagration had taken place two years earlier, when fighting resulted in retaliation against Badawi's Qsasiya lawyer, Ramadan Sayyed Ahmad. Although not initially personally involved, he was picked upon as a distinguished member of his community. While returning from Luxor he was beaten up by boys from al-Hurubat and thrown in the Nile, subsequently spending two weeks in the hospital to recover. The incident is still retold with a measure of glee around the foothills homes. Hostilities were eventually settled by Shaykh Tayyeb, who imposed a fine of LE50,000 on the initiator of any future fighting. Hassan maintained that he did not start this time, and is hoping for the help of two women witnesses.

Maneuvering for the most advantageous position, the decision of the Qsasiya elders to go to Sayyed Muhammad instead of Ali Hassan Ahmad may not have been in their best interests. Likewise receiving short shrift from him, they ended up going to Shaykh Tayyeb instead who, following his phone call, Sayyed Muhammad also refused to go and see. In a more receptive mood the next day, Sayyed Muhammad received fifteen Qsasiya elders, including lawyer Ramadan Sayyed Ahmad, but offered them no customary tea as a signal of his hospitality. He told them this was the "stuff of children," thereby not meaning that it is not an issue worth making trouble over and not worth not drinking tea for, but implying that peace can only be made when his nephew Hassan has settled the score. This is not fighting over property, when peace can return once the stolen item has been returned. There are issues of honor here. Hassan was attacked in the market by six or seven Qsasiya boys, in broad daylight, with Qsasiya elders now under the cover of darkness coming to ask for peace. The score is neither even nor in favor of al-Hurubat, and there is still the need for the party first attacked to reciprocate. Offers of peace can therefore not be accepted, a position in which Sayyed Muhammad is supported by four elders from al-Hurubat, who are willing to fight it out. Sayyed Muhammad agrees that al-Hurubat must first take revenge, but advises them to wait a week or so to instill extra fear in the Qsasiya boys, leaving them uncertain as to when an attack might take place. While Hassan Ali might be sleeping soundly now, his attackers will be worried and have trouble sleeping.

Yet, during this lull, his father, Ali Hassan Ahmad, possibly out of concern for his son's safety, had decided to make peace. Himself an accomplished fighter, his own safety will not have been at issue, despite adopting a vigilant stance by arming himself with his *khazarana* stick. No further conflict occurred during this period, no Qsasiya boys were sighted at the next several markets, and according to the attacking boy's father who had approached Badawi to mediate, his son was too afraid to leave the house. Yet, Hurubati were on their guard, including Badawi who, especially concerned for his *khawaja* being placed at risk, now made a habit of taking a stiletto knife with him when he went outdoors.

Ali's change of position demonstrates the degree to which such disputes quickly become political, leading to heated conversations, and polarizing Hurubati at the level of the community, across different age groups, and within families. Certain community members agreed with Ali Hassan Ahmad's peace overtures on the grounds that the Qsasiya boys may not have started the trouble after all. Hassan Ali could be found in the market every week, allegedly to look at the girls, and it was felt he may well have said something that was heard by and taken as offensive to the Qsasiya boys.[9] In any case, they argued, "those who want to fight it out are no good themselves. These are modern times, and revenge will not only result in continuation of the troubles, but also signal a return to the ongoing mutual violence of the past."

Village lawyer.

Dividing the community along age sets, and despite the position of the four elders, Hassan Ali and his friends were nevertheless not happy having to wait for a week, wanting to fight it out now, and leaving the old people to their peace deals. Intra-family, Sayyed Muhammad has the support of his sister and his nephew, who both disagree with Ali Hassan Ahmad. But the issue is also a personal one between Sayyed Muhammad and brother-in-law Ali Hassan Ahmad, who are close friends. Sayyed has a strong sense for justice and is extremely angry and offended by the unequal attack endured by his nephew. Sayyed and Ali are fearsome and proven fighters with both the *khazarana* and the *shuba*, the fighting sticks made respectively of cane and solid hardwood. Ali is known to have defended family issues with his stick in the past, and his peace initiative was seen as uncharacteristic, and distanced him from an "angry and sad" Sayyed.

Yet, even in the peace deal proposed by Ali Hassan Ahmad there was a strategic element that did not altogether exclude future reciprocal action. It was assumed that Shaykh Tayyeb would rule in favor of Hassan Ali, peace would be made, and the settlement money stipulated by Shaykh Tayyeb two years ago accepted; but a revenge attack would still take place in a few months' time. The peace money now received would then be paid back as part of the settlement terms set for that later attack, although such will only have been possible if any associated charity payments could be delayed. There was also the risk that Shaykh Tayyeb might set a higher penalty than expected, leaving al-Hurubat shortchanged.

Although positive reactions toward this strategy suggested both its past practice and practicality, many of the younger men still preferred to fight it out now rather than later, and heated discussion on the issue was still taking place just prior to the peace meeting at Shaykh Tayyeb's mosque in al-Hasasna. That meeting finally took place some full ten days after the initial market incident. The expected traditional scenario for such reconciliation councils required ten representatives chosen from different Hurubati families and ten Qsasiya representatives to go to Shaykh Tayyeb, and deposit LE50,000 per delegation on the table in front of him. Swearing their "*wallahi al-'azim*" oath on the Qur'an (only possible if clean and not menstruating), Shaykh Tayyeb would first invite the two women witnesses to speak. After hearing the protagonists' arguments, Shaykh Tayyeb would withdraw with the twenty representatives and any additional impartial elders chosen from other villages to discuss the merits of either side. Alternatively, he may choose to make the judgment alone. The party who began the trouble must pay the LE50,000 stipulated two years ago. The vindicated party is not to keep the money but will allocate the funds to some charitable purpose, giving it to a hospital for medicines, or any mosque for carpets, paint work, and so on. If the offending party refuses to pay, Shaykh Tayyeb will involve the police, who will act on his judgment of the case. But if such was the general expectation, proceedings turned out differently.

The nature of these meetings being public, a gradually swelling crowd of some hundred people attended, mostly Hurubati, their presence for these proceedings providing the clearest picture yet for the social overlay of these archaeological surroundings: an undulating sea of Qurnawi turbaned heads; dressed in *gallabiya*s varying in shades of brown, black, and gray to pastel-green and blue; seated on wooden *deqa*s against a background of courtyard trees; the houses of al-Hasasna looming above the canopies; to the right and in the background, the rocky tomb-strewn crest of Dra' Abu al-Naga; the road leading to Dayr al-Bahari and Hatshepsut's Temple at our back.

After a brief appearance, Shaykh Tayyeb first made a—possibly strategically placed—half-hour *wajib* visit to Qsasiya, thus demonstrating his impartiality in the dispute. Upon his return, he motioned Hassan Ali and two of the attacking Qsasiya boys to take up their positions in front of him. He listened to their accounts before—possibly influenced by the presence of a *khawaja* anthropologist—lecturing them that their petty behavior did not befit their village, which is renowned the world over because of the names of Tutankhamun and Hatshepsut. Indicating his verdict, Shaykh Tayyeb requested the two Qsasiya boys to kiss Hassan Ali's head, gestures promptly protested by Hassan. Instead, it was agreed that the boys would kiss Hassan Ali's shoulder, his height providing a convenient excuse to prevent embarassment for all parties. The truce was sealed by the boys shaking hands, Shaykh Tayyeb's on top, the boys' faces expressing not much of a desire to be amicable and appearing distinctly reluctant to go through these motions. There was no mention of the fine, the penalty imposed two years ago still in force, thus depriving al-Hurubat of any financial incentives to retaliate. The greatest deterrent for further hostilities on the part of Qsasiya was delivered to the attacking boy's father, a butcher, who was reprimanded by Shaykh Tayyeb for not better instructing his children, leaving "the inside of their heads as empty as the heads of the buffalos you cut."

That is where the entire affair, at least for now, ended, defusing the situation and also bringing a measure of relief in Badawi's family affairs. For, although involved by being related to Ali Hassan Ahmad, the conflict between al-Hurubat and Qsasiya also affected Badawi personally, demonstrating how such seemingly external issues can cut across related families. Tensions had been simmering for some time between Badawi's wife Amira and Samiha, her brother al-Azeb's wife. Samiha had been commenting on Amira visiting her parents' house in al-Tarif after meeting her two children from a previous marriage. Feeling that Samiha was placing her in an unfavorable light, the issue was a sensitive one for Amira. The meetings with her children were openly conducted at the house of a woman friend who also lived in al-Tarif, but she interpreted Samiha's comments as an attempt to portray these meetings as secret, which might upset Badawi were he to accept them as true. Samiha said she was only joking, but the issue had reached the point where Badawi was no longer invited in for tea by Samiha's father in al-Tarif. Amira did not want to see her own brother and his wife for now, as a result of which she had not visited her own parents in al-Tarif for some time. Just days before the market incident, al-Azeb and brother-in-law Mansur had come to Badawi and Amira's house to make peace, resulting in a settlement of sorts and with *al-Fatiha* pronounced upon departure. But Samiha's father had declined to represent his daughter, and the situation remained tense. Badawi still felt Samiha spoke ill of his wife, and viewed her peace offer as "an apology from someone who killed you." According to Badawi, Amira's family was now angry for al-Azeb having married her, and expected the marriage not to last. He also claimed that Samiha's family was "no good" and that it was for this reason that cousin Mahmud Hassan, Ali Hassan Ahmad's younger brother, had lost interest in Samiha's sister, even though she was a "nice girl," and it was Badawi who had introduced him to her in the first place. That these feelings could accumulate to this degree was in large part due to the recent hostilities between al-Hurubat and al-Tarif, Samiha and her family being Qsasiya. Shaykh Tayyeb's resolution of the case not only diminished the incentive for either party to escalate hostilities, but by retaining social relations with the offending party as symbolized by his last-minute—and therefore not altogether fortuitous—*wajib* visit, Shakyh Tayyeb also extended an invitation to other families to resolve any difficulties associated with this case.

Competition over tourism resources: al-Tarif versus al-'Atyat

Conflict over economic resources other than land may manifest itself among the operators of souvenir stalls (bazaars) located at tourist-intensive locations throughout the Theban Necropolis. One such dispute between a family from al-'Atyat and a family from al-Tarif also involved al-Hurubat—the latter family being related to Badawi through his father's half-brother. Members of the two opposing families operate adjoining bazaars at the entrance to the Valley of the Kings, and got into difficulties with each other when one operator offered a scarab for less than the other to the same tourist. Since 1979 there has been a rule that sellers may not compete for the same customer and that, if a dispute results, both operators will be arrested. With that in mind, the stallholder from al-Tarif let the matter rest, but waited for his competitor while on his way home. When his opponent passed by on his motorbike, the merchant from al-Tarif clubbed him on his arm and head with his *shuba*. The victim ended up in a hospital in Luxor, where he told his doctor that he had fallen off his bike, thereby circumventing the need to report the attack to the police.

The next morning, the father of the injured man and some eleven others from al-'Atyat attacked the compound of the family in al-Tarif who, in a pitched battle involving some fifty people, fought them off with sticks and stones, chasing them back all the way to the foothills road, and leaving in total another nine people in hospital. The father from al-'Atyat was subsequently summoned by Shaykh Tayyeb, who instructed him to make peace, but the father was rude and walked off, to which Shaykh Tayyeb responded by calling in the police, who arrested members of both families.

As an indication of his further displeasure at the father's behavior, Shaykh Tayyeb cancelled the original peace meeting, and ordered to have it reconvene the next day at the small al-Sualim mosque, on the opposite side of the foothills road. Proceedings commenced with the al-'Atyat father being fined LE2,000 for his rude conduct toward Shaykh Tayyeb. In this charged environment, the practice of fining those who speak out of turn was strictly enforced, leading to people quickly raising their hands if they wanted to speak. Shaykh Tayyeb had already found both parties to be at fault (al-Tarif for attacking the motorbike rider and al-'Atyat for attacking al-Tarif) and had drawn up a peace contract that stipulated that each party would pay LE17,000 if hostilities recommenced. The names of those people injured were also included in the contract and should they seek revenge for their wounds, their reprisal would be subject to the same penalty.

At the village level, these two episodes demonstrate in some tangible manner the degree to which even small-scale incidents may lead to larger-scale conflicts between communities and to tensions within them. They provide a contemporary remnant of, and offer a measure of insight into, the mechanics by which tribal conflict manifested and perpetuated itself. Despite such periodic disturbance, many Qurnawi nevertheless affirmed during interviews that "this is a quiet place" and considered it preferable to other places they know about because here there is "no stealing, fighting and killing."[10] If communal relations at al-Qurna are indeed relatively stable compared to other areas where feuding may still present problems, then the two operative forces guiding conflict and stability are those of the religious, socio-political leverage embodied in Shaykh Muhammad Tayyeb—who by means of the *majlis al-'arab* traditional system of gover-nance is able to defuse tension and manipulate intermittent conflict into renewed cycles of social harmony—and *wajib*. The opposition between conflict and stability is inherent in the way these two forces interact, with *wajib* a mechanism toward maintaining friendly social relations as much as it is a driving force in the perpetuation of communal tension, and tradi-tional governance mechanisms as a means toward conflict resolution.

Shaykh Muhammad Tayyeb, Khalwatiya, and the efficacy of *majlis al-ʿarab*

The particular spiritual expression of Sufism—the collective name for the many mystical orders *(tariqa)* that also exist in Egypt alongside formal Islam and where adherents in their devotional practice seek some direct personal experience of God—as represented by Shaykh Muhammad Tayyeb and his family, plays a significant part in the efficacy of Shaykh Tayyeb's particular style of local governance. This is not the place to present a technical analysis of Upper Egyptian religious experience as manifested in the lives of Upper Egyptian Sufi adherents. Such may be found in the work of Rachida Chih (1997; 1998; 2000), who worked closely with Shaykh Tayyeb and his brother Dr. Ahmad Tayyeb, the previous Grand Mufti of Egypt and the current Grand Shaykh of al-Azhar University in Cairo. A few comments may be made, however, to situate the Tayyeb dynasty squarely in the contemporary foothills landscape.

The presence of the mosque at al-Hasasna, at the intersection of the main foothills road and the road that leads to Hatshepsut's Temple, has been a landmark in a social and a vernacular sense. A new mosque has now been built several kilometers to the north at al-Suyul, accompanying the relocation of Qurnawi away from the foothills, but its move will not likely affect the spiritual or legal influence of the Tayyeb family. The spiritual roots of the Tayyeb family represent a mixture that demonstrates the fluidity that can exist between formal Islam and the Sufi schools. The family traces its roots back to Morocco and claims noble descent. Family records suggest that they settled in al-Qurna around 1865, which confirms Qurnawi claims that the al-Hasasna clan is of more recent date than the surrounding communities. The present generation is the third in a line of al Azhar–educated religious scholars. This formal aspect is intertwined with adherence to the Sufi order known as Khalwatiya to which an earlier generation was introduced while studying in Cairo. The Khalwatiya order in fact only allows shaykhs who have studied at al-Azhar to exercise spiritual leadership. As a result of this stipulation, the order is much more closely aligned with formal Islam. Emphasizing a degree of orthodox austerity, the musical aspects that form an integral part of Sufi devotion are largely absent here. Much of the esteem that surrounds the position of the present Shaykh Muhammad Tayyeb derives from two sources. First is the powerful *baraka*—the possession of spiritual gifts and the ability to bestow blessings—associated with his late father. Second is his function as the dominant player in *majlis 'urfi*, the traditional dispute settlement mechanism, which sees people come from afar to have their cases adjudicated by him rather than through the government's legal and law-enforcement means. One group of informants claimed to have also benefited from the spiritual leadership and personal *baraka* of the current Shaykh Muhammad Tayyeb, while others suggested he was still too much interested in politics and has not yet acquired the spiritual gifts that his late father had been endowed with.

William Adams has characterized Sufism as "dominated by . . . unorthodox and sometimes anti-orthodox elements" (Adams, 1977: 574), thereby positioning Sufi adherents somewhere outside the formal acceptance of orthodox Islam. It seems plausible that, through the particular quality of the Khalwatiya order, merging formal religious tenets with the acceptance of popular spirituality and incorporating rather than condemning local religious practice, a suitable vehicle emerged through which ethical precepts could be conveyed and directed toward social cohesion. Shaykh Tayyeb enjoys a legitimacy grounded in the spiritual reputation of his father on the one hand, while still embodying orthodox al-Azhar and state-approved Islam on the other. Although the shaykh—through personal political influence—is able to draw on the security apparatus of the state, he typically exercises his influence largely through the *majlis 'urfi*. Thus, a religious leader of Shaykh Muhammad Tayyeb's stature, equipped with a measure of personal tact and wisdom, can demonstrate a capacity for preventing conflict from escalating and for converting episodes of communal tension into cycles of renewed social stability. In the past, or elsewhere in Egypt today, tribal elders may have been less equipped to stop intertribal or intra-communal disputes from developing into open and uncontrolled violent conflict. In this sense, under Shaykh Muhammad Tayyeb's leadership, al-Qurna may indeed well be the "quiet place" Qurnawi claim it is.

Entangled relations: Obligation, reciprocity, social harmony
Wajib
Above, we have made the claim that the two dynamic forces mediating conflict and promoting stability in Qurnawi society are the religious socio-political leverage exercised by Shaykh Muhammad Tayyeb—especially through his use of the *majlis al-'arab* traditional system of governance and dispute settlement—and *wajib*. It is to the latter aspect that we shall now turn.

Notions of *wajib* are fluid to a degree. They will extend to close family members and more distant relations alike, the latter often also being neighbors. What expressions of *wajib* have in common is that they involve social obligations to all of them, and that the reciprocal fulfillment of those social obligations by all is in fact a duty: *wajib*. Because of this very fluidity, *wajib* takes on many forms, covering the range from what seem like simple courtesies to matters of life and death when notions of duty merge with perceptions of extended-family honor. It is in this latter form where *wajib* becomes a driving force in the perpetuation of inter-family disputes and any associated violence. Because of the myriad ways in which *wajib* is expressed, and because of the range of intensities along this 'courtesy-honor' continuum, *wajib* is more than a complex phenomenon: it is the single most salient structuring feature binding Qurnawi society together. Because of its importance, and rather than simply establishing its connections with issues of honor and conflict, in the following paragraphs the concept will be discussed in greater detail.

In their most tangible form, obligations of *wajib* involve the making of contributions toward the cost of staging public gatherings surrounding life-cycle events such as births, circumcisions, weddings, illnesses, and funerals. Offering *wajib* is not seen as a function of either wealth or poverty, although there is the potential for additional financial hardship if one is impoverished, but at its various levels of materiality *wajib* nevertheless offers a mechanism whereby community support can be expected toward both the cost and the labor required for such events. In terms of communal cooperation, the collective practice may be seen to reflect west bank Bedouin origins, where small itinerant bands will have been dependent on the cooperation and support of group members to survive in a hostile environment, both socially and physically.

People generally describe notions of *wajib* as a way of maintaining friendly relations in the village. Extending the small courtesy of paying the fare of good friends or extended family encountered during a ride in the collective taxi does maintain such friendly relations, and through reciprocated payments—a wife will tell her husband who will return the favor in due course—a measure of social cohesion is guaranteed, although the practice may be equally embarrassing for a person who finds he has insufficient funds on him to oblige. Obligations of this type will be remembered rather than recorded. The same applies to the labor of a woman, who will readily volunteer her time to neighbors and relatives to assist in the baking of bread and the preparation of food required for large-scale meals offered to guests attending celebrations or commemorations of one kind or another: she can expect to be assisted in kind when it falls to her family to stage a similar event. However, a woman's labor cannot be used as replacement for material gifts in instances where these are required.

Wajib as indebtedness

The above level of obligation contrasts with more formally treated expressions of *wajib*, where a material gift is offered in the certain expectation that a more substantial gift will be returned at an appropriate future occasion. Where occuring within the immediate family, there is a fine line between an unencumbered sharing in each others' grief and joy, and expectations of reciprocated *wajib*. When news broke that Ali's buffalo had unexpectedly died—a major financial loss of some LE2,000—Badawi and Amira, Ali's sister, immediately went to see him to offer their sympathy. No customary gifts of tea and sugar were involved this time, as there was evidently no 'account' outstanding, and there was no felt need—or available finances—to open a new one. However, when Mahmud, Badawi's brother, bought a new refrigerator for his family, his wife's sister came to offer her congratulations in the form of a crate of Fanta soft drink, a gesture recorded for future repayment.

Similarly, Ahmad Muhammad Ahmad will have kept note of the assistance offered to his family during his time in prison, establishing a new level of obligation between him and Badawi. But when Ahmad returned from having served his jail sentence in Armant, this was also an opportunity for Badawi to repay debts. When his brother Mahmud married, the family received LE10 from Ahmad, and when Mahmud returned from hospital after sustaining serious injuries during the massacre at Hatshepsut's Temple, he received two chickens, ten kilograms of sugar, four boxes of tea, and a box of rice and macaroni. After having been to Ahmad the first time to welcome him home, Badawi's second visit was to return at least a part of the products previously given. However, Badawi will return the money gift only on the occasion of the marriage of Hassan, Ahmad's eldest son, who, at fifteen, would leave that debt unpaid for some time yet.

In cases of sickness, *wajib* is offered upon a person's homecoming rather than in hospital, as used to be the case. Even so, hospital visits form part of *wajib* expectations, and occur with regular frequency, as do incidents of hospitalization. Europeans resident on the west bank have typified this tendency as attention seeking, but its certain institutional-ization—in any case limited by a family's financial position—is only one aspect of the *wajib* regime that allows Qurnawi society to perform its socially expected responsibilities, its families in due course receiving the benefits of any associated reciprocity. The noted occurrence of overpre-scribing by doctors may likewise be culturally based and not be simply a result of pharmaceutical companies' marketing strategies. Qurnawi are simply not satisfied with a doctor if they do not also receive a bag full of medication, a subconscious but legitimizing proof that the medical condi-tion indeed warranted the necessary *wajib* visits.

Wajib gifts presented to colleagues who are sick at home consist of the regular tea, sugar, cigarettes, and increasingly, packaged fruit juice. However, when one of Badawi's colleagues has to go to Cairo for medical treatment, a collection may be taken up among his workmates to help him and his family with any related expenses. While among colleagues it is considered a duty to participate, the individual gifts are not recorded, the understanding being that the patient would do the same for some-one else. The money will not be presented as a gift from colleagues but, under cover of some note written by an antiquities inspector, pretend to be a special payment from the Supreme Council of Antiquities to help its employee with expenses, this certain secrecy being one way to prevent any specific obligation of the recipient toward individual colleagues.

Depending on the individual, arrangements involving *wajib* within the family can become messy affairs, requiring flexibility among its mem-bers not to develop into resentment of one kind or another. A bachelor brother with a job and no significant commitments may give a generous present when his favorite sister gets married, but unwittingly places a burden on the extended household of her husband when the time for repayment arrives. This may be several years later, when there are chil-dren and increased expenses, which make it impossible to afford a LE140 *wajib* repayment from a monthly wage of LE150.

In a different scenario, when al-Azeb, Badawi's brother-in-law, pre-pared to marry Samiha, his Qsasiya bride, it became evident that he had budgeted insufficiently to buy his five sisters new dresses for the wedding day, expected *wajib* for the groom. Having bought a good dress for one of them, and a cheaper one for a second sister, there were no funds left for the remaining three. For the third girl this was no issue, as she had already bought herself a dress, and the fourth girl said she would do the same and not be angry, but the fifth sister was left to fend for herself. At least in part encouraged to forget about his duty toward that fifth sister by the two sisters happily making their own arrangements, matters of *wajib* may nevertheless affect relations among family members especially because of a wedding's intra-family political connotations. Elements of dress and associated prestige are important for families on display before the rest of the community, and occasions such as weddings present an opportunity for the women to show their jewelry for that very reason. For Badawi this was doubly significant, as Amira's gold would be an indication to the family of her first husband that she was being properly looked after.

Especially during weddings the complex protocols surrounding gift-giving and its reciprocal expectations emerge. Weddings are the most prominent occasion where *wajib* is 'traded': duties received on earlier occasions are repaid, with the possible exception of those received upon a birth or during sickness that may be held over for a later occasion. To this end, all parties involved keep strict records of what presents and what monies have and are being given to and received from whom, with individual gifts often dating back years. Gifts received on previous occasions must be repaid in kind with a more valuable gift when opportunities such as weddings arise. Long-standing debts may thus be settled, but the increase will again be recorded as the first new gift, thereby establishing again a relationship of indebtedness. *Wajib* gifts traditionally consist of sugar, tea, cigarettes, and money, but other food items and even goats or a buffalo calf may also be presented. Flour was previously given as *wajib*, but is now considered too heavy. Money is only given at weddings. Part of the tea and sugar will be consumed in the course of the festivities, but most will be kept for later use or directed toward similar gifts on future occasions. Because of their durability, tea and sugar may also be sold for cash. The payment is made by the head of the household, on behalf of its members, although the gifts themselves are taken by the female members of the household. Thus, a procession of women, either in small groups or individually, may be seen walking in the direction of the house where the wedding takes place, their black *fustan* a stark contrast against the sunlit limestone, one arm raised, supporting plastic bags with tea and sugar on their heads.

Wedding festivities take place on Wednesdays, Thursdays, and Fridays. On Thursday the bride and groom hold respective parties in their parents' homes, with only those attending who actually know the bride

Musicians performing at a wedding on the evening of the first day. Such small rural musical ensembles performing at weddings are now increasingly being replaced by disc jockeys playing earsplitting recorded music.

or groom or their families. Invitations to attend a wedding may come by mouth or via a printed invitation, but will always be closely linked with the recorded names of those to whom the bride or groom and their families had previously presented gifts. Upon arrival, gifts of tea and sugar are brought and handed to the mother of the bride or groom who, assisted by family members taking turns, records the amount of *wajib* and the name of the giver in a notebook. Although the household is represented by one of its women, she may indicate individual names of household members who have offered the gift, and it is their names that are recorded.[11]

Come Friday morning, the newlywed couple will be situated in the house of the groom, that is, the house of his father. Now gifts of money only will be presented, again by a female representative, to the mother of the groom and the mother of the bride respectively. She places the money in a box, indicating the amount and specifying the names of contributing family members to an attendant who keeps records. Despite this distinction between contributing members from the one household, eventually all monies so recorded will repay an old debt or

Sister and father of the groom receiving and recording *wajib* gifts of tea and sugar.

create a new one against the relevant household, rather than specific occupants or family members.

When Badawi's brother, Mahmud, returned home from hospital in Cairo after having been seriously wounded during the Luxor Massacre, Sayyed 'Abd al-Rasul presented the family with ten kilograms of sugar and four boxes of tea. These gifts were not for Mahmud personally, but were presented to the extended household of elderly parents and two married sons. Since he is the eldest and therefore the head of the household, the responsibility to repay would fall to Badawi. With Sayyed 'Abd al-Rasul's wedding, the time came for Badawi to repay his debt with fifteen kilograms of sugar and six boxes of tea. If Badawi has money, he will settle his outstanding *wajib* payments and any additional gifts that have to be offered. If he has no money he will sit down with his brother Mahmud and his mother to discuss who pays what.

The role of the mother here is important, both because she is old and wise, but also because she is the mother of the two boys who still share the house together. This form of maternal dispute settlement is not specific to Badawi's family, but occurs Qurna-wide. Her mediation would be especially valuable at this time. Tension between Badawi and Mahmud had arisen from Mahmud's interest in moving his family to a new house that the Luxor City Council and the Supreme Council of Antiquities had offered him at al-Suyul, in exchange for leaving the necropolis. Such a move would disadvantage Badawi, who already has a reduced income because of alimony payments he has to make to his first wife. When living in separate homes, it would have become Mahmud's responsibility to repay any gifts received as the head of an independent household. But were he to move now, repayment of the gifts received during Mahmud's homecoming to his former al-Hurubat household would still be Badawi's responsibility. If Mahmud were to do the honorable thing and be a "good boy," he would offer to help repay outstanding *wajib* associated with his homecoming. But Badawi could not ask for his help, leaving it to his mother to subtly mediate for Mahmud's awareness and cooperation.

In the absence of money to make the repayments, and if on friendly terms with the family to whom *wajib* is owed, arrangements can be made to make the payment in, say, two months. If such cannot be arranged, then money may be borrowed, the children's gold earrings and some of the women's gold jewelry may be sold, or sugar and tea may be purchased on credit from one of the small grocery shops that a number of people operate from within their homes. If repayment of outstanding *wajib* commitments is refused altogether, seven days will be allowed to pass before the mother of the bride will come over to the debtor's house to ask why he (or his wife or mother) did not come to the party, and the outstanding *wajib* will be claimed. To heap greater shame on the person, he or she may be addressed by the bride's mother in the market, for everyone to see, with families having long memories about such incidents: Amira's maternal aunt had once addressed a person this way, grabbing the lady by the front of her dress and obviously making a scene to attract as much public attention as possible. Such stories also have a didactic purpose, instructing children about the sensitivities and possible punishments if long-standing conventions are ignored. As such, these conventions are inherently social, binding the community together through bonds of mutual obligation, with those who decline heaping shame upon themselves. Even so, sentiments among the younger generation about *wajib* remain ambivalent, with several who consider themselves 'modern' having dropped the custom. Two of these, brothers, see in their mother and brother sufficient traditional representation, an implicit acknowledgment that they nevertheless find a sense of security in its continuity. Others in the same age group, by contrast, actively pursue the tradition.

Wajib monies are used by the parents to pay off debts incurred by them in preparation for the wedding, with money going to the mother of the bride and the father of the groom. Before the wedding, the father of the groom checks how much money he has, which was saved from the groom's income toward his own wedding expenses. The wedding in total may cost him LE6,000 or LE7,000. If he only has LE3,000 available, he buys what he can, including the bedroom furniture, with the groom deciding on style and decoration. The outstanding balance is to be paid on the Friday afternoon following receipt of the *wajib* monies. Beforehand, the father counts his records to see what he can expect from *wajib* repayments. Any monies received from the sale of sugar will go toward the outstanding balance.

As a case study, the arrangements made for Badawi's first wedding in July 1984 are instructive. His mother participated in the various arrangements rather than his father, who was less business-minded. Expenditures included: LE700 for bedroom furniture; LE500 to the father of the bride; LE300 for the party; LE200 for clothes for himself, parents, sisters, and their children, which Badawi was required to buy; LE200 for two pairs of

Musicians performing at a wedding on the morning of the third day.

gold bracelets; LE100 for cigarettes and taxis; with LE100 kept by Badawi to pay the Qur'an reader and to have money in his pocket for incidental expenses during the first seven days of marriage. The total projected expenditure was LE2,100. Badawi contributed his savings of LE800, and a count of family *wajib* records revealed some previously contributed LE600 that was expected to be returned as LE1,000. This left LE300 still needed, which Badawi's mother borrowed from private contacts of hers, using these funds as down payments for the various other purchases to be made. Each month Badawi repaid her LE25, which his mother in turn repaid to her creditor. No interest was charged.

Gift-giving associated with *wajib* at al-Qurna is not looked upon as a redistribution of wealth. In fact, it often places considerable hardship on households when repayments need to be made: weddings are frequently celebrated during the hot summer months, exactly at a time when foreign archaeological missions are absent from the necropolis and tourism revenues experience their seasonal downturn. Yet, gift giving through *wajib* contributions do represent an element of saving, with the anticipated return of those accumulated savings a central resource in the planning and financing of some future family event. If there are no unforeseen

The bridal couple present themselves on the morning of the third day.

incidents—illness being one catalyst for the untimely return of those savings—then one could indeed plan for the future marriage of a child although, as with all savings, financial constraints will still limit the extent to which new 'accounts' can be opened.[12]

If savings represent a strategic use of money designed to meet some future purpose, then *wajib* conventions may also be manipulated politically in order to control access to funds. Generally, these are the little tactics designed to hasten or delay the repayment of outstanding debts, or to foster money-saving or money-generating forms of interpersonal goodwill.

At the lower end of the scale and at the margin of formal *wajib* requirements, incidental presents may be given to cement friendly relations, as a result of which some future benefit may be expected. Some cigarettes and whiskey purchased for a young policeman on duty near Ramose's tomb was ostensibly to repay the gift of hospitality which his father, who came from al-Hurubat but who now lives in Cairo, had extended to Badawi when he had stayed in Cairo during his brother's hospitalization there. But receiving the goods on behalf of his father, the present was effectively for the policeman himself who, empowered to limit the activities of peddlers of whom Badawi was one, might thus be encouraged to turn a blind eye, his willingness to do so having direct economic benefits. Similarly, drinks bought by Badawi for a villager who was also an officer with the Security Police in Luxor helped to obtain leniency with his next quarterly payment to the children of his first wife. Unable to make the payment in one amount, the cost of a few drinks would enable him to make the payments in multiple and smaller amounts.

Closer to the spirit of *wajib*, a person indebted may assess to some degree the conditions at hand and the need for him to make repayments. For instance, if *wajib* might be contributed to one who organizes a *dhikr* on the occasion of *mulid al-nabi*, the month-long celebrations on account of the birth of the Prophet, then the obligation to bring sugar, tea, or money is less stringent, despite any outstanding debts, and there is not the same compulsion to repay as is the case with a funeral or marriage, especially if the *dhikr* host is rich. It may then be decided to reciprocate when there is such a situation, for example the wedding of a son or daughter. However, in these instances the principle requirement to fulfil *wajib* when invited is to attend, even if it is only to be seen shaking hands with the host. While there is a certain compulsion therefore to attend, irrespective of gifts, at least those functions that take place in outlying areas do guarantee a free meal. Which is not to say that the compulsion to attend *dhikr* in outlying places cannot have significant moral weight as well: attending a *dhikr* for a man who died a year ago in a town far south of the foothills was essential for Badawi, since the deceased man's son, who lives in Cairo, had never left Mahmud's bedside when he was recovering from his injuries in Cairo after the Luxor Massacre.

At other times, outstanding commitments may be 'cashed in' when there is the perception that the person to whom a loan was extended is in a position to make the repayment, especially when the initial benefactor is trying to make ends meet during a poor season. A variant on this theme would be when past favors extended to a relative or neighbor may be remembered, even if the debt has been repaid, and its goodwill used to ask for a favor in return. The fact that past or current creditors seem to appear out of nowhere when there are indications of financial capacity suggests that the phenomenon of *wajib* and the dominance of obligation, reciprocity, and communal expectations that characterizes the social environment at al-Qurna also serves as an equalizing force when relative prosperity and cyclical hardship are experienced within the community at the same time.

Wajib as service

One particular form of *wajib* contributions are those associated with the life of the *zawiya*, the communal space for use by extended families and neighborhood groups, with members contributing financially and with time and labor toward its material and social upkeep. *Zawiya* is also the name applied to those spaces that specifically pertain to the activities of the various Sufi orders, whose emergence and disappearance has been described by Rachida Chih (1997a). These were the very places that characterized spirituality in the necropolis, which, through the absence of formal liturgical architecture, caused such early archaeologists as Belzoni and Rhind to remain ignorant of Qurnawi spirituality.[13]

Any spirituality associated with the necropolis' *zawiya* during the late 1990s appeared of secondary importance, a situation possibly explained by the orthodoxy of the Khalwatiya order: Friday prayers were said either in the mosque at al-Hasasna, or in the small mosque near Ramose's tomb in al-Hurubat. At al-Qurna, a *zawiya* could still be used occasionally for the *dhikr*, the trance-inducing communal swaying and chanting that is the most visible act of Sufi devotion. These may be held at one of the *zawiya*s in al-Hurubat when particular individually experienced events—for example, acquittal in a court case—require a particular kind of spiritual celebration, which, through the associated expenses, is both feast and sacrifice. They are also held in August during the *mulid* of Shaykh 'Abd al-Qurna, one of the west bank village festivals, which, linked with the birthday or death day of locally revered holy men, are celebrated throughout Egypt (Atia and Sonbol, 1999).

The primary function of *zawiya*s at al-Qurna is for family gatherings after a funeral, when for a period of three days villagers, relations, and acquaintances from far and wide come to express their sympathy, the necessary *wajib* taken there by the men, or delivered to the house of the deceased by the women. Such death duty is paid to the eldest son or the immediate family of the deceased, but can be paid later if resources are not available. During these events, and assisted by non-kin neighbors belonging to a different *zawiya*, those who count themselves as members of the *zawiya* community act as hosts, their presence worked out on a rostered basis.

Unless otherwise known to guests, members of the *zawiya* community are indistinguishable from close family of the deceased and offer a welcoming handshake to newcomers, who may not specifically know or seek out close relatives to extend condolences. People quietly listen to the Qur'anic recitations, and softly converse during the breaks, with those in attendance offering glasses of water. When a person is ready to leave he arises and proclaims that *al-Fatihah* will be said, upon which everyone stands and joins in, barely audible and seemingly taking less time than the length of the passage would allow. Closing with *amin*, the person simply states a parting greeting—*salam 'alaykum*—and walks out.

Zawiya members are also jointly responsible for supplying large aluminum *sunniya* trays of food during mealtimes for the family of the deceased and those guests who live too far away to go home and eat. Relations, neighbors, or friends who have moved away from the mountain are still considered Hurubati in their new environment, and invitations in both directions must be responded to as *wajib*. For each of the ten *zawiya* members on duty, feeding such guests involves the preparation of four *sunniya*, two for lunch and two for dinner, to be equally distributed between the men in the *zawiya* and the women gathering elsewhere. The respective households on duty are to provide these meals from their own resources, as part of their *wajib* for the immediate family of the deceased, and in addition to the sugar and tea already offered to them. Served to guests and representing the hospitality of the *zawiya* community, the meal provided must be up to standard and include meat. Apart from the certain shame that noncompliance would incur, failure to fulfil these *zawiya* obligations attracts a fine of LE50 payable to the *shaykh al-zawiya*, which will be used by him for the further upkeep of the *zawiya*.

The entire process of managing the *zawiya* during times of public mourning has been one where, at least as perceived by outsiders, the *zawiya* community has effectively presented itself as one family. In the case of Badawi's *zawiya*, use of the proviso 'effectively' is especially appropriate, with a number of different families making use of, and jointly operating, their communal space. Still named after its founder, *zawiyat bayt Abu Ahmad Ali Raba*, who built it for his family, the *zawiya* now comprises thirty households, long since the result from a request by other Hurubati in the al-Khukha area to be allowed to use it. The *zawiya* itself consists of a walled area between the houses of Mahmud Ahmad Muhammad Yusuf and old Raba, its western end roofed to make two small rooms used for storing the public address system, to make tea, and for use by the Qur'an reader during the three-day wake.

Each family pays LE1 per month for the upkeep of the *zawiya*, their contribution called *jama'iya*, a term that conveys things done together. The money is collected by the *shaykh al-zawiya*, a title that is entirely secular in intent and significance, incorporating duties of both president and treasurer. He keeps the money at home, for ready use when there is a death in the community. At that time, ten kilograms of sugar, one kilogram of tea, and an additional amount of money are given to the family of the deceased. Only in recent years has the practice of offering cigarettes and tea to *zawiya* guests attending formalities on the occasion of a death ceased, in favor of a handshake and a glass of water only.

As and when necessary, representatives of the member families meet at the *zawiya* to discuss relevant issues, with Shaykh Ibrahim, the *shaykh al-zawiya* and one of the guards at Menna's tomb, acting as chairperson and a scribe taking the minutes. The *zawiya* meeting—also called *jama'iya*—of June 1999 was a lively affair, with a sizeable business agenda. Incidental expenses for upkeep in the form of blue paint for the *deqas* and other repairs had been incurred, the *deqas* costing LE75 for paint and LE30 for labor; the twice-repaired microphone LE35 and LE65; and the purchase of two new keys and locks LE30. These expenses were to be paid for separately,

Tarpaulin serving as shade cloth or partition in a *zawiya* during the three-day wake and commemorative *dhikr*.

with each member family having had to contribute LE14. In addition, LE10 was now requested to replace the old mud-brick kitchen with a new one. Further monies would be required to buy new glasses and *butagaz*, also for the new kitchen. All these issues required lengthy discussion, the most heated topic being the one that necessitated the new locks. Recently, items had been disappearing, including several mats that had been taken for use by a different *zawiya* but not returned. It was decided that Shaykh Ibrahim should be in charge of the keys, requiring his presence during which he could also count any items lent to others. Volunteers were invited to help collect funds and purchase the various items. The meeting concluded with an instantly organized team of volunteers commencing with the work of demolishing the old kitchen. Its members carried off the mud-brick rubble in equipment otherwise used by archaeological basket boys, water and tea was brought out to drink, sweaty arms turning the dust into mud and bringing a different discipline's fieldworker on board of what seemed like one of the mountain's archaeological excavation teams. A procession of donkey-pulled water carts bringing supplies to turn the finer rubble into mud for leveling the floor completed the building preparations for now. During the work the sounds of some other commemorative *dhikr* came drifting across the foothills. While both funerals and such a *dhikr*—held to mark the first forty days and the first year of a person's passing—constitute *wajib*, events that involve one's own *zawiya* community take precedence over attending those elsewhere.

Especially during the summer months there is intense social activity resulting from frequent weddings, but neither is there much reprieve throughout the remainder of the year, with episodes of sickness, death, the recurring commemorative *dhikr*, and the fulfillment of expected obligations in the community of the *zawiya* all making their demands in one form or another. Thus, life in the necropolis continues to be a procession of *wajib*, generating and relieving economic hardship at the same time as it establishes and maintains close social bonds both in the local hamlet and across the dispersed settlements of the Theban foothills as a whole.

Beyond the immediate economic implications of this regime, the significance of these *wajib* and *zawiya* institutions is that they unite the community both across extended family lines and between non-kin groups who are also members of the same *zawiya*. Social cohesion generated through mutual bonds of obligation and bonds of cooperation, however, can be a force for good as much as it has the potential to be an inflammatory factor during times of communal tension. For example, extended family and neighborhood networks aligning themselves in a perceived common cause, where defense of the group's honor and its members may be seen as a duty and thus equated with *wajib*, can quickly escalate conflict to proportions at which uncontrolled open violence will result.

It is during such circumstances that the political and spiritual influence of Shaykh Muhammad Tayyeb, and his role in the traditional dispute settlement mechanism of the *majlis al-'arab*, is made manifest. As such, it provides one aspect of the powerful position of the Tayyeb family in al-Qurna. Herbert Winlock, field director for the Metropolitan Museum of Art Egyptian Expedition during his excavations at Dayr al-Bahari had picked up on the powerful influence of Shaykh Tayyeb from his Qurnawi workmen but, as was argued in Chapter 1, only made reference to that influence in the context of his archaeological operations, glossing over the ethnographic context of his field site, seemingly neither cognizant of nor understanding the rich social dynamics of his surroundings (Winlock, 1942: 41).

Because of the *wajib* obligations they bring with them, multiple wedding invitations can impose a significant burden on the family budget, especially during the summer months when primary or supplementary earnings from tourism are likely to be reduced.

Also in Chapter 1, we observed how Christiane Desroches-Noblecourt, in her account of the discovery of the tomb of Tutankhamun, portrayed the Theban Necropolis as an area of "kings and brigands," where "its workmen and inhabitants regarded the old kings and their treasures as their own rightful heritage" (Desroches-Noblecourt, 1963: 56). But her observation that "such, then, was the setting, the atmosphere, in which the Egyptologists camping upon the west bank of Thebes lived and worked" (Desroches-Noblecourt, 1963: 57) was, not unlike Winlock's, necessarily distorted for her omission to adequately reflect some of the social dynamics that guide life on the west bank. This chapter has provided some greater definition of this setting, and we may now turn to the way 'the Egyptologists and its workmen and inhabitants live and work' in the necropolis.

8

All in a Season's Work: Egyptology-Induced Labor Relations at al-Hurubat[1]

Two houses and estranged neighbors

Among the houses of al-Hurubat, two earlier dwellings were imbued with symbolism. The two were very different. Sir John Gardner Wilkinson's house was essentially a tomb dwelling, expanded with mud-brick structures and partitions erected in the courtyard, as inspired by the practice of his Qurnawi neighbors (Thompson, 1996; 2010: 206–207). The nearby 1817 house built for Henry Salt's collecting agent Giovanni d'Athanasi ('Yanni') was a freestanding, aboveground, mud-brick structure, most likely constructed from ancient bricks obtained from the surrounding necropolis. Their difference was not only architectural, they were also in stark contrast conceptually. Wilkinson's tomb dwelling provided a base for an epigraphic study of the surrounding tombs, Yanni's mud-brick house was essentially a collecting point for and a staging post in the movement of antiquities. That the house itself had become central in the acquisition of antiquities is evident from a mid-1820s description by Edward William Lane, himself residing at Wilkinson's tomb house where he is likely to have penned these impressions:

> On entering this [Yanni's] house for the first time, I was surprised to see doors, shutters, shelves, &c formed of the materials of mummy-chests, covered with paintings. . . . Upon a table lay a small blanket full of round cakes of bread, also taken from an ancient tomb; & appearing quite fresh. Many other antiquities were in the room. (Lane, 2000: 339; also quoted in Thompson, 1992: 105 and Thompson 2010: 161)

Modern Qurnawi, the people whose very ancestors located and deposited in Yanni's house the antiquities observed there by Lane, have

219

been unable to fully extricate themselves from a history of having worked for Yanni and collecting agents like him. Its legacy, reinforced by other antiquities-related episodes, has clouded perceptions about them as a people and has influenced the rationale employed to justify their relocation from the foothills.

As part of this process, both houses in all their differences have come to serve as a metaphor for the spheres of interest that compete over the surrounding landscape. As has been mentioned, Yanni's house possibly came to represent an early blueprint for the gradually evolving aboveground village. But in their linked associations, Yanni's house may be seen not only as representative of the gradually developing vernacular urban infrastructure of the foothills hamlets. Ultimately, the phenomenon of these aboveground dwellings and their occupants has collectively also encompassed the negative perceptions attached to their involvement in antiquities. By contrast, Wilkinson's house and work have come to symbolize non-destructive epigraphic and archaeological research and the protection of the necropolis' tombs. By extension, opposing views with respect to the surrounding landscape may be seen embedded in the history of both houses, one signaling the perceived longtime, persistent, and resisting presence of a resident indigenous community steeped in a history of alleged illicit activity, the other signifying conservation and heritage management objectives.

Today, there is little to remind the informed visitor of the presence of Wilkinson's house other than the original tomb and a section of mud-brick wall that remains to the side of its courtyard.[2] In line with its above symbolic quality, the tomb of 'Amechu and designated as TT83 is now a closed and protected tomb. Maintaining the above opposition, and following the demolition of the foothills hamlets, the remains of Yanni's house were bulldozed in March 2009 by Luxor City Council workers. Its final destruction brought closure—the first house to be built, one of the last houses to be destroyed—to the much maligned human occupation of the foothills, and represented a further loss of a historically and culturally significant feature there.

Nevertheless, for those who know their location, the close spatial proximity of the two former houses continues to embody an element of the above-stated opposition, namely between resident or visiting archaeologists who, following the example set by Wilkinson, use regional west bank headquarters as an integral structural feature of their field operations, and the once tomb-dwelling population of Qurnawi who adopted vernacular architectural forms conceptually at least in part inspired by Yanni's house.[3]

Symbolized by the methodological opposition of both house types, and despite their shared history and mutual dependence, both communities—archaeologists and Qurnawi—and the different interests they represent, have largely viewed each other with suspicion. Practicing field archaeologists have long viewed the presence of a local community as an anomaly.[4] Qurnawi themselves have now been relocated into new communities at some distance from the foothills, where their red-brick and concrete houses continue to remind them of the economic and political power of the ancient monuments.

Elements of that suspicion may be found reflected in the derogatory tone of early-twentieth-century Egyptological writing, referred to earlier. Apart from the particular mindset and colonial sentiments of the time, which will have informed and colored such writing, as has been argued, the individual personalities of some of the principal characters involved may well have been as significant in this relationship as was the historical context in which the interaction with local community members developed and took place. The rather scathing language used by Sir Alan Gardiner could indicate that for some academics interaction with locals did not necessarily come naturally (Gardiner and Weigall, 1913: 8–11). As a philologist, he had spent much time among the Tombs of the Nobles, first alongside Arthur Weigall during the 1909–10 season, and by himself during the 1911–13 winter seasons (Hankey, 2001: 135, 163, 172, 195), working on their co-authored *Topographical Catalogue of the Private Tombs of Thebes*. Despite their close collaboration and personal friendship (Hankey, 2001: 139), the introductory text was written by Gardiner and the tone of the language was his. Notwithstanding the shared fieldwork experiences that underpinned its content, the documented history surrounding its publication indicates that there was little or no literary influence on the part of Weigall (Hankey, 2001: 195–96). Given the opportunity, Arthur Weigall, as inspector-general of antiquities for Upper Egypt and responsible for the protection of the Theban tombs, might have had cause to similarly express himself in strong terms. Yet, when he did eventually write about Qurnawi, and despite his at times condescending attitude, Weigall nevertheless maintained a generally sympathetic attitude toward and "in defence of the Theban thieves" (Weigall, 1923: 224–35; 258–77).[5]

In fact, Weigall's attitude may well be the more typical, reflecting those of other Egyptologists who also worked there and who were personally acquainted with the inhabitants of the surrounding villages. Zakaria Goneim, who was chief inspector for the west bank from 1943 and chief inspector of antiquities for Upper Egypt during 1946–51, initially "hated them bitterly" but acknowledges that "having worked among them for so long, I have come to like them, in spite of myself" (Cottrell, 1950: 144). A contemporary of Gardiner and Weigall—and on the evidence of it something of a mentor for Weigall in his relations with local communities (Hankey, 2001: 50)—Howard Carter spoke their language, lived among them, and socialized with Qurnawi. He reflected in his writing less on the relative merit or otherwise of their society and he also adopted a more sympathetic and seemingly less critical stance (James, 1992: 94–95, 130–31). Carter's account of being offered to buy antiquities from a pharaonic tomb and the subsequent negotiations over the location of the tomb of Amenophis I in Dra' Abu al-Naga with Gad Hassan, a Qurnawi from al-Tarif, is indicative of his non-judgmental attitude and demonstrates his ability to obtain satisfactory outcomes for both parties:

> My problem, therefore, was what would be an adequate reward for a tomb open in all probability since dynastic times and thoroughly plundered? . . . I therefore made up my mind to offer a sufficiently tempting though comparatively small sum for showing me the tomb, with a promise that if anything of real value was found in it he would be adequately repaid. . . . "Good!" I said to Gad Hassân, "Go in peace! Make up your mind, and come and tell me your decision to-morrow!" Adding, as a parting word, "Of course you will be engaged to oversee the work!" . . . And here I must observe that my surmise was correct. For early the following morning Gad Hassân was outside my house awaiting me. (Carter Notebook 17, autobiographical sketch XI: 204–205, 209–10)[6]

Carter's approach also suggests that interpersonal and relational differences will have caused opportunities to go begging in instances where archaeologists were less accommodating and sympathetic than Carter: by their failing to tap into local knowledge, by not accepting the reality of local illicit activities, and by not negotiating outcomes that left something for both sides.[7] The use of condescending language to depict the activities of local villagers may have been inspired by Gardiner and Weigall's personal attitudes and particular experiences or by more broadly held views current during the early decades of the twentieth century, but it also reveals that not all Egyptologists working on the Theban west bank had the flexibility to make the best of a bad situation.

Also because of these dynamics, archaeological labor in the past has not always been dependable for Qurnawi. Indeed, William Flinders Petrie bypassed Qurnawi workers altogether, preferring excavators from the village of Quft whom he had trained personally, thereby establishing the historical basis for an ongoing animosity between the two communities (Petrie, 1897: 2; 1909: 1).[8] Today, work for Egyptian and foreign archaeological missions contributes toward the household budgets of many families and, along with other archaeology-related employment, represents an important element of village economics at al-Qurna.

Two archaeologies: Foreign missions and the Supreme Council of Antiquities

During a time when foreign archaeological practice was still synonymous with colonial influence, foreign archaeologists worked under the auspices of the French-controlled Service des antiquités. After Egyptian independence in 1922, archaeological practice was increasingly brought under the control of Egyptian government officials.[9] Today, a clear distinction may be made between archaeological practice conducted by the Egyptian Supreme Council of Antiquities (SCA)[10] and seasonal foreign archaeological missions working in Egypt. For Egyptian officials, in political and administrative terms the distinction does not exist: the SCA—an autonomous body within the Egyptian Ministry of Culture—controls and views itself as executing all archaeological research and heritage management operations. It accepts foreign research proposals and has discretionary powers in issuing excavation concessions. It approves the individual members of foreign archaeological missions, and it stipulates the conditions (including reporting and publication as well as technical and conservation requirements) under which these missions carry out their work. All finds are retained by Egypt, although a specimen may be temporarily exported for purposes of dating or other technical investigations if facilities that are unavailable in Egypt are required to carry out the task. The Egyptian media releases issued to the international news agencies will generally advise that discoveries have been made by the SCA, even if the project was one conducted by a foreign mission. Reports and specialist publications by those foreign missions credit the SCA, even if in practical terms—other than the necessary approvals and the presence of an SCA inspector—their involvement has been negligible. However, the SCA also conducts its own field operations, which are entirely independent from the work of foreign missions. Different approaches to fieldwork practice by foreign and Egyptian teams also include aspects of Qurnawi employment, and in the following the distinction between Egyptian and foreign archaeological work will be maintained.

Working for *al-Athar*: Qurnawi and the Supreme Council of Antiquities

According to the 1981 World Bank-funded Arthur D. Little consulting study of tourism development on the Luxor west bank, "the Antiquities Organization (Gourna Inspectorate) has a long policy of hiring, as far as possible, west bank inhabitants in guarding and repair/construction positions" (ADL, 1981a: XIII–8; 1983: VIII–3). The study documents that at that time, out of a total of 208 positions, 196 were occupied by west bank inhabitants. It is likely that there were some Ba'irati included in the west bank group but it was most likely predominantly Qurnawi (ADL, 1981a: XIII–9; 1983: VIII–4). During 1998–99, that figure approached some five hundred west bank employees: 196 guards; 115 conservators/restorers; seventeen inspectors; twenty administrative staff; 150 engineering department personnel, the latter including excavation laborers, and construction laborers maintaining access paths and protective walls around tomb entrances; tomb cleaners; drivers; and a number of unskilled laborers or those charged with certain general duties ("getting water for the trees outside the *taftish* office"). The figures are somewhat fluid, especially among conservation, engineering, and excavation staff, due to the casual employment of extra personnel for projects that may only last until the end of the fiscal year (June 30). The available budget for the west bank inspectorate during 1999–2000 totaled LE5 million: LE2 million for conservation and restoration work; LE2 million for maintenance and engineering work; and LE1 million for archaeological excavation projects. Regular government salaries come from the Ministry of Finance, and do not affect the SCA's west bank operational budget. Tourism and Antiquities Police fall under the Ministry of the Interior.

Rather than being stood down, casual workers may choose to continue to work without pay beyond June 30, thereby retaining their positions until the new budget has been announced. They are keen to obtain permanent contracts, which means increased pay, paid annual leave, and periodic bonus payments, or *hawafaz*. Permanent positions for guard vacancies at archaeological sites are advertised annually during April in the national press, requiring the applicant to go to Cairo to register, before receiving an invitation to apply formally and sit for an interview. Casual workers are employed from local contacts and people already known to the SCA's west bank inspectorate.

Guard duties are distributed across three zones, each under the responsibility of a *shaykh al-ghaffir*: (1) Valley of the Kings, al-Tarif, Dra' Abu al-Naga, and Seti I Temple; (2) Hatshepsut's Temple, Ramesseum Temple, and the Tombs of the Nobles; (3) Valley of the Queens, Malqata, Madinat Habu, Dayr al-Madina, Qurnat Mar'ai, and the Memnon Colossi. Staffing numbers will vary per site,[11] but guard groups assigned to the Tombs of the Nobles at al-Hurubat generally comprise four persons for a group of tombs allocated to them. The guards work twenty-four-hour shifts from six in the morning to six the following morning on alternate days. Their daytime duties carried out between six in the morning and six in the evening are rotated every two to three hours. The daytime tasks include two guards assigned to active tourist duty whenever a tomb is open to visitors; one guard inspects tickets and the other guard accompanies visitors inside the tomb. Two guards are assigned to general tomb surveillance and cooking duty in the *ghaffir* hut, during which they take turns to rest. The remainder of their shift consists of two watches, one from six in the evening to midnight and another from midnight to six in the evening. The guards divide the night watches between the two-man groups. During each watch period, one party patrols the tombs while the other party sleeps. Their group is reinforced by two armed guards during the night shift: one a member of the Tourism and Antiquities Police, the other an SCA guard armed with a large-gauge shotgun, as we have already seen in the case of Ahmad Muhammad Ahmad. The placement of guards at respective sites is not dependent on seniority, even though the guard at the tomb of Tutankhamun is always an older person. During 1999, the then chief inspector for the west bank favored relatively short rotations across the various sites.

The calculation of permanent wages is complex. Badawi works as a conservator/restorer on the maintenance and conservation of temples and decorated tombs. He receives a base salary that is defined by his employee rank number, which relates to his years of service: the lower the number, the greater the years of service. Every six years of employment reduces the rating by one rank. The relative rank defines not only the base salary, but also the annual pay increase. Thus Badawi, who by 1998 had fourteen years of experience and is ranked number nine, earns LE150 per month (an arbitrary average, given the variables, listed below, that operate), he receives an additional monthly bonus payment of LE70 (in Badawi's case, the maximum possible, also see below), and an annual increase of LE6. However, his colleague Mahmud Ahmad Muhammad Yusuf, who has seventeen years of service and is ranked number eight, receives a basic wage of LE180 per month, an additional bonus payment of LE70, and a yearly increase of LE14.

At 1998 levels, Badawi's monthly base pay consisted of LE68.50, which includes deductions of LE6.50 for medical insurance and LE7 for old-age pension entitlements. Additional payments include a LE10 children's allowance, a supplement of LE10 for each of his first three children (living with his first wife from whom he is separated), and LE10 toward the cost of three train journeys to Cairo per year, amounting to a total basic monthly wage of LE118.50. The monthly bonus payment is variable and appears relative to SCA tourist receipts. Bonus payments at rates of 100 or 80 percent of base pay (LE68.50) are not uncommon but cannot be relied upon and may sometimes not be available altogether. If he were paid 80 percent of his net base pay, Badawi's monthly salary would amount to no more than LE173.30. Maintenance payments to his first wife of LE90 (LE30 for her and LE20 to each of the three children from his first marriage) would leave him with a net expendable income of LE83.30 for the month. Sharing the family house with his elderly parents and married brother, Badawi's contribution toward the upkeep of the house is payment of the monthly electricity bill, which at LE17, leaves him with only LE66.30 per month to support his new wife and their two young children, including food, schooling, *wajib* commitments, transport, cigarettes, and payments to his lawyer in al-Tarif who mediates between Badawi and his former wife. Since a divorce-settlement payment to be made to his ex-wife would be in the order of LE800 and well beyond his carrying capacity, there would be little opportunity for Badawi to reduce the monthly maintenance payments. Against this background, and in the absence of any land ownership or agricultural involvement, Badawi's reliance on supplementary income derived from peddling artifacts to tourists at the nearby tomb of Ramose becomes understandable. Upon retirement he would receive a lump-sum payment amounting to seventy-two months of his last received base pay, and a monthly pension equal to the value of his final salary's base pay. It is because of these provisions that formal government work is popular on the west bank, providing a degree of old-age security after a career where most other informal income-earning activities were either unpredictable or seasonal, and in most cases insufficient to prepare for retirement.

As a restorer with fourteen years of experience, Badawi has traveled to various archaeological sites around Egypt to participate in conservation projects, including the temple of Abu Simbel. But his career is primarily focused on the monuments of Thebes, where different projects may have him posted for several months at a time to Madinat Habu, Dayr al-Madina, the Ramesseum, or individual tombs in the foothills. During 1999, his work was concentrated on the tomb of Amenemope (TT41), a monument of considerable importance and extensively published (Assmann, 1991; Kampp, 1996: 235–37). The project was conveniently located in close proximity to Badawi's house, which enabled him to get tea for his colleagues during the morning break. The objective of the conservation was to clean and stabilize the tomb structure and its decorations. Apart from its significance for Egyptology, TT41 is also beautiful and it is possible that the tomb of Amenemope will be opened for tourists to visit once the work of conservation and restoration has been completed.

While the work requires specialist skills, it is not labor-intensive, and Badawi himself acknowledges that "we don't work so much, because restoration is slow work." Such may especially be the case at temple sites, where workers proceed under the supervision of a *ra'is*, a foreman, but often in the absence of an antiquities inspector, and where a day's work may comprise no more than half or one hour of dedicated activity: "If the inspector comes while you sit back, you look at your work and you say you are thinking about it." This is not to say that the work of tomb conservation proceeds any faster. Although another *ra'is* under whom Badawi had worked previously was keen for him to return to Dayr al-Madina to assist in the restoration of tombs damaged by the 1994 floods, the *ra'is* at TT41 seemed inclined to go slowly rather than change to a less convenient location.

In contrast with temple sites, at TT41 the inspector is always present, since he is the one who has the key to open the tomb. Pending

Supreme Council of Antiquities restorers at work in the tomb of Amenemope, TT41, the inspector at left.

his arrival in the morning, the workers group together in a shady spot, and at 7:30AM their names are registered in an attendance book kept by a clerk from the *taftish* office, who visits the foothills locations anywhere work is in progress. Not infrequently, the inspector fails to turn up, having been assigned for the day to some other location requiring his supervision, such as the demolition of a recently vacated foothills house.[12] Since he does not have the authority to send his restorers home, there is no point for him to travel to the other location and inform the workers that there will be no work on that day, and they are simply left waiting until it becomes evident no work is going to be done on that day and they all go home. The restorers accept this for what it is: doing nothing is no problem for them, and they are content to "sit in the shade, taking our rest, talking."

But when restorers do work, they acknowledge that they "work hard," even if only for short spells, after which they may either forego their morning tea break to stop work at half past ten in the morning, or take it easy. As government workers, they see themselves as not very different from clerical staff in government offices, "where people do some work, then sit around for long times," and suggesting a reasonably relaxed work environment also for those employed as restorers with the Supreme Council of Antiquities.

The routine completion of the attendance register is easily manipulated. If Badawi turns up late, his *ra'is* may vouch for him. Or the *ra'is* can choose to be flexible, and will regularly allow Badawi to leave work after signing in. Not only is the foreman aware that there are responsibilities outside work—for example, Badawi having to handle administrative matters on behalf of his brother, who was injured during the Luxor Massacre—he himself will occasionally need time away from work too and will therefore not deny it to his workers. Similarly, if *wajib* duties are required, a worker will sign in, and then the *ra'is* will allow him to leave. Ultimately, each will have his *wajib* duties to attend to, including the *ra'is*, and being given unofficial leave this way is simply the way it is done here. Were requests for unofficial leave to get out of hand, then the *ra'is* can always impose the requirement that official permission be sought from the inspectorate office.

Regular annual leave is twenty-one days, plus an additional seven days that may be taken for incidental needs. Yet, SCA employees may take a month or two months off, especially during the winter, to take advantage of the busy tourism season. Rather than using regular annual leave, a bribe of LE50 or LE100 will persuade a doctor to write a prescription for some illusionary illness, which, when signed off by a pharmacist, effectively serves as a medical certificate. Periodic visits to a doctor may extend the period, or be used to further legitimize the period of illness by obtaining a clean bill of health before resuming work. The visibility of a 'sick' person's activities during such times will nevertheless impose its own limitations: while a feigned illness may be fruitfully employed by a limestone carver working from home, the process is unsuitable for an SCA worker intending to publicly peddle artifacts, or using his 'recovery' period to work for foreign archaeologists.

Having "worked hard" for the short spells that they do, SCA restorers justify their periods of inactivity on technical grounds: working with chemicals requires them to take breaks for fresh air, or they credit the slow processes involved with restoration work generally, the various stages in the treatment requiring periods of time to dry. The chemical cleaning of paint-decorated surfaces and structural restoration techniques have been developed between Cairo University, the Supreme Council of Antiquities, the Getty Conservation Institute, and input from foreign archaeological missions. The techniques also incorporate knowledge gained from the Getty-sponsored restoration of the tomb of Nefertari in the Valley of the Queens by Paolo Moro and his team of Italian conservation experts. Wall-surface and structural repairs are made with a matrix obtained from natural materials *(heba)* occurring within the vicinity of the tomb, thoroughly washed and dried to extract any salts, then mixed with water to make a mortar: "no cement, only the pharaonic way!" A local *ra'is* like Muhammad al-Tayyeb or Abdu-Sittar Ahmad Abed combine their experience and advice received from Cairo University and members of foreign archaeological missions with what they call the "sensitivity of the mountain," a 'feel' for local materials, and conditions they attribute to having been born here.[13]

Restoration work mainly concerns the known temples and tombs, and restoration teams have few dealings with their excavating colleagues, although experienced people like Badawi may be called upon to make assessments of the conservation requirements when new tombs are discovered. Archaeological excavations conducted by Supreme Council of Antiquities teams have little in common with the precise operations of the seasonal archaeological missions conducted by western universities. Excavating teams appear essentially in the business of clearance, with no obvious recording taking place, baskets of skeletal remains and other finds carried away to be put in storage elsewhere. Western archaeologists complain that whatever reports are prepared are below standard and written in Arabic, thereby making them largely inaccessible for western researchers. Senior officials themselves, when asked, could not remember the names of the relevant SCA publications used for such reporting. During his term in office as secretary general of the Supreme Council of Antiquities, Dr. Gaballa Ali Gaballa reinstituted the publication of *Annales du service des antiquités de l'Egypte* (ASAE), but its authorship is virtually entirely composed of western academics.[14] It certainly does not act as a published record of work undertaken by the SCA's Egyptian excavators. As Dr. Gaballa acknowledged during interview, the SCA excavations in the necropolis are entirely "routine," and not designed to "make discoveries to attract tourists," adding: "When you have an army, you sometimes have a war," suggesting their relevance as government-sponsored employment schemes rather than targeted research.

The inspectors in charge of these operations have, nevertheless, obtained university degrees in Egyptology,[15] but in practice their duties in 1999 were more concerned with supervising excavation work gangs; implementing Antiquities Law No. 117 of 1983, Article 20, which prohibits the construction, expansion, or renovation of Qurnawi dwellings inside the necropolis (EAO, 1984); accompanying Luxor City Council engineers negotiating the exchange of necropolis dwellings for units in one of the new communities, measuring the house and establishing the priority of relocation in relation to any nearby tombs; and supervising the demolition of vacated houses, rather than actively engaging in research. Although courses in archaeology will have touched on research and fieldwork practice, the reality of an inspector's work in the Theban Necropolis and the 'routine' clearance of tombs being what they are, the absence of a targeted research agenda with academic requirements of methodological excavation, accurate recording, conservation, and scholarly publication are evidently not considered as relevant. Maybe such is all that can be expected of a junior inspector's wage that does not exceed LE260 per month. As one foreign archaeologist commented, "there is no reporting, there are no files for reports to be put into, there are no publications. What was published proved an embarrassment, such as one report on a Roman site of only two pages, but accompanied by fifty pages of photos, four of that showing cigarette wrappers as evidence that the site was robbed."

Other than the evident lack of objectives in Egyptian-conceived excavations, and the wonderment about the scientific rationale and chosen methodologies behind such work on the part of foreign field archaeologists working in the necropolis, they also cite other incriminating evidence: the tomb of Mentuemhet, TT34, was SCA-excavated, with pieces of wall decoration appearing on the international art market, and the tomb is now "in pieces."[16]

Additionally, and beyond any tensions inherent in the opposition between Islam and Egyptology (Silberman, 1989: 159–60), there is both anecdotal and published evidence that SCA inspectors are less than happy in their work. Being posted to the Theban Necropolis imposes its own hardships for those who come from the city (Silberman, 1989: 164–68). Therefore, according to one foreign archaeologist "many people hate their jobs, they just sit there, the only time they get excited is when told to destroy houses at two in the morning, coming back the next morning with a glint in their eyes thinking they have achieved something."

It is as a result of these circumstances that the relationship between Qurnawi and the antiquities inspectors is generally, albeit in tacit fashion, negative. When prompted, Qurnawi will offer views about inspectors who are not from Qurna that implicate them in illicit antiquities dealings, their sole motive for coming to Luxor to get rich quickly, upon their departure reportedly driving in an expensive car in their home village:

> they get rich by being offered money by foreign archaeologists who pay bribes to keep some of their prize finds; when the [foreign] archaeologist is absent, the workmen consider the inspector the "owner" of the tomb and give him finds which are never recorded; by stealing from the storage areas; and by receiving bribes to allow illegal construction.

Senior SCA officials for Luxor and the west bank are not exempt from this treatment either, allegedly being given their higher degrees from certain Eastern European countries without actually having studied there, but by "only going to the embassy." Allegedly, their dissertations were either written for them by academics from the countries involved, and inscriptions were translated by German or American colleagues,

Excavation conducted by the Supreme Council of Antiquities, the *ra'is* at right.

because the inspector involved "did not read hieroglyphs so well," or the findings of foreign archaeologists were plagiarized. Although foreign archaeologists may possibly benefit from currying favor with senior inspectors as a way of preserving excavation concessions, this is not the place to either attest their veracity or otherwise argue the merit of these allegations. Here these accounts are simply reported for their diagnostic value and suggestive of the mutual distrust that exists between Qurnawi and antiquities officials, with senior SCA inspectors readily countering that "the problem with Qurnawi is that nobody speaks the truth." While at least in part these allegations will inevitably be based on innuendo, half or dated truths, or simply be inspired by malice, they do reflect a degree of discontent present in the relations between local workers and their SCA superiors.

Working for *khawaja*: Qurnawi and the foreign archaeological missions

When Muhammad 'Abd al-Rasul in 1881 revealed to antiquities officials the location of the Royal Cache at Dayr al-Bahari, the family was not any worse off because of it:

> Mohammed Abd er-Rasul was rewarded for his confession with £500 and was appointed rais of the excavations at Thebes. . . . to this day they exercise an effective control on the employment of the men of Gurneh as guards of the monuments of Thebes or as workmen on excavations. (Wilson, 1964: 84)[17]

'Abd al-Rasul informants indicated that they and members of their family had been guardians since their grandfather, suggesting that if not hereditary, there are certain benefits to be had from their family name and that they get "*shughl alatul*," ('work straightaway'). But it is now no longer true that the 'Abd al-Rasul family "exercise an effective control" over west bank archaeological labor.

Although different missions will have differing approaches when contracting personnel,[18] all of them on some level will have to negotiate the desires of the west bank chief inspector, the appointed inspector, the appointed *ra'is*, and the local guards, each of whom may either represent a certain motivation or a particular—often kinship-based—constituency that needs to be considered.

There are a number of ways in which local archaeological workers may be selected: (1) through the local guard in whose area of responsibility the mission's excavation site is located; (2) through the *shaykh al-ghaffir*; (3) through the supervising inspector, who may not accept workers who already have other government work, reserving the positions for "poor people"; (4) through the *ra'is* if he is a Qurnawi, who may likewise favor poor people in combination with those he considers good workers; (5) through the recommendation of the foreign director of the excavation; and (6) through a person like Badawi, who has many years of employment with the SCA and who may, once he becomes aware of a planned mission to his local area, recommend a person to the inspector if the latter is well known to him. The representation of these various constituencies is a potentially political exercise, and a certain balance is needed.

One foreign mission field director complained that, increasingly since 1999, the chief inspector for the west bank and his "mafia inspectors and *ghaffir* . . . monopolise employment of their clients saying that these and those other people are 'bad' people unacceptable as antiquities work-men. If I insist, [the chief inspector for the west bank] threatens with closing the excavation." Occasional bribe taking by the *ra'is* to nominate certain individuals for employment has been alleged, especially in cases where that *ra'is* is also an SCA employee and was appointed by the chief inspector of the west bank, the use of such handpicked SCA person-nel evidently being seen as a measure restricting the use of traditional kinship-based labor-procurement contacts and networks. Yet, other mission directors appeared to have remained unaffected by such SCA interference: "our normal practice is to decide how many men we want and then ask for about 80 percent of that. Thus, with the extras 'forced' upon us we end up with about the right number. The *taftish* did once force a *ra'is* upon us, as they did not like the one we had, but overall there has not been much influence."

If the mission is in its first year, the field director or project leader will speak to the appointed inspector about the necessary workers. Advice is taken from both the inspector and the appointed *ra'is* regarding any trusted persons to serve as core group. But even without these, word gets around quickly that a mission is employing staff, and some twenty extra men may turn up, arguing with the project leader, the *ra'is*, and among themselves in order to be given work. According to one field director, the entire process may take "a week or ten days to settle down." According

Qurnawi basket boys working for Howard Carter in the Valley of the Kings during his search for the tomb of Tutankhamun in 1922. Photograph by Harry Burton. © The Griffith Institute, the University of Oxford.

to another, "if I need fifty men, I take about ten of my own and let them argue among themselves for the rest. This may take two hours of the first day with shouting and it may sometimes come to a near-fight." Historically, men have been known to come from areas of al-Qurna lying within one hour walking distance of the excavation. Today, distance is less of an issue in terms of selecting workmen from nearby hamlets, and those coming from al-Suyul or al-Tarif will use the collective taxi.

During subsequent years, the excavation's field director, the foreign archaeologist in charge, contacts the *ra'is* at the start of the season who—even if he is new to the mission—has a list of the workmen from previous years. The *ra'is* may in fact be a person who is also a local guard employed by the SCA, obtaining leave from his government job to work privately for the foreign mission. Alternatively, as suggested by questionnaire respondents, he may have been given time off work at the instigation of the chief inspector or the inspector allocated to the excavation, thereby acting as a further covert SCA form of control over the mission.

Generally, the labor requirements will vary according to the nature of the project and, in the experience of one field director, has been anywhere between seven and fifty men. The project leader will decide the number of workers required, although not all from last year's list will be available, with some now working for other missions, others recruited by the army. As a rule, if some twenty-four workers are needed, only two-thirds may initially be selected. Further requirements will then be filled from contacts of the inspector, the *shaykh al-ghaffir*, the *ra'is*, or the community of workers and guards: "it gives you what you need, but keeps the locals happy." The ultimate number will be a function of both the scale of the project and the funds available, with especially the number of basket boys capable of manipulation: "the work will not necessarily be slower, as the speed increases when there is more walking involved." Other teams may choose to leave out the sifting of debris, but this will result in "less accurate archaeology."[19]

One of the foreign missions working among the Tombs of the Nobles in al-Hurubat during the 1997–98 season employed a crew of twenty-seven workers, including one *ra'is*, four excavators, eighteen basket boys, three workers sifting debris at the dump site; and one person washing and assembling potsherds. This was their sixth season, the last season before work for Qurnawi would effectively cease, as the actual work of excavating tomb shafts and chambers comes to a close. At this point other missions might retain some local personnel for specialist functions including the assemblage of pottery, but such would not be the case here, the remainder of the work carried out by a few foreign specialists busy cataloguing and analyzing finds on the tables located in the tomb's courtyard or involved with recording and conserving tomb decorations.

Excavation controls consist of a reliable core group of those who do the excavating and those who sift the debris, carried there by a train of basket boys, at off-site dumps. It is especially the composition of this group of untrained basket boys that may fluctuate. They tend to slow down during the changeover of their baskets at the debris dump and have to be kept on track by the *ra'is* or the excavation director. The entire process is supervised by an SCA inspector who is well dressed and qualified but who, as likely as not, appears intent on not getting his hands dirty and thus offers little by way of practical support. The excavators selected from the core group of trusted workers also supervise those who put the rubble to be sifted in the baskets, with the project leader likewise supervising all tasks in order to impose visible controls. It was acknowledged that, nevertheless, some pilfering will occur. In certain respects, the field director will have to trust in the integrity of the core group, but it may never be known what was lost.

Also for foreign missions, work cannot start inside the tomb until the arrival of the inspector, who holds the key, but work in the courtyard and the excavation of tomb shafts can proceed without his presence. Work will start at six in the morning with a half-hour breakfast break at half past seven and conclude at one or one-thirty in the afternoon. During the holy month of Ramadan, work may start at seven in the morning and finish at half past twelve in the afternoon, the shorter times also compensated by the lack of a break. Compared with SCA excavations, foreign missions will impose longer working days, but since the money is better, more is expected.

Wages are paid every ten days at the end of that day's work, the money having been counted in advance and placed in envelopes. This prevents any questioning over amounts owed (for example, workers may argue about sick pay and the cost of medicines when they were encouraged to go and see a doctor) and gives a degree of formality that stifles argumentation. Some field directors operate according to the principle "do not upset the local economy," and when commencing operations inquire with other foreign missions what pay raises may have affected this year's rates. Pay for a five-and-a-half-hour day will range between LE13 and LE17, although certain specialist tasks may attract slightly higher wages, with the *ra'is* receiving LE25 for a day's work. At the end of the season the project leader may choose to give baksheesh, varying in amounts from pay received for one day, 1.3 days, or in one case the "equivalent of three to four days work." Since it is simply a gift, workers cannot argue, although those working at the bottom of a tomb shaft may get more, those who habitually turn up late, less. Some mission directors do not differentiate payments between differing responsibilities: "the workmen often change roles, and the best of these are ready to do different kinds of work." Instead, a system of progressive payments provides both a stimulus, and a way of averaging these varying responsibilities, the pay commencing at the beginning of the season at the lower end of the scale (LE13) and increasing as the work progresses to LE17. Taking an average

Income earned from employment with foreign archaeological missions continues to be an important and much sought-after component of household budgets for Theban west bank villagers.

pay of LE15 over a ten-day period, the LE150 in earnings compares very favorably with the government's monthly wage of the same amount. The difference explains why Qurnawi who work for the SCA are keen to take time off work and spend a month working for a foreign archaeological mission, as a number of them do. While the supervising inspector may be keen to reserve this labor for his connections, 'poor' or otherwise, the influence of both a *ra'is* of long standing and the stature of a field director may favor and enforce the services of trusted antiquities personnel with whose work they have many years of personal experience.

The financial stimulus that archaeological work represents must be seen as considerable. The names of "Current and Recent Foreign Missions" listed on the Supreme Council of Antiquities website (see: http://www.sca-egypt.org/eng/FMR_CURRENT-MISSIONS_MP.htm) provides an indication of the ongoing scientific interest in the west bank. Additionally, several foreign archaeological missions operate from an established west bank mission base (the German Institute of Archaeology, the Polish Archaeological Mission), and while the base is not used throughout the year, it continues to provide employment for permanent caretakers. A small sample of reported amounts of foreign archaeological funding injected into the local economy for seasonal excavation work among the foothills' Noble Tombs includes:

Expenditure by Foreign Archaeological Missions in the Theban Necropolis			
Year	Mission	Funded Items	Total Local Expenditure
2001	Mission '1A' of 35 days' duration	Maximum 50 workmen Water Cartage of debris into the desert Inspector's salary	LE24,000
2001	Mission '2A' of unspecified duration but given as average per week of $500 for labor during 2000–2002 seasons	Labor costs for 33 workmen Household servants	$825[20] $100
2002	Mission '1B' of 18 days' duration	Maximum 50 workmen Water Cartage of debris into the desert Inspector's salary	LE15,000
2002	Mission '2A' of unspecified duration but given as average per week of $500 for labor during 2000–2002 seasons	Labor costs for 20 workmen Household servants	$500 $100
1992 to 2002	Mission '3'	Qurnawi workers increased in numbers from 20 in 1993 to 32 when excavating finished in 1998. Total expenditure could only be indicated as "the cost of the project in the field has been in the region of."	£UK64,000[21]

Sample of foreign archaeological mission budgets benefiting the local economy.

Some respondents reported "by purpose and ʳolitics" not to establish a "particular relationship to individual Qurnawi," as these relations in the experience of "group members were felt in the end as too demanding and ended with disappointment." Others did "regard such as a little patronising" or worried that personal friendships and any support such might involve could "backfire on us or on the family in question." Nevertheless, personal relations between Qurnawi and visiting Egyptologists on occasion do become established as longer-term friendships that for some may mean that "I bring presents, I buy sweets for the women in 'my' family and at the end I leave a considerable 'extra' which is explained as not coming from the mission." For others, the support moves beyond gifts and contributes both to life-cycle events and the general well-being of the family:

> Yes, I have established friendly relations with the *ra'is* and his family: I know them since 1972 and assist their family events. Each year I bring some gifts to each member of the family (the *ra'is*, his wife and four children): shoes, tools, dress, sweets, etc., treating these as my private gifts. When visiting them in their homes, I may sometimes bring some local sweets, and I am ready to help them with medical expenses as well. I think this may be quantified altogether, since 1999 [that is, during a period of approximately three years], at about $400.

Those foreign Egyptologists with whom friendly relations of this kind are maintained will also assist with periodic financial support, as evidenced by correspondence involving the transfer of funds shown during home visits.

'Secret knowledge': *Antikas* and the trade in illicit antiquities

One measure of the continuing trade in ancient Egyptian art and artifacts is provided by the pronouncements of the Egyptologists themselves. Although some respondents were most emphatic in their reticence to comment on the phenomenon, discussions with others and evidence from the published record indicate that the Theban Necropolis continues as a source of supply for both small-scale collectors and the international art market. Inherent in the distinction between these two is the differentiation between small items pilfered from excavations to be offered for sale to knowledgeable visitors to the necropolis, and the damaging techniques used to extract wall decorations and tomb statuary. Their removal, transport, and export more specifically operates in the world of the international trade in antiquities and fine arts, which in turn are possibly linked with other criminal activities and associated money laundering.[22] The (edited)[23] account of one respondent will serve to situate both categories with respect to the Theban Necropolis:

Even during excavations, "things" vanish into thin air. Sometimes they appear again and you have to fire the workmen involved. Of course, nobody of us would mention these things because it would be the end of the mission for ever! The workmen have such quick hands and you always have to keep an eye on them! There are always only a few reliable persons and of course one wants to have only those people excavating with the trowel. But these incidents concern only small items. I think the really valuable things are going in a different manner. There exists a kind of mafia, and in the early 1990s the story of a kidnapping incident between two well-known families did the rounds, it being rumoured that the issue at stake was in fact an ancient statue.

Although many stories, innuendo, and aspersions customarily circulate throughout the west bank,[24] archaeological observation indicates that there may be some truth in such rumors:

It was clear from our excavations in this tomb that the robbery of the wall decoration of the broad hall took place in the early 20th century and probably not later than 1920, as suggested by the design of some matchboxes we found. The robbery of the heads of the statue group in the chapel seems to be of more recent date, as evidenced by the absence of bat-droppings on the broken surfaces. We also found the access-route which the robbers used, enabling us to conclude that the robbery took place during the past twenty years, and possibly not long before our arrival in 1990, when we closed the illegal entry.[25]

The distinction between the above two categories may also be found reflected in the accounts and actions of Qurnawi. Evidently, the nature of the trade being what it is, this is secret knowledge, and to that extent any inquiries made will rarely elicit a frank response. Yet, dealing with members of the wider peddler community, and meeting some of the better working craftsmen, one may get a glimpse, which, while not so much as providing an insight, nevertheless at times leaves the observer with a sense that something is going on. Some of this may be based on inferences made from the drift of a particular conversation, or indeed by just sitting around and observing certain things unfold.

On occasion, an incidental letter, one among the many that the fieldworker may be asked to write to some overseas tourist with whom friendly relations are maintained, may take an interesting twist, and be interpreted as not simply referring to an order for commissioned modern statuary, but also alluding to clandestine excavations:

> You asked me to fax the news for you and I can say I have been able to find what you wanted me to get for you and your friend. If you can please send me $1,500 via Thomas Cook Company in Luxor in my complete name [as stated]. If you please can send the money first, as the people who work with me want payment in advance. If you can please send me the money within the week because I must return the item after one week. As the final cost of everything is still not clear, we will finalize everything when you come in September. Please don't forget the sun-glasses, binoculars and head-torch when you come, as well as the four dust masks. Thank you for everything. My family sends greetings to your family and we miss you all. Please send a fax by return in confirmation of these arrangements. (Field Notes, al-Hurubat, July 9, 1999)

Obviously, the amount of $1,500 (LE5,100) would be insufficient to buy any substantial genuine antiquities, but the request for equipment invokes a scenario taking place both in bright sunlight—a sentry using sunglasses, scouting the surroundings with binoculars—and those exploring the caves and passages of the mountain, engaged in activities that leave no free hands to handle a torch and which require protection from dust.

Pieces pilfered from excavation sites or obtained from clandestine excavations may include amulets or fragments thereof; small plain deep-blue and indistinct faience *shabti*s,[26] mass-produced from a mold; fragments of broken *shabti*s; necklaces made up of porcelain tubular mummy-beads and assorted individual beads (transparent quartz, white-gray striped onyx, orange-red carnelian) reassembled into a necklace, without authenticity other than that the beads themselves are old. Generally such items are mixed with modern replicas made to look old and sold to tourists inquiring after antiquities with tomb-side peddlers who will take them to their home if they themselves keep items or, if not, to a friend or relative who does. During 1999, small amulets and *shabti*s might sell for LE1,300 to LE1,500. Displayed together with 'good copies,' these might also be sold as genuine and attract similar prices. Most peddlers operating in the Noble Tombs area will have access to such small *antikas*, either personally, or in the form of a small network of sales contacts, who will pay them commission for each concluded sale.

Both the peddlers and those who make it a business selling *antikas* claim that they can distinguish real ones from those that are fake when small items like amulets and *shabti*s are involved. They acknowledge they cannot distinguish a fake from an authentic antique when it concerns those items made by several Hurubati master craftsmen who produce limestone carvings and paintings made on stuccoed mud, in imitation of mural fragments. One of them is a craftsman who prides himself as the last surviving workman from Dayr al-Madina. He privately admits that some of his limestone pieces are now in museum collections, including the Cairo Museum and the Louvre, after having been checked by experts for their authenticity, and evidently conceived and executed by him as genuine pieces rather than 'good copies.' But local peddlers rarely engage craftsmen of this calibre: their work is targeted at the international fine-arts market and beyond the interests and financial means of the tourists peddlers deal with.

By contrast, the peddlers and their sales contacts obtain many of their artifacts from excavation sites where supervision may be slack, with a *ra'is* allowing one of the basket boys with an item hidden in his *gallabiya* to have a toilet break or to go and buy cigarettes, thereby providing the opportunity to dispose of the item for later retrieval. Those in the know claim it does not make much difference whether an excavation is Egyptian or foreign as "they are all easy." Foreign field directors may claim they select only trusted people as *ra'is* and those who do the excavating, but this simply means that instead of the field director receiving three pieces he may only be given two: "it is the Egyptian way." Usually several people are in on it, often including the *ra'is*. Smaller pieces may be put in the pocket of a *gallabiya*, any larger pieces placed in a basket and covered with rubble, to be found by the 'trusted' people sifting at the dump site and temporarily hidden in a hole from where it will be recovered later: "there are many ways."

Other artifacts may be purchased by them from persons who have been secretly exploring the area underneath their house, especially at Dra' Abu al-Naga. According to dealers, during earlier times the *'umda* at al-Hurubat conscripted the locals to excavate for him, which is the reason Hurubati now claim there is "nothing left." Instead, Qurnawi living at Dra' Abu al-Naga are claimed to be getting rich because supplies there have not yet been depleted, although such distinctions between different hamlets may simply serve to disguise what is also going on at al-Hurubat. Badawi would point to a particular nearby house, indicating that the son of its owner was a peddler like himself only a few years ago, but now appears wealthy. His father has renovated the house and bought three others nearby. The son is a half-owner of one of the souvenir stalls at Hatshepsut's Temple, and also owns a commercial business in al-Tarif. During household interviews, the apparent affluence was not explained, with the revenue from the souvenir stall understated and ownership of the commercial business not indicated. There is no sense of jealousy on the part of other Qurnawi when they point out such wealth: "if you can do it like this, and not damage the tombs everyone knows about, then it is okay." When asked about the potential loss of scientific information where such wealth was obtained from previously unexplored sites, informants seemed indifferent: "Sure!"

Major pieces discovered in this way, and capable of generating the evident fortunes in a family's material circumstance, are not the pieces sold by peddlers and their contacts, such small items as amulets and *shabti*s simply being referred to as 'presents.' Pieces of importance require a middleman who has a network of clients and the contacts to facilitate export overseas, and it may be inferred both from responses provided and observations made that several of the better craftsmen may be in this position. In some cases their artwork may be used to conceal authentic pieces, with the stuccoed mud paintings a successful medium, although by its nature imposing certain limitations on the size of artifacts so exported. In other cases, an artist's business contacts—"men in Cairo, men dressed in suits"—may provide avenues to dispose of a piece. One craftsman indeed acknowledged in conversation that he was capable of delivering "any piece, anywhere." While being an excellent and evidently successful artist, as demonstrated by a casually shown wad of banknotes resulting from a recent sale, his personal wealth could be said to be out of character with what local artists producing for the tourist market might be able to accumulate. Significantly, when a piece said to be authentic and claimed to have come from outside al-Qurna—a late-period stuccoed mummy mask—was made available locally for an attempted sale in this high-density tourism area, it was one of these knowledgeable craftsmen who was called upon to give his verdict on its authenticity, his acknowledged ability—"everybody knows"—to offer help and advice allowing certain inferences to be made about his relative position in the scheme of things.

While government officials may have their suspicions, they can only make a case if there is hard evidence. But even then, such evidence is not necessarily conclusive, as in the case of one craftsman who two years earlier had been imprisoned on suspicion of antiquities dealings but who was released after having had to produce evidence of his own work, while in prison, to establish his innocence. Nevertheless, a person capable of maintaining a credible cover to explain his standard of living, and only concerning himself with several authentic pieces every year, may evade detection: "If somebody wants to buy, he may take a piece from a secret place and bring it to his house. If there is no sale he will return it there. What can the inspectors do? If they go to his house they find nothing!"

Similarly, sudden changes in the standard of living experienced by those working in the privacy of their homes may not go unnoticed by antiquities inspectors who survey the foothills for illegal building activity, but Qurnawi remain secure in the knowledge that any suspicion will be found groundless: "there is nothing they can do, they will not find any pieces in the house." If inquiries are made, it will be stated that any visible change in personal fortune results from personal relationships with tourists or from some other involvement in the tourism business.

Items hidden in newly created artwork may not only be those substantial pieces clandestinely excavated from underneath people's houses or stolen from known tombs: antiquities inspectors who have access to the *makhazin* storage areas in the necropolis may also be implicated. An interview session with a local inspector was interrupted by a Hurubati craftsman coming to collect not only a design for a stuccoed mud painting copied by the inspector on tracing paper from a book in his library, but also a plastic bag with items, the outdoor inspection of which the author was barred from attending. Subsequent inquiries revealed that the artist supplies stuccoed mud paintings to the inspector who has business dealings with 'tourists' who come to the house, selling "expensive" items, a relationship in return for which his overseas friends provide him with all-expenses-paid annual European holidays. Although not constituting proof in a legal sense, the entire scenario invites speculation and must lead to the conclusion that there is more to the mud paintings commissioned by the inspector than meets the eye.

Incorporating the above illicit antiquities-related practices, we may devise a conceptual schema to offer a framework for contemporary concerns with designs inspired by ancient Egyptian themes. These may be categorized as ranging from fake to genuine, and incorporate artisan and antiquities practices at various levels: (1) cheap representations that are often fanciful interpretations rather than purporting to be imitations; (2) better representations that through the application of various age-ing techniques may be sold as genuine *antikas*; (3) genuine small *antikas* pilfered from archaeological excavations and sold as 'presents' to tourists who wish to own some authentic part of ancient Egypt; and (4) the sale and smuggling of higher-order pieces obtained through damaging extractive practices from known tombs, clandestine excavations, or stolen by antiquities officials who have access to storage areas or locations known to contain in situ specimens.

Where the trade in authentic ancient artifacts operates under a legitimizing cover of newly created modern art by resident Qurnawi craftsmen, this is not to say that all contemporary artisanal production in the Theban Necropolis serves illicit purposes. The first two categories in the above framework indicate that the production of art also operates in its own terms. In the following chapter we will discuss the phenomenon of west bank commercial artistic expression more specifically.

9

Faked *Antikas* and 'Modern Antiques': Artistic Expression in the Villages of the Theban West Bank

The early antecedents of contemporary tourist art in the Theban Necropolis

The archaeological work discussed above has historically had close connections with the tourism industry. Archaeological artifacts uncovered by Qurnawi have been items of interest to western visitors since at least the second half of the eighteenth century. There is a fine line between Qurnawi offering items for sale to a visiting person like Charles Sonnini, and to an early scientist like Vivant Denon engaging Qurnawi guides when exploring the necropolis to draw monuments and collect antiquities. The latter activity would eventually evolve into the large-scale explorations of Belzoni and Rhind, but the archaeological practice that gradually emerged from such operations will have been largely lost on Qurnawi. For them even such early research essentially concerned the provision of ancient artifacts to foreign visitors in exchange for money.

As a result of these excavations during the nineteenth century, the quantity of antiquities available for sale to individual travelers diminished, and we have already discussed how the apparent lack of antiquities during times of continuing demand gave rise to a new Qurnawi industry, namely the "concoction of spurious antiquities" (Rhind, 1862: 251). This industry has also contributed to al-Qurna's bad name with tourists for the stated objection of tourists to peddlers' constant overtures, also around the Noble Tombs of al-Hurubat. But the specific objects they peddle and the production and sale of al-Qurna's artisanal output more generally have received little attention, as a result of which Qurnawi artistic expression itself has remained largely understated.

The representation of Qurnawi artisanal activity in the literature, in common with the description of foothills sociality more broadly, is sparse. The range of artistic quality tends to be expressed in opposite extremes. Wilkinson mentioned that "particularly scarabaei . . . are so cleverly imitated, that it requires a practised eye to detect them" (Wilkinson, 1847: 325). Henry Rhind in 1862 encountered many "unwieldy imitations" of the same, classifying Qurnawi art as comprising a very limited repertoire of "small rogueries [which are] within the limits of their slight artistic ability" (Rhind, 1862: 252), yet acknowledging that some copies "are singularly good" (Rhind, 1862: 254). Ninety years later German art historian Kurt Lange observed that while "most [imitations] could be regarded as completely harmless . . . a fine sandstone head . . . would have been placed on exhibit . . . had it been found in the stores of a German museum" (Lange, 1952: 152). Lange's chapter is exceptional in that he spends the odd paragraph discussing the artistic merits of Qurnawi art, and how their work—by mixing characteristic stylistic features from different ancient Egyptian periods—can in most cases be readily distinguished from authentic antiquities.[1] But even his account loses focus by diverting attention to the quality of imitations found elsewhere, especially Cairo (Lange, 1952: 155–57), a literary device that bedevils the few extant accounts purporting to concern the abilities of Theban west bank artisans (Ammoun, 1993: 124).

Interpreting alleged mischief: Falsification and storytelling as marketing strategies

Before detailing the practices more specifically, something must be said about the often-stated assertion that Qurnawi art is the art of forgery, their creation bordering on the criminal, as suggested by Rhind's "small rogueries" (Rhind, 1862: 252). Ammoun indeed refers to the Luxor west bank art market as "*un marché de dupes*" ('a market of deception'), operated by "*artisans-faussaires*," that is, 'forger-craftsmen' (Ammoun, 1993: 121). Certain practices may have given cause for this ascription. Wilkinson describes the breaking up of complete papyri, the fragments used to coat the outside of false ones in order to give them a semblance of authenticity (Wilkinson, 1847: 325). Although such practices now no longer occur due to the simple absence of complete papyri, the breaking up of such texts under contemporary antiquities legislation would indeed constitute a crime. But such would not prevent Qurnawi probing the probable gullibility of many a visitor not sufficiently expert in the recognition of authentic antiquities when attempting to sell a 'modern antique.'

The process is one that cannot be divorced from the archaeological landscape of the necropolis, or the role that indigenous actors have played in it. Beyond access to 'good copies,' the combination of these two factors is crucial for many of the peddlers operating in the al-Hurubat area of the Tombs of the Nobles. As has been discussed, the reputation of Qurnawi as "inveterate" (Gardiner and Weigall, 1913: 8) illicit excavators leans heavily on the 1881 'Abd al-Rasul incident. Further reinforced through the pilfering of artifacts from excavations where they and other Qurnawi were employed as laborers (Petrie, 1897: 2), a popular understanding of local subsistence being concentrated in this specific form of economic specialization was cultivated, giving rise to the 'village of the tomb robbers' characterization.

To the extent that at least part of what it means to be a foothills Qurnawi has been shaped by a history of and a dependence on the resources of the archaeological landscape, the 'Abd al-Rasul history has served the villagers of the foothills well, affording them a certain identity that provides marketing support for the community's craft production. Qurnawi themselves are therefore happy to nurture and maintain their alleged involvement in illicitly procured antiquities. This will inevitably mean that genuine artifacts may still be traded, even though such items will be small and not be in the same category as the destruction of entire wall panels in decorated tombs. Yet, because of antiquities legislation which makes any such activity illegal, even antiquities business on this small and incidental scale will be covert, and it is therefore very difficult to ascertain how widespread such practices still are, or to what extent peddlers' expendable income may have come to rely on them.

Depending on the knowledge that individual tourists may have of that history, it will not be uncommon for visitors to come to the cemeteries with a hidden agenda of hoping to buy some small authentic antiquity from peddlers awaiting them at popular tombs or from local guides who show tourists items for sale in the privacy of their homes. Many visitors will have stereotypical expectations of Egyptian art, or what it is they like best, not anticipating that a seemingly 'bad' artifact may be 'good' and a 'good' one a fake. The difficulty of distinguishing between fake and 'real' when confronted with both a good modern copy and an authentic fragment of poor quality reinforces what could be called a locally practiced 'discourse of the uncertain.'

A prospective buyer can never be absolutely certain, but may ultimately give villagers the benefit of the doubt through assumptions which merge Qurnawi expertise with a tourist's personal knowledge of the history of 'tomb robbing' here. In this environment of uncertainty, where time and the evidently covert nature of proceedings impose their own pressures and constraints, there is always the nagging doubt that the artifact *might well* be genuine. Thus, it is only through the continued availability of clandestinely excavated or sporadically pilfered and marketed genuine artifacts that this 'discourse of the uncertain' can be maintained, that the difference between modern and ancient can be blurred, and that a framework of mystification can operate within which all modern copies—treated with the host of falsifying processes that this sort of marketing strategy requires—can be peddled as genuine in order to attract the hefty prices they do.

This blurring of genuine and fake categories is evidently dependent on the continued presence of the people within the landscape. It is the geographical presence of that archaeological landscape, which, in historic and spatial terms, is intrinsic to aspects of Qurnawi identity. Thus, a Qurnawi identity grounded in locally present archaeological remains was forged from the interplay between the landscape and the historical place of Qurnawi within that landscape. This identity exists by virtue of its association with historically situated practices of tomb exploration and antiquities dealings. Economic practices are structured by a strategic exploitation of this aspect of Qurnawi identity. These economic practices manifest themselves in, and ! come to depend on, the range of artistic expressions and manufacturing processes that aim at creating credible representations of ancient Egyptian themes of known local origin, that can be sold as genuine to those visitors who feel sufficiently convinced by Qurnawi storytelling, which aims to establish the authenticity of the pieces, to accept them as such.

At least where artistic output is sold in the 'alabaster factories' that line the foothills road, or when produced for the tourist bazaars in Luxor, Kurt Lange in his art-historical assessment of al-Qurna craft production correctly recognizes that most pieces are not forgeries and are indeed 'harmless.' He perceptively realizes that much of Qurnawi production simply constitutes tourist art, satisfying a demand for souvenirs rather than representing an interest in authentic antiquities. Lange also explains locally operative business conduct, employing an orientalist perspective on negotiation and bargaining, elaborating on some of the cultural rules that guide such behavior, and countering perceptions that overpricing constitutes deceit (Lange, 1952: 149–51). But he fails to explain the dynamics that operate between customer and Qurnawi peddler when it comes to the sale of artifacts—even if these are crafted in other centers of production such as al-Tarif—which in the particular surroundings of an embodied necropolis become imbued with archaeological qualities. The account presented here offers a holistic understanding of this process, merging artistic forms with such equally important operative factors as spatial location, the embodiment of landscape through the legacies of past social actors, and the persuasive power of story to create a 'discourse of the uncertain.' These dynamics may leave one-time prospective buyers to wonder about their decision to turn down the opportunity to buy an artifact, which may well have been authentic after all.

But in a contemporary assessment of these practices, their political dimension must also be stated. The Qurnawi's identity as 'tomb robbers,' and their effective exploitation of inherently associated sales strategies, also relies on geographically situated continuities between past and present. This continuity will be broken if Qurnawi can no longer claim to live in the landscape from which they allegedly obtain their artifacts, and will discredit their marketing strategy by undermining the effectiveness of their 'discourse of the uncertain.' Such reduced effectiveness will translate itself into decreased credibility with respect to the possible authenticity of items offered for sale, and will make the extreme concern on the part of certain artists to produce convincing imitations—which through a variety of falsification techniques represents a distinct aspect of contemporary Qurnawi craft production—superfluous. It is only one of the cultural practices to have evolved from a dependence on the archaeological landscape, and is likely to diminish in significance after having been severed from the very geographical essence that fed it now that relocation away from the archaeological zone is complete. Rather than to protect a livelihood based on illicit excavation and a trade in illegal antiquities (Rakha, 1999) it is for reasons such as these—combining economic pragmatism with the art of storytelling—that many Qurnawi have long been opposed to leaving the necropolis.

The classification of Qurnawi artistic expression

The above characterizations of deception, falsification, and tourist art, and the possibility that a 'good copy' to be sold as a 'modern antique' may be accepted by a buyer as archaeologically authentic, suggests that there is indeed a degree of fluidity in the way Qurnawi artistic expression can be categorized.

A framework for the classification of indigenous art applicable to "Fourth World" contexts has been established by Nelson Graburn (1976), and we may fruitfully apply parts of his schema to the artistic output of al-Qurna. Graburn defines the "Fourth World" as

> [T]he collective name for all aboriginal and native peoples whose lands fall within the national boundaries and techno-bureaucratic administrations of the countries of the First, Second and Third Worlds. As such, they are peoples without countries of their own, peoples who are usually in the minority and without the power to direct the course of their collective lives. (Graburn, 1976: 1)

Applying this notion to the field of art and craft production entails more than the study of seemingly fixed indigenous cultural expressions: the loss of isolation has caused indigenous art to become modified, the people involved often having become "dependent part-societies whose very thought and culture reflect the differences from, and accommodation to, the realities of the majority peoples surrounding them" (Graburn, 1976: 2). Because of this accommodation, Fourth World art adjusts itself to prevailing situations and is one of continual change: "of emerging ethnicities, modifying identities, and commercial and colonial stimuli and repressive action" (Graburn, 1976: 2).

In such changing environments, the gift to express oneself artistically becomes particularly important. Graburn identifies two categories: (1) art for internal use, intended to reinforce the ethnic identity and social cohesion of the group through the display and transfer of values held as important by its members (Graburn, 1976: 4–5); and (2) art for external, or commercial, use, which, apart from its economic function, maintains the intergroup boundaries that lie at the root of the perceived ethnic identity (Graburn, 1976: 5). As such "all-human social groups . . . need symbols of their internal and external boundaries; the practical and decorative arts often provide these essential markers" (Graburn, 1976: 5).

In the case of al-Qurna, we may indeed observe that its identity as a community of craftsmen is one of the characterizing features that distinguishes it from such neighboring and mainly agricultural communities as al-Ba'irat. Furthermore, its historical origins are squarely located in "colonial stimuli," its contemporary artistic output remains entirely commercial, and it is continually subject to innovation and change.

Graburn's schema recognizes six different stages within the above two types. These stages document the many directions through which artistic expression can be channeled: (a) non-commercial traditional or functional fine arts, which have remained unaffected by European contact, and which serve internal purposes such as the transmission of symbolic meaning; (b) commercial fine arts that may include objects that conform to the standard of (a) but which may be sold under certain conditions ("pseudo traditional arts"); and such less meaningful items as (c) souvenirs; (d) reintegrated arts; (e) assimilated fine arts; and (f) popular arts (Graburn, 1976: 5–6).

The two classifications relevant for al-Qurna are (c) 'souvenirs' and (d) 'reintegrated arts.' 'Souvenirs' are those artistic expressions that serve commercial tourism purposes, their production driven by economic rationales, intending to be pleasing to the buyer, but holding no artistic satisfaction for the producer, who may even operate at a loss of his own aesthetic standards. These artistic expressions, also known as 'tourist' or 'airport' art, "may bear little relation to the traditional arts of the creator culture or those of any other groups" (Graburn, 1976: 6). 'Reintegrated arts' represent syntheses between traditional and post-contact, European-inspired designs, materials, and production techniques. Some of these may lead to new traditions or new forms of commercial art in their own right (Graburn, 1976: 6–7).

On the surface, these two stages of Graburn's schema only roughly apply to al-Qurna's artistic output, and we may make some further observations to obtain a better fit. All art produced at al-Qurna serves commercial purposes and, in common with most Fourth World art, is "rarely produced for their own consumption" (Graburn, 1976: 1). In fact, what has been observed elsewhere also applies to the Theban west bank: "I know of no [villager] who produces carvings for his own amusement, to display such items in his household for his own pleasure" (McCall, 1980: 127). At least from early travelers' records, there is no attested evidence of Qurnawi indigenous artistic expression, although the symbolic hand stencils and *al-'arusa* clay figurines imprinted on west bank ovens and mud storage cylinders may be taken to reflect Graburn's category of art for internal use, and are likely to be of early origin. Beyond these, contemporary Qurnawi artistic expression cannot be said to have a direct, unbroken "relation to the traditional arts of the creator culture" (Graburn, 1976: 6). Immediate continuities between ancient Egypt and contemporary population groups inferred from postulated direct descent (Goneim, in Cottrell, 1950: 144) and resulting in claimed "analogies" (Blackman, 1927: 280–315) cannot be conclusively argued. In this sense, the Theban west bank artistic output is "reintegrated," and constitutes a synthesis between traditional ancient Egyptian motifs familiar to Qurnawi from their immediate village surroundings, and the external, post-contact and initially European but now fully international demand for such designs. The fact that such "reintegrated art" in Graburn's schema may also give rise to new traditions or forms of commercial art in their own right is also evident at al-Qurna: the production of imitation antiquities that has emerged since the early nineteenth century, and that continues to manifest aspects of technical and stylistic innovation, helps to explain the fluidity we have already observed, which may exist between such categories as a readily recognized 'modern antique,' a 'good copy,' and a convincing fake.

These fluid dimensions of artistic expression at al-Qurna also provide a theoretical corrective to Graburn's concept of "tourist arts." They come into play especially in archaeological contexts of culture tourism, where tourists' demand for locally obtained art merges with a demand for artifacts that have desirable archaeological attributes, and where artists' objectives become the creation of 'modern antiques' that can be identified as ancient artifacts obtained from allegedly authentic archaeological contexts. Where such applies, and evidently it not always does, rather than being simply 'souvenirs,' for the buyer concerned items obtained in this category will have the additional dimension of collectable antique. While its true nature will be known to the Qurnawi artist or peddler, the distinction will in many cases not be evident to the tourist, and it is the objective of Qurnawi production and sales strategies to blur the boundary between contemporary artistic expression and ancient artifact as much as possible.

At the margin of these practices, no longer concerning 'true' tourist art, and certainly not operating 'at a loss of his own aesthetic standards,' is the astronomically priced work of the master craftsmen who create faithful labor-intensive copies of ancient carvings commissioned by international connoisseurs familiar with their work, or variant interpretations sold as forgeries to unsuspecting overseas collectors and antiquities dealers. Artists of this caliber were consistently evasive when asked to show their work. The seemingly covert nature of their operations involves an understated process of referral through local and international contacts, which brings wealthy prospective buyers to their doors and which ultimately results in consignments of works of art shipped to overseas destinations. Possibly because of the speculation about more sinister business that such operations invite, these artists remain otherwise inaccessible to individual visitors of evidently insufficient means, including the resident anthropologist.

So many artists, so many ways: Form and method of Qurnawi artistic expression

Contrary to the image evoked by the grinders of alabaster ware encountered outside roadside tourist shops, artisanal production at al-Qurna is entirely a cottage industry, with all locally produced items destined for sale to tourists and created by men, women, and children in the domestic environment of their homes. The stylistic range and variability of artifacts produced is vast and the totality of production has moved well beyond the straight copying reported by Lange in 1952, when local artists seemed essentially guided by museum catalogues, with stylistic variability the unintended consequence of an inadvertent mixing of ancient Egyptian period-specific stylistic features (Lange, 1952: 152). Today the copying from illustrations in catalogues, popular and scholarly publications, or even picture postcards takes place, but the carving of limestone wall panels and assorted statuary especially appears to postdate Lange's observations, their introduction both reflecting the shifting tastes of visitors and the adaptive artistic skills of Qurnawi craftsmen. They form part of a range of innovative designs and manufacturing practices that have evolved, and no doubt will continue to do so, in evidence of people's inventiveness and the inspiration obtained from the surrounding environment. Where Lange could observe that the demand for these 'harmless forgeries' would diminish because people with "greater understanding of the true value of ancient Egyptian art [and] hardened by world wars would be less inclined to give in to romantic illusions" so as not to be "taken in" by these "naïve" forgeries (Lange, 1952: 153), the opposite has in fact occurred. The antiquities legislation–induced scarcity of ancient artifacts on the open market has forced any remnant trade to go underground. The consequent steep increase in prices asked for genuine *antikas* has placed the acquisition of authentic artifacts out of reach of all but the most serious collectors, thus creating the market niche for peddlers' 'modern antiques' and the host of imaginative substitutes capable of serving tourists' objectives of personal memento or gifts for loved ones.

It is not the intention here to give a detailed analysis of the range and stylistic variability of artisanal production at al-Qurna that has emerged from the above historical process. One limestone carver claimed that there were more than one thousand "good carvers," a figure that does not seem outside the range of possibilities, and that, at 5 percent of the west bank population and for limestone, soapstone, and wood carvers alone, can only be indicative of the total number of west bank craftsmen and women involved in the production of one type or another. Plates have been included under Appendix 6 to give the reader a 'flavor' of the quality and diversity of domestic craft production at al-Qurna. The photographs are of items obtained between 1995 and 1999 from craftsmen known to Badawi or several of his personal contacts and in that sense represent a random sample of the range of contemporary artistic practices that exist on the Theban west bank. Rather than categorizing production by material or design, the following paragraphs will briefly profile a small selection of working artists, their collective selection to be considered a framework for understanding Qurnawi artisanal production. Using this personalized framework, certain predominant details of design and artistic classification, as well as aspects of the social and material reality of their production, can be made explicit.

Tayyeb Muhammad Yusuf

Tayyeb, his brothers Mahmud and Yusuf, and their elderly father Muhammad are a family of alabaster carvers who are considered "the best ones" on the west bank.[2] Even so, this is not a family business and each works for himself, although their individual reputation at least in part also stems from that of their father. The work is labor intensive and does not allow for additional occupations. It is also specialized, and therefore, relatively competition-free: few who want to break into the business of producing tourist art will take it up as a new craft. But non-artist laborers will find employment in the alabaster industry and Tayyeb will engage some extra people to do the less specialized tasks for him. He has six children and his fifteen-year-old son Muhammad will help him after school and during his school holidays, thus acquiring the necessary skills from his father. Even though Muhammad aspires to be a doctor, Tayyeb holds the opinion that it is a father's duty to teach his son everything he knows. Even if a son will want to go his own way, he will still have his father's skills to fall back on.

Tayyeb does not deal with tourists directly and only produces for bazaars and tourist shops (also known as 'alabaster factories'). Many such businesses want to buy from him, but he can only work for three of them. By dealing with only these three clients, Tayyeb obtains the advantages that come with well-established relationships. He can rely on a 50 percent deposit from his clients when they place an order with him, and they know the quality of his work. Were he to change his customers, this would simply create hassles: negotiating pay conditions and inspections of his work. It is easiest to only work with those who are already familiar with him and his work. As is often the case in other tourism-related industries, there is no need to give special 'presents' to retain the business from these shops, and during the periodically experienced quiet times, for example, such as after the collapse of the tourism industry following the Luxor Massacre, he can rely on their help to make ends meet. Even so, he has not chosen the shops he works for without consideration. One of his daughters is married to the owner of one to whom he has chosen not to sell, so as to prevent any potential business dispute compromising either his relationship with his daughter, or her relationship with her husband; all business must remain business, with family links being seen as potentially counterproductive.

Tayyeb may receive orders for some twenty-five pieces every forty days, with orders comprising a variety of different pieces. Tayyeb has fixed prices based on a pricing structure for each item, their aggregate defining the amount for the order, rather than the order being specified for a total amount. Tayyeb's price is based on the size and number of days' work for each piece, rather than the design only, although the time spent will be defined by the size and the detail of its design.

Tayyeb orders his alabaster once a month from stone merchants who obtain their product from the Esna region, having it delivered to his house at LE350 per ton. When he was seventeen, he once went along, using donkeys in the desert where cars could not go, along a dangerous route with

Tayyeb Muhammad Yusuf.

narrow mountain paths and deep valleys where donkeys have been known to fall and people die. Walking from seven in the evening to eight in the morning, extracting the rocks using dynamite and handpicks from eight in the morning to six in the evening, and then walking back again without sleep, the trip left him sick for the next two weeks. He now would not go even if people paid him, but workers who demonstrate alabaster carving outside alabaster factories will readily use such personalized accounts as part of their presentations to tourists.

The manufacture of alabaster stoneware is complex and laborious, consisting of sixteen different stages or processes. In summary, and grouping some of the individual stages together, these include: (1) shaping the external form of the chosen design; (2) gluing layers of protective linen on the outside to prevent cracking; (3) 'opening' the interior, representing different stages and using a range of swiveled handles fitted with three-pronged spikes and drilling blades of ever-increasing degrees of precision; (4) removal of protective linen and application of further glue to strengthen the crystalline calcite structure; (5) filing off glue, sanding, and polishing; (6) heating for five or ten minutes in the *furn* (oven) to enhance translucence; (7) coating with liquid candle wax inside and out (to bring out the color and crystalline pattern, as well as to smooth the uneven crystalline structure of coarser stones), cooling,

Design-labor ratio for Alabaster stoneware pricing structure			
Design	Size	Time	Price
Large cup	30 cm	10 days	LE350
Small cup	20 cm	6 days	LE200
Large globular 'vase'	25 cm	7 days	LE150
Medium globular 'vase'	20 cm	5 days	LE150
Small globular 'vase'	15 cm	4 days	LE50
Large open bowl	30 cm	6 days	LE150
Small open bowl	15 cm	4 days	LE50

Alabaster stoneware pricing structure based on design–labor ratio for Tayyeb Muhammad Yusuf. Manufacturing times will only be approximate, as multiple pieces will be at various stages of construction at any given time. Prices are as given, but such information being offered to a potentially buying 'tourist' may possibly not truly reflect the 'Egyptian price' charged to alabaster factories. Even so, Tayyeb's earnings will be substantial.

hardening, and removal of excess wax, followed by a final cloth polish. Working from home, Tayyeb himself first prepares the external shapes of some fifteen pieces, before arranging for a laborer to assist him for five or six days by doing much of the rougher grinding, counting the number of turns to ascertain and control progress. Tayyeb is in charge of configuring the various grinding tools, and wedging the different blades, which will define the shape of individual pieces, into position. It is immaterial to what extent these production processes reflect ancient Egyptian alabaster-production technologies. Some stages may, others may not, but in the development of the current process their manufacture nevertheless represents a significant and locally developed innovation—distinct from the machine-produced stonewares available in Cairo—provided in response to external market forces. The resulting products have artistic merit in their own right and will remind those who buy them of similar wares found in the ancient tombs.

Ascertaining a measure of Tayyeb's income during times of constant demand, we may average the price of the above tabled seven designs at LE157 each, with Tayyeb's gross turnover on twenty-five pieces produced over forty days amounting to LE3,925 or LE2,944 per month. Even as a minimum turnover, this is significant when compared to a net LE150-per-month government wage paid to antiquities guards, and the desire for

Tayyeb Muhammad Yusuf's order in progress.

Tayyeb's son to study medicine is therefore not unrealistic. For his part, and apart from living well, during good times Tayyeb will convert his savings by buying gold for his wife and daughters, which can be readily sold during lean times. The use of gold for 'banking' purposes also explains the significance of the gold shop in Genina, which does not simply serve the purpose of personal adornment but also constitutes a traditional form of reinvesting wealth.

Muhammad Ali Muhammad

Like Tayyeb, limestone carver Muhammad Ali Muhammad produces mainly for three different tourist shops, one of these being the small bazaar near Ramose's tomb, but he will try to accommodate other bazaars if they ask for his work. He may also produce special orders and sell to tourists directly if they are brought to his home by peddlers or local guides. His decision concerning what to make is based on what the sellers of his art require: the bazaar near Ramose will predominantly (but not exclusively) be interested in copies of the Ramose limestone reliefs, a seller in the Valley of the Queens is likely to buy carvings of Queen Nefertari.

During times when demand is high, usually at least one seller will come to his house every day to buy two or three pieces. Muhammad can produce seven or eight of his better quality carvings in a week, but can achieve twenty by dropping his standard to the lower quality also found in tourist shops, depending on what the seller requires or is prepared to spend.

Muhammad only occupies himself with the actual carving, although, while his own nine- and ten-year-old sons are still too young, he employs older boys to cut the limestone panels and perform some of the less precise work, paying them some money for the cutting but training them in the art of limestone carving at the same time. It was in this same way that he acquired his first skills as a youngster: sitting and watching. When he was older and wanted to learn specific skills, he would invite renowned carvers into his home to produce a piece for him to buy, learning as he watched. Muhammad also uses a laborer to come and hand-saw the slabs for him at a cost of LE15 per day, generally not a family member, but one "who can do the job well." These are cut to a thickness of 2 to 2.5 centimeters, ranging in size from anywhere between 16x33 centimeters to 29x35 centimeters. The back and sides are retouched with a chisel to suggest hand-quarried stone. Larger designs are possible on request, but the physical constraint will always be what tourists can take with them. Muhammad works from a collection of photocopied designs, tracing the outline through carbon paper onto the surface of the limestone slabs, but only partially—he knows the designs well enough to confidently fill in the details by hand. Resting the slab on a low table, Muhammad carves the designs with a set of ten finely-graded chisels. Working on a 'Ramose,' he periodically wets the stone with a sponge to prevent irregular splintering, and uses the sharp corner of a four-millimeter chisel to draw freehand such design details as eyes and hair. Carving the latter, he does so with a deft, zigzagging motion, sometimes continuous, at other times only interrupting himself to adjust the angle of the limestone panel, and not in the least distracted when answering questions, sipping tea, or having his son play around him.

Other than working in limestone, and to relieve the certain monotony of his routine carving duties, Muhammad also explores other media such as soapstone and ceramics. When he was younger, he was trained by Muhammad al-Haw, who was then a famous scarab carver. Muhammad initially applied himself to carving only scarabs for four years, and his now infrequent soapstone specimens are still among the loveliest to be found. Combining his talents as a carver with a desire for continual innovation and improvement, Muhammad also experiments with the manufacture of ceramic *shabti*s, using a genuine antique specimen in his

Muhammad Ali
Muhammad.

possession as an example, employing various mixtures of clay, ground white glass,[3] *dinkar* (potassium carbonate, K_2CO_3), and powdered soapstone in differing drying and firing regimes to achieve results that range from red earthenware to white porcelain. His differing applications of crushed glass, copper pigment, and salts attempt to achieve the blue-green glaze of ancient faience.

Muhammad has fixed prices, based on size and the degree of difficulty—raised relief being somewhat more expensive than sunken relief—as well as the speed and the quality of his work. Although reticent to clearly indicate price categories and earnings, a larger quality carving representing a day's work would sell for LE200, while small- to medium-sized work in varying degrees of quality would range in price up to LE50. Discounting possible low-grade work sold at higher volume but lower price, and assuming only a production of seven high-quality pieces sold for LE200 each per week, this would provide a maximum income of LE5,600 for a given four-week period. Subject to seasonal downturns and other unforeseen periods of low demand, Muhammad's potential earnings, like Tayyeb's, thus compare very favorably with the government wage of an antiquities guard, and explain his move to a new red-brick three-storied house in the Gezirat al-Qurna area, which he shares with his elderly parents and two married brothers, while keeping the vacated family house in the foothills to be strategically exchanged with Luxor City Council for the future benefit of his and his brothers' children.

Ahmad al-Harazi

His job as an antiquities guard at the Noble Tombs in al-Hurubat, working shifts of twenty-four hours on, twenty-four hours off, provides Ahmad al-Harazi with the time to invest in his soapstone (gray or green steatite) sculpture business of thirty years. In addition to his shifts, his job allows him to take a total of twenty-eight days' leave per year, offering him the flexibility to take time off work to fill orders when demand is high. He cannot carve or sell to tourists in the necropolis during his working hours. Guarding two hundred tombs requires him and his three colleagues to make a round every two hours, leaving little time in between, their alertness in any case inspected by the *shaykh al-ghaffir* and Tourism and Antiquities Police. As a result, peddlers and bazaar owners come to him for stock. His sales network does not rely on family connections, but was established by Ahmad initially approaching sellers, looking for people who can "do good business for me." His network now consists of some fifteen to twenty men, six of whom have the Noble Tombs as their base, but his contacts range as far as the bazaars in the Red Sea resorts of Hurghada and Sharm al-Shaykh. Ahmad's prices are all different due to the varying amount of work involved, although the price for each type is set: his buyers know his prices and there is no bargaining. The selection of types of items is decided by Ahmad's buyers, who have knowledge of what tourists in their area will be likely to buy. They in turn will set their own sales prices, which is as much as the tourist is prepared to pay in order to get the highest profit margin.

The quantity Ahmad can produce in a day or a week will vary depending on the size of each piece and the amount of detail. During times of high demand he has two people who cut rough 'blanks' for him, who are picked for their ability and paid per piece or per day. In a good week

Ahmad may earn three to four months' worth of his monthly government wage, that is, LE450 to LE600, providing him with an extra gross maximum income of LE2,600 per month. But his guard job is nevertheless important for the security it provides: a predictable income during poor tourism seasons and the surety of a government pension upon retirement. During his earlier years he did not produce as much, nor did he work every available day, but he was content with a reduced income. Now that he has a family, and no revenue from agricultural activities, he never stops carving. Since he works from home, his overhead costs are relatively minimal, including LE250 for a carload of one thousand kilograms of soapstone, and the expenses for additional labor, fuel, color pigments, and other chemicals. No tax is payable on work done from home, and only deducted from government wages or levied if the business is a 'factory' or has a shopfront.

He initially learned basic skills from another carver, but soon developed his own style and repertoire, including large scarabs and seated figurines. Scarabs may come in two varieties, those high on their legs, with the stone in between carved away, the so-called 'walking' scarabs,

Ahmad al-Harazi applying a final coating of *jamalaka* (lacquer).

taking him as little as two and a half hours to produce, and the 'resting' scarabs. His larger and more complex figurines may take a day to carve. To give permanency and further character to his work, Ahmad subjects his carvings to three additional processes, first hardening the soft soapstone by firing his statues in a *faghura*, a traditional dome-shaped kiln consisting of dried dung cakes that Ahmad stacks underneath, over, and around a collection of finished carvings. A *faghura* measuring approximately 100x70 centimeters may contain some twenty-one carvings, representing ten days' work. Controlling the oxygen flow through the structure by plugging any developing holes with pieces of dung cake, a *faghura* will burn for one to one and a half hours, depending on size and the quantity of carvings. Stones with flaws will break, the pieces recovered by Ahmad to glue, although his clients will inspect his work for cracks. Because of Ahmad's stylistic diversions, these statues cannot be sold as faked antiques, where a fracture may be used to good advantage, but will ultimately be bought by tourists simply wanting an interesting piece. Like a potter, these firings are regular events in Ahmad's working week, as is the expense of buying the dung cakes at LE6 a bag, since he has no animals to produce his own: "my five children are all at school, so who would be there to look after them?" Retrieved from the ashes with tongs while still hot, each sculpture is immersed in a large bowl containing a quarter of a kilogram of dissolved *bermanghanat* (potassium permanganate, $KMnO_4$, LE16 per kilogram), fuming and spattering, first turning the stone white, then, upon prolonged immersion, greenish-brown. When it is taken out its flashes of pink and purple gradually turn darker as the stone cooks, then cools on its metal tray. The final stage involves applying an additional red ochre pigment with a sponge, and a final layer of lacquer serving as a fixative, softening the red into a polished, warm brown.

Ahmad's sculptures are only marginally inspired by the ancient designs, often somewhat surrealistically so—two figures seated back to back, their faces indistinct, the column that separates them ending in a lotus flower—and they are neither totally conventional, nor always well proportioned. Replicas they are not. Even so, his 'seated captives,' positioned back-to-back, their arms bound together above their heads, are said to be "from Tutankhamun," which may be true thematically, but stylistically only vaguely so. His work is not necessarily that of a skilled artist, but the work of one who, using basic skills and working in soft stone, has arrived at a particular style and, having developed a sales network that has evidently tapped a certain niche for this kind of work, has contributed a degree of artistic innovation to the total commercial output of the Theban west bank artisan community.

Abdu Muhammad Ahmad

Abdu, at fifty-two years old, has only been carving limestone statues for fifteen years. He initially learned the trade from a friend by observing him while he worked and then trying it himself, breaking pieces as he learned. He used to copy from photographs, but now has it all "in his head." Abdu is a colleague restorer of Badawi, and works at the temple of Madinat Habu. His working hours allow him to carve during much of the afternoon, usually between two and six in the afternoon, although he will work until midnight when there are orders to fill. During seasonal downturns and when tourism unexpectedly collapses, as it did during the winter of 1997–98, Abdu still continues to work, building up stock for better times. Limestone is delivered by the carload carrying one thousand kilograms and costing him LE250. One load provides a sufficient supply for two months' work when business is good. He hires somebody to cut the blocks into manageable pieces, paying the worker LE5 per piece. Abdu's selling strategies are less structured than those of the above-mentioned artists. He sells to several tourist shops, and will take orders from them. But he also supplies local shops operated by middlemen where peddlers go to buy their wares, and will also take occasional orders from peddlers themselves, or supply to tourists who are brought to his door by local guides. He may even travel to Aswan to sell to the tourist bazaars there.

Speaking about his choice of subject matter, he confesses that he is "good at everything," and "looks for his business" rather than his own preferences. The degree of difficulty and the amount of detail for three-dimensional work being roughly similar, his prices are generally guided by their size and the time taken to produce. A seated female figurine approximately forty centimeters tall takes four days to create and sells for LE200 to a tourist shop, or for LE150 to one of the local shops. Middlemen may arrange to have the statue painted, and would in turn sell it to tourist bazaars for LE250. Pieces between twenty-five and thirty centimeters tall take two days to complete and may be sold to a tourist bazaar for LE120 to LE150. Assuming that during good times Abdu would have orders for at least one such large and one smaller piece, this would provide him with

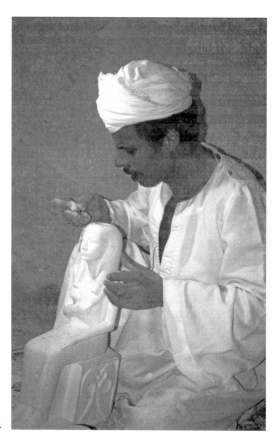

Abdu Muhammad Ahmad.

six days of work, although he may well be working on multiple pieces at the same time. Sold to tourist bazaars at top price, his government wage could be increased by LE350 per week, or roughly LE1,500 per month.

Abdu works with the *daburra*, the double chisel fitted like a small pick-axe, to carve the outline of his statues by taking large flakes off the raw block. He periodically moistens the stone for a few minutes to 'soften' it and make the cutting easier. Alternate use of the *daburra*'s differently sized ends allows for ever-increasing precision, the ultimate forms and features carved with the finely graded chisels also used by Muhammad Ali Muhammad. Entirely conceived by eye and without the use of draw-ings, Abdu's pieces are confidently and masterfully crafted, the odd pencil markings providing all the guidance he needs, the human form beauti-fully proportioned—even if somewhat stylized—and gifted with serenely smiling faces.

Abdu Muhammad Ahmad at work in his courtyard.

Such, indeed, seems to be the contentment of Abdu's life. In a happy second marriage with four young daughters, his artistic skills have enabled him to adequately provide for his family and to achieve the lifestyle he desires. The seated female figure was sold as soon as it was finished, notwithstanding that this was an otherwise disastrous season. The earnings were used that same day toward some new clothes for his daughters, purchased in Luxor, even though they were not necessarily happy with what they received: "they now all want jeans." Such is the dichotomy of the necropolis, where ancient skills enable aspects of modernity. Abdu is not worried, and accepts that such external influences are the same as those that generate demand for his business. He smiles a welcoming smile at his returning children, then resumes his work on the statue at hand, seated in his regular spot:

> [N]ext to the front door in the warm light of the setting sun, framed by the mud-brick wall that is his home, turkeys parading and chickens scurrying around the yard, a wife's beautiful smile, Abdu creating beautiful things. The children telling their Luxor stories to friends in the street, Abdu's father sitting to one side, fingering his beads, the call to prayer sounding from the nearby mosque.[4]

Abdu Muhammad Ahmad and family: Ancient designs as a way of making a living and the modernity it affords.

Sayyed Mahmud Ali Abu-Sherifa

When Sayyed was eleven years old his father began to teach him the skills of the trade. Sayyed represents the third generation in a family of carvers. He acknowledges that he can make "everything," and he has no preference for any particular material. After his father's death in 1964, Sayyed continued the family business, with bazaar owners familiar with his family's tradition seeking him out to fill their orders, some coming from as far as Aswan. He also received orders from tourists who made enquiries after seeing his work in bazaars, one of these resulting in a commission worth several thousand Egyptian pounds for a number of large sculptures to decorate a mansion in Germany. During a regular season, Sayyed has people coming to his house every day, both shop owners and local guides who bring interested tourists to his door. Even during the quiet 1997–98 winter, in the week when fieldwork visits to his house took place, incidental sales of items to unexpected visitors accompanied by local guides amounted to at least LE500, representing no more than four days' work, and despite commission payments still well in excess of the monthly wage of an antiquities guard.[5] Additionally, and recognizing that times were quiet, owners of large bazaars would come to his house to order a little stock, now that he was not so busy, rather than having to wait for a week to have their orders filled as they would during times of high demand.

Also in line with his family history, Sayyed is a professional, working during busy times from seven in the morning to three in the afternoon, then from six to midnight. He has four sons and one daughter, all of whom are still in school, but he also teaches his sons, beginning when they are nine or ten, by allowing them to perform small tasks. At sixteen, his oldest son has been fully trained, is capable of teaching his brothers additional skills, and may thus guarantee a fourth generation of craftsmen.

Other than limestone, Sayyed uses wood regularly, possibly because there appears to be an oversupply of limestone carvers, and wood is popular with travelers due to its lighter weight. Soft palm wood is favored, it being relatively easy to shape while its porous structure presents no impediment for fine detailing, as most statues are plastered and painted. But a harder variety called *ghimiz* presents no technical difficulties for Sayyed either. 'Open' statues, such as those of striding figures with limbs extended, are crafted as composite constructions when they are larger than fifty centimeters. This composite method is imposed by the size of the available wood, and serves as a means to use up smaller pieces. This method also makes carving easier and produces less waste. The various separate parts are dowelled to the torso, with any visible seams filed smooth and hidden by plaster and paint. Once coated in plaster and sanded smooth, Sayyed uses pencil to mark the areas to be painted by his wife. He eventually adds the finer details to the coloring himself. Yellow and red ochre, green, and black pigments are mixed with water and applied with a brush made up of several pigeon feathers tied in a bunch. A final coating stabilizes the water colors, but *jamalaka*, the alcohol-based lacquer, is more than a fixative: mixed with salt, soil, and limestone dust, the carvings are given a gritty appearance and 'feel,' as if they have only recently been excavated. Although such 'embellishment' would suit the stories told by tomb-side peddlers, this treatment seems out of place for items sold in bazaars. There, such treatment is not intended as 'story,' but simply to add to the character of the ancient theme, which is as much a part of the object as is its physical shape: offered in the commercial environment of the bazaars, the statue represents a package that sells not simply a memento of a one-time holiday, but the essence of Egypt as "an antique land" itself.[6]

As an artist, Sayyed is also a keen businessman and little inclined to discuss his financial dealings in detail. Yet, as we have observed, sales to buyers coming to his house indicate that he can generate money almost at will, allowing him to maintain a decent lifestyle, to the point of—as it was rumored by some—at times being excessive in his personal preferences.[7] Since the researcher felt that the routine production of tourist mementos might not be sufficiently indicative of his true skills, and to 'test' the artistic ability behind his evident business success, Sayyed was persuaded to carve a wooden *shabti* in the likeness of Tutankhamun, whose features are readily recognizable. Sayyed dismissed the use of a photograph, as "he has it 'all in the head,'" indeed shaping with chisel and file the figurine with deft, calculated but free-flowing, masterly strokes, achieving lovely curves and everything exquisitely proportioned, . . . continually blowing the chips and dust away with little puffs as he works."[8] The piece was finished in two hours, entirely charming in appearance, sufficiently credible to evoke Tutankhamun, yet failing to fully replicate the distinctive nose and lips. Although the soft but coarse palm wood will have imposed its own limitations, given a harder material, more time and a sufficiently large financial incentive that might come with a substantial formal commission, there is little doubt that Sayyed, especially when permitting himself to work from a clear illustration, would be capable of recreating a true likeness. However, other than from incidental commissions by knowledgeable collectors, such does not constitute his main business, and for his part Sayyed is content to make as many commercial pieces in as little time as possible, producing quantity orders for his bazaar clients or, not infrequently, selling any available piece at commission-inflated prices to such French or German tourists as may be guided to his door.

'Distressing' the fake: Chemistry as a marketing strategy[9]

Sayyed's standard practice to coat his painted carvings with some earthy mixture in order to give it a certain patina appealing to tourists is common throughout the necropolis. In generic terms, the process is known as *ghubuwa*, a practice locally explained in a range from "changing its quality" to "making it look old." The concept applies equally to Ahmad al-Harazi's innocent chemical soapstone treatment, changing the color of his pieces to suit his artistic inclination, to the gritty 'package' patina of a Sayyed Mahmud Ali Abu-Sherifa creation, and to those pieces so treated to be sold as real *antikas*. As suggested by the one generic term applied to varying categories of application, individual craftsmen such as Ahmad and Sayyed will have their own *ghubuwa* 'recipe.' Others, like Abdu Muhammad Ahmad, sell their pieces untreated, leaving any additional interpretation of their work to the bazaar middlemen, or to those who have made a specialization of concocting particular *ghubuwa* mixtures.

These latter *ghubuwa* specialists may be commissioned by bazaar middlemen, but are also used predominantly by peddlers who work at certain popular tombs, who have a limited capacity to carry large pieces, and who are in the business of selling some realistically carved small item as a genuine *antika* to any tourist who is interested in buying antiquities and capable of being persuaded, *ghubuwa* being the visible and physical attribute of their story. Those peddlers who invite potential customers to the security of their homes to inspect *antikas* there will invariably have a mixture of small genuine items mixed with pieces of more recent date, the latter suitably altered through *ghubuwa*, the former as much for sale as they add legitimacy to the rest, confounding the non-expert and feeding the 'discourse of the uncertain.' Needless to say, both categories will carry a price tag that reflects the absence of antiquities on the open market, starting at LE1,300 for a small amulet or *shabti*, a situation that marks the difference between the time of such observers as Kurt Lange in 1952 and today.

Some peddlers may buy their pieces unaltered and apply their own preferred *ghubuwa* treatment. But many will come to al-Hurubat to see Hassan Sayyed Muhammad who, in keeping with the academic community that frequents the village surrounds, calls himself 'Doctor Hassan,' for good measure announcing himself as "*professeur de ghubuwa*." Rather than in the artists themselves, it is in the craft of a person like Hassan that we may encounter what others have called the 'forgers' of the necropolis (Ammoun, 1993; Lange, 1952): artists probably less so, but artisans who ply a specialized trade nonetheless. Hassan lives next to his older brother, who is also a limestone carver. In close proximity to Yanni's house, Hassan's house is an assemblage of sorts: part mud-brick structure and partly constructed from palm-frond crates filled with rubble, the structure first served as animal space for the family home subsequently occupied by his brother. After he married, Hassan moved out and converted the animal quarters into his home. His standard of living is both indicative of his limited government restorers' wage, and the makeshift practice that is his *ghubuwa* trade: making things look less than what they are, rather than improving them into what they could be, 'distressing' rather than embellishing.

Although Doctor Hassan freely shared his knowledge and unselfishly demonstrated several of his practices, the researcher to whom such access is given is nevertheless limited by ethical constraints that inhibit disseminating what are essentially the secrets of his trade. Although realistically forged objects will contain their own power of persuasion, and public knowledge of forgery techniques will not necessarily compromise the livelihood of a person like Doctor Hassan, preserving informants' integrity and honoring their confidence by treating their information in a certain sense as 'secret knowledge' is nevertheless a duty that binds the ethnographer—not unlike insiders' knowledge of illicit antiquities dealings. But the repertoire of Doctor Hassan's practices in broad terms is indicative of the range of methods employed by others who similarly 'distress' contemporary foothills art, and we may therefore make some general observations about some aspects of that repertoire. In any event, and as can be observed in the work of Sayyed Mahmud Ali Abu-Sherifa, applications of *ghubuwa* are not only intended to 'forge': in most cases they innocently serve to provide the piece with an atmosphere that is

'Spurious antiquities' are now part of a package that sells not simply a memento of a one-time holiday, but the essence of Egypt as 'an antique land' itself. A range of recipes are employed to give modern tourist art a 'feel' for ancient times.

'Distressing' the fake: Chemistry as a marketing strategy   273 evocative of ancient times and that is therefore in aesthetic terms not very different from applying painted decorations.

Because of the peddlers' need for small portable objects, many of the practices concern small limestone items such as scarabs and heads. If color is deemed necessary, then it is applied first, consisting of pigments dissolved in alcohol, the color absorbed by the porous stone. Epoxy glues and natural resin can be used as coatings to control the degree of absorption. Corrosive processes then applied, either by means of chloric acid ($HClO_3$) or through boiling in liquids that contain copious amounts of kitchen salt, will cause surface erosion also in the painted areas, its existence indicated to buyers as proof of age. Additives during boiling may further include tea, henna dye, any surplus prescription medicines, soil, and limestone dust. Important ingredients used by several producers of *ghubuwa* are pulverized *mumiya* and mummification linen, obtained from ancient commoner burials still contained in the many caves and passages of the Theban Mountain and periodically accessed for this purpose by those who require these additives. Doctor Hassan is careful with their use, covering his hand in a plastic bag for fear of contamination by unknown ancient mummification chemicals, but in the process also protecting himself from any of the other chemicals that may affect his skin. Carvings may be left in this liquid mixture for several days, upon which they are slowly heated for one day in the oven after the weekly baking of bread (or fired specifically for that purpose) in order to dispel moisture from the limestone and to add extra patina. Wooden carvings may likewise be subjected to different treatments. One method requires a painted carving to be left buried for a period of one month in soil "underneath the donkey." A different method involves wrapping the carving in ancient mummification linen, painted white and provided with a copied inscription, the entire assemblage buried for one month in the limestone dust of the hillside, the hole backfilled with a mixture of kitchen salt and *nitrokima* fertilizer, the area regularly watered, the resulting heat-assisted corrosive impact considered sufficient to convince a non-expert of its authenticity.

Doctor Hassan's lifestyle suggests that this is not a lucrative business. At best, he may earn LE10 a piece for applying paint and *ghubuwa* for the owner of a carving who, if he is a peddler, may indeed dispose of it to a tourist for whatever price that person is prepared to pay. If the piece is sufficiently convincing, and the peddler's "intelligent" stories are equally persuasive, an individual sale for LE400 can indeed be realized. But by then Doctor Hassan's involvement with that piece will already have been concluded and he will likely be concocting a new mixture for his next project.

However, tourists on their way to Menna's tomb may stop to inspect some of the limestone panels exhibited on his brother's stepped display stand, as a result of which Hassan meets many visitors, and he too, like a peddler, may from time to time be able to charm a tourist into an occasional sale. To this end, Doctor Hassan also experiments with differing mixtures of shale, clay, and crushed glass to create ceramic and porcelain figurines. Since he is not a carving artist, he may obtain a modern carving and make a mold in order to make his own castings of such small items as *shabti*s and the inscribed ends of funerary cones, the ceramic cylinders that were originally inserted as a frieze above tomb entrances.

On other occasions he obtains an authentic piece, either for consideration as a purchase or lent to him for a night, both opportunities which he uses to obtain a mold for creating his own castings. Doctor Hassan claims such pieces come from excavations, although other scenarios possibly involving SCA antiquities inspectors and their access to the *makhazin*—formal storage areas located throughout the necropolis—may not be beyond contemplation either. The opportunity to produce a fake of this type may come only once a year, but rather than selling to the next person who comes along, Hassan will keep it for one who is looking for "something special" and who is prepared to pay for it, generally not less than LE500, even if it takes eight months. Even so, the incidental sale of such items does not make Doctor Hassan a wealthy man. Indeed, these sales are more likely to help him repay some accumulated debts or assist with periodically recurring expenses, such as buying new clothes and shoes for his children at the start of the school year, than they are regular and predictable income, providing consistent support for the household budget.

To overcome the periodic budgetary troughs resulting from irregular sales, and if there are no immediate financial needs, then any incidental surplus earnings Doctor Hassan makes from his *ghubuwa* practice or his ceramics sales may be invested in *jama'iya*. This is indeed the same term as used for the communal upkeep of the *zawiya*, but the notion of group cooperation is here exclusively applied to mutual financial support. Those villagers whose income is not sufficient to invest excess earnings in gold, such as is done by Tayyeb Muhammad Yusuf, may form a savings group with surrounding neighbors, colleagues, and related or befriended households: *jama'iya*. The practice is not particular to al-Qurna, but is widespread throughout Egypt, and may even be used by children among their friends. Arrangements per group will differ depending on the structure agreed upon by its members, but they all involve a set contribution over a certain time span and a periodic payment of accrued funds to one member at a time, the collecting of funds and keeping of records performed by one member of the group. According to one scenario, some seven members may decide to put in LE2 per day for a period of seventy days, with LE140 distributed every ten days according to a list of names obtained by ballot at the beginning of the cycle to establish the payment sequence. Thus, being number four in line, LE140 will become available after forty days. Other schemes may require an agreed-upon contribution of LE20 per month, with a payout made each month to one of the members. Depending on one's relative place in the sequence, such funds are generally unavailable for immediate needs, but other funds can be borrowed, or goods purchased on credit, against the security of accruing *jama'iya* payouts becoming available in due course. While not exactly micro-credit, *jama'iya* allows members to save toward future expenses such as weddings or *wajib* commitments, invest in stock when peddling artifacts to tourists or toward any other business purpose, and arrange credit or funds to cope with more immediate family needs. The schemes are flexible and as many members as are interested may participate, the agreed amount based on what everyone can pay. If individual members can pay more, they may enter multiple times, as long as they make the contributions required. If a sudden financial problem arises during the course of the cycle, a request can be made to the group to be placed at the head of the list, or one can exchange places with someone else for an earlier payout. In this sense, and rather than being simply a savings scheme or an alternative to formal banking, *jama'iya* is seen as a way to "fix a problem" and to even out the differences between the highs and lows that will inevitably punctuate household budgets, especially for Qurnawi such as Doctor Hassan and peddler Badawi, whose regular wages are low and for whom additional income earned from participation in the tourism business is either insubstantial or unpredictable.

One final observation that may be made from Doctor Hassan's *ghubuwa* business is that, rather than characterizing the Qurnawi art industry as a "market of deception" (Ammoun, 1993: 121), the existence and application of *ghubuwa* techniques generally, place in a social and technical context the legitimate production of all contemporary necropolis art. The test to which Sayyed Mahmud Ali Abu-Sherifa was subjected, reported above, revealed that, while he was judged to be entirely capable of producing a faithful likeness of an ancient design, his work nevertheless failed to completely and accurately achieve this. While the particular context of that commission and the somewhat charitable nature of his effort may have been reasons why he did not produce his best, the role of the *ghubuwa* phenomenon must also be considered. Individual pieces from different artists encountered by the researcher, which were totally satisfying and entirely charming in their newly carved state, lost much of their appeal as works of art in their own right once they had become—literally—'distressed.'[10] It must thus be concluded that artists technically capable of producing totally convincing pieces will rarely live up to their ability and generally be satisfied with something less than perfect, not only because they know their craft will still earn them a decent income, but also because they realize that striving for perfection will ultimately be useless for the socially-motivated mutilations inflicted upon their creations under the requirements of *ghubuwa*.

Point of sale: Purchasing tourist art in the Theban Necropolis

The covert way the few Hurubati master craftsmen conduct their business contrasts with the generally public way in which visitors to the west bank obtain their souvenirs and gifts: through tourist bazaars, stalls at particular archaeological sites, itinerant peddlers near popular tombs, and local guides mediating contact between individual travelers and local artists.

Package tour groups arriving by coach on the west bank will have their first experience with the material reality and artistic forms of the west bank artisan community while en route to Hatshepsut's Temple or the Valley of the Kings. By arrangement with the owner and in exchange for a hefty commission of between 40 and 60 percent of sales,[11] tour guides will stop the coach at 'their' respective 'alabaster factories,' which are concentrated along the foothills road opposite Dra' Abu al-Naga, to spend precious visitors' time not in temples or tombs but in the gallery atmosphere of these commercial establishments. Headlight signals from approaching touring coaches prompt the workers into action—"*shughl*!"—"work!" Disembarking tourists are treated to a display of alabaster carving in front of the building, which gives them the impression that the alabaster ware sold inside is made on the premises, and explaining why this type of business is generally referred to as an alabaster 'factory'. Their origin dates back to the early 1970s, when Tayyeb Abdullahi from al-'Atyat conceived of the idea to move the trade away from peddlers and concentrate sales in one particular point, at the same time providing a demonstration of the production process. The method was taken up by others when seen as successful, with people pooling resources to rent or build premises and obtain stock.[12] Although it was said that during the early years these were true places of production, with mothers keen to send their young sons there for apprenticeships, the diversity of stock lines today underscores that these are indeed bazaars, tourist shops, rather than places of alabaster production. The alabaster manufacturing techniques exhibited outside only marginally contribute toward stock, but serve to attract tourists and to provide photographic opportunities supplementing any alabaster purchases made inside.[13] The practice is locally known as 'cinema' or, to use Doctor Hassan's term, 'soap opera,' earning the workers outside some LE100 a month, working from seven in the morning to one in the afternoon, but leaving the bulk of production to those like Tayyeb working from home.

The concentration of these establishments below Dra' Abu al-Naga is remarkable and in stark contrast to their relative absence from the foothills road further south. As with many things at al-Qurna, stories circulate, overt or by innuendo, repeated by some, contradicted by others. According to one of these, antiquities are allegedly still found and sold illegally at Dra' Abu al-Naga, with proceeds invested in alabaster factories, such money laundering accounting for their proliferation in that area.[14] In turn, alabaster factories may serve as a front to cover up illicit antiquities dealings by explaining away any relative increase in personal wealth. Thus, alabaster factories constitute one example in a small repertoire of strategies to cover up antiquities-related earnings, as do intimate relations with and marriage to foreign tourists. In one instance, a long-term relationship with a 'poor' German girl allegedly served to disguise wealth and real estate financed from illicit antiquities found by her partner's father. Financial support obtained from intimate relations with westerners is not uncommon, and can be manipulated to divert the attention from antiquities inspectors by blurring distinctions between legitimate and illicit means of financial prosperity.

Tourist shops, including alabaster factories, are generally called bazaars, a term that also applies to the sales kiosks located at major archaeological sites such as the Valley of the Kings, the Valley of the Queens, and Hatshepsut's Temple. Their history is vague but probably linked with the issuing of licenses to itinerant peddlers in attempts both to limit their numbers and to restrict their operations to specific areas. The World Bank–funded west bank tourism development consulting study situated 64 percent of visitors' feelings about the local population in the "offensive," "too aggressive," and "harassing" practices of licensed and unlicensed peddlers at archaeological sites (ADL, 1981b: 28; 1983: II–12). Solutions offered included ...e allocation of specific areas near tourist sites from where sellers could operate, and improvements to the supervision over "ambulant peddlers" by Tourist Police (ADL, 1983: V–26). Although the ADL studies do not always clearly distinguish between these "ambulant peddlers" and the apparent practice of their stall-holding counterparts to hawk their wares, it may be assumed that visitors' discontent resulted in greater regulation working against the interests of licensed itinerant peddlers, and leading to the increased institutionalization of permanent souvenir stalls at archaeological sites. Although these bazaars are built by the Luxor City Council, the rights to operate them are purchased, and can be handed down from father to son, or even be sold. Increased regulation to control the sales overtures of roaming vendors has nevertheless been only partially successful, and has resulted in a new generation of unlicensed, ambulatory peddlers at most sites.

A peddler's existence: Competition and corruption at Ramose's Tomb

It is in the nature of these peddling activities, rather than in the activities of working artists or even those whose business it is to change the appearance of things, that many of the negative aspects of contemporary Qurnawi in their relations with foreigners are located, and it is in this way that travelers' age-old ambivalence toward west bank villagers is being kept alive. For tourists keen to simply concern themselves with the monuments and evade all contact with locals, any overtures made by a tomb-side salesman will be considered an intrusion; those who are persuaded to buy faked *antikas* may or may not eventually realize that they 'have been had'; while in the occasional sale of small items of real antiquity, peddling Qurnawi maintain the reputation of theirs being a community making a living through an illicit trade in ancient artifacts. Some indeed draw on the history of that reputation by feigning to belong to the 'Abd al-Rasul family, in an effort to enhance the persuasive power of their presentations.

Efforts to limit the operations of unlicensed peddlers have not prevented this trade from continuing. Police presence (in all forms: Tourism and Antiquities Police, or plainclothes Interior Ministry Security Police) are essentially ineffectual in preventing peddling and for reasons of personal gain are instrumental in its continuation. Police are non-locals who view a posting to a tourist location as a means to obtain their share from that industry. Qurnawi implicate them as being interested in nothing else but obtaining kickbacks of as much as 50 percent from unlicensed peddlers.

Other than as part of a general characterization of the peddlers who "are located at each of the sites" (ADL 1981a: XIII–14), the Tombs of the Nobles area, in which al-Hurubat is located, was not specifically identified in the ADL studies as an area where peddler activity raised concern (1981a: IX–10; 1983: IV–36), even though it could be expected that the close proximity of Qurnawi houses would lead to increased contact between tourists and locals. The density of tourist traffic at such sites as the Valley of the Kings and the negatively experienced interaction with peddlers there explains why such was less the case at the Tombs of the Nobles, where tourist traffic is much reduced. In 1999, a touring company's message on the notice board of the Novotel Hotel in Luxor placed the Noble Tombs, 'time and energy permitting,' as last on a list of activities:

West bank Tour: A very full half-day of the famous West Bank of Luxor. Cross the Nile to the Necropolis of Thebes to see not only the Valley of the Kings and Queens, but also Artisan Tombs, Queen Hatshepsut's Mortuary Temple, the Colossi of Memnon and, time and energy permitting, the Valley of the Nobles. An early morning start and you will need to take sunhat, sensible walking shoes and water, but an experience not to be missed! See your [tour leader] for additional information.

As a result of this lower visitor ratio for the Noble Tombs area and its consequent reduced impact of peddling, regulation in the form of souvenir stalls was never considered. A local family operated such a stall near the tomb of Ramose, mainly catering in shaded seating, cold drinks, film, and postcards. There were also three small alabaster factory-type shops in the Shaykh 'Abd al-Qurna foothills, but on the whole, the area is one where peddlers have been left relatively free to operate.

To understand how tour groups think they can do justice to an area with the world's greatest density of archaeological sites in "a very full half-day" excursion requires an appreciation of the nature and scheduling of international mass tourism to Egypt. Generally, a two-week package tour will involve several days in Cairo to visit the Pyramids, the Egyptian Museum, Khan al-Khalili, and the Islamic quarter; then fly to Luxor to board one of the 'flotels' (floating hotels) for a Nile cruise to Aswan; before or after which they may spend two days visiting sites in and around Luxor. It is as a result of the limited time available, and the saturation exposure to ancient monuments, that the Noble Tombs can be squeezed out of an itinerary.[15] Hurubati peddlers thus find themselves outside the mainstream and are dependent on the intermittent tour group that does come along, including groups on day trips from the Red Sea coastal resort of Hurghada, tour-group participants who decide to come back during their scheduled day off (a minority, as most will choose to go shopping in Luxor), and independent travelers. Because of these dynamics, those who expect to supplement their income from sales of artifacts in the vicinity of the tombs of Menna, Nakht, Ramose, Rekhmira, and Sennefer will find such employment unpredictable at best, and outright unreliable during the hot summer months, when tourism is down in any case.

Other than these tourism-structural features affecting peddlers' operations, local constraints that have an impact on sales come in the form of tour guides accompanying groups, and the presence of police and other security personnel. Tour guides are held in low esteem by the Hurubati guards and peddlers around the tomb of Ramose. A discussion on the topic of tour-guide practices between two of them, Ramose guard Mahmud Jabr Daramali and peddler Khalid Muhammad Usman, will quickly turn to some of the excesses they have experienced. Guides may come from all over Egypt, but are essentially in the business to become rich quickly. They keep the petty cash given by their companies for themselves, rather than give the money as tips to the guards on behalf of their group, then asking group members for additional money since he "has spent all the money on the guards." Furthermore, according to Mahmud, the guides strongly discourage the giving of baksheesh to the guards, indicating to their groups that they already get good government money and advising them that the giving of baksheesh is therefore a sign of disrespect and an affront to them. In reality, any money spent on the guards cannot be spent by tourists when purchases are to be made in the alabaster factories later. For the same reason, they claim, tourists are taken by their guide often to one tomb only, even though they may give access to as many as three tombs on one ticket: any time spent here might take from available time spent in the alabaster factory, and affecting his or her commission on sales there. According to Khalid, if peddlers offer their wares, the guides advise members of their groups not to buy here, asserting that the quality of the work is inferior and that they know of a better place, that is, the alabaster factory they are associated with.

In all these allegations, distinctions between tour guide and tour leader are blurred. As a representative of the foreign travel company, it would be expected that the tour leader would have the company program for that day, that they would dictate the itinerary, and that the scheduled

German tourists and peddlers at the tomb of Ramose.

tombs would therefore be visited rather than time spent unnecessarily in alabaster factories for purchases that group members could make during their free day in the Luxor bazaars. In reality, although not always, tour leaders may be Egyptian representatives of foreign travel companies, and a degree of fluidity between the two roles, possibly inspired by common financial objectives, may facilitate the practices described. There is likely to be a measure of truth in all these variant stories if their time depth is of any significance: peddler and tour-guide relations were also identified in the 1981 West Bank Social Impact Study (ADL 1981a: XIII–14).

But no matter how they are reflected in the literature, for the peddlers themselves the implications of these stories are real, and their truth is what affects them economically. Taking a day off work to sell his scarabs at Ramose, Badawi sold none, despite the many tourists. Incommunicative upon his return, the cause for his bad fortune required no elaboration: "because of the tour guides." The absence of such sales does affect the family budget, and at any given time there may be little money to go around, making LE2 for the tailor to have a *gallabiya* repaired something of a luxury. What money is available until the next monthly government salary is due, will be kept for market day, with all other essentials, including cigarettes, to be bought on credit from one of the small family stores—often no more than a cupboard—which operate from neighboring houses. Topping off what was already a bad day, Samiha, Badawi's young daughter, broke one of his scarabs while playing.

But bad fortune never lasts forever, and on other days Badawi may be as likely to make a sale as he is not. The following Friday, his weekly day off, Badawi sold four scarabs in a two-hour period, his earnings of LE40 reduced by an LE10 'payment' to the policeman who had turned a blind eye to him carrying out his business. Nevertheless, his earnings were still sufficient to afford some necessary household items and invest in a further three scarabs, to be purchased at the 'Egyptian price' for just a few pounds each from a local store in al-Tarif. During that two-week period, and including these four scarabs, Badawi sold a total of six scarabs, which left him with LE40 profit. On a monthly basis, this could translate into LE85 or 57 percent of his basic government wage. Although he would have had more time for his peddling activities had he not been involved with the present research, even these incidental earnings do indicate the relative importance of his tourism-related work, without which it would be impossible to satisfy all his household needs.[16]

Peddlers' shop in al-Tarif.

Obviously, in all these dealings peddlers will be keen to maximize their profits, but it would be facile to say that they simply settle for the highest amount possible. While setting a price and bargaining until some midway point is reached between seller and buyer may occur, a more complex way of price determination operates in the foothills, one that is as much culturally situated as it is driven by economic pragmatism. It is argued here that in the *wajib* conventions we have already discussed, we may also locate the basis for some of the present-day commercial behavior taking place between Qurnawi and tourists, and many of the pricing strategies that underpin their financial transactions with visitors. Essentially tribal in the way it regulates social relations between kin and non-kin groups throughout the wider community, *wajib* practices instill an ethos that dictates that for any service provided there must be something in return, preferably with an increase in value. In the contemporary context where tourism offers opportunities to supply a range of services—hospitality, providing information or acting as guides through the necropolis, and the sale of artifacts—price negotiations will often not be based on bargaining, but will be open-ended arrangements where a price is negotiated on the basis of what the buyer thinks is fair.

The standard invitation to pay "as you like"—encouraging uninformed foreigners to overestimate the value of goods or services supplied, and in this context indeed intended as a redistribution of wealth—is reminiscent of the open-ended additional payments that establish new degrees of indebtedness in the *wajib* cycle.

Likewise reminiscent of *wajib*, a motivating factor remains the maintenance of good relations. In the tourism context this means that the visitor must be made happy if he is ever to return. Were he to discover that a 'good copy' is not the *antika* he thought it was, only because he never asked if it was a 'good copy,' peddlers will simply say that nowadays (that is, in 1999) it is impossible to buy such authentic artifacts for LE100, LE200, or even LE1,000, that fifteen years ago *antika* may have been the price of a 'good copy' now, but no longer so, thus preserving their own integrity in the expectation that the customer will see some humor in his own naïveté.

It is also for reasons inherent in the *wajib* philosophy that the various forms of police presence, and their alternatively facilitating or obstructing role in peddlers plying their trade, is generally accepted by Qurnawi as fair practice. By contrast with the tour guides who are held in disdain,[17] cordial relations with police and other security personnel may be established. They may turn up in an off-duty capacity at weddings and other communal functions, where they may be seen smoking *bangu* and sharing some locally brewed spirit with peddlers whose tombs they police. Rather than perceived as 'drinking with the enemy,' there are clearly reciprocal objectives involved, with the expectation that any *bangu* freely shared will result in favors being returned and the business at the tomb will be made a little easier, even if such interaction was stated as being separate from business. These relations are not entirely without risk, and there are remembered instances where security personnel who had been drinking with Hurubati the night before found themselves transferred to the Valley of the Kings the next morning.

On a bad day, when such reciprocity evidently fails to operate, police and security personnel may use any reason—a fracas between peddlers competing for the same tourist, or aggrieved by having received insufficient kickbacks as a result of disguised earnings—to suspend trading, round up the peddlers, and take them by car to the west bank *taftish*, the antiquities inspectorate's office, where charges of unlicensed peddling are recorded. Processed by the Tourism and Antiquities Police in Luxor,

offenders may receive a small fine of LE10 after one or two months. Peddlers seem unfazed by these occurrences, and joke among themselves
about how one of them missed out on all the action while relieving himself "in the mountain."

Blessings of happiness and prosperity

One final touch of color must be added to the tapestry that Qurnawi
sociality imposes on the Theban landscape, and colorful it is: the young
girls in their bright dresses selling their equally brightly colored little rag
dolls to whichever tourist is charmed by them. Yet, small groups of heavily competing girls keen to sell their wares—jostling each other, waving
dolls in front of the person's face to attract attention and to convince the
tourist of this doll's particular merit—can be as invasive to an unsuspecting visitor as any harassing peddler. Such scenes of pandemonium can
attract police and security personnel who, in the absence of any bribes to
be expected on so limited a turnover, will equally chase away any visitor-
accosting vendors.

The images symbolize happiness and prosperity and are modeled
on the traditional *al-'arusa* design of the bride figurines found on mud
storage bins. Their history goes back to the late 1960s and early 1970s,
when several local girls made some as home decorations. Likely purchased by a visitor, their sale will have been seen as a new market niche,
soon inspiring others. Colored cloth fans mounted on a stick like flags
were similarly sold, but went out of fashion during the mid-1980s. Some
girls start making the dolls when they are as young as seven and only
'work' when they are of prepubescent age. The girls may sell one or
two per day during the summer, four or five per day during the winter,
or none at all. New material is bought by the meter in various colors,
the simpler constructions taking half an hour to make by an older sister
or at night by the girl herself. Roaming the foothills rather than staying with a particular tomb, the girls will sell the *'arusa*s for one or two
pounds each, and their ability to "speak good" is a stated advantage.
Girls will generally give the proceeds to their mother, to pay for additional material when necessary, the rest going toward household needs.
Individual girls may seek to innovate the standard design in order to
get a competitive advantage over the other girls, and a variety of forms
may now be encountered: a camel, a man with a camel, a woman with
children on the arm.

Competition set aside until the next tourist comes along: girls peddling cloth *'arusa* dolls in the necropolis.

Such, then, is the artistry of al-Qurna, where the artisans and peddlers of today produce and sell the imagery of the past, and where the generations of tomorrow—following the best social requirements of *wajib*—bestow on visitors the symbols of prosperity and happiness. Despite government schemes resulting in cultural homogenization, such is indeed Qurnawi sympathetic magic, which will continue to bring visitors back to the Theban west bank, their expected arrival the driving force initiating a new cycle in the continuing expression of modern Thebes' artistic vitality.

10

Contemporary Spirituality and Traditional Beliefs in the Theban Necropolis

Mulid!

Compared to other annual *mulid* celebrations, the August *mulid* of Shaykh 'Abd al-Qurna is a relatively small-scale affair but it is nevertheless significant. Not only do the celebrations take place in the midst of al-Hurubat and the Noble Tombs, they also provide a visible and contemporary expression of the spiritual quality that has characterized this landscape for millennia. In keeping with that spirit, and possibly reflecting the vernacular and uncomplicated approach of its community toward such things, the fair-like commercial atmosphere of other *mulid* events is entirely absent. There are no entertainment professionals here with their circus-style equipment, and the sweet tables with sugar dolls and other assorted paraphernalia masquerading as merchandise are likewise missing. The highlight for the children is the announcement parade, where a leading vehicle, fitted with loudspeakers and followed by several tractor-pulled trailers normally used for sugarcane but now loaded with children, travels around the dispersed west bank communities to announce that the *mulid* of Shaykh 'Abd al-Qurna will commence that afternoon.

Celebrations begin with a procession to the saint's shrine high up on the hill to fit the symbolic tomb with a new green cloth cover. When the formalities have been completed, the level plain below Ramose's tomb becomes the location for displays of horsemanship. Later in the afternoon the men exhibit their skills with the *khazarana*, the cane fighting stick, which in the context of these festivities should be a ritualized, almost danced, performance, but where aging men still keen to show their prowess do at times hand out heavy blows, demonstrating both the skills required and the lethal qualities of this traditional weapon. Late in the evening the bull is slaughtered for the next evening's communal meal, an event that in itself is neither a great spectacle nor a festive occasion, but that does encapsulate some of the organizational measures that allow the *mulid* to take place. Purchased the year before, the animal was raised by the *Shaykh al-mulid*, a local antiquities guard who is also the caretaker of the saint's shrine and the *mulid's* principal organizer. Money collected from the people of al-Hurubat during the coming weeks will likewise be used to purchase a new animal to be raised for next year's celebrations. The *mulid* concludes on the evening of the second day with the *dhikr*, the Sufi devotion, which takes place in one of the family *zawiya* and in close proximity to Menna's tomb. Distinct from the austerity of the Shaykh Tayyeb *dhikr* that took place during the *mulid al-nabi*, celebrating the birthday of the Prophet, the people of Hurubat may hire any Sufi

The procession to the shrine of Shaykh 'Abd al-Qurna located above al-Hurubat marks the formal part of the *mulid* of Shaykh 'Abd al-Qurna. One of the prayer stations for the guards of the necropolis is visible in the background.

shaykh, the identity of the particular order he represents considered less important than the musical qualities of his performance. It is especially during such religious festivities that the haunting sounds of the *nye*, the flute, evoke an atmosphere in the Theban hills that connects the willing listener with the ceremonial and processional events of ancient days.

Arguing the sacred in the Theban Necropolis

If time, then, has no meaning and the layering of different beliefs has always been a defining character of the Theban landscape, how may we view and interpret that aspect of the Theban Necropolis and the sur-rounding fields and villages today? What are the spiritual claims and what are the cosmological views that compete for attention, access to, and ownership of the physical landscape of the Theban west bank?

Egyptologists have described the landscape here indeed as sacred, not simply in recognition of the notion that funerary soil in some way is consecrated and thus sacred ground, but also because of the place that the Theban Necropolis holds in human cognitive evolution. John Romer has described its significance most eloquently:

> These royal tombs, then, hold in them one of the first detailed maps of the universe man ever made; a description of the life that follows after life on earth and a description of all its ways and workings. The Valley of the Kings is one of the places where modern notions of sacredness were first examined and defined. In these caves was born something vital to all modern religion. Not specifically the Judaeo-Christian god—but part of the language, of the vocabulary, by which that god is understood. This is where part of our perception of deity itself was born. . . . The landscape here, then, is not a dramatic formal statement, either of art or faith. Nor were these tombs created to provide a baroque celebration of the rituals of a faith designed to entertain and overawe a mass of people. This is nothing less than the creation of a new universe of being, a universe that we still partly hold within us today; hold as a deep, deep metaphor of part of human thought and impulse. (Romer, 1993: 35, 38)

But when considering aspects of the sacred on the Theban west bank today, the concept may prove elusive, involving differing standards of assessments and different layers of significance, and be collectively divi-sive. The *mulid* of Shaykh 'Abd al-Qurna may be a reason to celebrate,

Displays of stick fighting during the *mulid* of Shaykh 'Abd al-Qurna. Old men are still keen to show off their prowess.

but its existence is grounded in a system of belief and ritual that is integrated in broadly understood notions of the sacred as a reflection of that other world, which for many complements and gives meaning to human existence. In this manner, the feasts and rituals of both formal Islam and the Sufi schools more broadly will likewise comprise aspects of the sacred for their adherents.

Those who are grounded in rather more worldy objectives and concerns may be seen as a profane contrast to those rituals. Differently attuned to the sacral character of the area, working field archaeologists may be driven in their motivations by a near-religious fervor to understand and preserve the tangible legacy of, following Romer, a defining phase in human cognition. The Supreme Council of Antiquities may trade domestic space in the necropolis for blocks of land in al-Tarif, which despite a lack of decorated tombs in that area equally constitutes consecrated soil and forms part of the larger necropolis. In addition, academic Egyptologists will view the presence of an indigenous community in a sacred landscape as something of an anomaly; they may even view an anthropological fieldworker as an intrusion in the sacred preserve they consider their own. Finally, many of those who live in the villages of the

Theban west bank, especially the women, have little awareness of the sacral character or significance of the surrounding monuments.

The point here is that the entire west bank archaeological zone may be conceived of as a sacred space that for demographic, political, and academic reasons will always also be a contested space, and where—for any of the constituent interest groups—certain things are, can, should, or should not be done. This has a bearing on such expressions of west bank spirituality as may still be practiced inside or in the immediate vicinity of the necropolis, where tangible elements of a belief system may also draw on the ancient monuments and where spiritual practices require the adaptive reuse of the archaeological landscape. Such practices will not only be focused on a specific monument or locality of archaeological significance, and indeed quite a few are not, but because in their totality these expressions take place within the archaeological precinct of Western Thebes, they may still be seen as a contemporary extension of the ascribed sacred nature of the Theban west bank.

But the process will be two-way and, adopting the argument of architectural theorists that it is "fallacious to conceptualise society . . . without reference to the physical and spatial material reality of the built environment: the built environment does not reflect social order, it constitutes much of that social order" (King, 1990: 404, also quoted in Tunbridge and Ashworth, 1996: 24), it may be taken that the adaptive reuse of ancient funerary spaces is not only limited to tangible edifices but also influences constructions of the mind. This interplay between the built archaeological environment and the development and manifestation of ideational constructs may be seen to operate in al-Qurna, where fertility desires and personally held fears may draw on, or be influenced by, real or postulated features in the archaeological landscape.

Thus, contemporary cyclical ritual and ceremonial practices build on, and offer a continuation of, local landscape use that belongs to the same world of sacred ideational constructs seen emphasized in the surrounding ancient Egyptian funerary architecture. Indeed, for some there exists a direct link between the modern rituals performed at the shrine of Shaykh 'Abd al-Qurna and the ancient worship of Meretseger, the goddess of the Theban Mountain (Goneim, quoted in Cottrell, 1950: 145). If attested archaeologically, the connection between an ancient worship site and modern spirituality in the same location again serves to demonstrate the timeless quality of the human experience here.

Qurnawi engagement with the surrounding archaeological landscape

Before addressing villagers' spiritual interaction with their surroundings, it is of interest to assess the engagement of Qurnawi generally with the archaeological character of the foothills. We will exclude here the involvement of the male population, which in our earlier discussion has already been sufficiently highlighted, other than to say that women whose husbands or sons work in some archaeological or tourism context are obviously aware that it is by virtue of the monuments and their international appeal that they, at least in part, can earn an income. But when asked during household interviews to what extent they themselves have an interest in, or have visited the surrounding tombs, less than half, 46 percent, report having done so. Given the archaeological and tourism employment opportunities, it may not be surprising that 79 percent of the women surveyed who have visited surrounding tombs also came from nuclear families with archaeological or tourism connections. However, and significantly, of the 54 percent of women in the sample who have never visited any of the tombs, 70 percent also came from nuclear families with similar employment connections. These figures suggest that tomb visitation by women is as likely to be a function of a breadwinner's occupational specialization as not, and that any association between women and the archaeological environment in which they live is defined by cultural rather than economic factors, with views concerning the place of women in society and the sometimes articulated need to know one's history located at either end of the spectrum. The fact that girls up to the age of fifteen in this latter group were generally allowed to visit tombs if their fathers worked there, but not when older, confirms a picture that is based on social mores rather than any privileges, artistic appreciation, or historical interest inherent in or derived from a specific form of employment.

Fertility: Beliefs, loci, and practice

The transferral of meaning from archaeological artifact to magical relic is commonplace in Egyptian folklore where, especially in Upper Egypt, the perceived life-giving power—*baraka*—of ancient monuments is still widely appropriated to influence some personally held concern. While such concerns generally operate in the realm of the social or the medical, at al-Qurna they also demonstrate that the linking of archaeological

Circumstances facilitating ancient Egyptian tomb visitation by Hurubati women		
Response	**Total**	**%**
Parent or husband working with foreign archaeologists or as SCA employee in any capacity (guard, restorer, driver, builder, etc.)	18	53
Family involvement with tourism (peddling, bazaar or alabaster factory operator, artisanal production, etc.)	8	23
Fertility practices (only one from family involved with archaeology or tourism)	4+1**C**	15
Not otherwise specified	2+1**C**	9
Total	**34**	**100**
Total respondents with archaeological or tourism connections	**27**	**79**

Reasons given for non-visitation of ancient Egyptian tombs by Hurubati women		
Response	**Total**	**%**
Not allowed; women do not leave the home; "it is not our way"; shame; seen to be "behaving like tourists"; no money	5+2**C**	17.5
No time; too much housework	13	32.5
Not interested; "wife not from here"	4	10
No brothers, no men to accompany	1	2.5
Not otherwise specified	10+5**C**	37.5
Total	**40**	**100**
Total respondents with archaeological or tourism connections	**28**	**70**

Incidence of visitation and non-visitation of ancient Egyptian tombs by women at al-Hurubat. Total sample n = 74; Tombs visited "Yes" = 34 = 46 percent; Tombs visited "No" = 40 = 54 percent. **C** = Coptic Christian. In households sampled, where differentiation was made between mother, sisters, wife, and daughters, these were counted per each of these categories (multiple sisters and multiple daughters counted as one sister or one daughter respectively, assuming that if tomb visitation was allowed for one, this would apply to all). Where simply "family members" was indicated, these were assumed to have included the women, and were collectively considered to represent one instance. Not included were instances where no obvious or implied reference to women appeared present.

Over 30 percent of those women who did not visit the surrounding tombs indicated that domestic duties prevented them from doing so.

artifact with some external and socially constructed focus is a recurring feature of a traditional worldview to which many Egyptians, overtly and covertly, subscribe. Winnifred Blackman has discussed these issues in relation to fertility beliefs in some detail (Blackman, 1927: 98–99, 106), but despite the advances in medical science and the saturation presence of pharmaceutical products in Egypt since that time, fertility practices persist.[1] At al-Qurna, a reliance on pre-Islamic ways to facilitate conception is still relatively widespread. Women may turn to them as a last resort when in fear of remaining childless, or when trying for additional children. The practice may be found existing alongside modern medical technologies, with women either choosing to 'bet' both ways, or persuaded to use traditional means, often under the influence of an older female family member, usually the wife's mother. Whichever is the case, women today may still be seen wandering around specific sites inside the necropolis to seek their mediating power in order to obtain *baraka* and thus improve their chances at conception.

It is indeed in the cultural context of these specific fertility beliefs that the visitation of tombs by women may take place. The incidence of such tomb visitation is probably higher than the above figures reflect, as it was not always indicated during household interviews whether tomb visitation was for fertility purposes, either because such purposes are not solely associated with tombs, or simply because the connection was not made clear. In instances where no particular cultural interest for visiting the tombs was stated as its specific, primary reason—"we are born here, it is like our house, we must see it"—such visits may well have involved fertility purposes, with archaeological or tourism connections facilitating or legitimizing factors influencing the choice of location. Similarly, reported instances in which women accompanied friends or relatives visiting from Cairo or other towns may be understood less for reasons of tourism than for the purpose of guiding the visitors through the steps of the relevant fertility rituals. In other cases, a male respondent may have been ignorant of such visits, or did not want to discuss women's issues. It may be that its somewhat sensitive nature may have prevented establishing precise correlations between all acknowledged tomb visits by women and any practiced fertility rituals. Therefore the more general question as to the efficacy of such "special beliefs and practices associated with life in the cemetery"[2] may give a clearer indication of its extent, soliciting thirty-five affirmative responses from sixty-eight respondents (51 percent). Visits that took place for other reasons have been excluded. Especially when taking into account the certain ambivalence expressed by those who nevertheless rejected the efficacy of fertility rituals, the result is well above the 46 percent obtained for all tomb visits taken together, discussed above.

Efficacy of fertility rituals affirmed $n=68$		
Response	Total	%
Affirms efficacy of fertility practices outright	25	36.5
Affirms efficacy, but has had no problems conceiving	4	5.5
Affirms efficacy, but respondent claimed to be "modern"	1	1.5
Affirms efficacy, but still the will of God; also now doctors	2	3
Affirms efficacy, but still has religious concerns	1	1.5
Affirms efficacy, but still *bil haz*, 'luck'	2	3
Total	35	51

Efficacy of fertility rituals rejected *n*= 68		
Response	**Total**	**%**
Ambivalent; no problems conceiving	1	1.5
No opinion, not applicable, as no problems conceiving	4	6
Rejects efficacy; no problems conceiving; but would have gone if necessary and when pressured by mother	1	1.5
Rejects efficacy, no further reasons stated	4	6
Rejects efficacy on religious grounds	14	20.5
Rejects efficacy for reasons it is all *bil haz*, 'luck'	4	6
Rejects efficacy; no problems conceiving	3	4.5
Rejects efficacy, but evidence of ambivalence	1	1.5
Rejects efficacy, respondent claiming to be "modern"	1	1.5
Total	**33**	**49**

Efficacy of fertility rituals affirmed and rejected.

However, the thirty-five affirmative responses become more mean-ingful when we consider that thirty-one respondents offered a total of sixty references to archaeological sites where such practices are carried out, and a further sixty-two references to other fertility rites or locations being used as well. This equal division between archaeological sites and these other locations or practices reflects the belief that fertility rites are not dependent on the ancient monuments alone, and may equally draw on the perceived power associated with the modern Muslim cemetery, or make use of small charms that derive from geological rather than archaeological contexts. The table on page 299 reflects the number of references for each of the archaeological sites, locations, and practices deemed efficacious in assuring conception.

Archaeological sites of ritual significance
Visits to archaeological sites by women can roughly be distinguished into two groups: those that require the woman to undergo a fear-inducing experience, and those that do not. Visits to the tombs of Shaykh 'Abd al-Qurna, the part of the foothills in which al-Hurubat is located, fall into the latter category. Apart from their close proximity to the houses

Archaeological sites and other locations or practices indicated by women as efficacious in assuring conception		
Archaeological site	**Location**	**Total**
Tomb of Amunherkhepshef	Valley of the Queens	16
Hatshepsut's Temple	Dayr al-Bahari	2
Tomb of Kheruef	al-'Asasif	5
Temple of Maat	Dayr al-Madina	1
Temple of Madinat Habu	Nag' Madinat Habu	25
Tomb of Menna	Shaykh 'Abd al-Qurna	1
Tomb of Nakht	Shaykh 'Abd al-Qurna	1
Tomb of Ramesses IX	Valley of the Kings	1
Tomb of Rekhmira	Shaykh 'Abd al-Qurna	1
Tomb of Sennefer	Shaykh 'Abd al-Qurna	2
Tomb of Seti II	Valley of the Kings	3
Tomb of Tutankhamun	Valley of the Kings	2

Other sites	**Location**	**Total**
Ka'bela	al-'Asasif	20
Muslim Cemetery	al-Tarif	2
Shrine of Shaykh 'Abd al-Qurna	Shaykh 'Abd al-Qurna	14

Other practices	**Total**
Agate	6
Entry into house of newborn baby	3
Powder from ancient substances	9
Shaykh visits	3
Stones from Muslim cemetery	3
Stones from tombs	1
Water	1
Total responses all categories	**122**

Archaeological sites, locations, and practices deemed efficacious in assuring conception.

and the fact that a relative or neighbor may be the guard in charge, these tombs are popular for their specific content as well. The Noble Tombs of the foothills are significant for their portrayal of scenes of daily life, and distinct from the religious iconography typical of the royal tombs in the Valley of the Kings. Egyptologists have explained these depictions of daily activities as symbols of rebirth, the representation of all manner of daily activities replete with signs, which, by means of sympathetic magic, could mediate the creation and maintenance of life in the hereafter (Manniche, 1987: 29–63). Qurnawi women are not conversant with the finer points of ancient Egyptian cosmology as understood by Egyptologists, but they will instantly recognize in the detail of the wall paintings aspects that are also pertinent to them: family life, children, food, animals, and agricultural production, and they will associate the survival of the images with an inherent vitality that may also translate into the reality of their daily lives, if claimed. This is what Qurnawi women do by entering the tomb seven times in succession. A similar rationale applies with the iconography of the tomb of Ramesses IX in the Valley of the Kings and the temple of Hatshepsut. In the former, religious elements in the astronomical ceiling, depicting the king in the company of goddesses, are interpreted by villagers as "the king and queen during their wedding night." The portrayal of divine conception by her deified father Thutmose I, her pregnant mother Ahmosis, and the birth of Queen Hatshepsut in the northern intermediate portico or 'birth colonnade' of her memorial temple at Dayr al-Bahari is likewise considered to hold procreative powers.

Although only known to the accompanying older woman, visits to the stepped well in the temple of Madinat Habu and to the tomb of Kheruef in al-'Asasif are intended less for their archaeological context than for the significance of giving the younger woman a fright, with both locations providing the opportunity to do so. Women generally visit Madinat Habu in the morning because the site is closed for visitation from four in the afternoon until the following morning. Ostensibly to collect water from the well that is considered efficacious and to be taken home in a bottle for bathing, the woman descends the flight of steps down to water level when a complicit guard tosses a pebble through a hole in the surface structure above, frightening the unsuspecting woman as it splashes in front of her. A little more gruesome, in the 'Asasif tomb of Kheruef the *ghaffir* on duty hides behind and confronts the woman with a 'walking' mummified torso, at times frightening her to the point of momentary incontinence. According to Winnifred Blackman, the element of fear is said "to cause the blood to circulate quickly through the body, making the womb expand, with the result that she will conceive more easily" (Blackman, 1927: 102).

The use of ancient human remains, however, also derives significance from the simple fact that they have survived at all, and must therefore possess *baraka*. Such is the motivation at least behind visits to the tomb of Amunherkhepshef in the Valley of the Queens, the tomb of Seti II, and the tomb of Tutankhamun in the Valley of the Kings, as well as to the Maat Temple at Dayr al-Madina before the human remains located there were moved into storage. The tomb of Amunherkhepshef, one of the sons of Ramesses III, contains a small display case with the remains of a fetus excavated elsewhere in the Valley of the Queens by the 1903–1904 Italian Archaeological Mission. Qurnawi women wait until late in the afternoon, when the tomb closes for tourists, to approach the guard for access, upon which they circle the display case seven times. A similar scenario applies to the tombs of Seti II and Tutankhamun. In the former, women walk around the mummified remains of an unidentified man placed on one of the shelves in the first pillared hall. In the tomb of Tutankhamun, they walk seven times around the sarcophagus, which until recently contained the coffined

Ancient human remains are a fact of life in the necropolis.

royal mummy. According to one elderly Hurubati who had been a guard for twenty years stationed in the *ghaffir* hut just above that tomb, "many" women visited the tomb for this purpose during his years of duty.

Muhammad, for one, will get his future wife to do these things if she does not become pregnant soon enough: "If women do not conceive, it is a problem and we will do anything." However, initiating such action will not be up to him, as a husband will never tell his wife to go, nor will the wife take the first step herself: if after two or three years of marriage a woman still has no children, her mother will come and advise her to visit the sites. A daughter-in-law will not ask her mother-in-law, this being embarrassing for a wife who is already considered as "first trouble" for her husband's parents: she took their son and, where they share the same house, she would now unsettle them with the anticipation of noisy children running around the house. Instead, her own mother or any other woman can fulfill this role, provided she is sufficiently advanced in years to be of post-menstrual age. Any young accompanying women must wait outside the tomb. Women make the visits on the last day of their monthly cycle, wash themselves, and then go to the tomb. Upon returning, they should have intercourse that night. Also because of this, there is no secrecy in her actions and she will tell her husband of the visits, although in several reported instances the husband had no knowledge of it. Zeneb had been married for sixteen years and had remained childless, on account of which her husband divorced her. Her ex-husband remarried and had children. Zeneb subsequently married Hassan and visited the tomb of Rekhmira trying to conceive. Since Hassan had in fact married her because he desired no further children, she did not tell him. She gave birth within a year of her visit to the tomb.

Other sites of ritual significance

Shaykh 'Abd al-Qurna is the locally revered legendary shaykh whose historical antecedents are unknown (Nims, 1965: 12; Winlock and Crum, 1926: 16), but his simple commemorative shrine that overlooks al-Hurubat from the upper ridge of the hill that carries his name continues to play an important function both in the life of the community and that of its individuals. Because the shrine figures prominently in a girl's wedding festivities, women regard it as the most important of all the sites.

The shrine is a simple, roofless, blue-washed mud-brick structure. All that its wooden door hides from view is a light frame covered by

A bridal party visiting the shrine of Shaykh 'Abd al-Qurna on the day of the wedding.

green cloth symbolizing the saint's tomb, a box to make small coin offerings, a box containing some soil to be tied up as charms in locally stored pieces of material, and a niche placed in one of the mud-brick walls. Accompanied by girlfriends and—anticipating the chocolates that may come with such festivities—a throng of hand-clapping and music-making children from the village following in their wake, young Qurnawi women visit the shrine on the day of their wedding. A woman ensures both marital happiness and fertility by placing burning candles in the niche recessed in the wall, making some small offering, and taking a little soil from the box to wrap and suspend from a string as a charm around her neck. Less ceremoniously, married women will repeat the ritual if they do not conceive quickly enough, or when they are seeking to expand their family. The intervention of Shaykh 'Abd al-Qurna is considered highly efficacious. As a result, the shrine is among the most frequently visited fertility ritual locations. This faith in the power of the shaykh's intervention also helps explain why the annually celebrated *mulid* of Shaykh 'Abd al-Qurna and the festivities surrounding the renewal of the green shrine cover is a much anticipated event on the Hurubati social calendar.

Other sites of ritual significance   303

A bride burning candles at the shrine of Shaykh 'Abd al-Qurna.

The most frequently visited site that has no other recognizable archaeological context concerns what women call Ka'bela, a level area in al-'Asasif, which also functions as the village soccer field. Here, behind the posts that constitute the eastern goal, women roll themselves seven times through the dust, with the accompanying older woman sprinkling henna on the surrounding rocks and leaving some shaykh's written spell known as *kitab* (book) among the crevices. Soccer-playing boys are persuaded to leave the area by means of chocolate bribes, as during the process the woman's ankles may become visible.

Finally, the Muslim cemetery located opposite the Seti I Temple and marking the southern boundary of al-Tarif is also considered to hold procreative powers.

Ritual objects and other practices

Other traditional means considered efficacious include *agig*, strings of agate beads passed from family to family and possibly comprising ancient components; archaeological or unusually shaped geological objects serving as charms; seven stones collected outside a tomb; seven stones collected from the modern Muslim cemetery, to which end the woman is required to cross the length of the cemetery seven times; or even gold objects. On the last day of a woman's cycle, the agate is placed in a glass or bowl either in the house of an elderly woman, or on the roof and exposed to the night sky. The seven stones are immersed seven times in a bowl of water, and then likewise left submerged overnight. The water is to be used for bathing the next morning, with intercourse to follow that night.

Apart from traversing the modern cemetery, visits to certain shaykhs occur frequently, and for all manner of reasons. In all cases, the shaykh will provide a written magical or Qur'anic spell, which, in the case of fertility desires, a woman may carry as a charm suspended from her neck, or insert as a *kitab* among the rocks when visiting Ka'bela. In a different practice claimed to be effective, when a family member or neighbor has

What is there to lose? Enhancing the chance of conception at Ka'bela.

died, a barren woman may step seven times over the aluminum *tasht* with water used to wash the dead person's body before burial, and thus enhance her chances of conception. Likewise, it is considered 'good' to enter a house where there is a newborn baby, who is not more than forty days old. 'Good' means that the entering woman will soon conceive, although the practice is dangerous for the baby's mother, and was claimed to likely affect her capacity to breastfeed.

When confronting informants with the observation made by Winnifred Blackman that "women sometimes beg to be allowed to remove small portions of the decorated walls in ancient tomb-chapels to assure their bearing children" (Blackman, 1927: 99), and asking them if powder was also scraped from temple walls and columns or painted tomb surfaces at al-Qurna,[3] in seven out of eight cases women vehemently denied such practices, their denials expressed in such semi-verbal exclamations as "ckckck" and "wah," emphatic negations that in al-Qurna carry connotations ranging from forceful rejection to utter indignation: "If you cut your arm it is not like the tombs, your cut will heal, but it is not possible to replace a picture cut from the tombs and damage is hard to repair." One respondent remained ambivalent by saying *"mumkin"* (possibly), when asked whether this may have happened, stating that it had *"min zaman"* (a long time ago), but that such was now no longer possible

Intercessory *kitab* placed in the crevices among the rocks at Ka'bela.

because of the *ghaffir* (the guards). The woman indicated that she had heard about it from her mother and other old people although, again, they did not follow these practices themselves and had only heard about them. Yet, it cannot necessarily be ruled out that occasional occurrences do not persist. Following a process of reverse psychology, the intensity of the denials may well suggest that some material from ancient monuments may from time to time be taken still, especially when seen in the context of women's general tomb-visitation record and their lack of identification with the cultural significance of the tombs.[4] This may not necessarily be to the detriment of the art-historical record: decorated ceiling remnants still visible in a collapsed and destroyed tomb at al-Khukha evidence scratch marks, which, judging by their density and shape, could well be the result of an intentional scraping rather than damage sustained by the tomb's collapse. But it is impossible to determine their age.

Apart from the continued cooperation of the guards at archaeological sites, and their disseminating information of other efficacious tombs they have heard about from colleagues, the survival of these practices rests with the current generation of elderly women who are both the repository of this knowledge and the initiators when it comes to inducting the younger generation of married women. When exposed to these ways, younger people recognize rather than question that "the older generation may not know where these things come from or why they are still here, but that they were taught that way and accepted what they heard from their parents." There is nevertheless recognition by women that all these practices, either individually or in combination, as deemed necessary or desired, constitute "old ways," and that modern ways facilitated by education or television and involving doctors, medicine, and if still unsuccessful, a different doctor in a different city, become increasingly important. Thus, even an unmarried girl, clearly embarrassed for speaking about such things, acknowledges that she is modern, when asked if she will follow the old ways. Women claimed that two or three out of every ten women may still practice the traditional ways, a figure that is conservative when compared to the 51 percent of respondents who affirmed the efficacy of traditional fertility rituals. Informants, then, remain ambivalent, acknowledging that the old ways worked, but that now it is often a matter of money, with poor women adopting traditional practice rather than having to face the expense of doctors and medication: "It is the way for poor people; the rich people go to a doctor." But even when married women visit doctors many times over and no treatment offered appears effective, they may choose to accept an old neighbor's or a relative's suggestion of alternative ways. Even when barrenness persists and medical science provides an understanding of the cause, a return to traditional approaches may not be ruled out. What, after all, is there to lose? Whether *bil baz* (by luck), or through the will of God, what is destined to be may be effected through these means: "*Insha'Allah!*" Thus, with any new generation inducted in these ways, further enhanced by the propagating effect of Hurubati kin resident in other villages and cities as far away as Cairo, the 'seeds' are sown for a new generation of eventually aging women to persuade and pass on their knowledge to those who come after them.

Encounters with *Qabus*: Fear, possession, and exorcism

If the reaction of women confronted by the 'walking' mummy in the tomb of Kheruef is one of fear, then this emotion also characterizes situations that are less confronting, less immediate, and, in fact, almost expected. For there is a latent fear in many Qurnawi that some ill effect may be made manifest at any moment: walking past the house of a person who reputedly has the evil eye, a family will quicken its step and protectively cover the face of the baby the woman is carrying while murmuring the few *Allahu Akbars* that are appropriate in such a situation.[5] Less predictable, some ill-intended spell commissioned from a powerful shaykh by any opposing individual may equally have negative consequences. But thankfully, such malevolent spells may be averted by protective countermeasures. Following his divorce, Badawi complained of sore legs, attributing these not to a possible cold, but to his previous wife having gone to some shaykh for a spell to make him unwell. The cure to neutralize the spell was to burn an unpleasant-smelling mixture over charcoal and fumigating himself under his gallabiya, around his head, and throughout the room. Collected by his mother, the mixture was equally potent and would have been up to the task: garlic and onion leaves, scraps of old shoe and material fabric, and desiccated canine feces. Similarly, when Badawi remarried, there was the fear of a bad influence by the first wife, who may go to a shaykh to obtain a spell that would render her former husband ineffective in bed, and "like a woman." As a countermeasure, before signing the wedding document, the groom would obtain some fishnet material, tying a small piece with string around his stomach and a small piece similarly around one of his upper arms, under the gallabiya. The bride would likewise tie a piece to one arm, the belief being that the net will serve as protection and catch the bad spell. The time of the document signing was kept strictly secret, as the former wife's spell only works if written at the same time the wedding document is being signed. Beforehand and independently, the two mothers-in-law went to separate shaykhs to also obtain a protective spell, to be kept by the bride in her pocket, and placed by the groom in the room during the wedding night. Since the spell is Qur'anic in origin, care must be taken that such documents are not touched after intercourse until after one has bathed.

But such measures and countermeasures are the consequence of known human interaction, they form a part of everyday life, and are therefore in most respects expected and acted upon. In a certain sense, and especially following the appropriate countermeasure to render a malevolent spell inactive, the presence of spells—although stemming from fear—generally result in a personally experienced improvement, as in the case of Badawi, who now enjoys a second marriage. Even the anxiety experienced by Qurnawi women when visiting the well at Madinat Habu and the tomb of Kheruef in al-'Asasif will benefit the individual concerned if conception ultimately follows.

But there exists a different form of psychological distress afflicting Qurnawi, which is rather more sinister in nature. Like the above 'household' spells, experiences of this type also belong to a religious cosmology that merges pagan pre-Islamic with Islamic beliefs and which, while not fully recognized by either orthodox Islam or the Sufi schools, nevertheless form a part of folk religion in Egypt: "Among these are the belief in black magic, the evil eye, and an assortment of *jinn*s and other spirits. There are numerous formulae . . . for averting or exorcising these evil influences" (Adams, 1977: 574–577).

Eighteen out of sixty-three respondents of the households and individuals interviewed attested to being visited on a recurring basis during their sleep by what they call *qabus*. Interpretations of what this was varied from simply a nightmare, albeit one out of which people found it difficult to wake up, to a confrontation with a monstrous creature, which at least a number of respondents felt had to do with the fact that their village was located inside a place of the dead. Although many committed Qurnawi Muslims denied the phenomenon, for others such subconscious apparitions were neither *'afrit* nor jinn, the spirit-beings who enjoy a degree of formal recognition within orthodox Islam, and for those so afflicted they mostly formed a terrifying reality that could neither be totally explained nor escaped from.

When Ahmad Muhammad Abdu Rahman was asked if he knew where his friend Sayyed was, he knew he had gone to a cool tomb to sleep during the heat of day. When showing Sayyed's family the place, they found him there asleep, a full ten hours after he had gone to take his rest. When awake, he stated he had been unable to wake up because "something heavy sat on him." Although ten hours was exceptional, similar experiences are common, the weight described as being "heavy as the mountain," and the sleepers call for help but are not heard. Their condition typically lasts between two and fifteen minutes, yet they wake immediately when they are touched by someone.

Other experiences involve a man or a woman with an ugly face trying to strangle the sleeping person, who calls for help but is not heard, the fear eventually waking up the person. These accounts of strangulation occur frequently within the repertoire of such experiences, as recounted by Hussein Hassan al-Hashash:

> 'It' comes to me every night, when I am dozing, and still not deeply asleep: It is not like a dream. There is a breeze in my ears, making a sound like the wind blowing, hissing. A man tries to strangle me and I fight him, I call for help and can hear my own voice, but nobody else does. When my arm touches something I wake up. The man may have different faces, and sometimes I may see someone trying to kill my mother. At times, before I married, I could keep the light on when afraid, but this is now difficult with my wife. 'It' may come to me in other places, like in Cairo when I was in the army, but not as often as here. Some nights I do not sleep at all. My heart will be pounding as if I have been hard at work. It used to happen to my father when asleep outside, in the *zawiya*; I now do not sleep there at all. It started when I was a boy, and I am now used to it and no longer really afraid. Sometimes it may come to my wife too.

Although sometimes consisting of a female body only, without a face, at other times it cannot be said if the attacker is male or female and, while human in body, in appearance it may possess "something like the face of a buffalo." Some regard it as a *shaytan fara'un*, a devil from the time of the Pharaohs, or a devil who is an *'afrit min al jinn*, a ghost or spirit-being, and therefore more difficult than a normal *shaytan*, who knows fear. It lives off the dead and therefore presents itself "like a picture of the dead," showing only its back, approaching from behind and pressing a victim's folded arms against his or her chest. Others consider it a jinn that is distinct from the ancient cemetery, capable of appearing "everywhere, for anyone." Yet, it is not the same as 'afrit, which "you see when awake, although now less often because there are now many lights in the evening, and people and children are everywhere." In any case, you must already be afraid to see 'afrit: "When you are strong in yourself and you walk alatul (without delay), you will not see it." For others still it is simply a nightmare, although such dreams are also considered to come from shaytan.

As with Sayyed, for some qabus may come when one is asleep in a tomb during the heat of summer. For others, it will happen differently in different rooms and victims will sleep in some rooms but not in others. If it becomes difficult to sleep, rooms may be changed around. Children sometimes experience qabus but cannot tell the difference between these encounters and a dream. Some think that the reason why others are not affected is not because of the people, but because of the location of the house, on the assumption that there is a connection between a house and nearby tombs or still hidden human remains.

Different preventative measures may be taken by those whose sleep is disturbed by these apparitions. A kitab containing a magical spell from a Muslim or Christian shaykh may be carried on the body to ward off any evil afflictions, or the shaykh may write inside a plate, which is to be filled with water and left to stand outside overnight, the water to be taken before breakfast the next morning. Others may recite a memorized sura from the Qur'an, or keep a Qur'an in their bedroom, to read from either before going to sleep, or after an apparition to stop being afraid and to prevent it from coming back.

Modern medication in combination with a shaykh's traditional medicine may also be used, although the one incident encountered may not have been typical. 'Aysha claims she was relaxing but not certain whether or not she was asleep when she was alone in the house only eight days earlier. She was found lying on the floor by a visitor who took her to a local doctor and was diagnosed with an intestinal or stomach problem. She was given an injection and prescribed medication.[6] In addition, she visited a shaykh who prescribed asal naghl, honey, and a film container filled with a spicy and greasy substance obtained from a shop in Luxor, two drops to be taken at a time with a teaspoon of honey.[7] She had no recollection of what had happened, but was lucid when interviewed.

Different accounts involving otherworldly creatures concerned the alleged presence in several households of protective jinn, which prevented occupants from searching for antiquities within their homes. In Muslim cosmology, jinn are fiery beings who complement both humans and angels. Accounts do circulate in al-Hurubat about how those who became rich on the sale of illicit antiquities suffered at the hands of such jinn who, upon discovering that antiquities had gone missing, caused episodes of spontaneous combustion inside the house which eventually forced the owners to move.

Such accounts are still current. One of Badawi's al-Khukha neighbors, Ibrahim Abd al-Rahim Awad, whose house is approximately one hundred meters from Badawi's house, had experienced such fires only last year. The fires were stopped by a shaykh's spell, but his daughter who was also involved in the episode had only recently been declared dead by a Luxor doctor before being revived and was now still seriously ill. She had been possessed by a small boy-jinn, allegedly after her father Ibrahim had employed a shaykh to constrain a guardian jinn while he was excavating for antiquities inside his house. Upon discovery of the theft, the guarding jinn entered his daughter, while she was standing in the doorway. His presence in her enabled her to spit fire, although that had not been the cause of the house fires. The boy-jinn had also shown himself briefly to women who were visiting the house, including Badawi's mother and wife, both of whom jumped up and ran.

The incident had an unexpected follow-up during July 1999, when a shaykh who had been further treating the Awad girl in her house was called upon by Badawi's immediate neighbor, whose relatives in al-Tarif had a daughter suffering from periodic paralysis and who had been advised by their relative in al-Hurubat to come over so as to benefit from the shaykh visiting the village. The girl was about eleven years old, dressed in an orange-white World Cup, soccer-logo emblazoned tracksuit that she had been wearing while playing outside only an hour earlier. She was lying on a mat, her head supported by a pillow, punctuating her crying with "aboyaboyaboy" exclamations at the moments of her greatest distress. The shaykh, a young man, was bent over her, a copy of the Qur'an and a string of prayer beads nearby. People were milling around, women and children outside the room looking in, men inside, assisting or looking on and smoking *shisha*. The shaykh massaged her legs and knees, periodically slapping her shins and thighs, so giving cause to her distress. At other times he placed her hand on her forehead and recited in a whispering voice religious utterances from which only the name of Muhammad could be distinguished. Although seemingly ineffectual, with the girl still incapable of standing up, after some time the shaykh proclaimed that she would be fine by Friday, after which her family took her and left by car.

The account that subsequently emerged indicated that the girl's problems were similar to those of Ibrahim's eldest daughter in that, like her, she seemed to have become caught up in an unsavory business in which she herself was entirely innocent. Although not well known in al-Hurubat, the driver of the car was recognized as the girl's uncle, who was effectively her step-father after her own father had deserted his family. Her uncle had been recognized by some as a person of dubious stature and just as likely to be involved with illicit antiquities dealings as not. Not unlike Ibrahim's case, the scenario that caused the girl's afflictions was one in which allegedly a shaykh was called in to exorcize the 'pharaonic' jinn or *shaytan* (these terms being used interchangeably when it comes to the protection of antiquities) guarding hidden antiquities. The medium through which the shaykh acts is a young boy or girl of ten or eleven years. The uncle may have brought the girl into his presence for this purpose. The shaykh would have read the Qur'an to her for a lengthy period of time, asking her intermittently what her name is. If she correctly answers, he knows that the *shaytan* has not yet entered her. If she at one point mentions a name other than her own, the shaykh knows that the *shaytan* has now entered her, and that it is no longer she who is speaking. Once the *shaytan* has responded to the shaykh's call, he is in his service and must do as the shaykh pleases. Prompted by the shaykh's patron, the girl's uncle, he will ask the *shaytan* for directions to hidden antiquities, by requesting both indications of distance and descriptions of items. After following up this information and extracting the antiquities, the shaykh will order the *shaytan* to exit from the girl's body. When excavation of the antiquities is accomplished, the *shaytan* will find the treasure he was guarding gone, and awaiting the departure of the shaykh, he will re-enter the body of the boy or girl in revenge. Although there are other circumstances that would cause a *shaytan* to enter a person, knowing something of the person and character of the girl's uncle, the reigning consensus around al-Khukha was that this had happened to the girl. Rumor further had it that the uncle was now a worried man: having caused his niece's distress, he had taken her to different doctors in Asyut, who failed to establish a diagnosis. Now having to use a shaykh, the exiting *shaytan* might also accuse him as the cause of all the girl's problems.

These accounts are not unique incidents, simply stories, or even innuendo, but they occur with some regularity and in their own manner provide a provocative and other-worldly perspective on any alleged illicit antiquities-related activities in the Theban Necropolis. They all contain similar motifs, although they do occur in variant forms. One of these relates to Abdu Rahman Muhammad, whose sudden increase in his family's standard of living had already been pointed out by Badawi.[8]

In this instance, some two years earlier Abdu Rahman had asked a shaykh to point out to him where in his house he might find antiquities. The shaykh indicated three rooms, only to have his further involvement terminated by Abdu Rahman, who feared he would have to share the proceeds with him. Out of spite, the shaykh invoked a powerful protective *shaytan* to work against anybody who might dig in those three rooms. In the meantime, Abdu Rahman had let his son-in-law in on the secret of what might be hidden. Confiding in a partner appears good practice, for if something tragic were to happen, the knowledge would not be lost. When Abdu Rahman subsequently commenced with excavation, it was the son-in-law on whom the *shaytan* turned, paralyzing his arm and changing his voice and personality. A different shaykh was called in, improving the victim's condition, but finding the *shaytan* too strong to be evicted from the ground in which he lived to protect the antiquities against the greed of Abdu Rahman Muhamm?

In these accounts, as they do with other *shaytan* experiences, the role of the shaykhs figures prominently. They may be able to work things for good or for evil, using Qur'anic verses or magical spells of a darker nature. The assistance of Shaykh Muhammad Tayyeb may be invoked, or Qurnawi may choose a shaykh of some reputation with the type of case they need assistance with, often from places at some distance and not excluding Coptic Christians, and often on a commercial basis. Concerning the phenomenon of *shaytan*, according to the local Sufi Khalwatiya leadership in al-Hasasna, and following orthodox Islam, everyone has an invisible evil companion against which protection may be sought from the Qur'an. Shaykhs of the stature of Shaykh Muhammad

Tayyeb may show people the correct way through teaching and prayer, and may also write down protective verses from the Qur'an. As such, they, unlike many Qurnawi, see no connection between personally experienced fears and the influence of ghosts from pharaonic mummies still buried in the necropolis. They are simply representative of that part of Muslim cosmology against which religious protection may successfully be directed: *shaytan*.

But if a shaykh's mediation remains ineffectual, for any affliction, sufferers may attend a *zran* ritual. Distinctly non-Islamic and its meetings covert to a degree, their objective is the opposite of exorcism: *zran* are black-magic gatherings where those possessed seek to make contact with *shaytan*. Qurnawi may invite the Luxor-based woman medium to come to one of the foothill houses, for a fee, or they may visit her house in Luxor, which opens on Saturday and Tuesday for the sick. Playing her drum, she invokes the presence of *shaytan*; the participants dance, accompanied by the chime of their silver ankle bracelets. In a state of trance, they seek to appease whatever it is that has offended *shaytan*, petitioning what it is that they must do to find relief from their particular condition, with *shaytan* speaking through them and indicating what it wants in order to be pacified. Gatherings are mainly frequented by women, although some men may attend. Proceedings can be unpredictable, and the state of trance may result in some participants removing items of clothing. Orthodox Islam rejects such involvement with *shaytan*, holding the view that evil, once invited to influence one's condition, will stay with that person for the rest of her life.

Despite the interpretations and explanations offered by Muslim cosmology, for many people in the necropolis there are nevertheless strong associations between the spirit world and the physical, archaeological environment in which they live. Making ethnographic observations of the above type does not require a religious scholar or one who is acquainted with issues of the paranormal. When referring to the fears that are held and experienced by Qurnawi, one can only suspend the inevitable disbelief and adopt a relativistic mentality, acknowledging that which is true and meaningful for Qurnawi. These are simply the concerns that people have expressed and they must be reported as such. Independent of whatever merit they may hold for a western mindset, these accounts do reflect the preoccupations and anxieties experienced by people in this landscape.[9]

With the passing of the last generation of elderly people who have experienced pre-modern times, knowledge of the history and the old ways of life in the foothills will no longer be taught to the generations of the future.

The power of story

Irrespective of any underpinning belief structures, the question that must be asked is if there is any broader social significance in the mainte-nance of these accounts, and of their association with antiquities. A story recounted by one elderly Qurnawi tells of a shaykh who was engaged to open a tomb for a family who wanted gold, but the tomb closed while the daughter was still inside, and the shaykh's assistance could only work once. On the level of folklore, these literary narratives may not simply recount mythical or remembered accounts of illicit antiqui-ties searches, but during an earlier illiterate era they will have served didactic purposes as well, if only to warn youngsters of the dangers of the mountain.

Today, under the influence of formal education and television, the significance of storytelling as a means of educating the young has all but disappeared, and when asked, few could actually remember the stories they would have heard in their youth.[10] Despite formal education—the

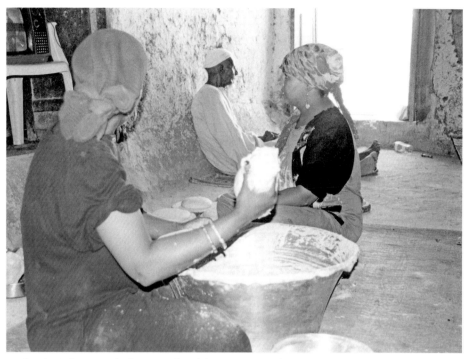

Under the influence of television, the old stories are no longer being told and the voices of the elderly are falling silent. . .

naghlu ummiya government-sponsored literacy program among women, or the Qur'anic village *kuttab* schools that children may attend—al-Qurna still remains only semiliterate. Many older people, women, and even children of large families who cannot afford the associated expenses incurred by schooling are unable to read and write.[11]

In situations where there is a degree of disinterest in, or ignorance about, the broader cultural significance of the surrounding archaeological monuments, as we have established at least in the case of many women, the vernacular association of certain observed pathological conditions—irrespective of their medical basis—with forms of antiquities-related behavior that are at least publicly viewed as socially deviant[12] may still serve an educational role. More formal awareness campaigns "to improve local capacity in site management and urban conservation" for Qurnawi have been recommended by UNESCO (1999, 2001) but have not been implemented. In their absence, traditional understandings about cause and effect, and the recounting of tales which detail the personal suffering

The power of story   317

of those who are innocent—like the girl buried alive in the tomb—may serve as the only worthwhile and truly local instructional device to prevent illicit archaeological activities.

Had they known—and mediated by such indigenous cosmology and experience—policymakers, heritage managers, and antiquities inspectors might have recognized that an ongoing symbiosis between 'man and monument' could have been possible. Such has not been the case, and we will now turn to the most recent chapter in the history of the necropolis' occupation, the removal of its inhabitants, and the demolition of their villages.

11

The Ethnography of Eviction

A single relocation event and its impact

On March 8, 1999, sixteen Coptic families moved from their large housing compound in al-Hurubat to the new settlement of al-Suyul. Comprising around one hundred people, the move represented the largest single relocation event from the central Noble Tombs area at that time. Apparently voluntary in character but effectively eviction by stealth, the desire for improved housing conditions was at least in part due to the declining standard of living resulting from standing prohibitions on maintenance and renovation, and a general deterioration in the appearance of the surrounding landscape caused by the discarded rubble from earlier demolitions. The event was particularly significant in that the relocation of such a large segment of the Qurna Coptic community—in any case representing only a small minority—in measurable ways reduced the Coptic occupation of the foothills.

The concentration of so many families and individuals occupying a single but large housing compound will be explained in both kinship and religio-sectarian terms. Although offering a dramatic example of the influence and scale of a single relocation event, its occurrence was comparable with other Muslim Qurnawi housing compounds where, to varying degrees, a similar sequence could unfold. An individual family might have either submitted a request to the Luxor City Council for alternative accommodation, or might be approached by representatives from the Luxor City Council and the SCA who made an offer for alternative accommodation, which the family could accept or reject. People might reject the offer being made if they felt that the space presented to them was not sufficient for their future family needs. This is in fact what often happened. But because construction prohibitions remained in force, the deteriorating structural condition of necropolis houses eventually forced Qurnawi to accept whatever accommodation was being offered simply because their present living conditions became unacceptable. As part of this process, neighbors (who were at the same time often close relatives) were also approached, as adjoining houses could become structurally unstable when a neighboring dwelling was demolished. This is one reason why the entire Coptic compound was vacated; on the surface the relocation appeared voluntary but in effect nearby occupants were given little if any choice. By virtue of this arrangement, their former house was returned to the SCA, who hold legal rights to the archaeological zone and who can unilaterally decide on the fate of the house, which invariably meant that it would be demolished (EAO, 1984: Article 17).

The destruction of the Coptic housing compound commenced on June 15, 1999. Under the supervision of one of the SCA inspectors assigned to the Noble Tombs area and assisted by a small army of SCA workmen, the process of reducing the houses to a state unfit for occupation took

The 1999 demolition of the Coptic compound was executed by means of manpower and the traditional *turia* adze. The supervising inspector stands second from right.

several days to complete. The traditional *turia* adze was used to break free sections of the walls, which were sent crashing down in clouds of dust by a combination of lever action and combined manpower. The method used stood in stark contrast with those of the first 1996 and 1997 campaigns, when houses at the northern end of the foothills were demolished with heavy earthmoving equipment. The use of bulldozers at that time caused indignation among local villagers who understood the destructive impact of such equipment on this fragile archaeological environment. Villagers would defiantly show photographs of the bulldozers, indicating that any subsequent damage would have been caused by the actions of officials and bureaucrats rather than the presence of Qurnawi.

By early September no attempts had been made to remove the rubble, its gray-brown stain clearly visible against the white limestone.[1] The chief inspector for the west bank explained that the mud-brick rubble could not be removed more speedily as it required careful excavation. His objective may have been the retrieval of any remaining ancient surface artifacts, but this would still have required the careful removal of Qurnawi occupation layers. The argument seemed curiously at odds with the then current archaeological practice that totally ignored any Qurnawi stratigraphy in the archaeological deposits, as was the case with the clearance of the area of Old Qurna around the Seti I Temple in 1998. However, his professional concern for any remaining surface finds was archaeologically valid. As we will see shortly, those concerns were of no consideration seven years later when demolition practices reverted to those of 1996–97, and the bulldozers returned to scrape clean the tomb courtyards and their surrounding perimeter.

"Here is my home and the tombs are our food: My family eats because of this!"

As will be evident from the above, the voluntary relocations of the late-twentieth and early-twenty-first century were ambivalent affairs. While they were accepted for one personal or practical reason or another, and thereby arguably forced upon them in so many ways, many Qurnawi, when asked about relocation issues, did indeed look forward to such basic domestic amenities as water, shower, toilet, and general cleanliness. But the move would come at a personal cost, as all trade-offs invariably do, the overriding sentiment expressed that they would still miss their place of birth, saying "Here is my home!"

If that was in 1999, then such is the case still. One married couple who voluntarily left in 2001 confided in November 2009 that they still occasionaly return at night to the location of their former house in al-Hurubat where they sit together, to cry and reflect. This was indeed their home and emotionally it still is. Their sense of loss revolves around knowledge of the family's history in al-Hurubat in general, the continuity of occupation in a specific house and location in particular, and the sense of identity found in memories and the knowledge of personal roots.

When asked in 1999, and demonstrating another aspect of their ambivalence, people were nevertheless conscious of why the government wanted them to move. However, Qurnawi pointed to the safety of the tombs as well as the people's economic dependence on them as reasons why they should not be made to leave the foothills:

> We know that the government must take care of the tombs because of their history, but it is not fair to accuse us of making illegal excavations: this is difficult as there are guards everywhere. If it is done inside the house, and my friends come, they will tell security and I will go to prison for twenty-five years. We must take care of the tombs for they are our food and my family eats because of this: if we break the tombs, the tourists do not come any more. Because of this, the guards do not like people to move: they will now be on their own and their job made more difficult as people in the houses cannot alert or assist them if there is trouble. If I hear dogs bark at night I look out of my window. It is not true that people damage the tombs. We take care of them but when we move all the tombs will be damaged. The tourists come to see al-Khukha, if they need help or water, who will help? It is good for the tourists who come here that people live here. Most people do not want to move because of business with tourists. Because the house is close it is easier to sell them carvings without a license, the house is like a license, the police make less problems because your house is here. It will be difficult to come here after we move and it will be difficult then to sell to the tourists. The water we use or the toilet is not the problem. The problem of water is at Polish [Archaeological Mission] House, at German [Archaeological Mission] House and the tombs which collapsed near the mosque of Shaykh Tayyeb because of the water, these are the problem. We do not use so much water and cause no such problems. Some will have toilets, for their women, girls and visitors, but many go to the mountain, even if this is now more difficult because of the guards.[2]

The general deterioration of the urban vernacular environment in the necropolis resulted from the implementation of Antiquities Law No. 117 of 1983, Article 20, which prohibits the construction, expansion, or renovation of Qurnawi dwellings inside the necropolis (EAO, 1984).

For others, these arguments were less valid. Mahmud Muhammad Hussein, an SCA employee, was born here, as were his father and grandfather, but he considered his ancestral history in this location of less importance than the future of his six children: "I will take a photograph and hang it in the new house. That will be my history!" He was generally in agreement to move to a new custom-built village in order to get a better house and services such as water and sewage for his children: "No renovations are now allowed, with antiquities inspectors looking at the houses, and if they notice we are fixing our homes, they notify the authorities and we will get five or six days in prison and fines of LE100, LE150, or LE200." Yet, he insisted he would only move with the entire community—"neighbors, parents, friends"—intact and not to al-Suyul, where the houses are poorly built, or to al-Qubbawi, where the houses feel "like tombs."[3]

By contrast, Sayyed Ali Muhammad does not have the luxury of government employment and is entirely dependent on his dealings with tourists to generate income. He is therefore only interested in moving if he gets a house sufficiently large for his family and his elderly parents, as well as a job: "The houses at al-Suyul are small and only people with small families will be willing to move. There are many big houses here and if you live in one of these now you will refuse to leave." Even if he gets a good house in one of the new communities but is still unable to secure a job, then he is not interested in moving: "We are poor people, but the government is only interested in the tombs, yet they come with bulldozers to destroy the houses. They can kill me and my wife and children, for what is there left if we are moved from here? In the new village there will be no tourist work, so how do we eat: sand from the mountain? UNESCO comes here and talks but only with government people, not to us, the people in the houses. They should speak also to Mubarak, he can change things."

Religious and political undercurrents

Thus, for Qurnawi, the social context in which relocation initiatives could take effect encompassed the two extremes seen represented in the attitudes expressed by Mahmud Muhammad Hussein on the one hand and Sayyed Ali Muhammad on the other: from harmonious compliance and peaceful adaptation to possible public disturbance and violent resistance. The vehemence of Sayyed Ali Muhammad indicated that the housing issue was sufficiently sensitive, also at al-Hurubat and, given the right conditions, capable of igniting into open conflict.[4]

Such a situation could be all the more dangerous because it appeared that the jurisdiction of Shaykh Tayyeb in matters concerning village relocation was not recognized: "If Shaykh Tayyeb instructs me to move somewhere else, I cannot, for Shaykh Tayyeb is not my father." Despite his spiritual pedigree, and the general Qurnawi recognition of his importance for the traditional dispute settlement process—including among members of the Coptic community and the police[5]—where matters of relocation were concerned, during 1999 Shaykh Tayyeb was seen as a politician and a member of the Luxor City Council whose first allegiance was to the government establishment: "We like Shaykh Tayyeb because of his *baraka* and Islam. We like him very much as he makes peace for us if we have a problem: he makes peace for all the people. But for his government job we do not like him at all."

Because of these political connections and connotations, both the Tayyeb family, and the surrounding community of al-Hasasna, where

Top: Ruined tomb dwelling in central Hurubat, a solitary *safat* (grain silo) in 1999 still representing one of the few surviving architectural markers of an earlier period in the occupational history of the Theban foothills. *Bottom*: This feature of the more recent stratigraphy has since been demolished, along with the nearby housing compounds that gave the area its distinct settlement pattern.

spiritual allegiance to Shaykh Tayyeb was strongest, were therefore seen as in favor of relocation. Proof of that was cited in the form of the new mosque and religious complex being built at al-Suyul during 1999. This was allegedly funded by a LE2 million grant from the Ministry of Religious Endowments *(Waqf)* enabling him to move with the people. There were those who viewed it as a conflict of interest and as an 'incentive' used by the government for Shaykh Tayyeb to persuade Qurnawi to move with him.

Such relocation-related innuendo may or may not be grounded in the political and religious realities of the day. Significantly, those who considered themselves followers of a powerful Sufi of the Ghaleliya order—Shaykh Saleh Ahmad Muhammad Abu Ghalil, whose portrait is found hanging in many homes in the foothills and who has his base in Zagazig in Lower Egypt—claimed that their allegiance was entirely on the basis of Sufi adherence rather than an act of religious rebellion on political grounds. Additionally, many Qurnawi have no spiritual Sufi allegiance to either Shaykh Tayyeb, Shaykh Saleh, or anybody else,[6] and adopted a rather more pragmatic stance on issues concerning relocation, with personal feelings about roots, and the economic implications of access to employment considered rather more important.

Between 1999 and 2006, all these dynamics would feed into the kaleidoscope of permutations that eventually made the wholesale evacuation of the Theban Necropolis a reality: ongoing voluntary relocations to dispersed locations and the move of the religious leadership to the new mosque at al-Suyul, both contributing to the consequent fracturing of the foothills' social structure; a resulting weakening of social cohesion,[7] which allowed the Luxor City Council to render ineffective any remnant semblance of community consultation;[8] a newly appointed Luxor governor and the progressive implementation of Luxor-wide development projects, including the west bank; the emerging political will to advance evacuation of the foothills communities; and the associated construction of the New Qurna settlement in the desert at west al-Tarif.[9]

Diesel fumes, a world away
The absence of the diesel fumes did not make the experience any less real: Despite the variable quality of the international cell phone connection between Egypt and Australia, the rumble of heavy earth-moving

Demolition by bulldozer in 2007. Their vibrations are likely to have caused serious damage to the underground decorated tombs. Senior SCA officials have discounted such criticism, stating that "the backhoes did not go more than a few inches deep into the earth" (Mustafa Wazery quoted in Waxman, 2008: 95). Irrespective of any underground damage, removing the debris from the surface in this manner has also permanently destroyed the archaeological stratigraphy in these places, including both ancient and more recent deposits. Photograph courtesy of Caroline Simpson.

equipment was clearly audible in the background. It was the week before Christmas 2006 and, this being the winter season in Egypt when temperatures are favorable for such work, the excavation of the ancient burial grounds of the Theban Necropolis on the west bank of Luxor by foreign archaeological missions was now in full swing. But the archaeologist's Egyptological fieldwork tools should not include the use of bulldozers and trucks, and the noise that day was clearly not that of the foreman's occasionally shouted admonishments to keep the line of rubble-carrying basket boys moving.

"Our hamlet is gone!" shouted Badawi above the roar of the engines, when I rang him on that fateful day—as I periodically did to enquire

The 'sculpture gallery' of page 96, destroyed in April 2009, despite undertakings given by the secretary general of the SCA and the minister of culture that should have guaranteed its preservation. Damage was also caused to the façade of the *bayt al-hajar*, the adjoining tomb dwelling. In combination, this unique assemblage represented a vestige of life from an earlier era, demonstrating the particular settlement pattern of the necropolis and the cultural landscape qualities inherent in the adaptive reuse of this archaeological site.

about his family and to hear how life in the village was going. I had lived in his house when I was conducting fieldwork during the late 1990s and had kept in contact with him during the intervening years. Plans to relocate the community had existed for a long time. Despite voluntary relocation by individual family groups, until then there had not been the political will to either execute a large-scale forced eviction or put in place the logistics and organizational readiness to effect the demolition of the foothills hamlets. Until that week, that is.

From a world away, I could envision exactly where he stood. His back turned toward the Ramesseum, the memorial temple of Ramesses II, and facing his village, situated below the cliff behind which Tutankhamun still rests in his Kings Valley tomb: Badawi and his people, the ancient king's modern neighbors. As we both intermittently stopped to listen to the roar of trucks passing close to where he stood, Badawi continued to convey that some still did not want to leave and that most were sad and angry.

"No orders to the contrary"

Amid such noise, exhaust fumes, vibrations, and emotions, the relocations to the new northern communities situated several kilometers
away, and the large-scale destruction of Hurubat and the other foothills
hamlets of al-Qurna, continued apace until early 2008. By then, local
and international observers had already described the foothills as a war
zone,[10] with even the archaeological stratigraphy heavily compromised.[11]
The destruction included many houses that stood out either for their
vernacular aesthetics or for their historical significance. Some were over
150 years old and 'antique' in their own right. Elsewhere they would
have been considered worthy of protection.

On March 25, 2009, and again a week later, and as a final insult to
those who hold the view that cultural diversity, vernacular earthen
architecture, the social history of an entire community, and the history
of a prominent and popular academic discipline count for something,
bulldozers destroyed several properties that had been earmarked for
preservation. The signatures of the secretary general of the SCA and
the minister of culture who, in written agreements that allowed Qurna
Discovery, a private British initiative, to preserve some of the vernacular
mud-brick architecture of the Theban Necropolis, were ignored as Luxor
City Council workers operating the machinery claimed they had received
no "orders to the contrary."[12]

The demolition of those properties was all the more painful for the
loss of significant historical value caused by that destruction. It happened
before the British initiative to restore one of those houses could make
good on its intentions. Sadly, that house was Yanni's, discussed earlier.[13]
Despite direct and tangible links with major European museum collections, including the collection of Egyptian antiquities held by the British
Museum, its destruction both summarized and symbolized that, at least
for Egyptian officials, there is no benefit to be obtained from Egyptology's own history.

The demolition of Yanni's house also brought closure to a significant
era in the necropolis' modern history. It was the first house to be built and
one of the last to be destroyed, its demise effectively symbolizing the end
of human occupation of the foothills.[14] Before reflecting on aspects of life
in the new communities, we may provide some context to that closure
and ask pertinent questions that arise from the fact that "no orders to the
contrary" were given.

Yanni's house—left of center with gaping hole—was already in a ruinous state before its destruction on March 25, 2009, but plans were afoot to have it restored as part of the Qurna Discovery protected cluster of properties. Its destruction is a denial of history in so many ways as much as it symbolizes the demise of the necropolis social landscape.

Many questions, one answer

Egypt boasts the world's greatest density of archaeological monuments within its borders and is a State party to the 1972 United Nations World Heritage Convention. For Egyptian officials to act in ways that are contrary to what contemporary conservation theory considers as internationally acceptable approaches therefore seems remarkable. To ask questions about what had happened at al-Qurna and what had gone wrong in the Theban west bank's heritage management strategy is therefore entirely valid. There are many questions and issues, but here we will simply raise the most obvious ones.

Why was a vibrant and culturally distinct community relocated from its historical territory within the archaeological zone of the Luxor west bank, its interests considered subordinate to all other objectives? Why could the comprehensive site management plan called for by UNESCO not be prepared, one that recognized and holistically integrated the socio-historical and contemporary cultural aspects of the Theban land-scape alongside its archaeological features? Why, instead, did the The-ban Mountain simply have to be denuded of all its social features? Why engineer social changes that will result in a loss of cultural diversity and the homogenization typical of new communities elsewhere in Egypt? If the stated objective was to protect the ancient tombs by limiting the alleged damaging impact caused by human habitation, then why bring in heavy earthmoving machinery to destroy mud-brick dwellings that could have been demolished with the use of hand tools? In their dealings with the Luxor City Council, why did the SCA not veto the use of bull-dozers on the grounds that their vibrations would surely cause damage to the underground decorated tombs? Despite the absence of a holistic site management plan, why did trained SCA archaeologists not use their cultural and historical insights, rather than allowing the destruction not only of the entire vernacular cultural landscape, but also of those houses that were of particular aesthetic or historical significance? Why was the history of Egyptology ignored, the academic discipline that is central to part of Egypt's identity as a modern nation, its links with the surround-ing social landscape equally a part of the broader cultural landscape qualities? Why favor a form of heritage management that is effectively a scorched-earth policy?

The answer, most poignantly symbolized by the new wall stretching for kilometers below the now denuded and deserted foothills, creating separate enclaves for visitors and local communities alike, is simple: Tour-ism. In the scheme of things, Egypt's pharaonic identity (both as pro-jected politically at the national level and as perceived internationally) is too important for the national interest to be left underdeveloped. Despite SCA involvement in the conservation and management of Islamic and Coptic monuments, its main concern rests with its pharaonic heritage, that is, those monuments that are also the focus of international mass tourism that has Egypt as its destination. Representing an important one-third of Egypt's hard currency earnings, international tourism—alongside revenue obtained from the Suez Canal and oil exports—simply constitutes too important an element of Egypt's economic base for it to be beyond high-level government oversight and control. Especially fol-lowing the attacks on tourists by Islamic extremists during the 1990s and the consequent downturn in tourism revenues, capacity building through the protection and further development of heritage sites has become of

Top: Houses in al-Khuka; *Bottom*: Location of these same houses in al-Khuka, making a grown man weep: "Here was my house!"

The location of Nag' al-Rasayla, formerly the hamlet of the 'Abd al-Rasuls in the central foothills of al-Hurubat, showing no more than the footprint of the social landscape shown in the photograph on page 142. A wall now demarcates the City of the Dead from the villages of the living, effectively putting a barrier between tourists and Qurnawi, now moved out of sight, and making 'enclave tourism' a reality for the Theban Necropolis.

national importance. Heritage management in Egypt therefore is essentially politicized and mostly so for economic reasons.[15]

As a consequence of the inherently politicized context within which tourism, heritage management, and even pure Egyptological research by foreign archaeological missions in Egypt operate, there is little or no room for the sensibilities that "activists" lobbying for the safeguarding of cultural diversity and the rights of local communities might espouse.[16] Indeed, according to this view of the world, there is no place for local villagers in an area designated as an open-air museum.[17]

As it stands, the SCA was entirely in agreement with the plans drawn up by those who ultimately showed little concern for this fragile archaeological landscape.[18] While on the surface this was ostensibly for heritage management reasons, the political reality may have left little or no room for the SCA to voice dissenting opinions by arguing for more holistic and less intrusive heritage management initiatives. In this sense, the presence of the bulldozers may well be seen as a metaphor for the (lack of) voice and influence of the SCA in the wider scheme of things. The SCA forms part of the Ministry of Culture, which itself plays a subservient role vis-à-vis the Ministry of Tourism, for all the reasons indicated. It may therefore be expected that major decisions relevant to tourism development and therefore national economic interests will come from the highest level, including the prime minister and the president.

Decisions are enacted through the president's local representative, the governor of Luxor who is chairman of the Luxor City Council, in coordination and consultation with the SCA. Even so, the nature of the working relationships between Luxor City Council and SCA officials appears at times characterized by miscommunication, if not dysfunctional altogether, as demonstrated by the use of bulldozers above the decorated tombs and as evidenced in the case of the destruction of the protected 'Yanni House' and the nearby assemblage of mud storage features. Nevertheless, the Luxor City Council's current concern with modernization and sanitization is not at odds with the mandate and objectives of the SCA, that is, the protection, conservation, and presentation of Egypt's ancient monuments.[19] Alongside stated heritage management arguments, sanitization issues and improving the lives of Qurnawi generally have been constant themes in the rationale employed to justify relocation.

The Theban foothills are not alone in this respect, and indeed modern Egypt has considerable experience in relocating entire communities for the perceived greater good, including the destruction of the Nubian villages following the construction of the Aswan High Dam; moving local communities away from the proximity of Edfu Temple; and making room for further excavations between Luxor and Karnak temples.

In the latter instance, the historic and vernacular character of the previously existing urban landscape has been completely lost. Houses of historical significance, and in excess of one hundred years old, were destroyed in the process, the understanding of 'antique' apparently lost on SCA inspectors who reported back that their destruction was in order since no 'antiquities' were present. Additionally, local stratigraphy in the areas adjoining Luxor and Karnak temples was effectively destroyed, forever preventing insight into and understanding of the broader history of the area, including the adaptive reuse of these temple precincts by more recent (that is, at least during the past millennium) population groups. Apart from any archaeological objectives, these initiatives, dating back to development plans formulated during the late 1990s (Barsum, n.d.), also fit the Luxor City Council's current quest

With piped water installed in the new communities, Qinawi women do not have to make the daily trip to the roadside wells (a). In most cases, the *'arabiya* and donkey are no longer a part of family and village life, other than through the regular house calls of the *butagaz* merchant (b).

for modernization in and around Luxor, resulting in bland open spaces, alternately paved or grass-covered (the now paved and one time rural character of the west bank ferry landing is another case in point). Luxor Temple may achieve greater prominence and thereby suit the SCA mandate for 'presentation,' but the loss of the historic and vernacular character of the previously existing urban landscape and its associated scientific knowledge is immeasurable.

It follows that the role of the SCA as the national body of professional archaeologists and heritage managers has been compromised by national economic objectives that leave little to no room for their independent advice or heritage management initiatives. Where such advice might have been given but was not, the professionalism and underlying expertise of the SCA and its trained archaeologists must be questioned where it concerns their analysis and interpretation of local histories and broader cultural values. For a professional organization of its kind, and in relation to the Theban west bank, it should have been evident that relocation and destruction of the necropolis' hamlets would bring to an end a historic and uniquely specific hillside vernacular settlement pattern that was equally a part of the archaeological stratigraphy and therefore worthy of academic interest. Such was not considered by the SCA and its scientific integrity appears diminished for having approved rather than objected to the inappropriate execution of a tourism development project in this environment. Equally, and if preservation of the existing social landscape ultimately was not an option, professional practice would have required the SCA to have sought higher-level approval for appropriate and wide-ranging (that is, beyond pharaonic landscape use) archaeological investigations to be carried out prior to any modernization or tourism-development plans being put into place, but such did not occur.[20]

As it happens, economically motivated modernization and heritage management initiatives that center on changes in the presentation of pharaonic monuments, through an inescapable alignment of (tourism) objectives, also satisfy the aims of antiquities officials. However, and on the evidence, what in fact takes place is the favoring of one particular—pharaonic—heritage at the expense of the broader archaeological stratigraphy, which is destroyed in the process, and ignoring the history, ethnographic character, and diversity of other more contemporary cultural expressions in archaeological areas.[21] To meet tourism development targets, the scientific principles and commitment to protection and conservation—and thereby knowledge and understanding—were sacrificed on the altar of state-imposed and economically driven motivations and objectives.

In all these developments, UNESCO, through its Bureau of the World Heritage Committee, has proven itself to be a toothless tiger. UNESCO's Bureau of the World Heritage Committee—as well as its expert advisors from ICOMOS[22]—have been unable to prevent the destruction of the foothills hamlets or the changes in and around Luxor more broadly. This was despite several commissioned expert missions reporting on local heritage management issues that included the location and possible impact of the Theban foothills communities,[23] despite calls for comprehensive site impact assessment studies,[24] and despite requests made to the Egyptian government through the Recommendations and Decisions made at the annual Sessions of the World Heritage Bureau.[25] Despite the quality of some of their commissioned expert reports,[26] it is difficult to escape the impression that the scope of any UNESCO influence is governed by diplomatic convention and that any real clout to prevent serious adverse impact on its World Heritage–listed sites and practical positive heritage management outcomes are ostensibly constrained by a perceived fear of being seen as meddling in internal affairs. Such may be the cynical view, but in the face of much international lobbying on behalf of the Theban cultural landscape, UNESCO's efficacy rate in coordinating, managing, and enforcing holistic heritage management solutions for its World Heritage–listed Theban property has effectively been nil.

Equally worrisome is the silence with which the international professional body of archaeologists and Egyptologists have confronted these issues. In the case of Qurna, the astute observer will have noticed that while the bulldozers were busying themselves destroying both Qurnawi houses and the underlying stratigraphy in this archaeologically highly fragile environment, Egyptology's international practicing field archaeologists were working in their profession's meticulous fashion on any of the nearby Noble Tombs for which the SCA had granted them concession to excavate.

This is not to say that individual archaeologists will not have discussed relevant issues with either SCA or Luxor City Council officials if they felt the moment was opportune. Nevertheless, and this may again be the cynical view, one is inclined to think that the effective wholesale professional silence on the part of the international Egyptological community may at least in part have had something to do with concerns about excavation permits, with future renewal applications possibly endangered by any overt or perceived "activism" on the part of foreign archaeological missions. If there is ground for such cynicism, then, here too, professional integrity has been substantially compromised as a result of archaeology's politicized place in the Egyptian scheme of things.

Of course, acquiescing to the tourism-induced modernization of Luxor may be a relatively easy thing for Egyptologists to do. Given that they are primarily focused on the pharaonic monuments, Egyptologists' objective to preserve and protect those monuments is not at all different from what the SCA seeks to achieve, even if the SCA may be driven by other motivations, as has been argued. The disconcerting issue is that, as professionals, the international body of Egyptologists apparently has allowed itself to be shackled by Egypt's politicized views of the role and place of archaeology in that country, and caged itself in an inward-looking framework of academic practice that is more concerned with self-preservation than with frank and fearless debate and the exploration of ideas that may range beyond the immediate boundaries of its own discipline. Following from what was said in Chapter 1, maybe this is what was to be expected: Given its certain 'classical' philological focus, and despite its associations with archaeological anthropology, Egyptology has had a somewhat uncomfortable relationship with other social sciences, preferring to concern itself with its immediate—ancient—focus rather than adding measurably to and engaging itself actively with an understanding of self in the contemporary world.

The constraints imposed on foreign archaeologists working in Egypt as a consequence of the politicization of Egyptology in that country are not directly relevant to the work of the social anthropologist. For one thing, concerns surrounding the renewal of excavation permits do not apply and, although longer-term residence for the purpose of conducting social science research is subject to certain strict security requirements,[27] in the present case multiple fieldwork visits supported by introductory letters and the assistance of local and government officials facilitated ethnographic data collection in the hamlets of the Theban Necropolis. It is as part of that project that the above observations and comments have been made, not out of spite or in anger, but to document the political and heritage management dynamics that provided context to the issues and concerns experienced by Qurnawi between 1995 and 1999, and to serve as background to their recent relocation to the new communities. In closing, it is to life there that we shall now turn our attention.

Life in the desert at west al-Tarif: The social and economic consequences of relocation

Life in al-Suyul is not what it could have been. Demolition orders were reportedly issued in 1999 for several of the earliest houses built. Tendered out by the army to private contractors, they were not well constructed and were "falling down, quite literally" (Rakha, 1999: 17).

Such problems may be the least disconcerting and will be overcome in due course by people making the necessary changes to improve their accommodation, as has been happening with the small and inappropriate dwellings at al-Qubbawi. By contrast, the architectural and barrack-style urban plan designed by army engineers that typifies al-Suyul in its visual appearance demonstrates in maximum terms the degree of homogenization that may be expected from mass relocation events. Placed in row upon row of square, single- or two-story flats, the open space between neighboring units is walled off on both sides, enclosing the courtyard that separates domestic from public space. The linear settlement pattern thus created is repeated street after parallel street, and their only structural intermeshing is provided by the two doors located in the opposing courtyard walls that provide entry from and access to the street on either side of the row of units. Not only in the use of materials—concrete and red brick—do the houses stand in stark contrast with the hillside dwellings, but especially in the regularity of their arrangements that is so at odds with the scattered placement of the foothills vernacular architecture. Not only does the design shape the visual and architectural arrangement of the settlement pattern, it also affects the quality of social interaction inside as well as outside the spaces it creates and has brought to an end the courtyard lifestyle that typified life in the necropolis.

The enclosed nature of the domestic space at al-Suyul, although obviously not impenetrable, allows less for the customary invitations of *tafaddal* (welcome!), which in the open spaces of the foothills would be extended to any passersby, but which in this new community would exclude much spontaneously extended hospitality, effectively screening friend, neighbour, and relative from all other community members. This reduction in spontaneous social relations, even if the observance of extending welcome to those passing by is socially expected, has resulted in

House façade in al-Suyul. Those who have the financial means may render and color their walls, but for many who are faced with an already reduced income and increases in the cost of living, this is not an expense everyone can afford.

more confined social relations and has contributed to the development of a social distance characteristic of most urban settlements. In this way, the planning and design of al-Suyul has reinforced the breakup of the individual hamlets, their social structure already fragmented due to irregular voluntary relocation and the random resettlement of larger family groups. In November 2009, people complained they do not know their neighbors and they lock their doors at night, having grown suspicious of strangers, becoming security-conscious in ways that previously they were not.

One could argue that foothills Qurnawi on one level are well familiar with the more confined nature of such social relations. In fact, they reflect much of life typified by the enclosed social spaces of al-Tarif, where narrow streets and enclosed courtyards cause most domestic activity to take place away from public view. Through intermarriage and family visitation, foothills Qurnawi will have experience with, and may in some measure even be well-versed in, this lifestyle. While this may be so, the foothills courtyard lifestyle was, nevertheless, one of the characterizing elements that set the foothills hamlets apart from al-Tarif.

Al-Suyul street scene, located in the desert. The urban plan is one of linear regularity, with social relations largely taking place behind closed doors that are locked at night, and neighbors who are perceived as strangers.

An immediate outcome of the placement of tombs and their adjoining courtyards, the open courtyard lifestyle, and the social relations that they fostered, can be said to be one of the defining characteristics differentiating (at least the central) foothills population from those of the plains adjoining the foothills to the north. Traveler James Bruce (1790: 138) already alluded to hostilities between the foothills and the plains communities, hostilities that have persisted in the occasional feuds between members of the foothills communities and members of certain kinship groups residing in al-Tarif. Indeed, the particular psyche that separates foothills and al-Tarif communities may be traced back in this context to the very fact that Fourth Dynasty al-Tarif *saff* tomb architecture and location are sufficiently different for a contrast in communal psychology and attendant social relations to have developed. While we need a clearer picture of the historical development of the settlements at al-Tarif and their relationship with those in the foothills—including the impact of any relative tribal differences and/or common origins during the past several hundred years—to make conclusive statements about developing psychological trajectories of individual communities, the differences between the foothills and the plains communities appear articulate enough to attribute at least some significance to the specific social relations resulting from the distinct Eighteenth, Nineteenth, and Twentieth Dynasty tomb architecture that predominates in the foothills.[28] Reference has already been made to the defining relationship postulated by architectural theorists between the built environment and local sociality. In this sense, the distinctions between al-Tarif and the foothills may reflect specific solutions toward the adaptive reuse of different archaeological landscapes, and the certain social characteristics of their respective communities, which developed alongside and in tune with it.

In Qurna al-Gedida, 'New Qurna,' the most recently completed new settlement, some of the social patterning and spatial arrangements that evolved from the foothills archaeological landscape have been retained. Incorporating elements from the 1992–94 social survey, different areas follow the kinship-based nomenclature of the foothills in an urban plan designed to separately accommodate the communities of al-Hurubat, al-Hasasna, al-Ghabat, and al-'Atyat, with the objective that upon relocation close proximity might ensure the continuation of existing close neighborly relations. In reality, the fragmentation across three different areas—al-Qubbawi, al-Suyul, and Qurna al-Gedida—has compromised this objective. One further factor that may work against this urban plan is the poor quality of many of the houses, as a result of which families may decide to sell and, supported by increasingly available bank loans, build elsewhere. Apart from the reported use of cheap and poor quality materials, problems with many of the houses are structural and are generally caused by foundations resting on uncompacted or insufficiently compacted excavated soil. Walls are reportedly cracking and have to be rebuilt, three times in the case of one family.

The new settlement could have been a model village, demonstrating what can be achieved with appropriately planned and well-executed heritage management initiatives. But in many respects the results are evidence of all the ills that can bedevil building projects in Egypt when appropriate tender and procurement protocols, project management, contract supervision, and quality assurance processes are lacking to enforce relevant industry standards. The issue is compounded by the lack of appropriate training in the necessary trade skills and the practice of sub-subcontracting, with a drop in standard at every level. Additionally, there is the certain 'cultural' context in which public works projects in Egypt may be executed, with the presence of kickbacks and bribes at many levels enabling shortcuts and infringements of standards; and the disappearance of funds (through overpayments to contractors and other mechanisms), which—had they been appropriately spent—should have ensured better overall outcomes. As is evident with the problem of uncompacted soil, which should have been addressed when identified, in the case of al-Qurna, the issue was also political, with the Luxor City Council seeking to control all aspects of the project,[29] reportedly resulting in the misappropriation of funds, an apparent lack of oversight, and substandard execution. While meeting the objective of evacuating the foothills, what has nevertheless been achieved is by all appearances not the model village that was envisaged in the social survey–based architectural designs of the 1990s.[30] Nor is it what was promised to the villagers in the community consultation leaflet distributed in 1996. Apart from the structural quality of the houses, which, when viewed from the rooftops, have a flimsy rather than a solid appearance, the generally poor workmanship of its amenities leaves the impression that 'near enough was good enough.' It may be inappropriate to apply western standards here, but considering that the village is a central component in a high-profile heritage management initiative for a major World Heritage–listed archaeological site, expectations will have been different.

The issue of substandard workmanship may or may not place additional financial strain on villagers' resources. Those who can afford it or attach importance to sound structures and properly working amenities will pay for the improvements they desire; those who cannot afford them will make do with what they have until they have the necessary means. Either way, relocation to the new communities has come at a cost. Constructed from red brick and concrete, the houses are unbearably hot during the summer months, requiring electric ceiling fans and air-conditioning units to make them habitable, with higher electricity bills adding to other experienced increases, including those for employment and school-related travel (the latter alone totaling between 15 and 20 percent of a necropolis guard's government wage, depending on the number of high school–aged children requiring return travel by collective taxi) and despite less predictable income from tourism for many of those who previously supplemented their income in this way.

Among these are the peddlers who hawk their wares near popular tombs in the necropolis. Especially for the ones among them who hope to sell artifacts they claim to be authentic, the removal of the village from the archaeological landscape may well undermine the credibility of their claimed stories about locally found antiquities. Yet, Ahmad Muhammad Ahmad, when reflecting in 1999 on his future ability to still persuade tourists at the tomb of Ramose that his limestone heads were found by him "under my house" and that they are indeed authentic antiques, commented that "I will just have to make a new story . . ." Time will tell if peddlers like Ahmad are indeed successful in adjusting their sales strategies in this manner. If not, then the Qurnawi exploitation of a village-dependent tomb robbers' identity that could previously be used to good effect to blur the distinction between genuine and fake artifacts, and the financial benefits such stories could generate, will have died with the village.

Additionally, following the demolition of the foothills hamlets, opportunities for future visitors to allow themselves to be invited by Qurnawi to visit their nearby homes to drink tea and watch while the women in the household bake their traditional bread no longer exist, at least not to the same degree. Similarly, establishing beneficial longer-term relationships with foreigners will be compromised for lack of opportunity. The new communities are located at several kilometers' distance, and only the most intrepid visitor to the necropolis among those not bound by tight tour-group schedules will permit themselves time for such a diversion. But many visitors to Egypt already experience the lack of privacy and personal space as negatives. Unless they are hardened travelers with time on their hands and not persuaded by non-Qurnawi guides who claim (for their own financial gain) that it is dangerous to be with the locals, they are less inclined to respond to the overtures and invitations made by well-meaning villagers if these are likely to take them 'off the beaten track.' In any case, tourists may be less interested in visiting a standardized red brick modern home than in experiencing rural life in traditional earthen architecture.

For the community of artisans, their art is unlikely to change when they can no longer draw on the tombs for their immediate inspiration. Like those who already work in al-Tarif and at some distance from the foothills, they may use photocopies or, not unlike Ahmad al-Harazi, come up with new imaginative designs. Indeed, Hassan Sayyed Muhammad has already said that "I have my permission [identity card] and I can come here [to the tombs] if I want. I can make anything and change." Hassan Sayyed Muhammad's capacity for change may suggest that, at least artistically, Qurnawi artisans living in the new communities may not be directly affected by relocation. However, it remains to be seen if tourists accompanied by their Qurnawi guide will still want to travel the distance to visit a particular artist in his new home and make a direct purchase.

Despite the possible exception represented by the artists, the lack of additional earnings generated by contact with tourists generally consti- tutes one of the negative effects of the relocation experienced by many Qurnawi in the new communities. These tourism earnings are one of the typifying social and cultural facets that have crystallized out of the com- munity's former presence in the archaeological landscape of the necropo- lis. Now that this site-specific aspect is no longer an element of their particular identity, it is to be expected that these characterizing qualities more broadly may change considerably as a result of the relocation to the new settlements and that those specific to the environment of the necropolis may disappear altogether.

Indeed, the fragmented urban plan of the new settlements has resulted in both a greater physical and social distance for Qurnawi and stands in stark contrast with the physical accessibility and the resulting interper- sonal and familial closeness of the open courtyard lifestyle experienced in the necropolis. The resulting loss of social integration and the greater burden imposed by the increased cost of living has also made adherence to reciprocal *wajib* obligations increasingly difficult. More so than in the foothills, commitment to *wajib* for many of the poorer families now involves an extremely delicate balance between what they can afford—at times at a loss of basic necessities—and the risk of endangering interper- sonal relations of long standing across the community. During November 2009, some privately expressed the wish that the practice be abandoned. Were such to become the case, then it would be a further contributing factor in an evolving homogeneous society, where a group's individual identity and its relative contribution to some more broadly perceived cul- tural diversity is diminished through uniformity and rendered virtually indistinguishable from other population groups elsewhere.

By then simply another Luxor 'suburb,' and like so many suburbs in cities around the world, the former Theban foothills society will have conformed literally and metaphorically to the confined architectural spaces imposed on Qurnawi in their new settlements, living alongside, yet separate from, their neighbors whom they may or may not know well, but in the absence of the immediacy of any real and experienced sense

Twilight over Qurna al-Gedida. For the necropolis foothills' hamlets, the sun has already set, permanently . . .

of community. Such may be the future for those who once called 'home' the vernacular mud-brick architectural spaces and the tightly-knit social environment of the Theban Necropolis, where when passing the open-tomb courtyards adjoining the houses, the most often heard cry that rang out would be *tafaddal!*—'welcome'!

Conclusions and a Challenge

The historic and ethnographic material uncovered during the present study has revealed the Theban west bank as a rich and fascinating field site. Overshadowed and obscured by the practice and marginalizing dominance of a differently focused academic discipline and the wholesale global preoccupation with ancient Egypt that its practice and analyses continue to inspire, here we have attempted to return to Qurnawi the degree of historic and contemporary visibility that their place in this archaeological landscape warrants, and the level of academic interest that its social and ethnographic specificity merits on its own terms. Although the vernacular foothills hamlets are now gone and despite the major changes taking place in the collective life of the present generation, it is hoped that the preceding pages may serve as a starting point for further and future Qurnawi studies. Greater insight into the social history and contemporary cultural expression of the former inhabitants of the Theban 'City of the Dead' will further expose the color of the rich social fabric that this community of the living has brought and continues to bring to the Luxor west bank.

The preceding chapters have sought to provide both a baseline ethnohistorical record of the villagers who occupied the foothills of the Theban Mountain and to offer a first ethnographic account of contemporary life in this archaeological landscape. To this end, a synthesis of a selection of early travelers' accounts has been used to situate al-Qurna both historically and ethnographically, and a first ethnographic account has been provided of contemporary Qurnawi sociality, incorporating perspectives that include social, economic, and artisanal practices as well as traditional beliefs, maintaining in all of these an emphasis on the articulations that

347

existed in relation to the archaeological surroundings of the Theban foot-hills. An objective in both these historic and ethnographic foci has been to provide a corrective to the particular representation of Qurnawi in the Egyptological literature, which, beyond references to Qurnawi involvement in archaeological fieldwork practice and their being implicated in the trade in illegal antiquities, has to date largely ignored the essentially social character of the archaeological landscape in which Egyptologists working in the Theban Necropolis have operated ever since the early days of Egyptological exploration.

This issue has a long history, and the material presented here may also be seen to fill the certain void left by the work of such early-nineteenth-century Egyptologists as Robert Hay, Sir John Gardner Wilkinson, and Henry Rhind. Hay, while being a good draftsman and an astute observer, never prepared his Qurna diaries for publication; Wilkinson, while living for many years among Qurnawi, and beyond some economic observations on agricultural production, hardly concerned himself with the social character of the surrounding community; and Rhind, who set out to do just that, never reached the comprehensive level of description and analysis that he leads his reader to expect. Although professional demarcations may explain the non-engagement of subsequent generations of archaeologists with contemporary social life, their silence nevertheless has resulted in a misrepresentation of the social context in which archaeological fieldwork practice is carried out, and has contributed to the 'desertification' of this socio-archaeological landscape. The implications have been anthropological, social, and political.

For Qurnawi, the culmination of these latter historical and political processes has been the relocation to newly built settlements, initiatives that on an ideational as well as a practical level have been in train with varying degrees of intensity since the mid-1940s, but which mostly from the 1980s onward—through antiquities legislation–instituted prohibitions on construction and renovation, assisted by ever-expanding emergency accommodation following severe flooding in 1994, to the design and construction of custom-built settlements, and resulting in the wholesale relocations of the first decade of the twenty-first century—have reached a measurable degree of finality. Commentary on these aspects have been presented elsewhere (Van der Spek, 1997, 1998a, 1998b, 1998c, 1999a, 1999b, 2003a, 2003b, 2007), but also in the context of these political developments the historic and ethnographic material presented here represents a crucial starting point. History itself and the claimed absence of any time depth for indigenous sociality in the Theban Necropolis have become political tools, with the institutionalized denial of an indigenous presence and history by heritage managers and government policymakers used to advance their specific agenda. That agenda was the realization of their particular interpretation of the archaeological landscape, with the execution of the recent relocation campaigns designed to achieve that objective.

Indeed, it has been the absence of a more widely known Qurnawi settlement history that has permitted consultants during the 1992–94 government-sponsored architectural surveys in the necropolis to accept as fact that the community of al-Qurna derived from "the labourers who worked on the excavations [who] settled near archaeological sites with their families" (Rashed, 1994: 265). While containing some measure of truth, as settlement history such analysis remains shallow and is evidently inspired by the views of local council and antiquities officials, reflecting Egyptian bureaucrats' tendency to assign a rather more recent date to the necropolis' community, and using such views to legitimize the eviction of Qurnawi and the destruction of the necropolis' vernacular architecture.

Rather than subscribing to any politically-motivated time-shallow forms of sociality, Qurnawi history and ethnography discussed here should have provided an important corrective necessary in the formulation of heritage management and tourism development initiatives involving the resident population of the Theban Necropolis. In this sense, there is a subtext here that advocates social anthropological analyses as an essential component in holistic approaches to heritage management of World Heritage–listed sites inhabited by indigenous and so-called fourth world communities. The material presented here may serve as an archetypal case study for other similarly occupied World Heritage–listed sites, combining a broad range of historical, social, and cultural criteria of significance.

Regrettably, and although recommended by UNESCO and the World Heritage Committee, the Egyptian authorities ignored requests for a comprehensive site assessment study of the Theban west bank, which would have encompassed "geological, archaeological and geographical surveys and mapping, anthropological studies, assessment of the historical and cultural landscape qualities of the foothills and of the presence of Gurnah village in the site" (UNESCO 1999; Michaelides and Dauge, 2008: 7; both based on recommendations first articulated in Van der Spek, 1998c: 180).

Despite the disinterest on the part of the Egyptian authorities in such a holistic heritage management approach, and notwithstanding the destruction of the foothills hamlets, this study has nevertheless sought to formally situate Qurnawi studies alongside the archaeological study of the Theban west bank as an equally legitimate field of academic social inquiry. Given the recent vigor and finality of government-sponsored relocation plans, this study must be considered as timely: the history and ethnographic specificity of the foothills communities have now effectively ceased, at least in that location and where it concerns their more direct linkages with the particular qualities of the necropolis landscape. Surviving memories of past life in that environment will disappear within the lifespan of the current or next generation of Qurnawi.

The conjoining of the many components that form a part of these recent developments—history, ethnography, Egyptology, heritage management, demography, political and economic interests, eviction and relocation with their possible social effects impact—renders Qurnawi studies of significant scope and complexity. Inherent in this complexity and importance is the fact that many aspects of al-Qurna's history and society have to remain subject to further study before a fully comprehensive picture of local history and sociality can be established. This is likely to remain an open-ended project: Not only will life for most Qurnawi continue to be lived in an environment, which, through its linkages with international tourism, will continue to be affected by global and national forces in one way or another, the social changes that may be expected following their relocation to the new communities also warrants academic investigation.

The emphasis on the necessary historical context and the ethnographic material presented here has meant that other aspects of contemporary Qurnawi history and sociality could either not be covered in the present discussion or require future investigation. Following the relocation of the community, and further expanding the material presented here, such research should include observations of any social changes that may occur within the new environment. From a social perspective, an emphasis on women's roles and all those other aspects of women's lives that were inaccessible during the present research will be necessary to round out any gender imbalance that is inherent in the representation of Qurnawi society offered here.

What must be conducted alongside these more contemporary issues is further research into the historic context and early social adaptation of life in the Theban foothills, including a systematic survey of travelers' records. The identification and analysis of these records may, through their commentary on and responses to the behavior of west bank population groups, provide additional insights into early forms of local sociality. An accompanying survey of photographic records may provide a pictorial representation of facets of pre-modern daily life on the Theban west bank.

Gaining an understanding of the implications of life once lived in this contested archaeological landscape would involve a study of the history of heritage management in the Theban Necropolis; the politics associated with the heritage management approaches that were implemented, including a full history of the various relocation initiatives; and the issue of the politicization of the archaeological landscape to serve national economic ends. The evaluation of all these elements may offer global lessons for policymakers and heritage managers who seek insight into what went wrong in the Theban Necropolis. Beyond more recent historical studies, the following topics, some of which have already been flagged in the preceding discussion, are also suggested for future further research.

A detailed archaeological and historical study of Luxor similar to Jean-Claude Garcin's study of Qus (Garcin, 1976) is necessary to obtain local micro-historical information on the social and political events affecting Luxor and its west bank communities. Given the recent infrastructure changes to urban Luxor, the question arises if this is still possible. A related study, but one that can be conducted independently from it, is a study of local taxation and cadastral records as well as the records of legal proceedings involving west bank land disputes.

There is a great need for a study of the surviving built fabric of Qurna, including the surviving utilitarian mud structures in the foothills tombs and in al-Tarif, and incorporating early religious architectural structures such as the shaykh tombs in the Muslim cemetery, the locations of early places of worship, and other places of liturgical significance such as the prayer stations and *zawiya*. Collectively, these features may be able to establish a measure of local indigenous history and practice that is distinct from the recorded observations of early western travelers. As part of such a project, the 1992–94 architectural and social survey should be translated and published. This five-volume document was produced in limited numbers toward the design of the new village (Husseen, 1995). Its social survey data and architectural drawings of the hillside vernacular built fabric represent an increasingly important snapshot of life in the Theban Necropolis during the mid-1990s.

A historical study of the *mumiya* trade will further situate and give substance to a European demand for products that predates—and gradually feeds into—the demand for antiquities, its early involvement by European agents negatively impacting on relations with local communities. Where still possible, such a study should explore the detail of the *mumiya* operations, the organization of local labor by expatriate European merchants in Cairo, and any evidence of associated indigenous exploitation by foreigners, coloring their relations with westerners. Oral-historical research among Ba'irati may reveal the nature of the discord between the two communities and establish whether any difference results from a religious marginalization of Qurnawi located in historically situated aspects of the *mumiya* trade.

Distinct from the heritage management focus outlined above, historical studies of archaeological practice carried out on the Theban west bank may reveal much about this discipline's interaction with foothills Qurnawi and the early formational history of the necropolis' vernacular architecture. The archives of the SCA in Cairo should still contain much information about the history of the French-dominated Service des antiquités and their policy toward indigenous communities inhabiting archaeological sites. The operations of British archaeologists and antiquities inspectors, as well as the involvement of private excavators and philanthropists who paid for the cost of expropriating, excavating, and protecting the foothills' Noble Tombs, should provide much of the detail of policy and practice responsible for the expansion of the modern vernacular settlement pattern throughout the Theban Necropolis. Apart from the archives in the SCA, locating the private papers of philanthropists like Sir Robert Mond and others in this latter respect seems crucial. Likewise, a close study of Howard Carter's notebooks kept during the years when he lived among Qurnawi should be conducted for the observations of foothills sociality they contain, as should the personal papers of those of his colleagues who came after him, including Arthur Weigall and Reginald Engelbach, and such other long-term resident archaeologists as

Bernard Bruyère. Part of this ethno-historical study should also comprise oral-historical research to establish the extent of any true encroachment inspired by the increased building activity that followed the expropriation of tombs. Apart from the vernacular consequences of expropriation, if an influx of exogenous, new foothills occupants also resulted, then this has implications for how we historically understand who or what constitutes 'Qurnawi.' This oral-historical approach may also clarify the extent to which Yanni's account of a system of drawing lots did in fact exist, and the extent to which it, too, played a role in the physical expansion across the foothills of the necropolis' community.

If Qurnawi identity has long been associated with the trade in illegal antiquities, something that we have attempted to deconstruct here through an emphasis on the plurality of economic practices, then aspects of this practice must also be understood in terms of the global demand for antiquities by collectors of fine art. Similarly, the interplay between global and local conditions, and the degree to which the sale of antiquities at the local village level constitutes a strategy of economic resilience, must be considered. In this context, the historical impact of the 1929 world recession on the international art market must be evaluated, and the extent to which a wholesale collapse in the demand for antiquities did or did not in fact occur. The result of such a study will influence how we see the function of locally occurring antiquities and the degree to which they are viewed and utilized at the local village level as a resource during times of economic hardship.

But a study of the continuing demand for authentic antiquities should also analyze the demand and production of imitation antiques, which, likewise, are situated within the broader public interest for fine art. An ethno-historical study of the production and economics of fake antiques would provide not only the background to today's artisanal industry, but also detail a local response to global interests resulting from western archaeological practice. This study would focus on the external forces generating the demand for and its development in the context of depleting supplies of authentic antiquities; the interrelationship between east and west bank practitioners in the supply of examples and ancient raw materials; shifting customers' tastes and any corresponding stylistic changes and evolving artistic qualities, methods of production, and sales strategies; and the industry's prominent historical characters, including the intermittent role of Egyptological specialists.

The existence of a rich literary corpus in the villages of the Theban west bank is suggested in the writings of several Egyptologists. If it is not too late, and if it has not already been completely wiped out by the advent of television, this corpus should be explored and recorded and its social significance as a mechanism for educating the young should be evaluated.

Many of these research foci could be elements of inquiry in the Qurna Discovery oral history project suggested by Caroline Simpson, but it seems vital that initiatives be taken to collect and record these materials before the knowledge is lost through a combined passing of the older generation and the impact of modernizing influences. As Caroline has said, "There is work for so many disciplines, if they dare to touch it" (Simpson, 2000).

Let that be the challenge. Although the vernacular foothills hamlets are now gone, there should remain much local knowledge to record elements of the Theban west bank's more recent settlement and social history. But time may be running out and it is hoped that those researchers with the relevant Islamic Studies–focused expertise in historical, sociological, anthropological, archaeological, and architectural methodologies and who are fluent in Egyptian Arabic will come forward to take up the challenge to record and document the Theban west bank's rich social history and cultural detail before it is too late. There is indeed more than Egyptology here, and the 'glittering wrappers' of Qurnawi cultural expression continue to sparkle still . . .

Appendix 1

Ethnography in Sensitive Surroundings: Notes on Life and Work among the Tombs

Background to the research project

Reference has been made to anthropological objectives and the use of anthropological fieldwork methodologies. Something must be said, then, about how the material that formed the basis for the ethnographic discussion presented in the preceding chapters was gathered and under what circumstances. Advantaged by a long-standing interest in Egyptology and having prior familiarity with Qurnawi and their role in the history of Egyptological practice, my initial access into their lives was via the tourist 'path' which leads archaeologically-minded visitors to the ancient burial grounds of the Theban west bank. During November and December of 1995, I was made to feel welcome by Qurnawi from the Noble Tombs area of Shaykh 'Abd al-Qurna, where I first became personally acquainted with some of the villagers who were to become my hosts and informants during subsequent fieldwork.

Early observations of Qurnawi activities during that 1995 visit noted some of the strategies operating between tourists visiting the Theban Necropolis and members of the local community. The evident variety of formal and informal income-generating activities that seemed to be in contrast with the emphasis on tomb robbing in the Egyptological literature, the constraints imposed by protective heritage management measures on community life and on the urban infrastructure, and the political dimensions associated with life in this environment as evidenced by villagers' concerns about the outcome of that year's general elections, which had the potential to influence future relocation plans, were all observed. Crowding around a small black-and-white television set to hear news of the November elections, the anxiety experienced by the host family was palpable. That experience was in some sense no more than a preliminary fieldwork introduction providing early insight into local concerns. With dawning realization, these historic, socio-cultural, economic, and political elements—enacted against the particular background of the necropolis' landscape, in their totality—appeared sufficiently interesting to merit study in their own right. Indeed, the time had come for an ethnographic account that would move beyond the stereotypical and narrow portrayal of Qurnawi economic activity.

Residing with local foothills families, anthropological fieldwork was carried out during two field trips that took place between October 1997 and September 1999, with each field trip concentrating on a distinct focus. During 1997–98 much attention was paid to the social organization and production of tourist art. Following the November 17, 1997 terrorist attack, the local tourism-driven economy had collapsed entirely, leaving artists instantly deprived of their market and with ample time to both talk about and demonstrate their work. Boundaries between legal and illegal activities proved, for obvious reasons, difficult to cross, with those artists suspected of involvement in black-market antiquities dealings altogether unwilling to talk about even the legitimate artistic aspects of their work. Fieldwork conducted during 1999 included a focus on interviewing many of the households in al-Hurubat (Badawi's hamlet located on the slopes of the hill of Shaykh 'Abd al-Qurna). In addition to on-site fieldwork in Qurna between 1997 and 1999, several stays in Cairo served the purpose of archival research and meetings with government officials, non-government organizations (NGOs), and social science and architectural consultants. A week in Oxford during February 1998 focused on the personal papers of Sir John Gardner Wilkinson, who lived in Egypt between 1821 and 1833, much of it in al-Hurubat, and whose manuscripts are now preserved in the Department of Special Collections and Western Manuscripts at the Bodleian Library in the University of Oxford. A follow-up visit to the Theban west bank took place during November 2009, providing the opportunity to obtain first-hand experience of life in the new communities.

Simply *khawaja*: A foreigner among many

Although archaeological research has been carried out in the necropolis for the past two hundred years, the presence of a social anthropologist would be a rare occurrence that generates its own dynamics as a result of the particular requirement for the researcher to live in and with the community under study. Al-Qurna may be unique in this respect and some observations are warranted to shed light on the context in which fieldwork was conducted and for the supplementary ethnographic insights they contain.

The village of al-Qurna cannot be separated from the visitor interest that the surrounding archaeological monuments continue to attract. Qurnawi economic practices are to a significant degree structured by the resources that the constant arrival of tourists represents and almost all friendly relations with foreigners are motivated by business interests. For some, providing board and lodging to visitors, and thereby providing a west bank base to explore the necropolis and the experience of participating in family and village life, may be one in a range of income-generating strategies. Given the variety of these strategies and the extent to which they depend on relations with strangers, the argument can be made that, in the absence of a pre-existing relationship, the exchange of Qurnawi goods and services for money is essentially one of commodity fetishism. Here, the process of exchange masks and substitutes for the social relations themselves and the commercial imperative is to make the visitor feel happy, thereby encouraging his or her future return. Achieving this mental and emotional state in visitors is the Qurnawi take on Marx's doctrine of the commodification of social relations, and virtually all tourist-focused activity is directed toward it.

Against this background, a resident anthropologist is simply *khawaja*, a foreigner, whose presence points to a potential source of income, and who as such is indistinguishable from both the tourists and the archaeologists. For those who provide hospitality, in practical terms the distinction between these categories of visitors is effectively meaningless: They are all simply 'tourists' whom God in his benevolence has sent across their path, offering access to something more than a modicum of normalcy during what may well turn out to be a poor season. As such, the anthropologist is also *shughl*, work—*insha'Allah!*—and only marginally different from those visitors who are the target of the peddlers selling their fake antiquities at the nearby tombs. There exists something of a dichotomy here, for if these dynamics suggest a clear distancing between personal and commercial sensibilities, and relationships with foreigners may only have a semblance of friendship, then the closeness, trust, and inclusion in the intimacy of the family circle that is nevertheless projected, still forms part of the repertoire of strategies intended to ensure that the guest has "a good time" and does not "feel sad."

But the anthropologist remains a foreigner among many, the only difference being the unusual length of his stay, which, as the gossip reportedly had it, must have turned his host into a "millionaire." If such gossip suggests possible jealousies, then the process of cultivating and protecting these bonds of friendship with tourists may indeed lead to a cooling of relations between Qurnawi themselves, but is nevertheless recognized by the parties involved as acceptable mercenary behavior in a competitive industry that invariably and in due course will give both sides its turn. As has been discussed, local rules of hospitality were an important ingredient in the recorded early interaction between Europeans and Qurnawi, and they may still be recognized in the modern relations of individual rivalry over access to and protection of *khawaja* and the certain economic investment that the 'ownership' of their presence represents.

There are, however, also individuals in al-Qurna whose lives move independently from the tourists, and who will have nothing to do with them. For at least some of them, and particularly among the elderly, any involvement with tourists will represent the range of questionable practices that in their eyes are inherent in contact with foreigners. Practices that are considered not *nadif*, clean, may not simply relate to commercial transactions involving accommodation or the sale of artifacts, but also include sexual relations between Qurnawi and foreigners evidently motivated by financial gain. Marriage between young Qurnawi men and middle-aged European women, and homosexual relations between Qurnawi and European men, may offer an economic base for some, but is frowned upon by segments within the community who have come to equate such relations with tourism and foreigners generally. Indeed, one elderly woman approached for an interview indicated in no uncertain terms she was not willing to talk, calling her visitors *lutee* (homosexual).

Other community members may have been indifferent to such foreign influences but could not get themselves to speak to a *khawaja* by virtue of the perceived divide that separates their occupational specialization from the world of the tourists. This category included some of the Coptic silversmiths and the *dallal*, the village surveyor who measures agricultural fields in instances of dispute. At least one branch of an extended family group refused to participate because members of another branch of the same family, with whom they were at odds, had already participated. One person openly stated that, following the recent terrorist attack, fear was a tangible component of village sensibilities, and there will indeed have been those who declined to participate for reasons of perceived personal safety. Egypt has been under a state of emergency law since 1981 and there will have been the perception that the heightened state of police and army presence following the attack at Hatshepsut's Temple on November 17, 1997, was not only directed at any future terrorists but, at least in the minds of the villagers, also at the people of Egypt, Luxor, and al-Qurna.

Pecuniary demands of life in the tourist zone

The objective of anthropological fieldwork is to collect ethnographic data, that is, information to be used as the source material in an analysis and a description of the social and cultural life of a particular community of people. Anthropological fieldwork is characterized by so-called participant observation, where residence of some duration in the community under study enables the researcher to develop a view from the inside. Conducting such anthropological fieldwork in an environment where virtually all services provided to visitors come at a cost generates pressures quite different from those where anthropological fieldwork is conducted in areas that hold no tourism interest. Furthermore, through their long-time involvement with archaeological exploration, Qurnawi are familiar with the intellectual and funding relationships that exist between universities and foreign archaeological missions, and they therefore more generally equate the presence of university-sponsored research in the necropolis with income-generating possibilities.

For the present research, this has meant that gathering ethnographic data in many instances also involved some reciprocal arrangements. Most notably, and almost inevitable given the total absence of tourists following the Luxor Massacre on November 17, 1997, interviews conducted with craftsmen in the production of tourist art often necessitated purchasing samples of their work in order to provide them with a little income and thereby maintain the sort of friendly relations throughout the artisan community conducive to obtaining information about their methods of craft production and marketing strategies. At other times, an otherwise innocent interview session could end with the suggestion that we go and "take a rest," which always meant having a couple of beers in the Ramesseum Resthouse, the restaurant located next to the memorial temple of Ramesses II, and a popular meeting place for foothills villagers who also enjoy a bottle of Stella, Egypt's low-alcohol beer.

The certain reciprocity often expected upon the receipt of information will also and inevitably include favors. The writing of letters to former overseas visitors, ranging from the generic maintenance of 'brotherly' relations, to such pragmatic but calculated requests as financial assistance with the higher education of children, to overt—and sometimes explicit, but always strategically conceived—love letters, is pursued with a distinct commercial quality in mind and is therefore highly valued tender. One of the more amusing versions of this sort of reciprocity was the request to photograph a villager excavating his fake artifacts, in the expectation that the photographs would provide the necessary unquestionable proof of their antiquity when shown to prospective buyers. Yet, even then, strategies of this sort only go to demonstrate the long-standing participation of Qurnawi in both archaeological practice and their resourceful dependence on visitors.

This form of reciprocity was less the case with the household visits, where there was no real economic benefit to be gained by those who agreed to be interviewed. For lack of a tangible benefit, therefore, these household visits were in some way distinct from the visits to artisans, or even peddlers, where the potential for personal gain—be it through a sale, letters to foreign tourist friends, or business-enhancing photographs—formed a natural extension to existing commercial practices. If Badawi, by mediating a meeting, could procure a little business for a village artisan, then, generally, household participation was secured by him on the basis of kinship bonds, personal friendships, collegial or neighborly relations, or by simply approaching and persuading fellow villagers with what he often called "chocolate-talking."

Broadly, the presence of such fieldwork reciprocity suggests that one of the implications for the objective gathering of ethnographic data in a location where western funds are in many ways central to the local economy is that in such a situation ethnographic fieldwork tends to be slanted toward the immediacy of 'participating' rather than the distancing quality inherent in 'observing.' As a participant observer it is impossible, for theoretical or purist reasons that the academy might instill, to prevent or evade any impact on the observed, and to be totally removed from the practicalities of daily life.

The Theban west bank environment is characterized by seasonal or periodic fluctuations in visitor numbers, no more poignantly demonstrated than with the collapse of the local economy in November 1997. Those were exceptional circumstances, but also during the hot summer months, tourism to Upper Egypt is traditionally down. Visitor numbers to the Noble Tombs area will be fewer still: left until last, when tour groups have already been saturated with royal tombs and temples, and unless their guide is otherwise (that is, financially) motivated, tourists show little inclination or desire to leave the air-conditioned comfort of their coaches to climb the central foothills during the heat of day.

Thus, when tourism (read: the presence of foreigners) is down, and the fieldworker (read: foreigner) becomes the tourist, it is his or her presence that enables villagers to make ends meet. Such reciprocal arrangements cannot be otherwise. 'What if' questions may reveal strategies of coping during lean times, but detached observation would seem impractical, both for the difficult interpersonal relations that might result, and for the ethical questions that non-involvement would raise. The solution for Colin Turnbull may have been to become like one of them, "selfish, uncaring, and unloving" (Turnbull, 1994: 10), but such Qurnawi are not.

Consequently, participation in the life of the local community also integrates the researcher into the structuring framework of social responsibility and commitment, the system of reciprocal social obligations known as *wajib*, duty. It is a measure of the fieldworker's acceptance in the family unit and in the life of the larger community that he is also made subject to the expectations and obligations that such duty imposes, either through direct participation in certain communal tasks following the death of a neighbor or through participation in the regime of contributions that seek to cement community cohesion. In the same manner as these obligations undoubtedly provide a severe strain for many Qurnawi, especially during the lean summer months, so they were also a burden on the researcher's resources. In this respect I became a true Qurnawi, with any irregular supplementary income received by Badawi from involvement with tourists, and so alleviating pressure on the household's overall financial situation, being greeted by me with the enthusiasm of a tomb-side peddler on a better-than-expected day.

Interviews and the dynamics of home visitation

Fieldwork conducted during 1999 included a focus on interviewing many of the households in al-Hurubat and as such was conceptually different from the 1997–98 'season' of inquiry. Yet, while tangibly present, the two foci of the different fieldwork stages were not necessarily mutually exclusive. As the possibility for thematically focused 'structured' visits was facilitated by, and thus depended on, the availability of Badawi, such visits generally did not occur until later in the day. Badawi's—not always rigidly enforced—working hours provided ample time for other approaches and activities. These could include: time spent with and observing the activities of members of Badawi's household or other acquainted families; accompanying other villagers in their daily activities, be it to the agricultural fields or the ancient network of underground tombs and passages to retrieve mummy linen claimed to be an important ingredient in the chemical treatment of fakes; discussions with Dr. Boutros, who is a fount of knowledge of all things local, and more, in his west bank medical practice; observing peddlers at work at nearby well-known tombs; visits to archaeological missions working in the area, including the library of Chicago House, the Luxor headquarters of the Oriental Institute, the University of Chicago; discussions with staff at the local *taftish*, the west bank inspectorate of the SCA; visits to the Luxor City Council for meetings with officials there; visits to the Mosque at Dra' Abu al-Naga for discussions with the religious leadership; visits to local alabaster factories; and so on.

Similarly, time spent with Badawi was not always spent as *shughl* (work) either, and I participated as much in his range of activities as he spent being involved in mine. Often his movements centered on the ever-present need for *wajib*, duty, with frequent visits to hospitals or someone sick at home, attending wakes, funerals, and the commemorative gatherings at specified intervals upon a person's death. Other activities were an extension of home life, with regular visits to in-laws and other affines in al-Tarif, events that often were planned in such a way as to leave room for more structured activities, but which invariably took longer than expected, and generating at times a degree of vexation for the seemingly endless 'sitting around' involved in these visits. Yet, and in their totality, these experiences were not less important than the more structured aspects of fieldwork, offering scope for true participant observation, and watching everyday life unfold without being affected by the unconventional demands that my presence and its specific level of activity demanded.

That level of activity grew particularly intense during the many visits to individual households that took place between May and August 1999. The method of conducting interviews was favored over a comprehensive census, which was considered impractical for a number of reasons, including its logistical complexity given the extensive and scattered nature of the community of Qurnawi and the conseqent need for a number of research assistants, the associated expense of which fell outside my limited research budget. Beyond these, the alternative of conducting a series of household interviews in al-Hurubat had the added advantage of providing access to a number of households outside Badawi's immediate circle of relatives and acquaintances that might otherwise have remained closed to me: Being considered a member of Badawi's household, and in so many ways viewed as his *khawaja*, including all the commercial sensibilities surrounding that term, would have resulted in a certain 'hands-off' attitude toward me and will have inhibitcd people's openness and availability.

To give structure to the household visits in al-Hurubat, a list of 174 nuclear foothills family units was established from discussions with Badawi. Households were identified by the name of the male head and sequentially numbered from one to 174. The al-Hurubat area east of the road was not included for these household interviews, although several artists living there were visited during earlier fieldwork. Visitation itself did not strictly take place following this numbered sequence, but followed a random pattern often linked with whom Badawi met during that day to arrange a suitable opportunity for us to visit.

It proved ultimately impractical to interview each of the 174 households in al-Hurubat. Not only was this because of other opportunities that came up—separate sessions with a number of elderly people to record some of their stories, additional visits to artisans and other occupational special-ists, ad hoc visits to selected individuals to pursue certain specific lines of inquiry, and so on—and the consequent time constraints, but also due to the often unpredictable range of social dynamics within the community.

Out of the 174 Hurubati households, sixty-six households were vis-ited, while another fifteen comprised (often multiple) social visits to individuals or families where specific topics could also come up for dis-cussion. Among the sixty-six households were several larger compounds consisting of adjoining houses occupied by members of extended families, usually married brothers with their individual families. Here, often the oldest brother and head of the extended family, that is, he who "knows everything," provided the responses. As a result of these visits to larger family clusters, the varying range of affiliations between Badawi and the families visited, the certain number of refusals, and the number of actual visits completed out of the total number of possible visits, the sample of household visits can be considered relatively random, as follows:

al-Qurna Household Visitation May 15–August 31, 1999		
Total number of counted Hurubati households as of May 1999		174
Number of household interviews conducted	66	
Social visits only, with information obtained on specific topics	15	
Not interviewed, demographic and occupational information only*	49	
Not interviewed, no information available	24	
Refusals for security reasons	4	
Refusals on other grounds**	3	
Not visited for personal reasons Badawi/Households✝	7	
Houses unoccupied✝✝	6	
Total number of Households		174
* Demographic and occupational information for eighteen households provided by other siblings or family members at interview time or during social visits		
** Demographic and occupational information available for one household		
✝ Demographic and occupational information available for two households		
✝✝ Demographic and occupational information available for one owner		

Distribution of household visits conducted at al-Hurubat, May to August, 1999.

The sets of questions used in these interviews were structured around three different themes: (1) household membership and family demographics; (2) property and income; and (3) archaeological, domestic, and spiritual space. In their entirety, these served to canvas aspects of the domestic and economic usage of the archaeological landscape and the nearby cultivated zone, and villagers' relationship toward it, at times establishing unexpected connections.

What is not conveyed in the above clinically presented table and three-fold thematic interview structure is that, in the direct interaction with people during the process of anthropological data-gathering, there may be a degree of unpredictability that can direct and shape the nature of the information obtained. Due to exposure to previous questionnaires and home visits by architectural consultants and social survey data collectors, I had personally anticipated a certain antipathy toward clipboards, note taking, and the collection of socioeconomic and demographic data generally. But the last major survey had been completed some five years before the present research in al-Qurna (SPAAC, 1995) and those families who agreed to be interviewed were for the most part welcoming and willing to participate. Those who demonstrated a degree of antagonism will have had their unrelated reasons, as in the case of the retired plasterer, who found questions about his ongoing undeclared earnings particularly confronting. This case highlighted the unforeseen conditions that could arise at interview time and that had the potential to impact on the data-gathering process.

The range of such unpredictable social dynamics proved quite broad and it may be instructive to offer a few additional examples. For some, fear was a tangible component of village sensibilities, and there will have been those who declined to participate for reasons of perceived personal safety. One of these, a villager who worked at the *taftish*, the west bank antiquities inspectorate office, and who was responsible for maintaining the attendance register of personnel working on the restoration of the Noble Tombs, was especially unhelpful. Suggesting that foreigners now, via the internet, could send information abroad, he with so many words planted the seed in several people's minds that my inquiries did not simply serve the stated objectives but could well be used against the interests of the state.

Indeed, the heavy-handedness on the part of the police and security apparatus, as documented in annual human rights reports,[1] demonstrates that there is a tangible component to people's fears. Whether guilty or not, the suspicion alone of having been involved in a criminal offense, and the known risk of physical harm during any associated police interrogation and custody, offer a real incentive for people not to draw attention to their involvement in any activities that may be construed as running counter to the interests of the state.

This situation accounts for some of the dynamics that took place during the household interviews. At times, there was a tendency for Badawi to answer on behalf of the intended respondent, as if to shield him or her from a potentially embarrassing or even compromising question. At other times, questions that had a certain qualitative component often met with overly positive responses, as if to conceal that things could be otherwise. But there were also humorous aspects, as in the case of one elderly widow who in her responses as often as possible sang the praises of President Mubarak, thinking that I was a journalist who would surely report everything she said. The point subsequently made by Badawi, namely that many people here have very little education, seems valid, especially among the older generation who, despite explanations, may fail to distinguish accurately between occupational specializations readily recognized within literate society.

A different set of dynamics was inherent in the position of Badawi himself, who as my research assistant provided introductions to the families and individuals to be interviewed, who translated for me during the interviews, and who as a key informant himself provided information and acted as my sounding board when trying to understand the range of emerging issues. Since there was no potential for personal gain to be had for respondents who took part in the household interviews, these home visits, therefore, very much rested on an existing and ongoing relationship between Badawi and the person or family in question. There thus existed a degree of sensitivity, as any perceived negative impressions could have backfired on him socially, and his position as a member of the local community will therefore have required him at times to balance my interests with his own. It also explains why on occasion he displayed a tendency to answer on behalf of the intended respondent when suspecting certain sensitivities, mentioned above. To be sure, Badawi knew many of the families well and he may have represented their views adequately if he felt that the issues concerned were problematic. If, in doing so, he might have compromised the possibility of variable responses, additionally volunteered information, or the opportunity for me to ask supplementary questions, then such was simply the fieldwork context and in the end one works with whatever data emerges.

This is not to say that Badawi himself was never on the receiving end of negative reactions. Our association branded him in the opinion of one elderly lady as "homosexual." In another instance, and when discussing certain fertility practices, Badawi was told by the female respondent to go and ask his own mother. The nature of the woman's discontent was not totally clear. There may have been an issue between the two (related) families; maybe the woman took offense at the type of questions being asked by someone of the opposite gender, or she had simply had enough, also in view of her husband's recent return from hospital.

It was initially not obvious to me that such negative exchanges sometimes occurred. When the subject came up in private discussion with Badawi, it turned out that he had kept this information from me so as not to make me "feel sad." These episodes underscored the fact that also for him the boundaries between tourist and, in my case, fieldworker, were either not always clearly understood, or not consistently applied. In the end it was apparently just 'tourist work,' with the objective, again, to provide the visitor with as good a time as possible and demonstrating both the enduring nature of Qurnawi perceptions about tourism work and locally entrenched notions of what constitutes tourist satisfaction.

Once alerted by Badawi to some of the less positive dynamics of the interviews, certain relations of power within the family became at times obvious. Generally it was the man as head of the household who provided answers, although not necessarily to the exclusion of his wife. The women were found to have an unexpected degree of authority inside the house, in several instances showing displeasure at the proceedings and thereby making a husband less responsive, instructing him to discontinue responding altogether, or simply speeding up proceedings. At times where the husband was absent, the wife could also confidently and willingly take his place, although she might, as one instance demonstrated, be overruled by her teenage son who, considering himself the head of the household during his father's absence, would not allow his mother to speak. Thinking that this is how his father would have expected him to behave, the oldest boy in front of his brothers obviously felt compelled to apply restrictions that his father himself might not have imposed. The mother was called outside allegedly to attend to some domestic detail, but did not return, with the son offering responses from thereon.

On another occasion, even though the father had agreed to the interview, the session was taken over by his unmarried son, who proceeded to supply information that did not corroborate with known facts. As I was to learn later, the son had deserted from the army and was probably afraid his father might divulge details that could lead to his imprisonment. His father in any case did not read well and my introductory letter failed to clarify the intent of our questions, prompting Badawi to conclude that fear linked with the terrorist attack was the real issue, the assumption being that any information gathered might, despite my 'tourist' status, serve the interests of the security apparatus. If correct, his son's intervention may well have been a relief. But if the scenario was one of a maturing son gradually taking over authority from an aging father then this instance was not simply concerned with the shifting power relations within a family, but also carried overtones of delinquent behavior. Stories later emerged how this boy was indeed "no good." Previously, after having been refused a job with the German Archaeological Mission, he attempted to place the foreman in a bad light with the German field director by claiming he could only be offered a job in return for some chickens. Such variability at the level of the individual prevented any unrealistically expected homogeneity but made it at times impossible to direct the questions at the intended target group of respondents.

The above is to say that, beyond the research design itself with its methodological considerations and the reported findings that eventually result, there is another picture that can be presented. There is possibly a tendency in ethnographic accounts to keep the data separate from the sort of conditions under which they were gathered. Beyond some methodological observations, the emphasis on analysis and representation of the factual material takes precedence to the point of exclusion over the context of the range of social variables that at the time of fieldwork both guided and constrained the data-collecting process. But in practice, the fieldwork experience covers a range that includes the above vexatious 'sitting around,' the broad range of social dynamics and other unforeseen circumstances over which one has little or no control, to simply being occupied when other interesting things occurred elsewhere, and the painfully felt instances where opportunities were missed through such perceived personal shortcomings as indecision and misjudgment. Returning from active fieldwork, the anthropologist may indeed be left with an abiding sense that the organization of the data-gathering process is neither automatically error-free nor always self-esteem-affirming.

Collected under the wide range of variable social conditions and instances of unpredictable circumstance only marginally alluded to above, following post-fieldwork coding and analysis, and supplemented by personal observations and insights, the collective subject matter so gathered at al-Qurna became the basis—its detail distilled, considered, consolidated, and reintegrated—for the ethnographic picture of life in the Theban foothills as it has been presented in the preceding chapters.

Appendix 2

Theban Mapping Project
Aerial Photographs

Plates 1–9

Toward a cartographic representation of al-Qurna: Aerial photographs of the Theban west bank communities by the Theban Mapping Project (TMP), the American University in Cairo (AUC).

Aerial photographs of the Luxor west bank, the Theban Necropolis, and localities named in the text. Each photograph is a cropped section selected from digital images made available by the TMP at the AUC. The support of the TMP and its director, Dr. Kent Weeks, and TMP staff members Magdi Ali, Francis Dzikowski, Nicole Hansen, and Lori Lawson is hereby gratefully acknowledged.

Two digital images were made available: 1) a 123 mb composite tiff image made up of a number of digitally scanned original 25x25cm diapositives. This image has a north-south vertical axis, representing the sweep of the foothills in its correct southwest—northeast direction; and 2) a single 23 mb tiff image digitally scanned from the original 25x25cm diapositive which represents the Theban Necropolis along a horizontal axis. Image 1 has been used for Plates 1, 2, 4 and 9. Image 2 was used for Plates 3, 5, 6, 7 and 8. Although cropped from image 2, Plates 3 and 5 are represented in the general direction of image 1. Plates 6, 7 and 8 have been slightly adjusted from their general direction in image 2 to allow for better visual representation.

According to the TMP, the aerial photographs were taken between 01 April–30 June, 1979, between 1430 and 1530 hours. The original diapositives were produced for the TMP by the Remote Sensing Center of the Egyptian Academy of Scientific Research.

According to the TMP 1979 preliminary report:

> *"Two scales of aerial photography were required for the desired photo-grammetric mapping. For the general mapping of the necropolis, five flight lines were photographed at 1,700 meters (+ or –) above sea level elevation. For one-metre contour interval mapping, this results in a 'C-factor' (a limiting factor) of 1,600 (+ or –). This is well within the capabilities of today's photogrammetric equipment and techniques. The larger-scale mapping of areas of intense archaeological interest required nine flight lines at 900 metres (+ or –) above sea elevation. The C-factor for this photography is an optimum value of 850 for one-metre contour-interval mapping."*

Reproduction of these aerial photographs here serves the purpose of providing a cartographic representation of the Luxor west bank, the Theban Necropolis, and the interrelationship of the various hamlets and archaeological and other landscape features of Western Thebes. Given the relative age of the photographs (1979), certain differences can be observed by those familiar with more recent west bank topography. Not consider-ing here the major changes resulting from the 2006–2008 demolitions, we may notice the following: the road which lines the foothills was relaid dur-ing the early 1980s and now follows a trajectory beyond the Ramesseum which runs closer to the agricultural fields, before rejoining the section at Dra' Abu al-Naga; the boys' school at Qurna Hassan Fathy no longer exists; the Abu Shau bridge at Genina is yet to be built; the road to the new communities beyond al-Tarif is still only a track in the desert; and there is no evidence of developments in the desert at west al-Tarif. The location of present-day al-Suyul and the new communities at west al-Tarif (al-Qubbawi and New Qurna) fell outside the fourteen flight lines. Such, however, does not affect the generally accurate representation of the foot-hills communities prior to their recent relocation and demolition.

Despite these 'archaic' features, comparison with the 1922 Survey of Egypt maps, the last ones to have been made before the 1979 remote sensing project, indicates that the general 'footprint' of the hamlets cor-responds with the earlier record. This is not to say that the population had not increased or that a greater number of dwellings did not exist in 1979 than was the case in 1922. While a degree of fill-in construc-tion will have occurred, such will have taken place within the delineation already marked in 1922 as pertaining to a particular dwelling or family, thereby not greatly altering the previously mapped footprint of villagers' claimed domestic space. Mostly, however, the increase in living space will have been achieved by converting from single to double story households, often prompted by sons continuing to reside in the parental home upon marriage. Examples of such ongoing upward expansion were still in evidence during the early 1990s (Caselli and Rossi, 1992: 266-67), despite Presidential Decree No. 267 of 1981, and Antiquities Law No. 117 of 1983, which prohibited both new construction and the extension of existing buildings.

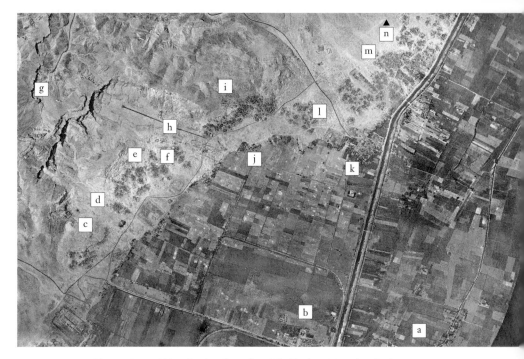

Plate 1. Luxor West Bank: Overview I © Theban Mapping Project

Plate 1
Luxor West Bank: Overview I

    a. al-Gezira (Gezirat al-Qurna), 'The Island,' its shape still discernible between the Nile and the al-Fadliya canal

    b. al-Qariya Hassan Fathy (Qurna al-Gedida [New Qurna], Qurna Hassan Fathy)

    c. Qurnat Mara'i

    d. Nag' al-Rasayla

    e. Shaykh 'Abd al-Qurna

    f. al-Khukha

    g. Valley of the Kings

    h. al-'Asasif

    i. Dra' Abu al-Naga

    j. 'Izbit al-Ward

    k. al-Genina

    l. al-Sualim

    m. al-Tarif

    n. To the new communities of al-Qubbawi, Qurna al-Gedida (New Qurna) and al-Suyul

Plate 2. Luxor West Bank: Overview II—Southeast Quarter © Theban Mapping Project

Plate 2
Luxor West Bank: Overview II—Southeast Quarter

a. Luxor
b. Local ferry landing
c. Tourist ferry landing (until 1997)
d. Gezirat al-Ba'irat
e. al-Gezira (Gezirat al-Qurna)
f. al-Qariya Hassan Fathy (Qurna al-Gedida [New Qurna], Qurna
   Hassan Fathy)

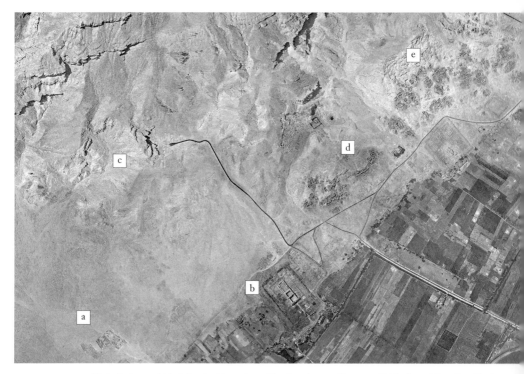

Plate 3
Luxor West Bank: Overview III—Southwest Quarter

a. Coptic Monastery Dayr Tadrus al-Muharab and Cemetery
b. Madinat Habu, memorial temple complex of Ramesses III
c. Valley of the Queens
d. Hill of Qurnat Mara'i
e. Hill of Shaykh 'Abd al-Qurna

Plate 4. Luxor West Bank: Overview IV—Northeast Quarter © Theban Mapping Project

Plate 4
Luxor West Bank: Overview IV—Northeast Quarter

a. al-Genina
b. ʻIzbit al-Ward
c. Draʻ Abu al-Naga
d. al-Sualim
e. al-Tarif

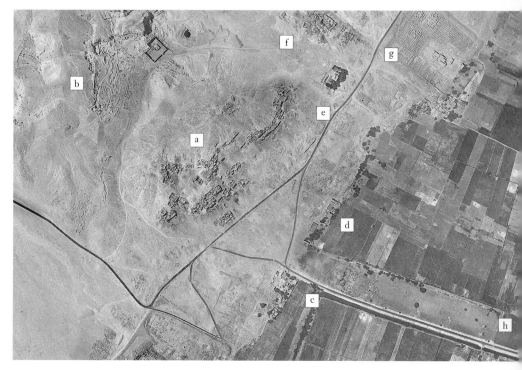

Plate 5. Luxor West Bank: Overview V—Qurnat Mara'l © Theban Mapping Project

Plate 5
Luxor West Bank: Overview V—Qurnat Mara'i

a. Qurnat Mara'i
b. Dayr al-Madina
c. *Taftish*, Supreme Council of Antiquities West Bank Inspectorate. Also the area of 'Castle Carter,' Howard Carter's house during his time as chief inspector of Upper Egypt (1899–1904)
d. Marsam Hotel (Hotel Shaykh Ali)
e. Expedition House of the German Archaeological Mission
f. Nag' al-Rasayla
g. Ramesseum, memorial temple complex of Ramesses II
h. Memnon Colossi (memorial temple complex of Amenhotep III)

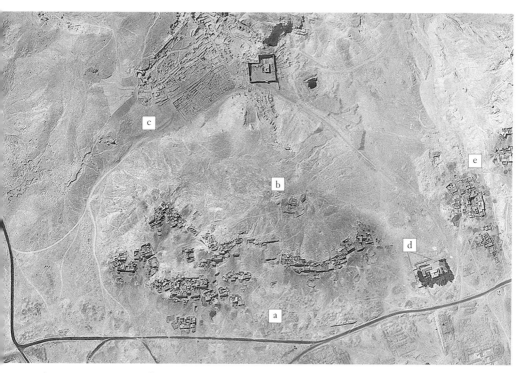

Plate 6. Luxor West Bank: Qurnat Mara'i © Theban Mapping Project

Plate 6
Luxor West Bank: Qurnat Mara'i

- a. Qurnat Mara'i
- b. Ruined Coptic Monastery of St. Mark at Qurnat Mara'i
- c. Dayr al-Madina
- d. Expedition House of the German Archaeological Mission
- e. Nag' al-Rasayla

Plate 7. Luxor West Bank: Shaykh 'Abd al-Qurna © Theban Mapping Project

Plate 7
Luxor West Bank: Shaykh 'Abd al-Qurna

a. Expedition House of the German Archaeological Mission
b. Nag' al-Rasayla
c. Ramesseum, memorial temple complex of Ramesses II
d. al-Khukha
e. General location of Bada⟩ house and 1999 fieldwork residence
f. Robert Mond and Norman ae Garis Davies Expedition House
g. Expedition House of the Polish Archaeological Mission at Dayr al-Bahari
   (formerly the Expedition House of the Metropolitan Museum of Art
   Egyptian Expedition, known as 'Metropolitan House')
h. al-'Asasif
i. General location of 'Yanni's House'
j. General location of Sir John Gardner Wilkinson's tomb house

Plate 8. Luxor West Bank: Dra' Abu al-Naga © Theban Mapping Project

Plate 8
Luxor West Bank: Dra' Abu al-Naga

a. al-Hasasna Mosque of Shaykh Tayyeb
b. al-Hasasna
c. al-Ghabat
d. al-'Atyat
e. al-Sualim
f. 'Izbit al-Ward and general location of 1997–98 fieldwork residence

Plate 9. Luxor West Bank: al-Tarif © Theban Mapping Project

Plate 9
Luxor West Bank: al-Tarif

a. Market area

b. Modern Muslim cemetery

c. al-Tarif (Saff al-Dawaba compound)

d. 'Castle Carter II,' Howard Carter's house during most of his association with Lord Carnarvon. Built in 1910, Carter lived here during the search for, and subsequent clearance of, Tutankhamun's tomb. The house has been used by Supreme Council of Antiquities inspectors but was restored during 2009 and is now open for visitors

e. The 1950 Hassan Fathy designed 'Stoppelaere House' on top of the hill 'Ilwat al-Diban

f. Area of west al-Tarif and general location of the new communities of al-Qubbawi and Qurna al-Gedida (New Qurna)

g. To the new community of al-Suyul

h. al-Madali

Appendix 3

English Translation of Carla Burri's Italian
The Anonymous Venetian Text[2]

To come back to what I wanted to tell you about the right bank of the river, I say that from Dendera to Gebelein, that means over a distance of two days, this is an area where the boat captains refuse to lodge you, and all go and put you on the other bank, for this area of land is inhabited by certain cursed tribes of insubordinate Arabs who do not want to see the Turks; and they kill as many as they can catch; even so the Turk is master there, but in a certain manner: he contends himself with levying taxes, but with a measure of goodwill; and they give these taxes to the Shaykh al-Arab, meaning the boss of the Arabs. In this manner, they preserve a sort of independence.

The Moors call that place El Chosas: It is situated in the heart of the Sa'id; it is the best [district] there is in the country because it is rich in villages; the mountain does not invade, so that you find a very beautiful countryside here. Each time the Turks have tried to attack, they have withdrawn themselves into the mountain, which is their fortress.

In this countryside, which belongs to them, opposite Luxor, I have seen a large expanse of land filled with ancient buildings; among those that have tempted my eyes two great colossi of mixed stone; I have not been able to admire them at close range because the countryside is completely submerged. It is because of this that I have only seen them from the bank of the Nile, which was at more than a hundred paces distance. Apart from those two statues, there was a rather large number of monuments.

Appendix 4

Extract from Howard Carter's Autobiographical Sketch V

Notebook 16
Sketch V
Pages 115–21

Summer Life and a Tale from the Coffee-hearth (Extract)

By this time I was able to converse with the people among whom I was residing with tolerable ease. So to while away the darker nights, when the pestilential gnats and midges tired me out of all patience, I occasionally indulged in the diversions of the Omdah's [Carter's footnote: "The headman or mayor of the village"] Mandarah ("guest-house"). There in the evenings the selectives of the village—the sheikhs and the fathers of the people—are generally gathered, and contrasting with these a fair representation of the community.

I must admit, however, that this practice was liable to serious criticism: some colleagues in the government service frowned upon it as a bad habit. They thought it degrading! But whether that be a fact or not, what I found was so valuable in this practice, or study, if it can be called such, was that it thereby brought me into contact with the people with whom I had to deal. It enabled me to study their manners and customs, and there can be no doubt that by it I acquired to a large extent their good opinion and at least some of their confidence.

At this coffee-hearth one could at times listen to reciters of romances, who, without book, commit their subjects to memory, afford attractive entertainment, and are often highly amusing. Some of their recitations contain a deal of history and romance. Moreover, they are told in lively and dramatic manner, but unfortunately many of their stories, such as fables of questionable moral teaching, are extremely indecent. They cannot therefore be repeated. But here in a nutshell is one from the coffee-hearth, which may be recounted in any drawing-room, and one, I believe, may be amusing to the reader.

"The Rat and the Snake"

On this occasion the evening conversation had drifted towards the subject of reptiles, their venom and their repulsiveness. Whereupon, one of the notables, Sheikh Mansûr el-Hashâsh by name, drolly remarked: "But forget ye not where horror is, there is fear, and fear is often more deadly than the venom of a Snake!"

This venerable Sheikh was a time honoured notable of the village, especially among the frequenters of the coffee-hearth, even though, years gone by, he had been deposed by the Government for his conduct towards the taxpayer, whom he had held under the river, sometimes too long, to collect for the second time the annual land tax—once for the Pasha and once for himself. Sheikh Mansûr was, in fact, a sage of fame throughout the villages, and his droll utterance caused a silence on the part of all those present. During this pause he re-settled himself upon sandy Mother Earth, dextrously sipped his steaming-hot coffee, and with pleasant gravity added: "Surely ye have heard tell of the quarrel between the Rat and the Snake?"

"No! But by the Reverence of your beard! Let us hear it!" exclaimed the assemblage in one voice.

So smoothing down his beard, old Mansûr replies: "Then hearken to the following strange event!"

When silence reigned once more, Mansûr then began: "'Twas on one of midsummer's days, when the heat of the sun, like molten lead, oppressed all life in the desert wâdis and tracts, there were met old disputants in bitter controversy—a desert Rat and a Snake!"

"In that intense heat neither Rat nor Snake had scarcely enough energy to fight, but gradually wrath dispelled their languor and the argument grew exceeding fierce."

"'Take care! O Cursed one! Lest I bite and slay thee!' hissed the Snake."

"'O my father! Thy bite indeed! To Gehenna with thy bite! It is true, Allah has given thee venom enough, but it's your ugly face that really kills! Though, poor creepy one, thou knowest it not!' exclaimed the Rat."

"Just then, a hot blast of wind, as from a furnace, made the disputants draw even closer under the scanty shade of a rock.

"'O father of insolence, clothed with hair, as with a garment, to guise thy impudence!' retorted the Snake. 'Thou knowest well, as all know, that life cease if I deign to bite!'"

"'Such indeed is the belief among the common folk of belly creepers, as the like of thee!' answered the Rat, assuming a philosophic air, 'Yet, if thou durst accept my challenge, I can easily prove my words to thee!'"

"'I accept what test thou will! For, by the Reverence of thy smellers, thou will soon learn how none can withstand the terribleness of my poison!' quoth the Snake."

"Other vermin of the desert were attracted by this heated conversation, but they kept a little apart from fear the Snake in his anger might strike at them. For they, too, at times, had had hellish orgies."

"'Will thou then agree,' asked the Rat, 'to descend to the black land, where men toil, and crops of every kind grow, to test the truth of what I declare?'"

"'Assuredly I will,' answered the Snake, 'for there the herbage is cool and pleasant, and there dwell fools as great as thee!'"

"And so in angry silence, the compact being made, they departed together, crossed the sandy desert tract in the heat of the summer afternoon. They trailed through a dusty burial ground, threaded their way among grave-heaps, glided under palm-groves, and at length they descended to the arable land, where the crops were green and fragrant. But they were careful not to linger in other places—no cover being perilous to them—lest men might espy them and deal a fatal blow. And so they wormed their way through bushes, and between the silence of the tall waxing millet, until they came to a suitable spot, a hole beside a trodden path amid the crops, where the Rat, who led, stopped and drank of the common juice of the earth."

"'It is here, O Snake,' said he, 'that our test shall be made. For here is a suitable hole in which for us to lurk!'"

"Then, when they had entered the hole together, the Rat proceeded: 'Thou see'st the path, trodden by wayfaring men, who pass at morn and eve. It is here that your power and mine shall be put to test. All that thou needest do is to bite the heel of him who first shall pass, return quickly into the hole, and await that which I shall do.'"

"And lo! Upon seeing some poor old man approaching, bearing a heavy load of fodder upon his back, the Rat said: 'Now is thy time, O Snake! Out with thee quickly. Bite his heel, and return at once to this hole!'"

"And behold the deed was done! With the extreemest speed, the Snake came out, struck the old man's heel, and was back in the hole unseen by him who felt the wicked fang."

"Stung with acute pain from the puncture caused by the poisoned fang, the old man leaped from the ground, dropped his load, and upon looking down beheld the Rat at the edge of the hole, cleaning his smellers!"

"Cursed be thy kind! Thou son of a dog! May thy race be burned for ever!' cried the old fellâh. And with that, he collected his load and passed on his way."

"Thou sawest what happened, O Snake.' Said the Rat: 'Thou hearest how he cursed thy race, and departed! But where is thy victory? How was it he was able to overcome the malignity of thy venom? Is there naught but pride in thy cold heart? Surely thou needest a lesson in humility. The next who passes by shall be bitten by me, and all I ask of thee is that thou showest him thy face!'"

"Such were the Rat's words to the Snake in the hole. But the Snake answered him nothing."

"Then there happened another thing! It chanced that within an idle hour a youth approached, driving his flock of sheep and goats before him. As he passed, the Rat sharply bit the youth's heel and disappeared into the hole, whence, as was agreed, the Snake thrust his head."

"The sting of the bite made the youth recoil. But when he looked down and beheld the wicked head and shining folds of the Snake, in terror he shrieked: 'O my father! O my misfortune! I have been bitten by a venomous Snake!' And then while uttering, like all good Moslems, 'It is by the Command of God!' he swooned and died."

"'What about your ugly face!' said the Rat in triumph to the Snake. 'Said I not truly? Was it not I who bit the poor youth, and did not thy face kill him? And after such a sight, what hope has he to live?—God bless and save him! O Snake, discard vanity from thy dark soul, and know thy lowly place among all created things that have form!'"

And then as the assemblage drew nearer to the coffee-hearth, Sheikh Mansûr el-Hashâsh muttered: "Alack and well-a-day, how dread a thing is fear!"

Appendix 5

A Petition from the People of Qurna to the Egyptian Government

A petition from the people of al-Hurubat which circulated in the central foothills during late 1996 and which was subsequently submitted to government officials with villagers' accompanying signatures, representing some seventy families. Translation courtesy of Caroline Simpson.

We, the people of Qurna, have recourse to every governmental official to give us our lawful rights concerning the great injustice that has befallen on us. We shouted, moaned, and complained.

We live in fear and worry as we are threatened with losing our own homes, when these homes are subjected to evacuation. You well know the suffering of refugees when driven away from their homeland. It is a devastating feeling of being a stranger in your own country, and an immigrant on your own land. We sometimes doubt our Egyptian nationality.

What is bewildering is the claim that we are offensive to tourism and the threat that our being on our own land is upsetting the security of our monuments. We are part of these monuments, we are born there and that is where we earn our only income. We cannot comprehend how we could threaten tourism in these sites when we care greatly, interact solely with tourists, and live off tourism work. Without the ruins, we cease to exist.

Tourists from all over the world can see and know that we form an integral part of the pillar of the industry of tourism in Egypt. The tourist season is our season. From that season we can marry off our sons and daughters. We eagerly wait for its arrival like a farmer waits the harvest.

More than ten thousand families live, inhabit, and work in Gurna. It is to us like water is to fish. We ask: Why move us away from the sites? What is it we have done wrong over a period of more than one hundred years here? We share next-of-kin tie with tourists. They, after all, are our source of bread. We believe we honor Egypt when it comes to our relationship with tourists. Expulsion and evacuation serves none but those who want to gain from our expulsion.

We give readily, with the help of God, our warmth and welcome. No matter how much preparation is made on receiving tourists, and money spent on investment in tourism; they will not suffice and take our place. We do not say no to sharing our source of income, but we do object to the denial of our livelihood. The security of the sites is a must, but we object to raiding our land and homes. Why declare a war against our livelihood?

When torrents of rain hit our villages, it was an omen to troubles ahead. Thankfully, the government gave us maximum support and aid. However, the case is different when these same villages that suffered the torrents are threatened by flattening bulldozers. The reality is clear to us. Some bodies are eager to lay hands on our source of income. They are far removed from excavation work or tourism.

Please have mercy on us and our children. Do not deprive us of our land and homes. Do not make us feel strangers in our own country. We have no doors on which to knock for help. Think and reflect on the prayers of those who are unjustly and wrongfully treated.

We would like you to remember our martyred heroes who fought when needed in times of war. Our people fought for Egypt bravely and thousands died willingly. However, we will take it into our hands to banish from our lands and homes whoever is responsible for our evacuation in return for personal profit. They are merely a handful of profiteers who are ready to drive away ten thousand families from their homes for personal gain.

We understand and comprehend God Almighty is there for the wrongly and unjustly treated, seeing those who take our livelihood and as written in the holy Qur'an: 'It is but the truth, just as you utter.'

May God bless you and show you the right path.

From the people of Gurna
Their representative
Abdul al-Salam Ahmad Souly
November 1996

Appendix 6

Art and Craft Production at al-Qurna
A Portfolio of Work 1995–1999

'Nefertari'
Limestone
Height of image 22.5 cm
Muhammad Ali Muhammad
January, 1998

'Nefertari'
Painted limestone
Abdelal Ahmad Ghalil
January, 1998

'Tutankhamun' shabti
Doum palm wood
Sayyed Mahmud Ali Abu-Sherifa
January, 1998

'Tutankhamun' shabti
Doum palm wood
Sayyed Mahmud Ali Abu-Sherifa
January, 1998

'Scribe'
Limestone
Abdu Muhammad Ahmad
January, 1998

'Mother and Child'
Ceramics, *ghubuwa*
Hassan Sayyed Muhammad (alias)
July, 1999

'Mother and Child'
Ceramics, *ghubuwa*
Hassan Sayyed Muhammad (alias)
July, 1999

Globular stone ware
Calcite ('Egyptian alabaster')
Height 14 cm
Tayyeb Muhammad Yusuf
January, 1998

Art and Craft Production at al-Qurna   391

Production line of 'walking' scarabs
Natural gray soapstone; *faghura*-fired,
dyed and lacquered gray soapstone
Length of *faghura*-fired and dyed scarab
9.5 cm
Ahmad al-Harazi
January, 1998

'Walking' scarab
Faghura-fired, dyed, and lacquered
gray soapstone
Ahmad al-Harazi
January, 1998

'Ramose'
Limestone
Muhammad Ali Muhammad
January, 1998

'Anubis' canopic jar
Crushed granite and epoxy resins
cast in a mold
Azeb Mustaffa Muhammad
January, 1998

Ibis
Doum palm wood, composite,
paint, and *ghubuwa* on stucco
Jahalan al-Azeb al-Tayyeb
Mahmud Hadraby
August, 1999

Peddlers' wares
Various materials:
ceramics, *faghura*-fired
soapstone, copper
pigment, *ghubuwa*
Various unknown artists
1995–99

Background: woollen
Upper Egyptian winter
scarf

Peddler's ware
Amarna period head
Painted limestone,
ghubuwa
Artist unknown
July, 1999

Peddler's ware
Shabti head
Painted limestone,
ghubuwa
Artist unknown
July, 1999

Peddler's ware
Shabti head
Painted limestone, *ghubuwa*
Artist unknown
July, 1999

'Hatshepsut'
Faghura-fired soapstone,
copper pigment
Total height 12.2 cm
Sayyed Mahmud Ali al-Matani
January, 1998

'Hatshepsut'
Faghura-fired soapstone,
copper pigment
Detail
Sayyed Mahmud Ali
al-Matani
January, 1998

Guardian statue
Doum palm wood, composite,
paint, and *ghubuwa* on stucco
Jahalan al-Azeb al-Tayyeb
Mahmud Hadraby
August, 1999

'Anubis'
Doum palm wood, paint, and
ghubuwa on stucco
Sayyed Mahmud Ali Abu-Sherifa
January, 1998

396   Appendix 6

Globular stone ware
Faghura-fired soapstone, glass paste,
and copper pigment
Height 8.5 cm
Ahmad Mahmud Ahmad
January, 1998

Imitation coffin fragment
Postcard, cement sheeting,
glue, mummification linen,
lacquer, *ghubuwa*
Adham Muhammad Esaman
January, 1998

Ceramic necklaces
Ceramics, copper pigment, dye
Women's crafts
Artists unknown
August, 1999

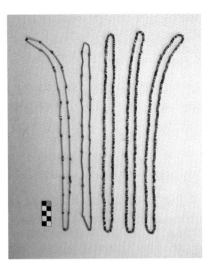

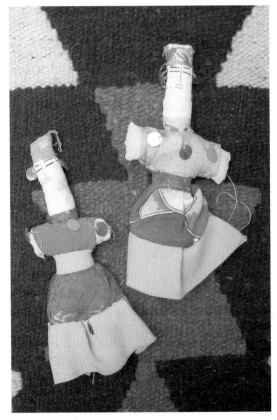

'Arusa dolls
Fabric, sequins
Women's crafts; girl
peddlers' wares
Height 24cm
Artists unknown
January, 1998

Background rug by male
Coptic weaver, al-Hurubat,
July, 1999

Notes

Notes to the Prologue and the Introduction

1   Thebes is the name of the ancient town and capital of Eighteenth Dynasty Egypt in the location of what is now Luxor, situated on the east bank of the Nile. On the west bank of the Nile are located the cemeteries of ancient Thebes, its memorial temples, and the village of the royal tomb builders. Although in popular parlance the area is more commonly referred to as the Luxor west bank, incorporating both the archaeological precinct of Western Thebes and a number of modern towns and villages, here the term 'Theban west bank' is used to integrate the houses of the modern village of Qurna more directly into the archaeological landscape with which it is historically closely associated. Even so, reference to the Luxor west bank and the Theban west bank may be used interchangeably in the chapters that follow.

2   The protective ancient Egyptian goddess of the Theban Necropolis was Meretseger, who as 'Mistress of the West' was associated with the land of the setting sun, that is, the kingdom of the dead. Her name means 'Beloved of him who makes silence,' a reference to Osiris, the Egyptian god of rebirth and resurrection (Lons, 1968: 116) or, alternatively, 'She who loves silence' (Wilkinson, 2003: 50, 224).

3   Other than the depicted musical instruments in the Theban tombs themselves (Manniche, 1975: passim), little is known of the role music played in the context of funerary processions and burial rituals. Considering the inherently religious nature of ancient Egyptian burial practices, it is to be expected that religious music will have accommodated funerary practices as well. Manniche has documented the use of percussion instruments (tambourine, drum) in funeral processions (Manniche, 1975: 3, 10), while deities significant in funerary beliefs (Anubis, Osiris) are associated with tambourine and trumpet respectively (Manniche, 1975: 4–5, 34–35).

4   UNESCO is the United Nations Educational, Scientific, and Cultural Organization. Its World Heritage Bureau is responsible for the 1979 World Heritage listing of the Theban Necropolis (UNESCO, 1972; 1979).

5   Conventionally, the article 'al' ('el') is often omitted in English transliterations. The names 'al-Qurna' and 'Qurna' will be used interchangeably. In contemporary usage, and depending on either the transliteration of the original Arabic, or the phonetic approximation of the spoken Arabic, 'Qurna' may also be rendered as Gurna or Gourna. In addition, eighteenth- and nineteenth-century early sources may offer such transcriptions as el-Ckoor'neh, Corna, Gorna, Gourneh, Gournei, Korna, Kurneh, and similar variants.

6   There is now a small catalogue of both published and unpublished titles that treat issues relevant to cultural and political aspects of the Theban foothills communities, for which see: Abu-Lughod, 1998; Chih, 1997a, 1997b, 1998, 2000; Colla, 2000, 2007; Hansen, 2004; Hassan, 1997a, 1997b, 2007; Meskell, 2000; Mitchell, 1995, 1998b, 2001, 2002; Parker and Neal, 1995; Simpson, 1997, 1999, 2000, 2001, 2003, 2004, 2010; Van der Spek, 1997, 1998a, 1998b, 1998c, 1999a, 2003a, 2003b, 2004a, 2004b, 2007, 2008; Wickett, 1993, 2010.

7   'Outstanding Universal Value' is a term defined by UNESCO as "cultural significance which is so exceptional as to transcend national boundaries and to be of common importance for present and future generations of all humanity" (UNESCO, 2008: 14). The concept underpins inscription in the World Heritage List. However, and contrary to the views of archaeologists working in the Theban Necropolis, the concept may go beyond strict archaeological features, as is evident from Article 1 of the 1972 World Heritage Convention (UNESCO, 1972) and as reflected in Michaelides and Dauge (2008: 7).

8   To the extent that Egyptological concerns through popular archaeological writings and the interests of the international tourism industry have set an unquestioned ethical and moral standard, heritage management concerns have indeed come to represent what Pierre Bourdieu calls *doxa*, where "the social world appears as self-evident [through the] quasi-perfect correspondence between the objective order and the subjective principles of organization" (Bourdieu, 1977: 164). According to this schema, the dominant view has "an interest in defending the integrity of doxa or, short of this, establishing in its place the necessarily imperfect substitute, orthodoxy" (Bourdieu, 1977: 169). In this environment, and by contrast, the ethnographer who seeks to advocate a more broadly defined 'cultural landscape' heritage category inclusive of human presence and agency over a singularly defined archaeological landscape will inevitably be seen to represent a dissenting voice, "pushing back the limits of doxa and exposing the arbitrariness of the taken for granted" (Bourdieu, 1977: 169), and be a heretic in the eyes of many.

9   Donald Reid foreshadows much of the historic, social, and ethnographic work that remains to be undertaken, opening up a wealth of opportunity for researchers if only they—and their funding bodies—were interested: "The uneven personal and regional benefits and costs of tourism, the tensions between insensitive tourists and conservative villagers, folk-beliefs about the fertility-inducing power of antiquities, and the antipharaonism of Islamist purists are all pieces of an as yet little-known puzzle" (Reid, 1997: 140).

10   The idea is not far-fetched. The United Nations 1972 World Heritage Convention in Article 1 defines 'world heritage' as including "archeological sites which are of outstanding universal value from the historical, aesthetic, ethnological or anthropological points of view" (UNESCO, 1972). Since 1992 the World Heritage Convention also recognizes and protects cultural landscapes, one of the objectives being "to protect living traditional cultures" (see http://whc.unesco.org/en/culturallandscape). Recommendations for appropriate studies that could feed into the Theban Necropolis' nomination as a cultural landscape were ignored by Egyptian officials, for which see UNESCO 1999, and Michaelides and Dauge (2008: 7).

11   Caroline Simpson has captured it succinctly: "Like hill villages throughout the world, there is something especially beautiful about the groups of houses nestling on the contours" (Simpson and Laven, 1997: 4).

12   The term is not inappropriate here, given that archaeological salvage is what tends to accompany large-scale government-sponsored development and relocation schemes, most famously the construction of the Aswan High Dam, with its associated archaeological salvage projects and the international campaign to rescue the Nubian temples. For an account see Säve-Söderbergh (1987).

13   The "Qurna Discovery" exhibition was a private British initiative, conceptualized, coordinated, and admininistered by Caroline Simpson and funded through the Friends of Qurna Discovery organization established by her. Alongside a number of information panels, the exhibition displays drawings that show Qurnawi going about their business. The drawings were made during the 1820s by Robert Hay, with copies donated to the exhibition by the British Library. Until May 2010, the exhibition was located in a small compound of surviving buildings in the central foothills. Formal approval had been obtained from Dr. Zahi Hawass, the secretary general of the Supreme Council of Antiquities, and Farouk Hosni, the minister of culture, for this compound to be restored and preserved to serve as exhibition space and information center documenting the social history of Qurnawi in the Theban Necropolis. Notwithstanding these approvals that should have guaranteed their preservation, several of the compound's structures were bulldozed by Luxor City Council workers during March and April 2009. On May 17, 2010, the secretary general of the Supreme Council of Antiquities ordered

the exhibition to close. On May 27, 2010, bulldozers moved in once more and demolished the two remaining buildings of the compound—one a restored foothills house, the other an adjoining *zawiya* that was in excess of one hundred years old and antique in its own right. The exhibition was handed over to Qurnawi and is now located in the Baladi Handicraft Center in al-Suyul but it remains to be seen to what extent visitors will make the effort to go and see it, if they know about it at all. Qurna Discovery and its Friends of Qurna Discovery organization were dissolved on October 2, 2010.

Notes to Chapter 1

1   In order to safeguard their true identities, the names of Mahmud, his older brother Badawi, their relatives, and other informants have been changed in accordance with established anthropological practice. In several instances where informants are also practicing artists, and where they are not being implicated in otherwise sensitive issues, their real names have been used in recognition of their artistic output, some of which is illustrated in this book.

2   Although the events of November 17, 1997, have become known as the 'Luxor Massacre,' the site of the killings, Dayr al-Bahari, the memorial temple of Queen Hatshepsut, is in fact located among the foothills hamlets of the west bank. Now a mortuary temple in the true sense of the word, an earlier ethnographic account of a neighboring village describes the temple in erroneous terms: "the stone reliefs and hieroglyphics might tell of wars and massacres, but the blood and misery was long past; now they were just pictures on a wall, and the ruins had the same soothing calm of the desert" (Critchfield, 1978: 217). Critchfield rather overstates the surviving imagery on the Dayr al-Bahari temple walls, seemingly having taken his inspiration from the battle scenes of the nearby Madinat Habu temple.

3   The 'Luxor Massacre' represents the saddest and most striking example of the politicized nature of Egypt's heritage. Responsibility for the attack was claimed by Gamaʿa al-Islamiya, who in their pursuit of an Islamic state seek to destabilize the political system. To the extent that tourism revenues are seen as contributing to the upkeep and legitimization of incumbent governments, attacks on the tourism industry by Islamic extremists were a clear means toward attempts at overthrowing the government. The attack at Hatshepsut's Temple took place on November 17, 1997, exactly one month after the final performance of Verdi's *Aida*. Performances had been staged at Hatshepsut's Temple from October 12–17, 1997 to mark the 125th anniversary of the opera's premiere but equally served the government's purpose of advertising Egypt as a safe tourist destination (Rousillon and Hajal, 1998; Saad, 1998a; Walker, 1997; Walker and Mekay, 1997). In that sense, *Aida* was a clearly politically motivated event that was intended to counter militants' objectives and secure vital foreign currency earnings by demonstrating that

Egypt was safe. Equally politically motivated, the attack on the very site where *Aida* had been staged, both symbolically and in all its horror, served to demonstrate that this was not so. The choice of *Aida* to mediate a political statement is clearly significant. As Rousillon and Hajal (1998) have pointed out, *Aida* figures prominently in the Egyptian consciousness and constitutes an important element in a nationally perceived identity that is linked with the history of opera in Egypt, and the nationalist aspirations inherent in the first Cairo opera building, which was to be the venue for the *Aida* premiere in 1871. As they do today, those aspirations centered on a desire to be seen as a western, civilized, modern nation, which, when they are transposed into the present, allow little sympathy for concepts of a strict Islamic state, which in terms of global politics and economics would be judged as backward and retrograde. The symbolic and historic elements of national identity that are encapsulated in *Aida* are further enhanced by the setting of Hatshepsut's Temple, which both glorifies Egypt's past and represents the archaeological heritage which is central to the tourism industry. The protection of that heritage was in large part initiated by Auguste Mariette, who instituted the Service des antiquités in 1858 and established the first Egyptian Museum. Significantly, it was also Mariette who wrote the libretto for *Aida*.

4   Although not using the term 'resilience,' in 1938 Henry Habib Ayrout described the psychological character trait among Egyptian peasant farmers that allows them to endure during and rebound from times of hardship. Ayrout views this personal quality as closely linked with the environment in which the Egyptian peasant lives and works, and where "the soil and the care of the soil render the fellah patient, long-suffering and tough. It has imprinted in him its own earthiness" (Ayrout, 1938: 146). For a discussion of Henry Habib Ayrout's psychological characterizations, influenced by the work of French social psychologist Gustave Le Bon, see Mitchell (1990). Despite the merits or otherwise of Ayrout's psychological analyses, reference to his work here is also appropriate for the political and economic context that underpins his study of Egyptian peasant existence, as demonstrated by Mitchell (1990: 136).

5   Despite Romer's claims, the first of the international displays of Tutankhamun's treasures toured the United States of America between November 1961 and January 1963 (Reeves 1990b: 212; Säve-Söderbergh, 1987: 78). However, Romer does allude to the political machinations involved with securing rights to the exhibitions (1993: 19). Intertwined with Cold War realities of the day, these earliest exhibitions must be understood first and foremost in the context of Egypt soliciting financial and practical support when faced with the permanent inundation of the Nubian monuments, resulting from the Soviet Union–funded construction of the Aswan High Dam (Säve-Söderbergh, 1987: 78). Likely, George Rainbird, who commissioned

the 1963 Desroches-Noblecourt work, correctly read the growing interest that made such a book a viable commercial proposition, in turn further propagating that interest.

6   The material is being published as the *Tutankhamun's Tomb Series*. The initial series, now closed, comprises volumes I–IX, but this core corpus continues to be augmented by subsequent individual monographs published by the Griffith Institute, the University of Oxford.

7   Desroches-Noblecourt was not the first to focus attention anew on the community of the necropolis; however, the popularity of her book and the widespread distribution of its sixteen translations guaranteed it an advantage over such other publications as Kurt Lange's (1952) and Herbert Winlock's (1942).

8   Seeking to establish a more interdisciplinary relationship between anthropology and Egyptology, an early collection of papers recognized "the current unwillingness of Egyptologists to deal with any but the details of their subject, and their lack of exposure to the analytical techniques of other disciplines that might assist in their explanation" (Weeks, 1979a: 1). In turn, "Egyptologists have frequently admitted confusion and discomfort with disciplines whose basic tenets and theories seem to change so rapidly" (Weeks, 1979b: 21). While providing a useful overview of the interaction between the various disciplines (Trigger, 1979: 24–32; 1993: 1–26), and applying some of the insights of anthropology to the interpretation of Egyptian data (Weeks, 1979c), the attempted synthesis between the disciplines has largely favored Egyptology. Given that the contributors themselves predominantly are Egyptologists, maybe it is to be expected that a discussion of this type is largely one-way: the interaction with other social sciences is ultimately used to enhance and refine Egyptological analysis, at the expense of applying insights obtained from Egyptology to contemporary social science perspectives.

9   For an example, see Jenkins (1999): "'You can't have donkeys and cows in a world-class archaeological site,' one high-ranking antiquities official exclaimed when questioned about the aesthetics of the village." For similar sentiments that view elements of west bank village life as "visual pollution," see Hawass (2009: 264).

10   The appropriation of archaeological data toward overt political objectives is now well established as a category of intellectual inquiry, and its relevance for archaeological practice is recognized. It is not the objective here to offer a wide-ranging and in-depth overview of the extensive literature on the subject. A regionally based introduction to the topic is offered by Silberman (1989), his ethnographically conceived account of a number of Middle Eastern archaeological field sites—including the Theban west bank—offering insights into the relevance for archaeological

fieldwork. Broad-based academic sessions on the topic were features of the 1986 Southampton World Archaeological Congress (WAC1) and the 1990 Barquisimeto Second World Archaeological Congress (WAC2), and have become the major concern of the World Archaeological Congress' ongoing activities: "The deconstruction of power inherent in the very act of controlling, or even of being able to claim to control, another group's or people's knowledge about, or of, the past" (Ucko, 1994: xiv). The theme's various aspects are covered in many of its proceedings volumes, most notably in Gathercole and Lowenthal (1990) and Bond and Gilliam (1994). In turn, both thematically and as academic event, the WAC has as its antecedent the Australian Academy of the Humanities symposium "Who Owns the Past?," which convened in Canberra, Australia, in 1983, (McBryde, 1984). Kohl and Fawcett (1995) and Meskell (1998a) draw together a wide range of regional perspectives, while Colla (2000; 2007), Meskell (1998b; 2005), and Mitchell (1995; 1998b; 2002: 179–205) exemplify the cross-disciplinary contributions that inform political discussions of cultural heritage management and the politicized appropriation and consumption of Egypt's ancient remains. Finally, Tunbridge and Ashworth (1996) have developed the theoretical model of 'Dissonant Heritage,' which articulates the contested nature of ideologically situated heritage selection processes.

Notes to Chapter 2

1   See Martin (1982b: 262 n) and Wilkinson (MSS, 1830, c.14).
2   According to Burckhardt, "This word means 'Corner,' as being at the northwest angle of the mountain, where it takes a more eastern direction" (Burckhardt, 1819: lxxvi).
3   This uncertainty about local designations and their meanings is not new. According to Wilkinson, "the largest of [the Theban tombs], and indeed of all the sepulchres at Thebes, are those in the Assaseef, one of which far exceeds in extent any one of the tombs of the Kings" (Wilkinson, 1843: 220). Wilkinson's subsequent description (Wilkinson, 1843: 220–22) invokes a labyrinthine funerary architecture, which, if considered a sufficiently dominant geomorphological feature, may have inspired local toponymy. Nims indeed suggests that the word 'Asasif' "perhaps" signifies "labyrinth," acknowledging that the word nevertheless is "obscure" (Nims, 1965: 12). This same ambivalence is evident in the personal papers of Joseph Bonomi, one of the artists employed by Robert Hay during his 1820s west bank epigraphic expeditions. Bonomi first held the view that al-'Asasif was named after a man called 'Asaf who lived in the general area but, not unlike Nims, later linked the name with the Arabic concept of "walking without direction," "to feel about like a blind man," and "going astray," ideas associated with "those dark winding passages underground [which] are so frequent [in Gorna]" (Bonomi

MSS, letter dated April 23, 1833 [annotated January 7, 1854], in the private collection of one of his descendants). Lane "perhaps" derives the name from the Arabic word for 'barren' and 'unproductive,' "as applied to land" (Lane, 2000: 332). Funerary architecture also informed local toponymy for the Birabi, the area enclosed by Dra' Abu al-Naga, the cultivation and the causeway of Hatshepsut's Temple: "*Birabi* is the plural of *birba*, an 'ancient temple,' but here the name is locally used more for a 'vaulted tomb,' of which many occur in the district" (Carnarvon and Carter, 1912: 2).

4   For an academic discussion on the possible origins and meanings of the name Shaykh 'Abd al-Qurna, see EEF Archives (2005).

5   For the location of most of the place names referred to in this section, see the Theban Mapping Project aerial photographs under Appendix 2. For those unfamiliar with the general location of Luxor west bank topographical features, the description in the text follows a route that commences roughly in the vicinity of the modern ferry, then moves west to the Theban Mountain, turning northeast to follow the road at the base of the foothills for some two kilometers, before turning east again toward the main irrigation canal (during previous centuries the bank of the river itself, and the landing place for early European travelers).

6   Caroline Simpson provides the following statistics for the hillsides: "In 1921 there were some 900 properties enclosing 1,008 tombs inhabited by about 5,000 people. In 1945 there were 7,000 people and nearly 1,000 houses. In 1993 there were nearly 1,500 properties and over 8,000 people" (Simpson and Laven, 1997: 3).

7   The settlement of 'Izbit Muhammad Salim that is indicated on the 1922 Survey of Egypt maps may have provided an early (late nineteenth-century) nucleus of habitation that subsequently expanded into larger Gezirat al-Qurna. For background on the 'Izba village phenomenon see, for example, Mitchell (2002: 54–79).

8   Usage of the name 'New Qurna' remains ambiguous. Its origin goes back to Hassan Fathy, who coined it in opposition to 'Old Qurna,' which he understood to mean the cluster of hamlets spread across the Noble Tombs areas in the foothills. Archaeologists, however, will understand Old Qurna as the site of an earlier village at the Seti I Temple at the northern end of the necropolis that was vacated toward the end of the eighteenth century, and consider the term in opposition to the subsequent occupation shift to the Noble Tombs areas. Despite the acceptance of the name 'New Qurna' in the English-speaking world to designate the village built by Hassan Fathy, local villagers are inclined to return a blank stare when confronted with its Arabic equivalent of 'Qurna al-Gedida,' referring to it instead as 'Qurna Hassan Fathy' to foreigners, or among themselves as al-Qarya Hassan Fathy or simply 'al-Qarya,' 'the village.' James Steele, Hassan Fathy's

unofficial biographer, employs 'Gourna al-Gadida' for the Noble Tombs hamlets, a usage that is less than helpful (Steele, 1997: 61). Following their 2006–2008 relocations from the foothills, Qurnawi are now accommodated in new settlements north of the Theban Mountain, one of which is indeed known locally as Qurna al-Gedida.

9   One member of the extended 'Abd al-Rasul family argued for a distinction between those who were 'true' 'Abd al-Rasul and those who were not. The distinction was claimed to be the result not only of intermarriage but also of non-'Abd al-Rasul settling at Nag' al-Rasayla and claiming 'Abd al-Rasul descent. Others denied the distinction. The issue may at least be partly inspired by jealousy as a result of differential economic success.

Notes to Chapter 3

1   Terry Wilfong applies the name 'Shaykh 'Abd al-Qurna' to the Theban Mountain (Wilfong, 2002: 1), that is, the Qurn. While incorrect, and possibly giving cause for confusion, the issue is effectively immaterial: although the density of monastic settlements is greatest in the hill of Shaykh 'Abd al-Qurna and its surrounding foothills, Coptic graffiti can also be found in the royal tombs in the Valley of the Kings, and the entire Theban west bank may be taken as the locus of intense Coptic spirituality and habitation (Wilfong, 2002: 1–22, 145). Following Wilfong, I have therefore taken the Theban Mountain, the Qurn, as the dominant geographical marker in the spiritual landscape of the Theban west bank's Coptic Christian communities.

2   I am grateful to Professor Wilfong for freely sharing his knowledge and opinions on ancient Jeme.

3   Somers Clarke visited the church on several occasions and measured its architectural plan on March 19, 1901. In his typology he categorizes the structure as "a good example of type C" (Clarke, 1912: 116), which is, "it must be presumed, more recent in its development than the types A and B, and, I venture to believe, did not come into being until after the Arab conquest" (Clarke, 1912: 32). Clarke, nevertheless, postulates certain stages in the development of the building, and it remains possible that Dayr al-Muharab has a history of modification that included earlier types, although to obtain archaeological verification would seem impracticable (Clarke, 1912: 118).

4   During 1998, bulldozers cleared vacated modern houses and recent Qurnawi occupation layers just to the north of the walled Seti I Temple area, permanently destroying the archaeological record of the original village of Qurna that is mentioned in seventeenth- and eighteenth-century travelers' records. Any opportunity for understanding or reconstructing this part of the history of occupation in this area is now irrevocably lost. Sadly, in its ambition to enhance the presentation of monuments or to uncover ancient

occupation layers, academic Egyptology has the habit of failing to record and destroying rather more recent settlement patterns, which, for their unique integration of ancient temple and funerary architecture with contemporary indigenous cultural practice, should merit equal academic topographical, archaeological, and anthropological interest.

5   A precedent for the persistence of local architectural practices was noted by Somers Clarke: "There are certain peculiarities in the methods of building used by the masons of ancient Egypt which differ entirely from methods made use of by the Romans. But in Egypt native methods have held their own. They are to be seen even in buildings which have some little of the Roman manner and style about them. Here, then, we have an intruding power absorbed, as far as its architectural development is concerned, by the subjugated race" (Clarke, 1912: 15).

6   Human Genome Diversity Projects (HGDP) aim at mapping human diversity by combining DNA samples with socio-cultural, historical, and linguistic data. Analysis of such data could chart migratory movements of past population groups and reveal the genetic makeup of, and the historical relationship between, different population groups. While ethnicity continues to be a cultural notion, the identification of genetic markers does demonstrate the biological reality of such past historical processes which underpin the formation of distinct ethnic identities. Opposition by indigenous peoples to HGDP suggests the inherent legal and ethical issues of such research in cross-cultural settings.

7   That is, the coastal region of North Africa, comprising the former Barbary states of Morocco, Algeria, Tunisia, and Libya.

8   Garcin sources the connection with Labid of the Sulaym to al-Qalqashandi: *Qala'id al-juman fi-l-ta'rif bi qaba'il 'Arab al-zaman*, edited by Ibrahim al-Ibiari, Cairo, 1963. The exact location of the 'Desert of Barqa' is not further specified, as are other geographical reference points, which makes it difficult to follow the trajectory of Bedouin migrations.

9   Elsewhere, Garcin identifies these "Berbères" as nomads from the Western Desert, or implies they come from the Maghreb (Garcin, 1976: 61, n6; 63, n2). Although not further specified, such differences in appellation and associated origins probably inform his use of the "convenient" distinction "Sulaym-Hawwara," which he nevertheless acknowledges is not always clear (Garcin, 1976: 469, n4, n5).

10   Representing early interests in Egypt, the legacy of their travels, and their antiquarian, ethnographic, and pioneering Egyptological endeavors have earned most of them—where known—a place in *Who was Who in Egyptology* (Bierbrier, 1995), which remains a comprehensive and indispensable resource. Since 1997, academic interest in these travelers has become something of a subdiscipline, encompassing both Egyptology and history,

through the activities of the Cambridge (UK)-based Association for the Study of Travel in Egypt and the Near East (ASTENE).

11   For the English translation of the relevant original Italian passages, see Appendix 3.

12   The Venetian refers to the "right bank," that is, the west bank. Sailing south (upstream) from Cairo, references to the 'right' and 'left' bank of the Nile mark the direction of travel when first approaching the towns and villages of Upper Egypt.

13   The relative extent of Qasas territory as indicated by Burckhardt remains ambivalent. By locating them "on the south" of the Hawwara who are "their determined enemies," Burckhardt implies neighborly status, but while Hawwara territory extends between Asyut and Farshut, that of the Qasas reached no further north than Thebes. It is conceivable that Burckhardt means 'Thebes' to denote the entire Theban plain, which can be taken to mean the entire 'Qena Bend' section of the Nile Valley. Garcin, however, reads 'Thebes' to mean the specific location of Luxor, commenting that the territory of the Qasas during the sixteenth century, that is in the account of the Venetian, extended further north (Garcin, 1976: 500–501, n2).

14   This is not to say that such a density was specific to Luxor only. Burckhardt describes Hawwara territory between Asyut and Farshut as "one of the most populated and well cultivated," counting in one instance "from the hill of the small town of Tahta . . . 35 villages within reach of the eye" (Burckhardt, 1819: 531). The cluster of villages near Luxor may similarly have demanded attention, if only for their unusual setting.

15   St. John in his work leans heavily on the writings of other travelers. His passage on the 'Rebellion of an Arab Prophet,' from which the above quotation is drawn, originally comes from John Madox, 1834. Also see Bierbrier (1995: 269).

16   Burckhardt reports that one clan of the Hawwara tribe, the Awlad Yahya, "were very conspicuous for their rebellious behaviour" (Burckhardt, 1819: 531), confirming not only that uncharacteristic unruly conduct was not entirely exclusive to the Theban area, but also that such behavior did indeed stand out against that of other tribes.

17   The word *mumiya* is of Persian origin (*mum* = wax) and its use was premised on the perceived therapeutic properties of bituminous materials in medicine. Through a "confusing process of transference and substitution," which saw the resinous substance of mummified human remains associated with similar, but medicinal, bituminous materials as early as the eleventh century, the term *mumiya* "was to lead eventually to the use of 'mumia' for a drug in Latin and to 'mummy' for an embalmed Egyptian corpse in English" (Dannenfeldt, 1985: 163).

18 For references to published sources documenting Muslim legends in relation to ancient cemeteries and the search for pharaonic treasure during the
Islamic era, see Garcin (1976: 11).

19 al-Bakri, *Kitab al-Mamalik wa-l-Masalik*, quoted in Garcin (1976: 12 n1):
"Entre cette ville (Qus) et Assouan, on trouve des cavernes creusées dans les
montagnes de cette région, qui contiennent des tombeaux des morts dont on
retire la mumiya odorante; on la trouve dans les os et les linceuls des morts."

20 For references on the mummy trade see those cited by Garcin (1976: 12).
For references on the medieval use of *mumiya* see D'Auria et al. (1988: 14);
Dannenfeldt (1959: 16–22); Dannenfeldt (1985); David and Tapp (1984:
3); Fagan (1975: 44–47); Ikram and Dodson (1998: 64–66); and Pettigrew
(1834: 3–12).

Notes to Chapter 4

1   According to Sonnini (1800: 649) he "arrived off Gournei on the morning
of the 29th [July, 1778]," spending an uncomfortable night there (Sonnini
1800: 652) before leaving for Nagada and Qus. Dates given by Sonnini for
his transit through nearby towns or villages and other internal textual evidence suggest he arrived at Qurna on July 19. Despite his stated difficulty
of finding a suitable guide as a result of inter-village feuding (Sonnini 1800:
654), it would appear he left on July 20. On July 23 he arrived at Qena via
Qus (Sonnini 1800: 666).

2   The travelers included in this discussion are among some of the more
prominent ones, whose accounts are formative in developing an ethno-
historical reconstruction of the Theban west bank communities. It is not
claimed here that this treatment is necessarily fully comprehensive or conclusive. During the nineteenth century, in part due to its 'Grand Tour'
appeal among the aristocracy and upper middle class, but also under the
influence of the beginnings of organized travel to Egypt through the pioneering work of Thomas ᴄ ᴐk, the number of visitors to Egypt steadily
increased. By consequence, ᴗᴗ did the number of resulting travelogues and,
more recently, the published correspondence relating to such journeys
(see, for example, Steegmuller, 1972, on the travels of Gustave Flaubert
and Maxime Du Camp, and Nightingale, 1987, on Florence Nightingale's
sojourn in Egypt). Among such travel accounts, many will make reference
to incidents experienced when visiting the Theban Necropolis, as did William Browne on his encounter with local women in 1792 (Browne, 1799:
138). Systematic research of these sources will no doubt reveal numerous
snippets of ethnographic interest and insight that would offer greater historical definition of Qurnawi society. However, a comprehensive analysis of
the nineteenth-century travelogue genre falls outside the historical scope
considered appropriate here. The primary intention here is to isolate and

synthesize certain historically situated ethnographic perspectives contained within the accounts of a number of early visitors, whose records may shed light on both the time depth and the cultural characteristics of Qurnawi society. Claiming for itself no more than a starting point, the rudimentary construction of this synthesis by its very nature invites additions, and welcomes corrections should other sources reveal new information. In the absence of a formally documented indigenous history, such an evolving Western reconstruction may be all there will ever be.

3   Having read Bonomi's personal and unpublished papers (Bonomi GIA), including those still in the possession of one of his descendants (Bonomi MSS), Caroline Simpson suggests the Qurna material may have been destroyed by Joseph Bonomi himself, either to eradicate the disagreements that existed between him and Robert Hay, or to erase any reference to Fatima, his Egyptian wife, after assuming a new life upon his return to England. On the difficulties between Hay and Bonomi, see Grutz (2003: 4, 6).

4   Some three decades later James Bruce is clearly frustrated with Norden's inaccurate identification and naming of geographical locations: "Mr. Norden seems to have very much confused the places in this neighbourhood . . . from what authority I know not; but the whole geography is here exceedingly confused, and out of its proper position" (Bruce, 1790: 140–41).

5   Precise years for dates given are hard to come by in Richardson's 1822 account for 1816–18. He states, nevertheless, that on "the 14th of January" he accompanied Mr. Salt "to view the antiquities which the diligent and faithful Greek had collected for the noble traveler, during his absence in Nubia, and with whose industry and success there was every reason to be satisfied" (Richardson, 1822, 2: 2). That "faithful Greek" can only be Giovanni d'Athanasi, who entered Salt's employ in 1817, making Richardson's observation datable to 1818.

6   This may be seen reflected in the account of Charles Sonnini, who slept in "one of the most unsubstantial of the cottages" in Old Qurna village on the night of July 19, 1778, during which he narrowly escaped injury when strong winds caused one of the walls "of this place of wretchedness and misery" to collapse: "our unstable cottage could not resist its violence" (Sonnini, 1800: 652–53; Simpson, 2001: 5). Even so, during January 1818, Robert Richardson observed that, while temporarily abandoned, the village contained houses "generally small, but some of them much larger and of superior workmanship to the average of ruined houses in this country" (Richardson, 1822, 2: 8).

7   Travelers use this term to refer to the excavated recesses in the mountain, the tombs, as well as to the more or less systematic search for antiquities taking place in the west bank cemeteries. For example, compare Denon's use above with Amelia Edward's "From the tombs above, we went back to the excavations below" (Edwards, 1877: 416). Reflecting earlier,

eighteenth-century vocabulary, Denon's usage leaves no room for ambiguity, since his term clearly predates the intensive antiquities operations characteristic of nineteenth-century travelers' objectives.

8   One feddan = 1.038 acres or 0.42 hectares. One *ardeb* = 198 litres = 5.62 US bushels (Hopkins and Westergaard, 1998: ix).

9   According to Dannenfeldt, a 1564 *mumiya* merchant in Alexandria was a Jew (Dannenfeldt, 1959: 19).

10   Also compare Gustave Flaubert's observation: "the ground under your feet is riddled with holes, like a sieve, and frightfully so" (Steegmuller, 1972: 174).

11   The damage inflicted by early scientists and collectors was severe. Champollion and his Italian colleague Ippolito Rosellini (Bierbrier, 1995: 362–63), under the auspices of their joint Franco-Tuscan Expedition, in 1829 removed portraits of Seti I from his newly discovered tomb in the Valley of the Kings (Romer, 1993: 109). Known as 'Belzoni's Tomb,' the royal sepulcher was discovered by Giovanni Belzoni in 1817, who was then still Henry Salt's collecting agent at Thebes. Champollion's actions caused concern among colleague copyists at the time, as evidenced in a letter dated August 3, 1829, now in the James Burton Manuscript Collection in the British Library and containing a July 1 report by Joseph Bonomi: "A few days ago Triantafellos came to me and told me that sawyers had arrived from Cairo to cut various pictures from Belzoni's Tomb—he requested me to join with him and try to prevent Champollion from cutting and taking away what he considered belonged to the British" (British Library Add. Mss. 25, 658). A subsequent letter to Champollion by Bonomi was to no avail, with the Frenchman refuting British ownership. Bonomi nevertheless made British presence felt, and eventually oversaw part of the operations. The spoils were divided between Paris and Florence. Champollion was neither the first nor the only one to have acted as role model for Qurnawi in this manner. Others include Cailliaud (1821) and Yanni (d'Athanasi, 1836), for accounts of which see Manniche (1987: 103–104).

12   The scarab or dung beetle, *Scarabaeus sacer*, was considered sacred in ancient Egypt as a symbol of rebirth and as Khepera, one of the forms of the sun god Ra. Scarabs are ubiquitous among the variety of contemporary artistic expressions that draw on ancient Egyptian themes.

13   Wilson's account is based on Budge (1920: 323–26). The collection was purchased for the Egyptian Museum in Cairo by Gaston Maspero some time between 1899 and 1914, but not being genuine antiquities, they were apparently not entered in the Journal d'Entrée (JE). A search by the author for scarabs entered in volumes JE VI–IX for the years 1899–1914, as well as an archival check of the scarabs in the Farouk Collection of Egyptian Antiquities in the Cairo Museum during November 2009, failed to establish their whereabouts.

14 Sonnini adds: "The disorderly behaviour of these troops, consisting of men who possessed none of the qualifications of a soldier but courage, infected the districts through which their parties passed. Themselves pillaging and laying everything waste, they left to others a free opening to pillage and devastation. Robbers stripped the travellers by land, while pirates stopped the boats upon the Nile. Tribes of Arabs revived old quarrels, and had frequent skirmishes with each other; village was fighting against village; in short, upon these occasions, disorder, tumult, and licentiousness, were carried to the highest pitch; and all authority being at an end, the unprotected foreigner could not fail of becoming a victim in the general confusion. It was impossible for me to remain longer on the spot where the proud city of Thebes formerly stood. This district, extremely dangerous at the most tranquil period, was upon the point of becoming impassable for every one but robbers" (Sonnini, 1800: 648–49). Yet, even at the "most tranquil" of times, the Nile remained a dangerous river to sail, as attested by Claude Sicard in February 1714 (Martin, 1982b: 68–69).

15 Usage of the term 'troglodyte' was not uncommon among eighteenth-century and nineteenth-century travelers, and can be found in the writings of James Bruce (1790: 138), William Browne (1799: 134), Sir John Gardner Wilkinson (in Thompson, 1992: 102; 2010: 207), and Henry Rhind (1862: 80, 310). At its most innocent it may simply denote the subterranean character of their dwellings, but in all likelihood it will also imply all the derogatory associations inherent in the term.

Notes to Chapter 5

1 Difficulties inherent in the tracing of local ancestries back to the time of the Muslim conquest of Egypt will be common for those trying to reconstruct orally transmitted Arab and Bedouin genealogies. This is not simply a matter of time depth. Complicating factors include the degree of admixture between different population groups and ethnic identities in the wake of the Arab conquest. The need for a distinct Muslim identity resulted in the practice of creating legitimizing genealogies rooted in Arab descent with claimed spiritual links to the Prophet. Thomas Kiernan has described such "geneologizing" as "an accepted form of status-seeking" (1975: 198, 207).

2 An attempt was made to construct a sequence for the 'Abd al-Rasul family, also in the light of claims made by one member of that family about those who allegedly were not 'true' 'Abd al-Rasul. Although several sequences were obtained, their reliability remains doubtful largely due to discrepancies in the information provided by different informants. Several non-'Abd al-Rasul Qurnawi doubted the veracity of the allegations made about those who were alleged to falsely claim 'Abd al-Rasul descent. It is possible that such claims are either grounded in economic rivalry or jealousy within the

larger family, or that they form part of the family's early history and relate to events that took place so long ago that they—like those many skeletons in cupboards everywhere—will likely be of little practical consequence today, other than in the mind of at least one individual. Beyond these observations, such projects as suggested by Donald Reid remain to be undertaken: "A multigenerational biography of Qurna's 'Abd al-Rasul family, who discovered the cache of royal mummies at Deir al-Bahri about 1871 and mined it for a decade before being caught, could make an illuminating social history. So could the century-old guild of skilled archeological laborers from Quft whom Petrie first recruited in the 1890s" (Reid, 1997: 139).

3   Not much is known about the house of Italian excavator Piccinini at the southern end of Dra' Abu al-Naga (Bierbrier, 1995: 333–34). Lane mentions it as one of only two houses "in the district," the other being Yanni's (Lane, 2000: 327–28). Jean-François Champollion stored luggage there when on his way to the Valley of the Kings in 1829 (Champollion 1833: 178). For an illustration by Nestor l'Hôte, who accompanied Champollion, see Simpson (2003: 248). Although seemingly solitary, it remains unclear if the Piccinini house was representative of a more extensive aboveground settlement pattern.

4   The precise year is debatable. Wilkinson's acquaintance with the Salt house dates to 1824, as stated in his letter to Mr. William Frankland Hood of Nettleham (Wilkinson MSS d.113, 71^v–72–72^v; Bierbrier, 1995: 207), although this may not mean that Wilkinson by that time had established his own house there. The likely year appears to be 1827: in correspondence dated June 28, 1827, Wilkinson mentions living in a tomb and from the middle of that same year visitors to the house report Wilkinson has adopted Qurnawi tomb-based architecture (Thompson, 1992: 102–103, 253). Depending on the frequency of such correspondence and visits, the house could arguably date earlier. Flynn (1997: 6–7) does not address the issue, while Thompson remains vague: "From the mid-1820's Wilkinson began spending much more time at Thebes, especially on the west bank. It was there that he did his best work and built his remarkable house" (Thompson, 1992: 100).

5   Although Wilkinson built a large private collection of antiquities, he was not a collector in the commercial sense and most of his research was epigraphic in nature. In essence, the distinction between Wilkinson's epigraphic activities and Henry Salt's collecting for financial gain was a methodological one, both in their different ways contributing to the advancement of science as it was then understood, even if most of the items collected were arguably "the visual footnotes of a growing academic library" (Romer, 1993: 86). Giovanni d'Athanasi initially supervised the Theban excavations on behalf of Salt, but later became a collector in his own right. He was critical of the working practices of some of his contemporaries and his understanding of antiquities

reflects an early concern for larger collections found in situ, the provenance of individual items compromised by the Qurnawi practice of selling items separately (d'Athanasi, 1836: xii–xiii, 10, 14–15). Even so, his own working methods were equally destructive (Manniche, 1987: 103–104). On the level of their individual scientific understanding, both Wilkinson's and Yanni's operations would have been mutually intelligible, even if their practice had little in common.

6   As indicated in the foothills panoramas of Robert Hay (Hay MSS), and according to the assessments made by Isabella Romer (1846: 291) and Henry Rhind (1862: 244).

7   This is not to say that the architecture of Yanni's house and its successors is European. Both Henry Salt and Giovanni d'Athanasi were familiar with mud-brick architecture from their travels through the Nile Valley. Conversely, subsequent Qurnawi mud-brick architecture drew on an established repertoire of styles and techniques typical of Upper Egypt (see Blackman, 1927: 24–28, figs. 4–7) and Nubia (Fernea and Fernea, 1991: ii–iii).

8   Broadly stated, an 1835 viceregal decree effectively placed all excavation under state control and restricted the export of antiquities. As evidenced by the many exemptions that enabled the manipulation of European collectors in return for services favoring government objectives, these earliest measures were more concerned with politics than with heritage management. Indirectly, and to the extent that they served to delimit the removal of antiquities from the necropolis, these measures were at least in some part aimed at the people of Qurna, who facilitated the movement of antiquities, although in practice the exemptions would have made the impact negligable. However, evolving protective measures were not exclusively directed at the removal of works of art and the trade in antiquities, but also at damage caused by the occupation of tombs. This double-pronged approach resulted initially in the placement of iron gates and, later, the eviction of Qurnawi from inhabited Theban tombs, resulting in the construction of aboveground dwellings. In historical terms, these early protective measures are on a continuum with present-day episodes of relocation and in their totality represent ongoing heritage management–motivated social, architectural, and settlement pattern changes affecting Qurnawi society. For the developing legal framework of Egyptian antiquities legislation see Khater (1960). For early-twentieth-century issues of conservation and protection inside the Theban Necropolis see Gardiner and Weigall (1913) and Engelbach (1924). For a particularly insightful—and damning—appraisal of early-twentieth-century Egyptological fieldwork practice and its implications for heritage management as viewed through the lens of Arthur Weigall's biographer see Hankey (2001).

9   The Theban west bank has always been a busy place, attracting the focused interests and resulting 'traffic' of different groups of people across time. The

comings and goings of archaeologists are equally a feature of that traffic, and their activities are as much intertwined with the local landscape and the lives of Qurnawi as the local landscape and its modern population are with theirs. Other than its intrinsically interesting qualities, the history of Egyptological practice and its attendant pursuit of suitable forms of heritage management (as distinct from the study of ancient Egypt itself) is important for the specific form of Theban west bank human activity it represents. Although in many respects a topic in its own right, the presence of archaeologists cannot be viewed in isolation from other expressions of human agency and action on the Theban west bank, and certain aspects of Egyptological practice with relevance to Qurnawi and the necropolis' social landscape are therefore also discussed in the text and its accompanying notes.

10   All references to ancient Egypt's chronology are based on O'Conner and Silverman, 1995: XXIX–XXXIII.

11   Human occupation in the Nile Valley is of ancient date indeed and ancestral human populations have been in the Qurna area for at least several hundred thousand years. Protohuman occupation of the Luxor west bank extended to the Lower Palaeolithic (1.6–0.4 million years ago) and tools distinctive of the period are common in the desert west of the Theban Mountain (Lange, 1952: 7–11; Renfrew and Bahn, 1991: 135, 142–43; Romer, 1981: 15).

12   This observation stands in contrast with more recent suggestions that at least one royal mummy obtaining from DB320 found its way to the United States as early as 1861, for which see Gibson (2000: 21). The 'Abd al-Rasuls may be implicated through the involvement of Mustafa Aga Ayat, who facilitated the sale. If correct, this would bring the discovery of DB320 forward by at least ten years.

13   Such landscape knowledge suggests that for Qurnawi the necropolis with time had become imbued with cognitive elements. The physical appearance of the surrounding hills became a mind map enabling the identification and appropriation of its economic resources. A function of the collective and transmitted memory of the embodied landscape, and beyond the tangible character of its funerary and vernacular domestic infrastructure, the presence of this cognitive ability is a further indication of the deep-rooted social character of the necropolis: "Before it can ever be a repose for the senses, landscape is the work of the mind. Its scenery is built up as much from strata of memory as from layers of rock" (Schama, 1995: 6–7).

14   Engelbach's assertion that the lack of effective wartime supervision resulted in comparatively little damage to the known tombs is only partially true. Although he acknowledges that "the natives of Qurneh had a most enjoyable time" (Engelbach, 1924: 6), which he mainly links with increased Qurnawi encroachments, clandestine discovery and consequent damage of unknown tombs also took place: "[This tomb] was first entered by a native, Muhammad

Salim, through a hole in the courtyard of his house. He, however, instead of giving notice of his find, entirely demolished one of the two inscribed walls in an attempt to cut away pieces of it to sell to collectors of antiquities. Fortunately, he was detected and punished by a month's imprisonment, before he had time similarly to destroy the second painted wall" (MacKay, 1916: 125).

15   James explains the conventions surrounding the trade in antiquities operative during Howard Carter's years of dealing in ancient Egyptian artifacts thus: "Objects acquired in a division with the Antiquities Service were in his day legitimately the property of the excavating authority or individual, and . . . it did sometimes happen that objects might be sold by excavators to finance further work, or to cover other costs. Objects that turned up on the market could in some cases be assigned with certainty to particular sources, even particular excavations, and Carter had a good record of trying from time to time to alert excavators when he came across pieces in dealers' shops that could be retrieved for the archaeological record. But most objects in the shops were not easily assignable, and they were, he surely felt, fair game for purchase" (James, 1992: 388). For an example of Carter alerting excavators to stolen items, see Hankey, 2001: 357, n13. During Carter's years of involvement in the antiquities trade, Antiquities Law No. 14 of 1912 regulated the operation of the dealers' shops and their supervision by the Service des antiquités, for which see Khater (1960: 291–93). For the regulations concerning the export of antiquities at that time, see Khater (1960: 293–95). Antiquities shops openly offering items for sale could still be found to hold pieces of importance as late as 1975 (Habachi, 1979: 32, 40). Such trade in antiquities was prohibited by Law No. 117 of 1983, Article 7 (EAO, 1984).

16   The numbers assigned to the tombs in the Theban Necropolis are prefixed by letters indicating their respective locations. Thus, KV identifies tombs in the Valley of the Kings; WV identifies the few tombs located in the so-called West Valley of the Valley of the Kings; QV denotes tombs in the Valley of the Queens; and TT (Theban Tomb) indicates tombs in the foothills, that is, the Tombs of the Nobles.

17   During the early years of Mond's work among the Noble Tombs, the archaeological supervision stipulated by the Service des antiquités was provided by Egyptologist Percy Newberry, Carter's trusted friend and peer (Bierbrier, 1995: 310; James, 1992: passim), who had first inspired Robert Mond to work in the necropolis. Gardiner confirms that Newberry "had made the study of the Private Tombs his special province, and had been very successful in stimulating interest in them" (Gardiner and Weigall, 1913: 7). In his 'Rapport' for 1901, Maspero reports that "Mr. Newberry had asked for permission to clear the tombs of Shaykh 'Abd al-Qurna, which he proposes to publish fully: it is a project of long duration that will take him several years. The tombs he has cleared will be fitted with gates by him and maintained

henceforth at the expense of the Service" (Maspero, 1912: 38). It is possible that the provision for the installation of protective doors at the end of each clearance, contained in Newberry's 1901 concession application, was his own. However, it seems likely that the idea, breaking new ground as much as characterizing what essentially was a private concession, came from Carter and resulted from his close cooperation with Newberry. The innovation will have reflected the requirements and personal standards of Carter himself, who as chief inspector was ultimately responsible for all work done in the necropolis. On at least one occasion, in 1904, Carter appears to have been more directly involved with the fitting of iron doors to protect tombs excavated by Mond (Maspero, 1912: 120). Ever pragmatic, Carter in those days was both a meticulous excavator and an accomplished engineer (see, for instance, Carter, 1901). The latter quality likely influenced Arthur Weigall, who, himself an energetic and efficient administrator (Bierbrier, 1995: 435), vigorously continued the work of protecting the Theban Tombs that Carter had started, but who nevertheless considered the necessary methodologies as rather self-evident (Hankey, 2001: 77). Instituting the 'TT' numbering system now in place for the Theban Tombs, Weigall expanded the rather limited requirement for protection applicable to tombs cleared under private concession (which explains the small number—eight—achieved by Carter) into a methodical program of protecting as many tombs as available funds permitted, totaling some 200 by January 1912 (Hankey, 2001: 78).

18 Sir Alan Gardiner scathingly states: "The inhabitants of Gurnah are inveterate and incorrigible tomb-robbers; they are by no means content with searching for portable objects, but will, with equal readiness, cut fragments of painting or sculpture from the tomb-walls for sale to any Europeans who are Vandals enough to purchase them. . . . It must be remembered that the natives of Gurnah are for the most part born and bred to the habit of tomb-robbery; there is no hole so small that a native will not creep into it, undeterred by darkness, dirt, or lack of air" (Gardiner and Weigall, 1913: 8–11).

19 T.G.H. James, commenting on the same period, by contrast, strikes a rather more balanced tone: "The idea of fitting protective gates on tombs was new, even though it was an obvious first step to preserve these ancient monuments from the destructive actions of visitors, especially antiquities hunters, and from illegal occupation of tomb-chapels by Egyptian *fellahin* who found the Theban tombs in particular very convenient ready-made dwellings. It seems inconceivable that less than one hundred years ago access to most tombs in the Theban region was unimpeded by anything more than a local guard, who was only on duty from time to time. Even then substantial numbers of visitors trod the archaeological trails to the Valley of the Kings and over the hills of Qurna which were honeycombed with finely decorated tombs" (James, 1992: 71).

20   The formulation of Antiquities Law No. 14 of 1912 had a long history, and a first draft was included in Maspero's 'Rapport' for 1902 (Maspero, 1912: 84–89). The 1902 document is in many respects very close to the final wording of the 1912 law and likewise forbids the adaptation of tombs for purposes of habitation or stabling animals (Maspero, 1912: 86). Since it was not enacted until a full ten years later, Weigall could not have legally based his actions between 1905 and 1911 on the existence of the draft law, even if revisions during 1903, 1904, and 1911 would have raised hopes that its promulgation was imminent (Khater, 1960: 112–13). That the Antiquities Service had high hopes about the draft's imminent acceptance is demonstrated in the printing in 1903 of a supply of brochures containing the text of the draft law. They were never brought into circulation (Maspero, 1912: 84).

21   Writing about Robert Mond and others who "contributed generously to the heavy expense," Gardiner throws light on what may well have been the single and most pragmatic of methods employed: "With these funds much restoration and protection was able to be effected, and many more inhabited tombs were expropriated. Weigall was fortunate in possessing in his Native Inspector, Mahmud Effendi Rushdy, a most capable and energetic assistant, whose services have proved particularly valuable in conducting the delicate negotiations for the purchase of tombs used as dwelling places" (Gardiner and Weigall, 1913: 8). Although not all tombs involved will have been inhabited, the process seems to have been quite successful: Gardiner reports that at the time of writing, the total of known tombs amounted to 252, "one hundred and sixty-one of which are now adequately protected" (Gardiner and Weigall, 1913: 8). For Mahmud Effendi Rushdy's dealings with Qurnawi, see Hankey, 2001:133.

22   One family in al-Hurubat is still identified with the nickname 'al-Samak,' 'the fish,' reflecting both their external origins and their past occupational specialization as fishermen. Strained relations between a Coptic silversmith and his Muslim neighbor in al-Hurubat were claimed to result from the fact that the Muslim neighbor was "not from Qurna." Despite this latter instance, intra-village relations between Qurnawi and these (relative) newcomers are cordial. They are accepted as community members and people share and participate in each other's life-cycle events.

Notes to Chapter 6

1   Acknowledging that "the natives prize these tombs immensely, though the conditions under which they live in them are unspeakably filthy," Reginald Engelbach describes Qurnawi strategies employed in their negotiations with the Commission of Delimitation as follows: "The encroachments and claims of the inhabitants grouped themselves into three [sic] categories: (a) The squatters occupied rock tombs as cave dwellings. (b) They had built

mud-huts and courts in which they lived and kept their cattle; in some cases these dwellings were substantially built of red brick. (c) They had built out from these buildings mastabas, nawwamahs and low walls, frequently with the intention of enclosing a further area. (d) They claimed extensive rights over undefined areas in front of their dwelling, often without visible act of occupation, sometimes dumping bricks, straw, manure, etc., over a part of the ground claimed. . . . The marking of the boundaries was done in a very liberal way, but the arguments and protests of the inhabitants could be heard half a mile away. Some of the situations met with were ludicrous in the extreme; one man was caught red-handed, preparing 'ancient' foundations below the soil in front of his house, to prove that he had occupied the part so exposed from time immemorial" (Engelbach, 1924: 9).

2   Several partly ruined and dysfunctional mud structures were measured. The sleeping platform of a *manama* or scorpion bed, small in size and probably made for children, measured 538 centimeters in circumference and 164 centimeters in diameter. Its supporting column measured 483 centimeters in circumference, a hatch measuring 46 centimeters wide and 40 centimeters high providing access to its internal space. The rim of the sleeping platform measured between six and nine centimeters in thickness. Its total height could not be assessed, due to surrounding rubble, but will have been low enough to give easy access. Grain-storage *safat* (a) consisted of a *dulab* for storing small items integrated in the upper part of the storage column proper, reaching 180 centimeters in height when measured to the roof's outer edge and 190 centimeters when measured to the center of its slightly domed roof. Because of the height of the structure it was not possible to eye the highest point properly, which may well have approximated two hundred centimeters. The circumference and diameter of the *dulab* measured 335 centimeters and 120 centimeters respectively, its opening (presumably to be closed with a—now missing—wooden door) measuring 55 centimeters high and 50 centimeters wide. The grain storage column itself measured 265.5 centimeters in circumference, an access hole in the base being 22 centimeters across. Grain-storage *safat* (b) likewise contained a *dulab* for loose items. If not used for grain, the structure may possibly have been used to house chickens at night, in view of the vent holes around its lower sides. The entire structure stood 140 centimeters high, its roof being flat. The circumference and diameter of the *dulab* measured 282 centimeters and 113 centimeters respectively, the size of its opening 49 centimeters high and 43 centimeters wide but its wooden door missing. The base of the grain storage column itself measured 224.5 centimeters in circumference, an access hole in the base measuring fifteen centimeters across, the vent holes measuring four to five centimeters.

Notes to Chapter 7

1   See Appendix 1 for notes about the distribution of household visits and interviews.

2   Hopkins notes a similar lack of distinction between owned and rented holdings (1987: 61). Any impact of the 1992 Tenancy Law has not been considered here (Saad, 1999).

3   Amounts in Egyptian pounds reflect 1999 prices. At that time, 1 US$ was approximately equal to LE3.4.

4   After Hopkins (1987: 61) and Hopkins and Westergaard (1998: ix).

5   This position is made possible because Ahmad is not solely dependent on income from agriculture. For the same reason, there was also no evidence that Ahmad availed himself of advance payments or cash loans offered by the sugar factory during the early stages of the growing season to help him cover costs, as reported by Mitchell (1998a: 25). Requiring some cost-cutting, he pays all expenses from his other sources of income, which allows him to look forward to being paid in full at harvest time.

6   Similarly, one elderly widow in her responses as often as possible sang the praises of President Mubarak, thinking that the researcher was a journalist who would surely report everything she said. For other instances of popular understandings of government knowledge, often mediated by print or electronic media, see Lila Abu-Lughod (1998: 150).

7   For an account of such documents, see Nielsen (1998).

8   Accounts of examples requiring the traditional dispute settlement mechanism to be activated may be found in Fakhouri (1987: 111–12) and Hopkins (1987: 165–69). More recently, Nielsen (1998) and Zayed (1998) have provided insights into the mechanics of these 'Reconciliation Councils' and some of the political aspects of local governance they comprise. The detail of proceedings in which such customary law is carried out will, in keeping with their 'vernacular' arrangements, be subject to some degree of inter-regional variability. In the case of al-Qurna, the sociopolitical legitimacy of Shaykh Tayyeb located in the spiritual leadership of his family, the centrality of the mosque at al-Hasasna as the locus of jurisprudence, and the resulting absence of such institutions as *rizka* money (Fakhouri, 1987: 110) appear to be features that distinguish the Theban foothills from other known cases. A more detailed study of Qurnawi *majlis 'urfi* practices remains to be undertaken.

9   Even so, the market does seem an accepted venue where contact between men and women can be established. One informant recounted how he himself was addressed by a married woman with child at whom he had been looking in the market, asking him why he was doing so. His response was that he was not interested in her, in order to prevent trouble if his looking was considered offensive. When it was put to him that her question could have implied that she was unhappy with her husband and that she

was interested in him, the response was that such was not necessarily so, "as maybe there could be something wrong with her clothing and she wanted to find out about it." It would seem, nevertheless, that such excuses provide a vehicle for people to establish initial contact, facilitating mutual recognition and renewed contact on a later occasion.

10   Which is not to say that other communities do not also take pride in the efficacy of their dispute settlement mechanism: "many pointed out to me how good it was that in Musha people had a way of sitting down to thresh out their problems so that they did not degenerate into violence; they used words instead of fighting" (Hopkins, 1987: 167).

11   During previous illiterate generations, *wajib* obligations were not recorded but remembered. Population density being less, one's extended *wajib* group might count no more than twenty or thirty families or individuals. Gifts were more standardized and easier to remember, consisting of tea, obelisk- and brick-shaped sugar (*sukkar gomma* and *sukkar gawakin*), and wheat or flour measured in *ruba* (a grain measure equivalent to 8.25 litres). Most people might give only half or one piaster, which was easier to remember. A rich person might give five piasters. Even if amounts were forgotten, people would still remember who came and women could ask the person concerned. Until the late 1980s, money was paid by guests who came to the *zawiya* to celebrate weddings or circumcisions, the money to be paid at the washing place before entering, the amount recorded, and a cigarette offered as a token of welcome. Called *kharz*, this process of collecting *wajib* was discontinued because it was "like asking for baksheesh," because people decided not to come and eat because of the money involved, it caused shame if a man were hungry but had insufficient money on him, and people did not respond to the invitation if they could not afford it.

12   *Wajib* commitments for Badawi during the summer of 1999 ranged from LE20 (comprising five kilograms of sugar, three packets of tea, and LE10 cash) for the wedding of a distant neighbor's daughter, to LE139.50 for the wedding of his next-door neighbor's son and the wedding of Sayyed 'Abd al-Rasul, both taking place in the same week. The *wajib* gifts for the latter two weddings were to be significant, as these constituted repayment of the gifts received by Badawi's family upon the return from hospital of Mahmud, his brother. Apart from twenty-one packets of tea and thirty-five kilograms of sugar, and his own cash gift of LE40, *wajib* also included LE40 given on behalf of Badawi's two young daughters and representing an investment in their own weddings in many years' time. To finance such amounts from a small monthly government wage, Badawi is dependent on his peddler work at the nearby tomb of Ramose. He may purchase the tea and sugar on credit from a small grocery store operated by one of his neighbors, he may solicit his brother's contributions through mediation by his mother, or he may

borrow money from a third party. Were Badawi to approach a third person to borrow money, this person's body language would convey the outcome of his decision: rubbing eyes and forehead would signify approval, scratching the back of the head a refusal.

13   Contrasting with Belzoni and Rhind, the observations made by another Egyptologist, William Adams, who in his monumental Nubian study gave a comprehensive overview of the levels of spirituality he encountered there, much of which applies to al-Qurna, demonstrate how practicing field archaeologists can also fruitfully engage in activities that are rather more ethnographic in nature, in the process clarifying why Belzoni never saw his mosque: "Apart from the annual celebrations at certain Shaykhs' tombs, most public worship takes place in 'mosques' belonging to the various orders, which are called zawiya mosques. They are very seldom distinguished by minarets or other features of liturgical architecture; often they are simple enclosures of mud or straw, with or without a roof. In them are performed not only the orthodox Friday prayers but traditional devotions (dhikr) prescribed for the orders to which they belong" (Adams, 1977: 574–76).

Notes to Chapter 8

1   Preferring the winter months for Egyptological fieldwork, foreign archaeologists working in Egypt traditionally refer to the time span of their annual excavations as 'seasons.'

2   This section of mud-brick wall is all that remains of one of the towers that formed part of John Gardner Wilkinson's tomb house. In the absence of Yanni's house—demolished in March 2009—it stands as a small but significant fragment of Egyptological history, which now may be equally at risk of demolition. Once gone, it will only survive in the pictorial representations contained in the Egyptological documentary historical records left by Robert Hay, Karl Richard Lepsius, William Prinsep, Henry Rhind, and John Gardner Wilkinson himself.

3   Archaeologists' west bank headquarters include (roughly from south to north) German Archaeological Institute House, Mond and Davies House (used by SCA inspectors), Polish House (formerly Metropolitan House), Theodore Davis House, Japanese Excavation House, and Carter House, also known as Castle Carter. This building is not Castle Carter I, located behind the *taftish*, the west bank antiquities inspectorate office near the temple of Madinat Habu, but Carter's second house, Castle Carter II, built by him during the winter of 1910–11 and located at the opposite end of the necropolis, at the northern extremity of Dra' Abu al-Naga. Stoppelaere House, designed by Hassan Fathy and built on top of the hill of 'Ilwat al-Diban in 1950, is sometimes mistaken for Castle Carter II, which is located

at its foot (James, 1992: 158; also compare Reeves and Taylor, 1992: 104 with Steele, 1997: 90, 94–95).

4   One view holds that "You can't have donkeys and cows in a world-class archeological site" (Jenkins, 1999). Many others would agree that the presence of Qurnawi has "proven disastrous to the survival of the tombs . . . because of the deleterious impact of the village upon the stability and preservation of the tombs (due to theft, erosion, building, and vandalism)" (Piccione, 1997).

5   As Weigall put it: "I here name him a thief, for officially that is his designation; but there is no sting in the word, nor is any insult intended. By all cultured persons the robbery of antiquities must be regarded as a grave offence, and one which has to be checked. But the point is ethical; and what has the Theban to do with ethics?" (Weigall, 1923: 258–59).

6   Carter Notebook 17, autobiographical sketch XI, "The Finding of the Tomb of Amenophis I." I am very grateful to the late T.G.H. 'Harry' James, former Keeper of Egyptian Antiquities at the British Museum and biographer of Howard Carter, for faxing me in 1999 his photocopies of the pages containing Carter's dealings with Gad Hassan. The autobiographical sketches were written by Carter later in life. As a literary source they are undated, other than their internal dates associated with specific incidents recounted. The episode of Gad Hassan is dated "in the late spring of 1912," although James' annotations suggest this should be winter 1910–1911 or spring 1911. For his general comments on their primary historical value, and their "tiresome" and "vexing" internally inconsistent chronology, see James (1992: 2). The autobiographical sketches are contained in Carter Notebooks 15–17, one of the extant sets of which is held at the Griffith Institute, the University of Oxford. I am grateful to Dr. Jaromír Málek, the archivist, for permission to use this material. A broader survey of Carter's interaction with Qurnawi as reflected in his manuscripts remains to be undertaken.

7   In Carter's Notebook 16, autobiographical sketch V, 'Summer life and a Tale from the Coffee-hearth,' he describes how he viewed his interaction with the local community to benefit his work as chief inspector of antiquities for Upper Egypt, despite criticism from other government officials: "So to while away the darker nights, when the pestilential gnats and midges tired me out of all patience, I occasionally indulged in the diversions of the Omdah's Mandarah ("guest-house"). There in the evenings the selectives of the village—the sheikhs and the fathers of the people—are generally gathered, and contrasting with these a fair representation of the community. I must admit, however, that this practice was liable to serious criticism: some colleagues in the government service frowned upon it as a bad habit. They thought it degrading! But whether that be a fact or not, what I found was so valuable in this practice, or study, if it can be called such, was that it

thereby brought me into contact with the people with whom I had to deal. It enabled me to study their manners and customs, and there can be no doubt that by it I acquired to a large extent their good opinion and at least some of their confidence." It was in this company that Carter was introduced to Qurnawi storytelling. His account of the "Tale of the Rat and the Snake" is reproduced in Appendix 4.

8   Stories abound among Qurnawi that involve allegations of Qufti stealing, Qufti coming forward to be paid twice, and Qufti generally getting rich on antiquities. Informants indicated that because of such instances, the use of Qufti workers and *ra'is* ceased some "twenty-five, twenty-seven years ago" (that is, around the mid-1970s). Kent Weeks offers a more pragmatic account, arguing that workers from Quft have moved into other professions and have effectively outgrown more recent developments in archaeological fieldwork practice (Weeks, 1989: 188–89). Possibly both accounts are true and represent related developments.

9   Following Egypt's independence from Britain in 1922, Egyptology and the culture and history of ancient Egypt were being appropriated by the forces of nationalism in Egypt itself. The discovery of the tomb of Tutankhamun during that same year was a powerful catalyst in that direction, if only for the symbolic qualities of that discovery in the context of emerging post-colonial British–Egyptian relations. The nationalist Wafd Party of Sa'd Zaghlul's inspired takeover of the tomb of Tutankhamun in 1924 represents the first tangible politically inspired appropriation of an archaeological site and, at least in terms of the practical implications for archaeologists, now stands as the birth of nationalist archaeology in modern Egypt (James, 1992: 274–306; Reid, 1985: 237). Since nationalism and colonialism are both sides of the same coin, the fact that such an event could occur in the first place was as much due to the maturation of national political sentiments as it was to archaeologists' control over, and reticence to let go of, a domain that they had historically viewed as representing an exclusively western prerogative (Colla, 2007; Meskell, 2000; Reid, 1985, 1997, 2002).

10 A first attempt at documenting the history of the Supreme Council of Antiquities (the name created in 1994, for what started in 1858 as the Service des antiquités and, after 1971, the Egyptian Antiquities Organization) is the paper by Dodson (1999). A comprehensive treatment still needs to be written. Other than Dodson, the history of Egyptian government-sponsored protection of antiquities must be distilled from the existing but periodically discontinued pages of *Annales du service des antiquités de l'Égypte* (ASAE) and a variety of dispersed works of which Bierbrier (1995), David (1994, 1999), and Khater (1960) are examples. Given the deterioration of record-keeping following the 1952 Revolution (virtually absent for Egyptian work done in the Valley of the Kings, according to American archaeologists working

there), it remains to be seen whether that task can still be accomplished. For studies of the indigenization of academic Egyptology in Egypt during the postcolonial period, in the context of which the operations of the variously named Egyptian governmental antiquities bodies must also be considered, see the work of Donald Malcolm Reid (1985, 1997, 2002).

11   In the period following the Luxor Massacre, twenty-five Supreme Council of Antiquities guards were on twenty-four-hour duty in the Valley of the Kings, reinforced at night by five armed SCA guards. During the day five security guards working for the Ministry of the Interior also patrolled the Valley. In addition, up to thirty army personnel kept around-the-clock watch from two army tents high up on the mountain. These have since become permanent army surveillance posts.

12   During the weeks when fieldwork observations also focused on the activities of the group of restorers working in TT41, the antiquities inspector failed to turn up on the following dates: June 19, 20, 27; July 6, 7, 8, 10, 14.

13   This is not to say that their work only involves traditional means, as suggested by the list of chemical substances used in the restoration process. Although this study is not about the technical aspects of ancient Egyptian tomb restoration, the process employed by Qurnawi restorers is nevertheless a locally practiced craft that merges traditional and modern technologies. The following extract from field notes dated August 1, 1999, serves to provide a flavor of this particular aspect of Qurnawi involvement with the archaeological landscape of al-Hurubat: "Other than the inspector and *ra'is* Abdu-Sittar, six restorers were present, three absent. Previously the team included also two girl trainees and two casual workers called 'pass boys' responsible for handing instruments to the restorers and washing the *heba* matrix. The ceiling is still black from fires even after cleaning with acetone and possibly suggestive of earlier Coptic occupation, but the blackening is widespread throughout the tomb, possibly so widespread that one wonders if this is the result from localized hearths alone. The fires mentioned by James Bruce in 1769 come to mind. The restoration is executed with an instinctive eye for what is ancient, even if the tomb's religious or art-historical significance is not understood. The tomb courtyard was previously open, but is now covered with a roof on steel supports. Yet, a mud patch, anciently used to shore up the façade to the left of the door, has been left in situ. There are several unfinished niches, possibly the beginnings of side rooms and left as they were found, their origins unclear: they could be unfinished parts of the original design; evidence of past robbers digging in promising areas; incomplete tomb extension after usurpation for use by secondary occupants; natural cave-in; or excavation associated with past human occupation. Where these areas are unstable, supports are built by cementing limestone pieces in place and rendering the

resulting surface. This task is not specific to the person doing it, and there are no distinct specializations within the team: 'each can do everybody's job.' Deep wall-surface damage is repaired by inserting small limestone pieces into the natural *heba* matrix. Small holes are filled with jute and epoxy resin. All wall-surface repairs are left slightly recessed, their color matching the surrounding areas. Small cracks and loose surface decorations are stabilized with epoxy resins, using a hypodermic needle. The work is tastefully done, a newly reconstructed door inclining to the top. The ancient tomb was never finished, as indicated by incomplete statues in the forecourt. One is still in a beautiful condition, and was strengthened by pouring a two-component hardener ('Ciba Speciality Chemicals, Performance Polymers, Hardeners HY1092 and HV1338 mixed 1/1') between the statue and its backing surface, effectively gluing it to the rock behind, the side gaps between the statue and the wall surface filled first. Qurnawi pride themselves in the stamp of approval given by Dr. Karl Seyfried, who worked on this tomb with Professor Jan Assmann, when here in April. Other restoration materials noted: CIBA-GEIGY EP-CA resin mix with hardener 1:1, for heavier stone; Beriman Primal Acrylic Emulsion 100% AC 33, Originale Rohm & Haas CTS, Prodotti Attrezature e Impianuti al servizio del restauro, colour additive for cement; OKAY Extra white plastic Poly Vinyl Acetate (PVA) dispersion adhesives; Polarite colouring fixative; acetone; ABC Araldite; jute."

14 Despite the stated objectives to provide an outlet for excavation reports by Egyptians, the list of seventeen contributors to the 1998 edition of *Annales du service des antiquités de l'Égypte* only includes four Egyptian names (ASAE, 1998: v, vii).

15 A typical four-year archaeology bachelor's degree at Sohag University covers during the first year: Egyptology, Islamic history of Egypt, prehistory, archaeology, hieroglyphic writing and ancient Egyptian languages, and English. During the second year students specialize by choosing between Islamic archaeology or Egyptology. In Egyptology, during subsequent years subjects include German, hieroglyphic writing and ancient Egyptian languages, including Hieratic, archaeology, and Egyptian history.

16 Other than simply hearsay, even if from an (undisclosed) Egyptologist, Kampp simply lists TT34 by name, location, and date (Kampp, 1996: 224), the lack of any other documentation indeed indicating that this was a previously unpublished (and therefore unexcavated) tomb.

17 Members of the family today also take pride in the existence of a gold medallion, struck to honor the family for their discovery and now claimed to be in the Louvre. Asked by the government of the day what he would like in return for his discovery, Muhammad 'Abd al-Rasul requested a gold coin with his image, expecting it to be used as currency and in general circulation.

18   This discussion is based on fieldwork interviews with foreign archaeological missions working on the west bank, supplemented by a questionnaire
relating to various aspects of archaeologists' labor relations with Qurnawi
that was distributed among the Egyptological community. The use of local
informants during social-anthropological research in al-Qurna, by virtue of
the archaeological qualities of the place, requires that the body of informants
with knowledge of local conditions ought not be limited to Qurnawi alone—
asking pertinent questions of Egyptologists both in person and through
cyberspace seemed an equally valid approach. To obtain a representative and
balanced perspective it was thought desirable that the information provided
by Qurnawi should be complemented with whatever records the archaeologists might have kept on their side of the labor relations they engage in
with members of the local community. The questionnaire was designed as
a follow-up to some of the discussions held with archaeologists working in
the necropolis at the time of fieldwork, as well as to obtain information from
missions that were not available at that time. Some of the questions will have
been sensitive. Making statements about operational arrangements, which
invariably involve members of the SCA, was something that western Egyptologists would not be inclined to view as overly beneficial to the safeguarding
of their concessions. While this was indeed confirmed by some respondents,
it will likely also have been a reason behind the limited number of responses
ultimately received. Thirty-two questionnaires were sent via mail and email,
and another thirty were handed out during an Egyptological conference
at the British Museum, London, in September 2003. Beyond face-to-face
fieldwork interviews, the questionnaires yielded a total of seven responses.
Separate from the questionnaire, but in content overlapping with it, were
email exchanges with two further Egyptologists. Because of the delicate
nature of some of the responses received, the authorship of the quotations
obtained from these responses and used here will not be further identified.
The limited number of responses received prevents us from presenting comprehensive findings. Such may in any case not have been feasible, as gathering sufficient data toward that end would involve a rather different sort of
project. However, presented as individual case studies, the data offered here
nevertheless carry weight for the type of practices they represent.

19   By which it is meant that some artifacts or ancient materials may escape eventual quantification and analysis. Even so, Egyptologists claim they get a bad
press from archaeologists working in Europe on account of "poor technique"
and "going for the goodies" at a loss to other aspects of stratigraphy and
general methodological precision. Egyptologists counter that archaeologists
working in regions where the quantity of materials uncovered is much less
cannot visualize the volume involved with a Noble Tomb excavation: thirty-
five thousand fragments of artifacts and materials apart from pottery sherds.

The numbers involved make Egyptology a "science of compromise," where arbitrary stratigraphy levels of twenty centimeters in depth may be established, at a loss of more scientific archaeology. Foreign team members will accompany Qurnawi excavators working in tomb shafts to assess changes in stratigraphy or finds that may be indicative of chronological changes.

20   During 2001 and 2002, the Egyptian pound would have traded at approximately LE3.97 and LE4.50 for US$1 respectively.

21   Using an average exchange rate for this ten-year period of LE5.55 for GBP1, £64,000 would convert to LE355,200 for ten years or LE35,520 per archaeological season lasting between four and six weeks each. If we assume that roughly one-third of this may have been toward the cost of airfares and hotel expenses for the principal mission members, as well as equipment purchased elsewhere, then this would leave an operating budget to be spent locally in the order of LE23,680. This is roughly what was spent by Mission 1A, the figure of LE24,000 thus representing a reasonable average for a medium- to large-scale archaeological season. In actual terms, the seasonal expenditure for Mission 3 would have been higher, as all local labor would have been concentrated in six seasons (1993–98) rather than ten. Although, taken this way, labor costs seem on the high side, the field director indicated that it was not possible to be more precise "without a lot of work."

22   For an account of the international trade in antiquities and fine arts, see Watson (1997). For attempts at restitution to source countries of the artifacts involved, see Waxman (2008).

23   Edited both for clarity and to remove any language use that might disclose the nationality of the respondent.

24   The expression 'by injection' is used to indicate the telling of some little half-truth or gossip, which, when spreading throughout the community, will pick up pace and eventually serve to incriminate the intended target. Antiquities-related subject matter is also used toward this purpose and thus, when receiving such accounts second- or third-hand, one may never be sure what the facts of the matter are.

25   The identity of the tomb owner and its TT number have been withheld here in order to disguise the nationality of the foreign archaeological mission responsible for excavating this tomb.

26   Mummiform *shabti*s or 'answerers' are ancient Egyptian funerary figurines intended to perform duties on behalf of the deceased in the hereafter when called upon.

Notes to Chapter 9

1   His chapter is also exceptional for the differing sentiments he expresses, including the sometimes condescending style reminiscent of earlier years: "One cannot imagine a more desolate, unromantic robbers' den. As if from

a falcon's lair facing the naked rock-desert, they look down upon perspiring tourists from all countries on earth. . . . All relations that can be entered into with them can only result in [their money] being coaxed out of them as fast and as thoroughly as possible." Yet, as an art historian he remains sympathetic of their overt ability: "they were industrious people, quiet, dedicated masters of their trade. I have often observed them with collegial respect" (Lange, 1952: 145, 151).

2   'Alabaster' is the contemporary generic term used for the semi-translucent globular calcite stoneware inspired by ancient Egyptian calcite perfume vessels. Termed 'alabastron' or 'alabastrum' by Greeks and Romans, and also known as 'Egyptian alabaster' or 'calcite alabaster,' calcite (calcium carbonate, $CaCO_3$) is distinct from true 'alabaster,' which is a calcium sulphite ($CaSO_4$). The etymology of the word alabaster is still debated among philologists (Eyma, 2007).

3   Obtained from any suitable material such as lightbulbs and empty whiskey bottles, the latter collected by Luxor hotel workers who sell them for this purpose to west bank artisans.

4   Entry in Fieldwork Diary, 'Izbit al-Ward, January 21, 1998: 447.

5   Commission is paid to the guide who brings the tourist to the artist concerned. Without the sharing of earnings through commission entitlements, a guide would have no incentive to give artists this kind of unexpected business. Payments will vary depending on general economic conditions, but can be expected to be anywhere between 20 and 50 percent, inflating the artist's price by as much.

6   Use of the turn of phrase 'an antique land' here was inspired by Amitav Ghosh (1992). Ghosh may similarly have found inspiration in the opening line of Percy Bysshe Shelley's poem "Ozymandias": "I met a traveler from an antique land."

7   Other artists commented that Sayyed's lifestyle and interests included smoking *bangu*, marijuana, and taking "medicines" ("Barconal"), claiming that it "did not allow him to concentrate or spend much time doing his work" and suggesting a degree of addiction. The taking of drugs for recreational purposes appears not uncommon on the west bank. Other than *bangu* and not infrequent references to medical prescription drugs, one elderly Hurubati was known to be an occasional opium user.

8   Entry in Fieldwork Diary, 'Izbit al-Ward, January 18–19, 1998: 398, 414. A camera containing film with photographs of Sayyed Mahmud Ali Abu-Sherifa at work was stolen while I was researching the John Gardner Wilkinson manuscripts in Oxford during February, 1998. When returning to al-Qurna in 1999, also due to the changed research focus, the opportunity to replicate those photographs was, regrettably, not taken: Sayyed Mahmud Ali Abu-Sherifa has since passed away. May the word-picture of his work given here be his epitaph.

9   The term 'distressing' comes from Richard and Sally Price's *Enigma Varia-tions* (1995: 23): "If it's anything like Africa . . . much of what's on the market today is fake and buyers have to be very, very savvy. I shan't bore you with anecdotes from my own trips to Abidjan, but it's common knowledge that a trader in Ivory Coast will take a newly made mask and smoke it for a few weeks in a cooking fire, let it weather for a while in a termite hill, and rub on soot—it's the process more technically known as 'distressing.' Then he'll tell the buyer that the mask has 'been danced,' which of course gives it much greater market value." Richard and Sally Price's work is grounded in their research among the Afro-American Maroons, the Bush Negroes of Suriname. Reference to their work here establishes meaningful connec-tions, as the present author lived in Suriname during the 1970s. The Prices' (fictionalized) account cited here is in turn based on James Brooke (1988).

10   "Nice scarabs are heavily treated with chloric acid, and I am still finding it strange that so many good carvings are being defaced, only to be sold not as real *antikas*, but as 'good copies.' I feel more money could be made by selling good carvings new, instead of as fake antiquities, their original beauty reduced by all these *ghubuwa* procedures and processes" (Entry in Fieldwork Diary, 'Izbit al-Ward, January 27, 1998: 507).

11   As a result of these high commission rates, allegedly much cheating takes place by the owner of the alabaster factory, disguising any payments made in US dollars, and only paying commission over claimed sales in Egyptian pounds.

12   The 1981 World Bank–funded ADL study indicates that there were then only "four or five showroom/workshops on the west bank" (ADL, 1981a: XIII–13) and that "products are made in the home and sold to the alabaster 'factories' on the west bank or to other wholesalers and retailers" (ADL, 1981a: XII–8).

13   Staff working inside will speak English, French, German, or Italian, cater-ing to the nationality of the visitor. Their stories are designed to achieve maximum prices at the expense of even the most basic qualities of a piece: light soapstone is said to be alabaster, fired soapstone is basalt, an so on, the marketing principle being that alabaster will attract a higher price than soapstone. The account is given weight by holding a light-bulb inside or behind the item to demonstrate the translucence of gray soapstone which is therefore pronounced as real alabaster, while the opacity of green soapstone devalues it to a cheap imitation made of gypsum. For his efforts, a salesman may earn between LE150 and LE250 for ten days' work, depending on busi-ness generally and any commission obtained from a particularly good sale.

14   As far as the original appearance of such alabaster factories during the 1970s is concerned, there is probably a degree of truth in these stories. The trade in antiquities was only prohibited by Law No. 117 of 1983, Article 7 (EAO, 1984), and antiquities shops openly offering items for sale could still

be found to hold pieces of importance as late as 1975 (Habachi, 1979: 32, 40). Antiquities police were concerned with damage inflicted upon tombs by extractive antiquities thefts, but they allowed, or at least turned a blind eye to, the sale of items discovered privately.

15 The World Bank–funded ADL study (1981a: III–3–5; 1983: II–8, 9) established relative visitation densities and visitation times for the west bank archaeological sites, with percentages expressing the number of tourists arriving on the west bank (=100 percent) visiting a particular site. The ADL Tourist Survey of visitors took place in June and July of 1981 (ADL, 1983: II–10), with visitiation density for the Noble Tombs area assessed at 10 percent, the visitors on average spending only thirty minutes there. Despite the summertime survey and probable real-time fluctuations, the unfavorable position of the Noble Tombs visitation numbers when compared with other high-density west bank archaeological sites may be taken to realistically reflect the relative interests of international tour-group visitors to the Theban Necropolis.

16 Badawi is not interested in investing in some higher-priced carvings on which he might make a larger profit. Cheap soapstone scarabs or cats represented only a small investment during times when he could afford them, and while sold to tourists for relatively little, they did guarantee a reasonably quick turnover, something that would be more difficult to achieve with more expensive pieces, and thereby offering him the surety of some near-predictable extra income to make ends meet.

17 Peddlers, who sell books of postcards only in the Valley of the Kings and whose wares represent no threat to tour guides' commissions, acknowledge that they often benefit from tour guides' explanations about certain tombs, the postcards of which tourists will be more inclined to buy as a result.

Notes to Chapter 10

1   For a medical account of traditional fertility-related beliefs and practices see Harer (1981). The definitive study on this subject is Inhorn (1994).

2   Question twenty-two in the list of questions asked during household interviews.

3   Egyptologists remain undecided about the origin or significance of cigar-shaped grinding-grooves visible on the walls and columns of temples on the Theban west bank and elsewhere in Egypt. These grooves may range in size from fifteen centimeters to in excess of thirty centimeters, suggesting the continual use of one and the same spot over time. While impossible to prove, at least some of these may have been associated with procuring ancient materials for application in fertility beliefs, although other uses, for instance the sharpening of digging sticks or plow parts used in agricultural contexts, may also be a possibility. Even so, not all such temple

structures are necessarily found in contexts where previous agricultural use was dominant, if it occurred at all, such as, for example, the Temple of Isis on the island of Philae (before the permanent inundation of that island and the relocation of the temple to nearby Agilka Island in Lake Nasser by UNESCO during the 1970s).

4   However, tomb visitation for fertility purposes may have an unanticipated educational benefit, with some women commenting that once in the Valley of the Queens, "they may also visit other tombs there, just to see."

5   Apart from this example, fears associated with the evil eye may encompass any personal, domestic, or business concerns: a lady broke her shoe when passing the house of a certain Azeb, the person in the village claimed to have the evil eye; a wife would hesitate to reveal the number of her geese for fear Azeb might overhear it and his knowledge of her wealth bring her bad luck; a taxi driver had his engine burst into flames near the west bank ticket office when one of his passengers was Azeb. The author experienced first-hand the reality of people's fears about such claimed unsolicited malevolence while taking photographs at a wedding. A newly loaded unexposed film of thirty-six frames suddenly and inexplicably rewound itself into its cartridge after just fourteen shots, resulting in a degree of anxiety on the part of the photographer, who now only had one unexposed film left to document proceedings. Given that the camera was new, malfunction seemed an unlikely cause. When he was told by Badawi the following day that Azeb was in the crowd and his jealousy was likely to have caused the problem, the experience provided an interesting perspective on fieldwork discussions on related topics that took place during May 1999. According to Badawi's mother, boys or girls obtain the evil eye when taken off the breast for a single week at age one or eighteen months, then offered the breast again: weaning a child must be done *alatul*, 'straight away,' for which it is recommended to crush an aspirin and put the powder on and around the nipple, the bitter taste weaning the infant for good after three days. (Field Notes and Fieldwork Diary, al-Hurubat, May, 1999).

6   Injection: Cevagine (ascorbic acid 1.0g, analgin 1.0g). Medication: tablets of Migaura (=metaclopramide hydrochloride 5mg, paracetamol 500mg) and *Motinorm suspension* (gastroprokinetic and antiemetic, each 5 ml contains domperidone 5 mg) (Field Notes, al-Hurubat, May 26, 1999).

7   Called *habb al-baraka*, a fingertip sample left an unpleasant and oily taste in the mouth.

8   See "'Secret knowledge': *Antikas* and the trade in illicit antiquities."

9   There is a historical basis for such accounts. Gaston Maspero recounts how his workers claimed invisible beings *("afrîts")* pulled them by the arm when descending the corridors and passages of the Theban Necropolis (Maspero, 1911: 165).

10   Yet there is evidence that there was once a rich oral literary corpus in existence in the villages of the Theban west bank, as is evidenced by such actual stories as "The Parable of the Sultan's Lion" recounted by Rhind (1862: 305–307); "The Tale of the Rat and the Snake" as told to Carter and his reference to recitations containing "a deal of history and romance" (Appendix 4; James, 1992: 94); Maspero's reference to stories "partly satirical, partly sentimental" (1911: 202–203); and the existence of "songs for every occasion" mentioned by Goneim (in Cottrell, 1950: 145–46). Never published before, and despite James' assessment that Carter's account of tales told to him over local coffee hearths is "somewhat 'literary' and contrived" (James, 1992: 95), "The Tale of the Rat and the Snake" has been included in Appendix 4. When asked about stories during fieldwork, informants appeared reticent to respond, arguably because of the political overtones of at least some of this material. If not too late, this corpus should be explored and recorded as part of a much-needed oral history project.

11   Several cases were encountered where children had made it through to high school or agricultural school, but were still incapable of reading and writing. In the case of Ahmad Muhammad Ahmad's son Muhammad, who was unable to write even his name, it was alleged that teachers had passed the boy through the primary school years in order to get rid of him. In another case, it was claimed that the minister for education wants everyone to pass in order to protect his own position.

12   Television now also serves to reinforce this message, although the emphasis will be less on antiquities than on advancing aspects of a national 'civics' program. Beyond disseminating ideas about "state culture" (Abu-Lughod, 1998: 150), television also perpetuates urban views about the backwardness of Upper Egyptians (Abu-Lughod, 1998). The phenomenon is not exclusive to television scriptwriters, but can also be encountered in the mainstream Cairene press, for an example of which see Rakha (1999). For a response see Van der Spek (1999a).

Notes to Chapter 11

1   Ironically, it will have been in part the demolitions-induced visual deterioration of the foothills landscape that caused the media at that time to decry al-Qurna as "derelict, hilly stretches populated by shadows," "the Egyptian countryside's most striking misfit," and "this pariah of villages" (Rakha, 1999: 16).

2   This statement combines a selection of responses offered by Hurubati during household interviews.

3   The name reflects the domed architecture of a shaykh's tomb.

4   On January 17, 1998, four people died at al-Tarif during a riot between Qurnawi and police which had its origins in housing and demolition issues. Also see EOHR, 1998.

5   The traditional dispute settlement process is also recognized by both the Luxor and west bank police force: "If there is a problem Shaykh Tayyeb fixes it and not the police. Some Christian people may go to the police, but if they do, the police will still contact Shaykh Tayyeb."

6   Qurnawi will say *"Allah bas!"* (God alone is sufficient), meaning that they have a personal relationship with God and do not need any mediation on the part of a Sufi shaykh. Asked why others nevertheless do, the general response is that people like Shaykh Tayyeb or Shaykh Saleh may teach you "how to pray," and that "according to the Qur'an, God does not look for your body but your heart; if your heart is good you can be close to God directly. If your heart is not so good, God is not so close. If you stop doing bad things and want to be close to God, then the *dhikr* and the prayer ways of different shaykhs can help."

7   Such was still in evidence in 1996 when seventy Qurnawi families from the Hurubat area signed a petition to the government (Simpson, 1997; see Appendix 5).

8   A process of community consultation was still in place during the mid-1990s, resulting in the distribution to foothills families of a leaflet containing a map and explanatory text of the new settlement that had been agreed to (Simpson, 2003: 249).

9   The history of those relocation initiatives could be the subject of a book in its own right. They date back to the mid-1940s, when renowned architect Hassan Fathy constructed the beginnings of his revolutionary 'New Qurna' concept of mud-brick Nubian-inspired vernacular architecture, for which see Fathy (1963; 1973). Later, after the failure of his project, a number of academic studies, social surveys, architectural design initiatives, and consultancy studies put forward ideas and designs that were never fully implemented (see, for example, ADL, 1983; Eldin Ibrahim Mohamed, 1995; Husseen 1995; LCC, 1992; Rashed, 1994; SPAAC, 1995). Severe flooding in 1994 prompted the construction by both army and private developers of the beginnings of new settlements: al-Suyul and al-Qubbawi in the desert north of the foothills and west of al-Tarif. Following the Luxor Massacre in November 1997, a review of security arrangements for the tourist zone resulted in the construction of a large base for army and security personnel at al-Suyul. Thus, the earlier core of flood emergency accommodation came to serve as a nucleus for later adjoining developments. In this sense, al-Suyul was never going to merely serve the immediate need of emergency relief, but contained within itself the seeds of ongoing west bank urbanization. Following the architectural design work of the mid-1990s and further design work by the engineering faculty at Helwan University, during 1999 the al-Qubbawi site was enlarged and prepared to accommodate a new village that was built during the next several years. Wholesale relocations from

the foothills to the new village commenced in December 2006, bringing to a close what had been a long and in many ways complex and convoluted process. In all these developments, alongside such accidents of history as the fallout of the 1997 terrorist attack and other political variables, the 'Act of God' 1994 flooding episode was a driving force. The sudden presence of new communities facilitated the initial and ongoing moves away from the foothills, and helped build the political momentum to further develop the desert west of al-Tarif and proceed with wholesale relocation. As a result, there are now three identifiable new communities: al-Qubbawi, its original domed but small houses increasingly built over with the standard concrete and red-brick two- or three-story buildings that can be found anywhere in Egypt; al-Suyul, the original 'flood' village that was gradually expanded to accommodate families who opted to relocate voluntarily; and Qurna al-Gedida, 'New Qurna,' the most recent complex of houses adjoining the al-Qubbawi site.

10   "Gurnah is demolished. The scene of ruined homes is that of a heavily bombarded war zone." Observation made by a dissenting SCA official, January 17, 2007, personal communication, identity withheld, used with permission.

11   According to a senior international heritage management NGO official: "Even if we do not consider the primary issue of the people living there, from a strictly archaeological point of view what has happened is terrible, as bulldozers have slashed through layers and layers of archaeological remains, probably going back to pharaonic times. Not even archaeology can justify what has been done to Qurna. What was there to discover and learn is gone." Personal communication, March 22, 2007, identity withheld, used with permission.

12   Caroline Simpson, in an email to the members of the Egyptologists' Electronic Forum, March 27, 2009.

13   ASTENE, the Cambridge-based Association for the Study of Travel in Egypt and the Near East, had pledged to provide funds and, through its membership links with British Museum Egyptologists, the relevant historical and archaeological expertise.

14   The three mosques at al-Hurubat, al-Hasasna, and al-'Atyat were demolished by Supreme Council of Antiquities and Luxor City Council personnel on September 23, 2010, thus removing the last vestiges of the foothills' contemporary spiritual character.

15   For a more elaborate discussion, see Van der Spek (2003a).

16   The term "activist" is used by Hawass (2009: 268).

17   Although not stated in so many words, the idea of a west bank open-air museum is not a new one and can be traced back to Gaston Maspero, director of the Service des antiquités between 1881 and 1886 and 1899 and 1914: "I hope that by advancing gradually we will succeed in returning

the entire hill to its past appearance but the task is more difficult than one thinks" (1912: XXXIV). Yet the concept that the necropolis was ever devoid of human activity is historically flawed. Occupation of at least a part of the foothills is evidenced in the existence of the ancient workmen's village of Dayr al-Madina (Lesko, 1994; Romer, 1984). While people did not actually live inside the cemeteries, the presence and diversity of human activity nevertheless suggests the degree of movement that took place there. Such is evidenced in the coming and going of family members of a deceased person or their appointed "Ka-servant—a priest learned in mortuary ceremonies, who was also the manager of the estates with which he endowed his tomb" (Winlock, 1942: 57), performing the ritual duties expected in the religious calendar. Such regular and periodic visits constituted a degree of occupancy of the necropolis, as some of these duties "called for night and day attendance, [and] there were times when the Ka-servant camped out at the tomb for several days on end" (Winlock, 1942: 57; James, 1962: 2).

18   See Hawass (2009: 266).

19   The very mandate of the SCA is closely linked with Egypt being a signatory State party to the 1972 United Nations World Heritage Convention: Article 5 of the World Heritage Convention stipulates the several conditions that are to ensure that "effective and active measures are taken for the protection, conservation and presentation of the cultural and natural heritage on its territory," including "one or more services for the protection, conservation and presentation of the cultural and natural heritage with an appropriate staff and possessing the means to discharge their functions" (UNESCO: 1972, Article 5b).

20   This is not the first time that issues surrounding al-Qurna have caused observers to express themselves in critical terms about Egyptian antiquities officials and this writer finds himself in respectable company. Hassan Fathy, the renowned Egyptian architect who designed and built the first relocation village during the 1940s, would later reflect on his experiences by commenting: "I have often heard responsible officials refer to the peasants as sons of dogs and say that the only way to handle them is to build them houses of any sort and bulldoze the old ones. The Department of Antiquities made no attempt to gain the cooperation of the peasants, and even seemed sometimes to side with them in opposing the scheme. The attitude of department personnel was one of callous brutality to the peasants in private talk among themselves, and timid procrastination in practice" (Fathy, 1973: 187).

21   Although not further developed in the preceding chapters (but see Van der Spek, 2007: 179–80), the tension that exists between the emphasized pharaonic character of the Theban Necropolis and the recent destruction of the history and cultural expression of its social landscape may be

reconciled by the phenomenological understanding of landscapes as pioneered by Christopher Tilley (1994) and Barbara Bender (1998; 2002) in their analyses of archaeological sites. The phenomenological approach with its "differentially understood" and "conflict-ridden" spaces, "created, reproduced and transformed in relation to previously constructed spaces provided and established from the past" (Tilley, 1994: 11), naturally evolves into the "dissonant heritage" model developed by Tunbridge and Ashworth (1996), where "the outcomes of the model described . . . are clearly not attempting any accurate revelation of the past as a fixed and describable truth. Heritage is obviously not the totality of the history of a place or even facets of that totality, expressed through preserved and presented artifacts and interpretations. It is, to restate the argument, a created phenomenon continuously recreated anew according to changing attitudes and demands" (Tunbridge and Ashworth, 1996: 10–11).

22   ICOMOS is the International Council on Monuments and Sites, an expert body of heritage managers, conservationists, architects, and engineers providing UNESCO with technical advice regarding the listing and maintenance of properties nominated for and/or included in the World Heritage List (UNESCO, 2008: 9–10).

23   For examples see Fonquernie (1995), Braun (2001), and Michaelides and Dauge (2008).

24   See UNESCO (1999) and restated by Michaelides and Dauge (2008: 7), both based on recommendations first articulated in Van der Spek, 1998c: 180.

25   Since the inscription of Thebes and its necropolis on the World Heritage List in 1979, the World Heritage Committee has examined and adopted decisions on its state of conservation in 1997, 1998, 2001, 2006, and 2007. For an overview see Michaelides and Dauge (2008). For an example see UNESCO (1999).

26   The concise assessment made by Michaelides and Dauge points to how a model heritage management plan for the area should have been approached and is painful for both the lost opportunity and the loss of history and culture that hides between its lines: "The information made available demonstrates that while the [changes in Luxor are] very much about cleaning up, improving image and conditions for tourists, renewal, sanitization etc., it is not about protecting the Outstanding Universal Value of the site. As a result, little attention has been given as to how best to maintain the complex set of historic layers that underlie the Thebes inscription on the List, and that indeed many significant parts of the site are being needlessly discarded. The demolition of some of the structures near Karnak, the later urban settlements between the two temples and of substantial parts of Gurnah are neither acceptable approaches within

contemporary conservation theory (which demands that changes be limited to only those essential to meet critical functional needs, and here, only where this can be done without loss to heritage values), nor respectful of the property's Outstanding Universal Value. Even if some of these places are not what would be described as 'antiquities,' they should be protected as being indissociably connected to the development of the site, and therefore worthy of the strongest protection efforts. In particular, the loss of Gurnah, whose residents have provided the bulk of the excavation effort at Thebes from the 19th century forward, would involve loss of a place of great importance within the original nomination. Removal of the population of Gurnah, and reduction of the village to a few surviving designated (and empty) historic br'' 'ings is an act that goes against all the principles of conservation. ICOMOS would note that in 1998, and then in 2001, the Bureau of the World Heritage Committee had recommended the 'launching of a co-operation programme encompassing geological, archaeological and geographical surveys and mapping, anthropological studies, assessment of the historical and cultural landscape qualities of the foothills and of the presence of Gurnah village in the site' and that the Bureau had also recommended 'the postponement of any further transfer of the population of Gurnah until these investigations had taken place'" (Michaelides and Dauge, 2008: 7).

27   In case of longer-term research, specific applications are required, for both residence purposes and security clearance. Research permits for archaeological research are issued through the SCA. Research permits for other research disciplines are issued through the Ministry of Higher Education (MHE). In case of the latter, the MHE would arrange affiliation with an academic relevant to the field of inquiry. SCA- and MHE-sponsored security clearance can take up to three months to arrange, while the MHE is known to disallow permits for social science research by foreigners. The complexity of arranging suitable research documentation is indicated by Gaffney (1994: 10), but appears not specific to foreigners: "some of these official papers are still in the process of approval. In reality I did my fieldwork without or with the minimum official approval, which was mainly because of personal contacts. The unofficial approval of the key persons helped" (Rashed, 1994: 228).

28   Based on limited oral-historical investigations, Caroline Simpson postulates a settlement history that saw people move from the *saff* tombs at al-Tarif to the northern foothills of Dra' Abu al-Naga, while the southern foothills communities originated from Old Qurna, the area of the Seti I Temple. She accepts as plausible that the past two hundred years will have seen the development of new ways, but also accepts that it "could be argued that the grouping of families in their communities on Dra' Abu al-Naga replicated whatever went

on in the multi-roomed *saffs*" (personal communication). It may be too late now to obtain any substantive oral-historical data on these issues.

29   Helwan University consulting engineers interviewed in 1999 expressed themselves in bitter terms about their dealings with the Luxor City Council following their removal as project supervisors. The following listed issues occur in the transcript of the record of interview: (1) The Luxor City Council sought to interfere in time frames and the development of architectural designs, questioning the need for nine house styles and instead wanting three; (2) Helwan University project managers refused to sign payments to contractors with bills LE870,000 and LE1.5 million in excess of their calculations. They were overruled by the then Luxor governor, who subsequently arranged for the Luxor City Council to take over the supervision and resulting in (3) contractors now being government contractors: "it is all an inside job"; (4) the Luxor City Council argued it had the right number and caliber of staff to take over the supervision and so cut costs. According to Helwan University, that might be true for a single two-story building, but not a project of this scope; (5) according to Helwan University, government architects and engineers work to different standards. They work from nine in the morning to two in the afternoon; they are not permanently on site and often work only part-time on government contracts because of other (university teaching and private consulting) commitments; (6) "As a result there is now no quality control. Back filling of excavated areas which should be done at fifty centimeters compacted, is now executed at three to four meters uncompacted. This will eventually lead to cracking walls. The designs will not be changed. Uncompacted soil can be rectified by increasing the structural building strength, chemical injection or re-excavation, but it is not possible to do all. The area affected by uncompacted material is 30–35%. It will only be rectified if there is external supervision. But the contractor is not voluntarily going to criticize his own work and make corrections. He will proceed according to his own plans" (Field Notes, Cairo, September 14, 1999).

30   The invitation extended by the SCA leadership to those who have been critical of the relocation to come and visit the new village certainly suggests that the SCA views Qurna al-Gedida as a model village (Hawass, 2009: 267–68). However, the question remains if a 'model village' was indeed possible. The original designs of the mid-1990s were costed in July 1999 by Usman Ahmad Usman Arab Contractors at LE350 million. The previous secretary general of the SCA, Dr. Gaballa Ali Gaballa, projected the cost at around LE500 million (Jenkins, 1999), but what was eventually spent was LE180 million (Hawass, 2009: 267). Ideas about Qurna al-Gedida being a 'model village' may acquire a degree of credibility when placed next to the observation that the houses in the necropolis were "not well built or kept up" (Hawass, 2009: 267), but what is not stated is that the often derelict situation directly

resulted from the restrictions imposed by Antiquities Law No. 117, which prohibited maintenance and renovation of those very houses. Such arguments sound at best ingenuous. Claims made by the secretary general of the SCA about the preservation of the architectural landscape of the necropolis have also proven to be incorrect. The architectural and historical integrity of the four SCA-protected Qurna Discovery properties had already been heavily compromised by the destruction of the 'Yanni House' and the bulldozing of the intact cluster of historically significant earthen storage structures in the courtyard of the adjoining tomb house during March and April 2009. The decision by the secretary general of the SCA to order the destruction of the two remaining buildings during May 2010 also suggests that the promises made to supposedly guarantee their protection and preservation were again, at best, ingenuous. Additionally, there is no evidence that "25 of the most historic buildings . . . chosen to remain as an important witness to the more modern history of the area" were ever selected and preserved (Hawass, 2009: 267–68). The reality is that—in contravention of UNESCO recommendations—no suitable assessment was ever made to identify which these historic buildings were. Those that would have qualified, to name just a few, include: the 'Abd al-Rasul house; the 'Yanni House'; the house of the *'umda* in Hurubat; some of the multi-dwelling compounds there; several of the tomb houses with associated surviving utilitarian mud storage features; a representative sample of the foothills' characteristic contemporary pilgrimage (hajj) wall paintings (for which see Parker and Neal, 1995); and a sample of the unique vernacular styles defined by the hillside contours as could be found in Dra' Abu al-Naga. These were demolished nonetheless. The future of the community at Qurnat Mara'i remains unclear. In November 2009, a parcel of empty houses at Qurna al-Gedida still awaited occupation, but villagers have opposed moving to the northern communities on the grounds of their economic (agricultural) identification with the south. One antiquities inspector claimed that the houses at Qurnat Mara'i are being preserved "for the film industry."

Notes to the Appendices

1   See EOHR (1998) and US State Department (1999, 2000, 2001).
2   English translation of the French version of the original Italian text as provided by Carla Burri (1971: 79–83). © Institut français d'archéologie orientale, reproduced by permission.

Bibliography

Abd al-Salam, Shadi, and Roberto Rossellini. 1969. *The Night of Counting the Years* (motion picture; original title *al-Mumya*). Cairo: Egyptian Cinema General Organization.

Abu-Lughod, Lila. 1998. "Television and the Virtues of Education: Upper Egyptian Encounters with State Culture." In Nicholas Hopkins and Kirsten Westergaard, eds. *Directions of Change in Rural Egypt.* Cairo: American University in Cairo Press.

Adams, William Y. 1977. *Nubia: Corridor to Africa.* Princeton, NJ: Princeton University Press.

ADL (Arthur D. Little International Inc.) 1981a. "Study on Visitor Management and Associated Investments on the West Bank of the Nile at Luxor." Interim Report. Unpublished Consultants' Report. Arthur D. Little International Inc., Egyptian Ministry of Tourism and Civil Aviation, Cairo.

————. 1981b. "Study on Visitor Management and Associated Investments on the West Bank of the Nile at Luxor. Technical Appendix." Interim Report. Unpublished Consultants' Report. Arthur D. Little International Inc. Egyptian Ministry of Tourism and Civil Aviation, Cairo.

————. 1983. "Study on Visitor Management and Associated Investments on the West Bank of the Nile at Luxor. Final Report." Unpublished Consultants' Report. Arthur D. Little International Inc. Egyptian Ministry of Tourism and Civil Aviation, Cairo.

Ammoun, Denise. 1993. *Égypte des mains magiques: Artisanat traditionnel et contemporain.* Cairo: Institut français d'archéologie orientale.

Arnaudiès, Alain, and Wadie Boutros. 1996. *Lexique pratique des chantiers de fouilles et de restauration. Français—Égyptien, Égyptien—Français.* Bibliothèque Générale XV. Cairo: Institut français d'archéologie orientale.

Arnold, Dieter. 1976. *Gräber des Alten und Mittleren Reiches in El-Tarif.* Plan der Nekropole von Josef Dorner. Archäologische Veröffentlichungen 17. Deutsches Archäologisches Institut, Abteilung Kairo. Mainz: Verlag Philipp von Zabern.

ASAE (Annales du service des antiquités de l'Égypte). 1998. *Annales du service des antiquités de l'Égypte.* Vol. 73. Cairo: Département des Publications Scientifiques du C.S.A.

Assmann, Jan. 1991. *Das Grab des Amenemope (TT41),* Theben III. Mainz: Verlag Philipp von Zabern.

Atia, Tarek, and Sherif Sonbol. 1999. *Mulid!—Carnivals of Faith.* Cairo: American University in Cairo Press.

Ayrout, Henry Habib. 1938. *The Fellaheen.* Repr., Boston: Beacon Press, 1963.

Barakat, Halim. 1993. *The Arab World: Society, Culture, and State.* Berkeley: University of California Press.

Barsum, Laila K. n.d. *The Comprehensive Development for the City of Luxor Project (CDCL).* Sponsored by the Ministry of Housing, Utilities, and Urban Communities (MHUUC) and the United Nations Development Program (UNDP). Cairo: Ministry of Housing, Utilities, and Urban Communities.

BBC (British Broadcasting Corporation). 2002. "Egypt Feud Ends in Carnage," *BBC News,* August 10. http://news.bbc.co.uk/1/hi/world/middle_east/2185164.stm (accessed on November 23, 2010).

Belzoni, G. 1820. *Narrative of the Operations and Recent Discoveries within the Pyramids, Temples, Tombs, and Excavations, in Egypt and Nubia; and of a Journey to the Coast of the Red Sea, in Search of the Ancient Berenice; and Another to the Oasis of Jupiter Ammon.* London: John Murray.

Bender, Barbara. 1998. *Stonehenge: Making Space.* Oxford: Berg.

———. 2002. "Time and Landscape." *Current Anthropology* 43, August–October, supplement: S103–S111.

Bierbrier, M.L. 1995. *Who was Who in Egyptology.* 3rd ed. London: Egypt Exploration Society.

Binder, Tony. 1914. "Village in the Desert, Upper Egypt." Postcard based on mixed media (charcoal and water color) drawing by the artist, signed "Tony Binder Luxor 1914." Wide-Wide World Series, Picturesque Egypt, Series XVI, "Photogravure." Postcard no. 4338. London: Raphael Tuck and Sons.

———. 1926. "A Golden View of the Theban Hills opposite Luxor." Postcard based on aquarelle by the artist, signed "Binder 1926." Postcard no. 35. Luxor: Gaddis and Seif.

Blackman, Winifred S. 1927. *The Fellahin of Upper Egypt*. Repr., London: Frank Cass and Co. Ltd., 1968.

Bond, George C., and Angela Gilliam. 1994. *Social Construction of the Past: Representation as Power*. One World Archaeology series, 24. London: Routledge.

Bonomi GIA. Bonomi Manuscripts. A collection of unpublished personal papers of Joseph Bonomi for the period March 25, 1829 to May 26, 1834. Held at the Griffith Institute, University of Oxford.

Bonomi MSS. Bonomi Manuscripts. A collection of unpublished personal papers of Joseph Bonomi, privately owned by one of his descendants.

Borghouts, Joris F. 1994. "Magical Practices among the Villagers." In Leonard H. Lesko, ed. *Pharaoh's Worker: The Villagers of Deir el Medina*. Ithaca, NY: Cornell University Press.

Bourdieu, Pierre. 1977. *Outline of a Theory of Practice*. Cambridge: Cambridge University Press.

Braun, J.P. 2001. *La question des villages de Qurna installés sur les tombes des Nobles de la Nécropole de Thèbes (Egypte)*. UNESCO-Commissioned Report. Paris: ICOMOS.

Breasted, James Henry. 1916. *A History of Egypt; From the Earliest Times to the Persian Conquest*. New York: Charles Scribner's Sons.

Brooke, James. 1988. "Ivory Coast: Faced with a Shrinking Supply of Authentic Art, African Dealers Peddle the Illusion." *New York Times*, April 17.

Browne, William George. 1799. *Travels in Africa, Egypt, and Syria, from the Year 1792 to 1798*. London: T. Cadell and W. Davies Junior.

Bruce, James of Kinnaird Esq. F.R.S. 1790. *Travels to Discover the Source of the Nile, in the Years 1768, 1769, 1770, 1771, 1772, and 1773, in Five Volumes*. Vol. 1. London: G.G.J. and J. Robinson.

Budge, E.A. Wallis. 1920. *By Nile and Tigris: A Narrative of Journeys in Egypt and Mesopotamia on Behalf of the British Museum between the Years 1886 and 1913*. Vol. 2. London: John Murray.

Burckhardt, John Lewis. 1819. *Travels in Nubia*. Repr. London: John Murray.

Burri, Carla. 1971. "Le Voyage en Égypte du Vénitien Anonyme: Août-Septembre 1589." In Carla Burri and Serge Sauneron, eds. *Voyages en Egypte des années 1589, 1590 & 1591: Le Vénitien anonyme—Le Seigneur de Villamont—Le Hollandais Jan Sommer*. Cairo: Institut français d'archéologie orientale du Caire.

Cailliaud, F. 1821. *Voyage à l'oasis de Thèbes et dans les déserts situés à l'Orient et à l'Occident de la Thébaïde fait pendant les années 1815, 1816, 1817 et 1818*. Paris: Edition Jomard.

Carnarvon, Earl of, and Howard Carter. 1912. *Five Years' Exploration at Thebes: A Record of Work Done 1907–1911*. London: Oxford University Press.

Carter, Howard. n.d. "Autobiographical sketches." Carter Notebooks 15–17. Oxford: The Griffith Institute, the University of Oxford.

———. 1901. "Report on Work Done at the Ramesseum During the Years 1900–1901." *ASAE* 2:193–95, plates I–II.

———. 1902. "Report on the Robbery of the Tomb of Amenophis II, Biban el Moluk." *ASAE* 3:115–21.

Carter, Howard, and A.C. Mace. 1923. *The Tomb of Tut.Ankh.Amen*. Vol. 1. Repr., New York: Cooper Square Publishers, Inc., 1963.

Caselli, Giovanni, and Alberto Guido Rossi. 1992. *Egypt*. London: Flint River Press Ltd.

Ceram, C.W. 1966. *Hands on the Past*. New York: Alfred A. Knopf, Inc.

Champollion, Jean-François. 1973. *Lettres écrites d'Égypte et de Nubie en 1828 et 1829*. Genève: Slatkine Reprints. First published 1833 by Firmin Didot Frères, Libraires.

Chih, Rachida. 1997a. "*Zâwiya, sâha* et *rawda*: Développement et rôle des lieux de sociabilités soufies en Egypte." *Annales Islamologiques* 31:1–14. Cairo.

———. 1997b. "Entre tradition soufie et réformisme muselman: La littérature hagiographique dans le soufisme égyptien contemporain." *Egypte-monde arabe*. Première série, 29: 23–36. Cairo.

———. 1998. "The Basis of Authority in Contemporary Egyptian Sufism: Succession and Spiritual Transmission in the *Khalwatiyya* Order." Paper presented at "Authority, Sainthood and Heredity," Middle East Studies Association conference, Chicago, December 3–5.

———. 2000. *Le soufisme au quotidien: Confréries d'Égypte au XXe siècle*. Paris: Sindbad/Actes-sud.

Clarke, Somers. 1912. *Christian Antiquities in the Nile Valley: A Contribution towards the Study of the Ancient Churches*. Oxford: Clarendon Press.

Clayton, Peter A. 1982. *The Rediscovery of Ancient Egypt: Artists and Travellers in the 19th Century*. London: Thames and Hudson.

Colla, Elliott. 2000. "Shadi 'Abd al-Salam's *al-Mumiya*: Ambivalence and the Egyptian Nation State." In Ali Abdullatif Ahmida, ed. *Beyond Colonialism and Nationalism in the Maghreb: History, Culture, and Politics*. New York: Palgrave.

————. 2007. *Conflicted Antiquities: Egyptology, Egyptomania, Egyptian Modernity*. Durham, NC: Duke University Press.

Commission des Sciences et Arts d'Égypte. 1802. *Description de l'Égypte: Publiée par les ordres de Napoléon Bonaparte*. Repr. Cologne: Benedikt Taschen Verlag GmbH, 1994.

Conner, Patrick. 1984. *The Overland Route of William Prinsep (1794–1874): A Pictorial Record of his Journey across the Desert from Koseir to Luxor and Down the Nile to Cairo in 1842*. Catalogue 37, Martyn Gregory Gallery. London: Martyn Gregory.

Cook, Robin. 1979. *Sphinx*. Repr. London: Pan Books Ltd., 1980.

Coquin, Rene-Georges, and Maurice Martin. 1991. "Dayr al-Amir Tadrus." In Aziz S. Atiya, *The Coptic Encyclopedia*. Vol. 3: 717–18. New York: Macmillan Publishing Company.

Cottrell, Leonard. 1950. *The Lost Pharaohs*. Repr. London: Pan Books, 1972.

Critchfield, Richard. 1978. *Shahhat: An Egyptian*. Repr. Cairo: American University in Cairo Press, 1988.

Dannenfeldt, Karl H. 1959. "Egypt and Egyptian Antiquities in the Renaissance." *Studies in the Renaissance* 6:7–27. Available online: http://www.jstor.org/.

————. 1985. "Egyptian Mumia: The Sixteenth Century Experience and Debate." *Sixteenth Century Journal* 16 (2): 163–80. Available online: http://www.jstor.org/.

Darnell, Deborah, and John Coleman Darnell. 1996. "The Luxor-Farshût Desert Road Survey: The Oriental Institute of the University of Chicago." *Bulletin de Liaison du Groupe International d'Étude de la Céramique Égyptienne* (BCE) 19:36–48.

————. 1997. "New Inscriptions of the Late First Intermediate Period from the Theban Western Desert and the Beginnings of the Northern Expansion of the Eleventh Dynasty." *Journal of Near Eastern Studies* 56 (4): 241–58.

D'Athanasi, Giovanni. 1836. *A Brief Account of the Researches and Discoveries in Upper Egypt, Made under the Direction of Henry Salt, Esq. To Which is Added a Detailed Catalogue of Mr. Salt's Collection of Egyptian Antiquities; Illustrated with Twelve Engravings of Some of the Most Interesting Objects, and an Enumeration of the Articles Purchased for the British Museum.* London: John Hearne.

Dauber, Maximilien. 1994. *Egypte: Un village au bord du Nil.* Avignon: Espaces, Éditions A. Barthélemy.

D'Auria, Sue, Peter Lacovara, and Catharine H. Roehrig. 1988. *Mummies and Magic: The Funerary Arts of Ancient Egypt.* Boston: Museum of Fine Arts.

David, Ann Rosalie, and Eddie Tapp. 1984. *Evidence Embalmed: Modern Medicine and the Mummies of Ancient Egypt.* Manchester: Manchester University Press.

David, Elisabeth. 1994. *Mariette Pacha, 1821–1881.* Bibliothèque de l'Égypte ancienne. Paris: Pygmalion/G. Watelet.

———. 1999. *Gaston Maspero, 1846–1916: Le gentleman égyptologue.* Bibliothèque de l'Egypte ancienne. Paris: Pygmalion/G. Watelet.

Denon, Vivant. 1803. *Travels in Upper and Lower Egypt (in Company with Several Divisions of the French Army, during the Campaigns of General Bonaparte in That Country; and Published with His Immediate Patronage).* Translated by Arthur Aikin. Vols. 1, 2, and 3. London: Longman and Rees, Paternoster-Row, and Richard Phillips.

Desroches-Noblecourt, Christiane. 1963. *Tutankhamen: Life and Death of a Pharaoh.* London: George Rainbird Limited.

Dodson, Aidan. 1999. "Protecting the Past: The First Century of the Egyptian Antiquities Service." *Kmt: A Modern Journal of Ancient Egypt* 10 (2): 80–84.

Dorner, Josef. 1976. "Plan der Nekropole. Blatt 1, Blatt 2. Maszstab 1:1000." 2 loose maps inserted in back cover inside sleeve of Dieter Arnold, *Gräber des Alten und Mittleren Reiches in El-Tarif.* Archäologische Veröffentlichungen 17. Deutsches Archäologisches Institut, Abteilung Kairo. Mainz: Verlag Philipp von Zabern.

Dziobek, Eberhard, and Mahmud Abdel Raziq. 1990. *Das Grab des Sobekhotep. Theben Nr. 63.* Archäologische Veröffentlichungen 71. Deutsches Archäologisches Institut. Abteiling Kairo. Mainz am Rhein: Verlag Philipp von Zabern.

EAO. 1984. *Law No. 117 of 1983 for the Protection of Monuments, Including the Decree No. 194 of 1984 of the Minister of Culture, Head of the Supreme Council of Culture, concerning Some Resolutions related to the Execution of the Protection of Monuments Law.* Egyptian Antiquities Organization booklet. Cairo: Egyptian Antiquities Organization.

Edwards, Amelia B. 1877. *A Thousand Miles up the Nile.* Repr., London: George Routledge and Sons, Limited, 1899.

EEF Archives. 2005. "Sheikh Abd el-Qurn: Who was the Sheikh of Sheikh Abd el Qurn?" Discussion thread in Egyptologists' Electronic Forum Archives, August. Available online: //www.egyptologyforum. org/archeef/EEFarchives.html

Eickelman, Dale F. 2002. *The Middle East and Central Asia: An Anthropological Approach.* Revised edition. Upper Saddle River, NJ: Prentice Hall.

Eigner, Diethelm. 1984. *Ländliche Architektur und Siedlungsformen im Ägypten der Gegenwart.* Beitrage zur Ägyptologie, Band 6, Veröffentlichungen der Institut für Afrikanistik und Ägyptologie der Universität Wien. Nr. 30. Vienna: H. Mukarovsky.

Eldin Ibrahim Mohamed, Diaa. 1995. "Technical and Design Criteria for Community Relocation Projects." Unpublished MSc thesis, Faculty of Engineering, Department of Architecture, Cairo University.

Engelbach, R. 1924. *A Supplement to the Topographical Catalogue of the Private Tombs of Thebes (Nos. 253 to 334) with Some Notes on the Necropolis from 1913 to 1924.* Cairo: Printing Office of the French Institute of Oriental Archaeology.

EOHR. 1998. *No Way Out . . . Fears of a New Stage of Social Violence: An EOHR Report on Incidents of Spontaneous Violence in Egypt during 1998 (Damarouh, El-Fawakhreya, El-Korna, Kafr El-Geraya, Belkas and El-Hamoul).* Cairo: Egyptian Organization for Human Rights.

Eyma, Aayko. 2007. "Egyptian Loan-Words in English: 'Alabaster.'" Egyptologists' Electronic Forum (EEF). http://www.egyptologyforum. org/AEloans.html. (accessed on December 12, 2010.)

Fabian, Johannes. 1983. *Time and the Other: How Anthropology Makes Its Object.* New York: Columbia University Press.

Fagan, Brian M. 1975. *The Rape of the Nile: Tomb Robbers, Tourists, and Archaeologists in Egypt.* New York: Charles Scribner's Sons.

Fakhouri, Hani. 1987. *Kafr el-Elow: Continuity and Change in an Egyptian Community.* 2nd ed. Prospect Heights, IL: Waveland Press Inc.

Fakhry, Ahmed. 1947a. "A Report on the Inspectorate of Upper Egypt: The Theban Necropolis—Destruction of the Tombs." *ASAE* 46:31–33.

Fakhry, Ahmed. 1947b. "A Report on the Inspectorate of Upper Egypt: The Theban Necropolis—The Project of the Expropriation of the Village of Gurna." *ASAE* 46:34–35.

Fathy, Hassan. 1963. "Planning and Building in the Arab Tradition: The Village Experiment at Gourna." In Morroe Berger, ed. *The New Metropolis in the Arab World.* New Delhi: Allied Publishers.

Fathy, Hassan. 1973. *Architecture for the Poor: An Experiment in Rural Egypt.* Chicago: University of Chicago Press.

Fernea, Elizabeth Warnock, and Robert A. Fernea. 1991. *Nubian Ethnographies.* Prospect Heights, IL: Waveland Press, Inc.

Flynn, Sarah J.A. 1997. *Sir John Gardner Wilkinson: Traveller and Egyptologist 1797–1875: An Exhibition at the Bodleian Library.* Oxford: Bodleian Library.

Fonquernie, B. 1995. *Landscaping of Archaeological Sites on Lake Nasser, Thebes and around the Nubia Museum in Aswan.* International Campaign for the Establishment of the Nubia Museum in Aswan and the National Museum of Egyptian Civilization in Cairo. Report prepared for the government of the Arab Republic of Egypt by the United Nations Educational, Scientific and Cultural Organization (UNESCO). Paris: UNESCO.

Foucault, Michel. 1980. "The Eye of Power." In Colin Gordon, ed. *Power/ Knowledge: Selected Interviews and Other Writings 1972–1977.* New York: Pantheon.

Gaffney, Patrick D. 1994. *The Prophet's Pulpit: Islamic Preaching in Contemporary Egypt.* Berkeley: University of California Press.

Garcin, Jean-Claude. 1976. *Un centre musulman de la Haute-Égypte médiévale: Qus.* Textes Arabes et Études Islamiques, vol. 6. Cairo: Institut français d'archéologie orientale du Caire.

Gardiner, Alan H., and Arthur E.P. Weigall. 1913. *A Topographical Catalogue of the Private Tombs of Thebes.* London: Bernard Quaritch.

Gathercole, P., and D. Lowenthal. 1990. *The Politics of the Past.* One World Archaeology series, 12. London: Unwin Hyman.

Geertz, Clifford. 1973. "Thick Description: Toward an Interpretive Theory of Culture." In *The Interpretation of Cultures.* New York: Basic Books.

Ghosh, Amitav. 1992. *In an Antique Land*. London: Granta Books.

Gibson, Gayle. 2000-2001. "Names Matter: The Unfinished History of the Niagara Falls Mummies." *Kmt: A Modern Journal of Ancient Egypt* 11 (4): 18–29.

Ginter, Boleslaw, Janusz K. Kozlowski, and Barbara Drobniewicz. 1979. *Silexindustrien von El Târif: ein Beitrag zur Entwicklung der Prädynastischen Kulturen in Oberägypten*. Archäologische Veröffentlichungen 26, Deutsches Archäologisches Institut, Abteilung Kairo. Mainz: Verlag Philipp von Zabern.

Godlewski, Włodzimierz. 1986. *Deir el-Bahari V.: Le monastère de St Phoibammon*. Centre d'Archéologie Méditerranéenne de l'Académie Polonaise des Sciences et Centre Polonais d'Archéologie Méditerranéenne dans la République Arabe d'Égypte au Caire. Warsaw: PWN—Éditions Scientifiques de Pologne.

Golding, William. 1985. *An Egyptian Journal*. London: Faber and Faber.

Graburn, Nelson H.H. 1976. *Ethnic and Tourist Arts: Cultural Expressions from the Fourth World*. Berkeley: University of California Press.

Graefe, Erhart. 2004. "Final Reclearance of the Royal Mummies Cache, DB320." *Kmt: A Modern Journal of Ancient Egypt* 15 (3): 48–63.

Grutz, Jane Waldron. 2003. "The Lost Portfolios of Robert Hay." *Saudi Aramco World*, March/April 2–11. Houston: Aramco Services Company.

Habachi, Labib. 1979. "Unknown or Little-known Monuments of Tutankhamun and of his Viziers." In John Ruffle, G.A. Gaballa, and Kenneth A. Kitchen, eds. *Glimpses of Ancient Egypt: Studies in Honour of H.W. Fairman*. Warminster, UK: Aris and Phillips Ltd.

Habachi, Labib, and Pierre Anus. 1977. *Le Tombeau de Nay À Gournet Mar'eï (No. 271)*. Mémoires publiés par les membres de l'Institut français d'archéologie orientale du Caire. Vol. 97. Cairo: Institut français d'archéologie orientale.

Hankey, Julie. 2001. *A Passion for Egypt: Arthur Weigall, Tutankhamun and the 'Curse of the Pharaohs.'* London: Tauris Parke Paperbacks.

Hansen, Nicole B. 2004. Posting on Qurnawi in the "Export of Antiquities, Collectors and 'Bandits,'" discussion thread, Egyptologists' Electronic Forum email discussion list, June 7. Also see the EEF Archives for May 2004, *Antiquities Export Records*, http://www.egyptologyforum. org/archeef/EEFarchives.html.

Harer, Benson W. Jr. 2002–2003. "An Exercise in Exorcism, Egyptian Style: Modern Medicine Expels an Ancient Demon." *The Ostracon:*

The Journal of the Egyptian Study Society 14 (1): 2–5. First published in December 1981 in *MD Magazine*.

Hassan, Nawal. 1997a. "A Village's Right to Live." *Al-Ahram Weekly*, May 8–14.

———. 1997b. "Gourna in the Collective Memory of Modern Egypt." Public lecture, American Research Center in Egypt, September 17. Lecture presented as part of the cultural festival, "Old and New Gourna: Treasures Under Siege." The Center for Egyptian Civilization Studies, Cairo, September–December.

———. 2007. "Killing the Goose." *Egypt Today*, January. http://www.egypttoday.com/article.aspx?ArticleID=7117. (Accessed on November 29, 2010).

Hawass, Zahi. 2009. *Life in Paradise: The Noble Tombs of Thebes*. Cairo: American University in Cairo Press.

Hay MSS. Hay Manuscripts. The Collected Personal Papers of Robert Hay. The British Library, London. Including his panoramas of the Theban foothills: Add. Mss. 29,816 fol. 83–86, 103–107; Add. Mss. 29,821 fol. 2–7, 111.

Henein, Nessim Henry. 1988. *Mari Girgis: Village de Haute-Égypte*. Bibliothèque d'Étude, vol. 94. Cairo: Institut français d'archéologie orientale du Caire.

Hirsch, Eric. 1995. "Landscape: Between Place and Space." In Eric Hirsch and Michael O'Hanlon, eds. *The Anthropology of Landscape: Perspectives on Place and Space*. Oxford: Clarendon Press.

Hirsch, Eric, and Michael O'Hanlon. 1995. *Anthropology of Landscape: Perspectives on Place and Space*. Oxford: Clarendon Press.

Hivernel, Jacques. 1996. *Balat: Étude ethnologique d'une communauté rurale*. Bibliothèque d'Étude 113. Cairo: Institut français d'archéologie orientale.

Hopkins, Nicholas S. 1987. *Agrarian Transformation in Egypt*. Cairo: American University in Cairo Press.

Hopkins, Nicholas S., and Kirsten Westergaard. 1998. *Directions of Change in Rural Egypt*. Cairo: American University in Cairo Press.

Husseen, Fahmy. 1995. "Project of Relocation of People of Qurna to New al-Tarif." Unpublished private consultants' report prepared for Ministry of Housing, Utilities and Urban Communities (MHUUC). ESC Engineering Systems and Consultants, Cairo.

Ikram, Salima, and Aidan Dodson. 1998. *The Mummy in Ancient Egypt: Equipping the Dead for Eternity*. New York: Thames and Hudson.

Inhorn, Marcia C. 1994. *Quest for Conception: Gender, Infertility, and Egyptian Medical Traditions.* Philadelphia: University of Pennsylvania Press.

Irby, Charles Leonard, and James Mangles. 1823. *Travels in Egypt, Nubia, Syria and Asia Minor during the Years 1817 and 1818.* London: privately published.

James, T.G.H. 1962. *The Hekanakhte Papers and other Early Middle Kingdom Documents.* New York: Metropolitan Museum of Art Egyptian Expedition.

———. 1992. *Howard Carter: The Path to Tutankhamun.* London and New York: Kegan Paul International.

Jenkins, Siona. 1999. "Destroying Ancient Way of Life to Save Antiquities." *The Irish Times,* December 12. http://www.irishtimes.com/newspaper/world/1999/1223/99122300045.html (Accessed on November 29, 2010).

Kákosy, L. 1995. "The Soter Tomb in Thebes." In S.P. Vleeming, ed. *Hundred-Gated Thebes: Acts of a Colloquium on Thebes and the Theban Area in the Graeco-Roman Period.* Leiden: Brill.

Kampp, Friederike. 1996. *Die Thebanische Nekropole: Zum Wandel des Grabgedankens von der XVIII bis zur XX Dynastie.* Theben XIII. Mainz: Philipp von Zabern.

Khater, A. 1960. *Le régime juridique des fouilles et des antiquités en Égypte.* Recherches d'Archéologie, de Philologie et d'Histoire, Vol. 12. Cairo: Institut français d'archéologie orientale.

Kiernan, Thomas. 1975. *The Arabs: Their History, Aims and Challenge to the Industrialized World.* London: Abacus.

King, A. 1990. "Architecture, Capital and the Globalisation of Culture." In Mike Featherstone, ed. *Global Culture: Nationalism, Globalization, and Modernity.* Special Issue of *Theory, Culture and Society.* London: Sage Publications.

Kohl, P.L., and C. Fawcett, eds. 1995. *Nationalism, Politics and the Practice of Archaeology.* Cambridge: Cambridge University Press.

Lane, Edward William. 2000. *Description of Egypt: Notes and Views in Egypt and Nubia, Made during the years 1825, –26, –27, and –28: Chiefly Consisting of a Series of Descriptions and Delineations of the Monuments, Scenery, &c. of those Countries; the Views, with Few Exceptions, Made with the Camera-lucida.* Edited and with an introduction by Jason Thompson. Cairo: American University in Cairo Press.

Lange, Kurt. 1965. "Op bezoek bij de vervalsers van Dirâ Aboe 'n-Naga."
Chapter 11 in Kurt Lange, *Egypte: Wonderen en geheimen van een grote
oude cultuur*. Dutch translation of *Pyramiden, Sphinxe, Pharaonen: Wun-
der und Geheimnisse um eine grosse Kultur*. Zeist: W. de Haan. Originally
published 1952 by Hirmer Verlag in German.

Lawson, Fred H. 1981. "Rural Revolt and Provincial Society in Egypt,
1820–1824." *International Journal of Middle East Studies* 13:131–53.

———. 1992. *The Social Origins of Egyptian Expansionism during the
Muhammad 'Ali Period*. New York: Columbia University Press.

LCC. 1992. *El-Gurna Region Resident Relocation Study and New el-Tarif
Village Planning through Community Participation: Terms of Reference*.
Luxor: Luxor City Council.

Lesko, Leonard H., ed. 1994. *Pharaoh's Workers: The Villagers of Deir el
Medina*. Ithaca: Cornell University Press.

Lippman, Thomas W. 1989. *Egypt after Nasser*. New York: Paragon
House.

Lons, Veronica. 1968. *Egyptian Mythology*. Middlesex, UK: Paul Hamlyn.

MacKay, Ernest. 1916. "Note on a New Tomb (No. 260) at Drah Abu'l
Naga, Thebes." *Journal of Egyptian Archaeology* 3:125.

Madox, John. 1834. *Excursions in the Holy Land, Egypt, Nubia, Syria, etc.* 2
vols. London: Richard Bentley.

Manley, Deborah, and Peta Rée. 2001. *Henry Salt: Artist, Traveller, Diplo-
mat, Egyptologist*. London: Libri Publications Ltd.

Manniche, Lise. 1975. *Ancient Egyptian Musical Instruments*. Münchner
Ägyptologische Studien, Vol. 34. Munich: Deutscher Kunstverlag.

———. 1987. *City of the Dead: Thebes in Egypt*. London: British Museum
Publications.

———. 1988. *Lost Tombs: A Study of Certain Eighteenth Dynasty Monuments
in the Theban Necropolis*. London: Kegan Paul International Limited.

Martin, Maurice, ed. 1982a. *Claude Sicard: Oeuvres I—Lettres et Relations Inédites*. Bibliothèque d'Étude, Vol. 83. Cairo: Institut français
d'archéologie orientale du Caire.

———. 1982b. *Claude Sicard: Oeuvres II—Relations et Mémoires Imprimés*.
Bibliothèque d'Étude, Vol. 84. Cairo: Institut français d'archéologie
orientale du Caire.

Maspero, Gaston. 1881. "A Hoard of Royal Mummies." *Bulletin de
l'Institut Égyptien*. Repr., series 2, no. 2: 149–53.

———. 1889. *Les momies royales de Déir el-Bahrî*. Paris: Ernest Leroux.

————. 1911. *Egypt: Ancient Sites and Modern Scenes*. New York: D. Appleton and Company.

————, ed. 1912. *Rapports sur la marche du Service des antiquités de 1899 à 1910*. Cairo: Gouvernement Égyptien, Imprimerie Nationale.

McBryde, Isabel. 1984. *Who Owns the Past? Papers from the Annual Symposium of the Australian Academy of the Humanities*. Melbourne: Oxford University Press.

McCall, Grant. 1980. *Rapanui: Tradition and Survival on Easter Island*. Honolulu: University Press of Hawaii.

Meskell, L.M., ed. 1998a. *Archaeology under Fire: Nationalism, Politics and Heritage in the Eastern Mediterranean and Middle East*. London: Routledge.

Meskell, Lynn. 1998b. "Archaeology matters." In L. M. Meskell, ed. *Archaeology under Fire: Nationalism, Politics and Heritage in the Eastern Mediterranean and Middle East*. London: Routledge.

————. 2000. "The Politics and Practice of Archaeology in Egypt." In Anne-Marie Cantwell, Eva Friedlander, and Madeleine L. Tramm, eds. *Ethics and Anthropology: Facing Future Issues in Human Biology, Globalism, and Cultural Property*. Annals of the New York Academy of Sciences, vol. 925, 146–49. New York: The New York Academy of Sciences.

————. 2005. "Sites of Violence: Terrorism, Tourism, and Heritage in the Archaeological Present." In Lynn Meskell and Peter Pels, ed. *Embedding Ethics*. Oxford, and New York: Berg.

Michaelides, Demetrios, and Véronique Dauge. 2008. *Report of the Joint World Heritage Centre/ICOMOS Reactive Monitoring Mission to the World Heritage Site of Thebes and Its Necropolis, April 18–24, 2008*. Paris: UNESCO. Available online: http://whc.unesco.org/en/documents/100786

Migdal, Joel S. 1988. *Strong Societies and Weak States: State-Society Relations and State Capabilities in the Third World*. Princeton, NJ: Princeton University Press.

Mitchell, Timothy. 1990. "The Invention and Reinvention of the Egyptian Peasant." *International Journal of Middle East Studies* 22:129–50.

————. 1995. "Worlds Apart: An Egyptian Village and the International Tourism Industry." *Middle East Report* 25 (5): 8–11.

————. 1998a. "The Market's Place." In Nicholas Hopkins and Kirsten Westergaard, eds. *Directions of Change in Rural Egypt*. Cairo: American University in Cairo Press.

———. 1998b. "The Heritage of Violence." Conference paper presented at the sixth biennial conference of the International Association for the Study of Traditional Environments, "Manufacturing Heritage/Consuming Tradition." Cairo, December 15.

———. 2001. "Making the Nation: The Politics of Heritage in Egypt." In Nezar al-Sayyad, ed. *Consuming Tradition, Manufacturing Heritage: Global Norms and Urban Forms in the Age of Tourism.* London: Routledge.

———. 2002. *Rule of Experts: Egypt, Techno-Politics, Modernity.* Berkeley: University of California Press.

Myśliwiec, Karol. 1987. *Keramik und Kleinfunde aus der Grabung im Tempel Sethos' I. in Gurna.* Mainz am Rhein: Verlag Philipp von Zabern.

Nafie, Reem. 2004. "We'll Get Them: An Upper Egyptian Vendetta Consumes Four More Lives, Including a Groom on His Wedding Day." *Al-Ahram Weekly*, February 26–March 3.

Nielsen, Hans-Christian Korsholm. 1998. "Men of Authority—Documents of Authority: Notes on Customary Law in Upper Egypt." In Nicholas Hopkins and Kirsten Westergaard, eds. *Directions of Change in Rural Egypt.* Cairo: American University in Cairo Press.

Nightingale, Florence. 1987. *Letters from Egypt: A Journey on the Nile 1849–1850.* Selected and introduced by Anthony Sattin. London: Barrie and Jenkins.

Nims, Charles F. 1965. *Thebes of the Pharaohs: Pattern for Every City.* London: Elek Books.

Norden, F.L. 1741. "Extract From my Own Journal, Containing Part of What Passed on the 12th of December 1737, N.S. Being the 25th Day Since my Departure from Grand Cairo." In *Drawings of Some Ruins and Colossal Statues at Thebes in Egypt with an Account of the Same in a Letter to The Royal Society.* London: The Royal Society.

———. 1757. *Travels in Egypt and Nubia.* Vol. 2. London: The Royal Society.

O'Connor, David, and David P. Silverman, eds. 1995. *Ancient Egyptian Kingship.* Leiden: E.J. Brill.

Parker, Ann, and Avon Neal. 1995. *Hajj Paintings: Folk Art of the Great Pilgrimage.* Washington. D.C.: Smithsonian Institution Press.

Petrie, W.M. Flinders. 1897. *Six Temples at Thebes. 1896.* London: Bernard Quaritch.

———. 1909. *Qurneh.* British School of Archaeology in Egypt and Egyptian Research Account Fifteenth Year. London: Bernard Quaritch.

Pettigrew, Thomas Joseph. 1834. *History of Egyptian Mummies, and an Account of the Worship and Embalming of the Sacred Animals by the Egyptians; with Remarks on the Funeral Ceremonies of Different Nations, and Observations on the Mummies of the Canary Islands, of the Ancient Peruvians, Burman Priests, &c*. London: Longman, Rees, Orme, Brown, Green, and Longman.

Piccione, Peter. 1997. Caption to *Tom Van Eynde: Tombs and Village of Sheikh Abd el-Qurna, Western Thebes. The Thebes Photographic Project of the Oriental Institute, the University of Chicago*. Chicago: Oriental Institute, University of Chicago. http://oi.uchicago.edu/gallery/tve_tpp/index.php/0726_58.png?action=big&size=resize (accessed on March 7, 2010.)

Pococke, Richard. 1743. *A Description of the East, and Some Other Countries. Vol 1. Observations on Egypt*. London: W. Bowyer.

Porter, Bertha, and Rosalind L.B. Moss. 1927. *Topographical Bibliography of Ancient Egyptian Hieroglyphic Texts, Reliefs, and Paintings*. 3rd ed. Oxford: Clarendon Press.

Price, Richard, and Sally Price. 1995. *Enigma Variations*. Cambridge, MA: Harvard University Press.

al-Qalqashandi. 1963. *Qala'id al-juman fi-l-ta'rif bi qaba'il 'Arab al-zaman*. Ibrahim al-Ibiari, ed. Cairo: n.p.

Rakha, Youssef. 1999. "A Yearning for Another Country." *Al-Ahram Weekly*, 435, June 24–30.

Rashed, Ahmed Yehia M.G. el-Din. 1994. "Public Participation in the Conservation of Historical Environments: A Case Study of Luxor City, Egypt." PhD diss., Institute of Advanced Architectural Studies, University of York.

Reeves, C.N. 1990a. *Valley of the Kings: The Decline of a Royal Necropolis*. London: Kegan Paul International Limited.

———. 1990b. *The Complete Tutankhamun: The King, The Tomb, The Royal Treasure*. London: Thames and Hudson.

Reeves, Nicholas, and John H. Taylor. 1992. *Howard Carter before Tutankhamun*. London: British Museum Press.

Reeves, Nicholas, and Richard H. Wilkinson. 1996. *The Complete Valley of the Kings: Tombs and Treasures of Egypt's Greatest Pharaohs*. London: Thames and Hudson.

Reid, Donald M. 1985. "Indigenous Egyptology: The Decolonization of a Profession?" *Journal of the American Oriental Society* 105 (2): 233–46.

————. 1997. "Nationalizing the Pharaonic Past: Egyptology, Imperialism, and Egyptian Nationalism, 1922–1952." In James Jankowski and Israel Gershoni, *Rethinking Nationalism in the Arab Middle East*. New York: Columbia University Press.

————. 2002. *Whose Pharaohs? Archaeology, Museums, and Egyptian National Identity from Napoleon to World War I*. Cairo: American University in Cairo Press.

Renfrew, Colin, and Paul Bahn. 1991. *Archaeology: Theories, Methods and Practice*. London: Thames and Hudson Ltd.

Reynolds, Dwight Fletcher. 1995. *Heroic Poets, Poetic Heroes: The Ethnography of Performance in an Arabic Oral Epic Tradition*. Ithaca: Cornell University Press.

Rhind, A. Henry. 1862. *Thebes: Its Tombs and Their Tenants*. Repr. New Jersey: Gorgias Press, 2002.

Rice, Anne. 1989. *The Mummy*. London: Penguin Books.

Richardson, Robert. 1822. *Travels along the Mediterranean and Parts Adjacent in Company with the Earl of Belmore, during the Years 1816–17–18*. 2 vols. London: Cadell.

Ridley, Ronald T. 1998. *Napoleon's Proconsul in Egypt: The Life and Times of Bernardino Drovetti*. London: The Rubicon Press.

Ritner, Robert K. 1998. "Egypt Under Roman Rule: The Legacy of Ancient Egypt." In Carl F. Petry, ed. *The Cambridge History of Egypt*. Vol. 1, *Islamic Egypt 640–1517*. Cambridge: Cambridge University Press.

Roberts, Paul William. 1993. *River in the Desert: Modern Travels in Ancient Egypt*. New York: Random House.

Romer, Isabella. 1846. *A Pilgrimage to the Temples and Tombs of Egypt, Nubia and Palestine*. London: Richard Bently.

Romer, John. 1981. *Valley of the Kings: Exploring the Tombs of the Pharaohs*. New York: Henry Holt and Company, Inc.

————. 1984. *Ancient Lives: The Story of the Pharaohs' Tombmakers*. Repr., London: Phoenix Press, 2003.

Romer, John, and Elizabeth Romer. 1993. *The Rape of Tutankhamun*. London: Michael O'Mara Books Limited.

Rousillon, François, and Toni Hajal. 1998. *Un Opéra sur le Nil*. Documentary film. Planète/François Rousillon et Associés.

Saad, Reem. 1999. "State, Landlord, Parliament and Peasant: The Story of the 1992 Tenancy Law in Egypt." In Alan K. Bowman and Eugene Rogan, eds. *Agriculture in Egypt: From Pharaonic to Modern Times*. The British Academy. Oxford: Oxford University Press.

Saad, Rehab. 1998. "Verdi's Aida Moved Back to the Pyramids." *Al-Ahram Weekly*, 375, April 30–May 6, http://weekly.ahram.org.eg/1998/375/egy7.htm (accessed on November 30, 2010.)

Säve-Söderbergh, Torgny. 1987. *Temples and Tombs of Ancient Nubia: The International Rescue Campaign at Abu Simbel, Philae and Other Sites*. Paris and London: UNESCO/Thames and Hudson.

Sauneron, Serge, and Maurice Martin, eds. 1982. *Claude Sicard: Oeuvres III—Parallèle Géographique de l'Ancienne Égypte et de l'Égypte Moderne*. Bibliothèque d'Étude, Vol. 85. Cairo: Institut français d'archéologie orientale du Caire.

al-Sayyid Marsot, Afaf Lutfi. 1985. *A Short History of Modern Egypt*. Cambridge: Cambridge University Press.

Schaffner, Franklin J. 1980. *Sphinx*. Film production. Hollywood: Orion Pictures Company.

Schama, Simon. 1995. *Landscape and Memory*. London: HarperCollins Publishers.

Silberman, Neil Asher. 1989. *Between Past and Present: Archaeology, Ideology, and Nationalism in the Modern Middle East*. New York: Henry Holt and Company.

Simpson, Caroline. 1997. "Gourna: The End of a Symbiotic Relationship." Public lecture, American University in Cairo, November 12. Lecture presented as part of the cultural festival "Old and New Gourna: Treasures under Siege." Center for Egyptian Civilization Studies, Cairo, September–December.

———. 1999. "The Jigsaw of Qurna." Conference paper presented at the third biennial conference of the Association for the Study of Travel in Egypt and the Near East (ASTENE), Cambridge, July 15–18.

———. 2000. "Searching for the History of Qurna on Thebes." Paper presented at the American Research Center in Egypt (ARCE), Cairo, November 8.

———. 2001. "Qurna: Who Saw it Where, When, and Why?" Paper presented at the fourth biennial conference of the Association for the Study of Travel in Egypt and the Near East (ASTENE), July 11–15.

———. 2003. "Modern Qurna: Pieces of an Historical Jigsaw." In Nigel Strudwick and John H. Taylor, eds. *The Theban Necropolis: Past, Present, and Future*. Proceedings of papers presented at an international colloquium held at the British Museum, London, July 2000. London: British Museum Press.

———. 2004. Posting on Qurnawi in the "Export of Antiquities, Collectors and 'Bandits'" discussion thread. Egyptologists' Electronic Forum email discussion list, June 2. See the EEF Archives for May 2004, *Antiquities Export Records*, http://www.egyptologyforum.org/archeef/EEFarchives.html (accessed on November 30, 2010.)

———. 2010. "Qurna: More Pieces of an Unfinished History." In Z. Hawass and S. Ikram, eds. *Thebes and Beyond: Studies in Honour of Kent R. Weeks*. Cairo: Supreme Council of Antiquities.

Simpson, Caroline, and John Laven. 1997. *Gurna: Living Villages in the City of the Dead*. Traveling photographic exhibition. Unpublished accompanying introductory text and photograph captions.

Smith, B. 1985. *European Vision and the South Pacific*. New Haven, CT: Yale University Press.

Sonnini de Manoncour, Charles Nicolas Sigisbert. 1800. *Travels in Upper and Lower Egypt*. Translated by William Combe. London: J. Debrett.

SPAAC. 1995. *Demographic and Social Survey of El Qurnah Community: New al-Taref Plan for Rehousing El Qurnah Community*. Social Planning, Analysis and Administration Consultants. Final Report, March. Cairo: SPAAC.

Steegmuller, Francis, ed. 1972. *Flaubert in Egypt: A Sensibility on Tour. A Narrative Drawn from Gustave Flaubert's Travel Notes and Letters Translated from the French*. Boston: Little, Brown and Company.

Steele, James. 1997. *An Architecture for People: The Complete Works of Hassan Fathy*. Cairo: American University in Cairo Press.

Stelter, Florian. 1991. "Das oberägyptische Dorf Gurna (am Hügel von Schêch Abd el-Gurna)." Unpublished manuscript, Hamburg.

Stephens, John Lloyd. 1837. *Incidents of Travel in Egypt, Arabia Petraea, and the Holy Land*. Repr. Norman, Oklahoma: University of Oklahoma Press, 1970.

Stewart, Stanley. 1997. *Old Serpent Nile: A Journey to the Source*. London: Flamingo.

St. John, James Augustus. 1845. *Egypt and Nubia: With Illustrations by J.A. St. John*. London: Chapman and Hall.

Strudwick, Nigel. 1995. Review of Eberhard Dziobek and Mahmud Abdel Raziq's *Das Grab des Sobekhotep. Theben Nr. 63, Journal of Egyptian Archaeology* 81:263–65.

Survey of Egypt. 1922. *El Qurna, Tourist Edition, Scale 1:10,000*. Survey of Egypt map 22/229H.

———. 1924. *The Theban Necropolis, Scale 1:1,000*. Survey of Egypt map 24/285, Surveyed in 1921, Revised in 1924, Sheets D–4, D–5, D–6, D–7, E–4, and F–3.

Thompson, Jason. 1992. *Sir Gardner Wilkinson and His Circle*. Austin: University of Texas Press.

———. 1996. "Tomb-dwelling in 19th century Thebes: Sir Gardner Wilkinson's House at Sheikh Abd el Qurna." *KMT: A Modern Journal of Ancient Egypt* 7 (2): 52–59.

———. 2010. *Edward William Lane, 1801–1876: The Life of the Pioneering Egyptologist and Orientalist*. Cairo: American University in Cairo Press.

Tilley, Christopher. 1994. *A Phenomenology of Landscape: Places, Paths and Monuments*. Oxford, and Providence, RI: Berg Publishers.

Trigger, Bruce G. 1979. "Egypt and the Comparative Study of Early Civilizations." In Kent R. Weeks, ed. *Egyptology and the Social Sciences*. Cairo: American University in Cairo Press.

———. 1993. *Early Civilizations: Ancient Egypt in Context*. Cairo: American University in Cairo Press.

Tunbridge, J.E., and G.J. Ashworth. 1996. *Dissonant Heritage: The Management of the Past as a Resource in Conflict*. Chichester, UK: John Wiley and Sons.

Turnbull, Colin. 1994. "Introduction to the Pimlico Edition." In *The Mountain People*. London: Pimlico.

Ucko, P.J. 1994. "Foreword." In George C. Bond and Angela Gilliam, *Social Construction of the Past: Representation as Power*. One World Archaeology series, 24. London: Routledge.

United Nations Educational, Scientific, and Cultural Organization (UNESCO). 1972. *Convention concerning the Protection of the World Cultural and Natural Heritage*. Paris: UNESCO.

———. 1979. *Convention concerning the Protection of the World Cultural and Natural Heritage. World Heritage List. Nomination Submitted by Egypt: Ancient Thebes and Its Necropolis. CC–79/ws/39*. Paris: UNESCO.

———. 1999. *Convention concerning the Protection of the World Cultural and Natural Heritage. World Heritage Committee Twenty-second Session, Kyoto, Japan, 30 November–5 December, 1998. Report of the Rapporteur. Annex IV—Decisions of the Twenty-second Extraordinary Session of the Bureau of the World Heritage Committee (Kyoto, 28–29 November 1998) with Regard* to the State of Conservation of Properties Inscribed on the World Heritage List, Noted by the Committee: Ancient Thebes with Its Necropolis (Egypt). WHC–98/CONF.203/18, January 29. Paris: World Heritage Centre.

————. 2001. *Convention concerning the Protection of the World Cultural and Natural Heritage. Bureau of the World Heritage Committee, Twenty-fifth session, Paris, France, 25–30 June 2001. Report of the Rapporteur: V.206–211 Ancient Thebes with Its Necropolis (Egypt).* WHC–2001/CONF.205/10, August 17. Paris: World Heritage Centre.

————. 2008. *Operational Guidelines for the Implementation of the World Heritage Convention, WHC.* 08/01, January. Paris: World Heritage Centre.

US State Department. 1999, 2000, 2001. *Egypt: Country Report on Human Rights Practices for 1998, 1999, 2000.* Washington: Bureau of Democracy, Human Rights, and Labor.

Van der Spek, Kees. 1997. "Another Place, A Different West Bank . . ." *Bulletin of the Centre for Middle Eastern and Central Asian Studies (CMECAS)* 4 (1): 3–6. Canberra: Australian National University.

————. 1998a. "Culture and Change: The Case of Shaykh 'Abd al-Qurna and Dra' Abu al-Naga." Conference paper presented at "Egypt under Mubarak: Politics, Economics, and Foreign Policy." Conference held at the Centre for Middle Eastern and Central Asian Studies, Australian National University, Canberra, May 7–8.

————. 1998b. "A Tale of Two Cities: A Comparative Perspective on the Political Economy of Contemporary Heritage Management Practices in Egypt and Jordan." Conference paper presented at "The Middle East: Fifty Years On," annual conference of the Australasian Middle East Studies Association (AMESA), Centre for Middle Eastern and Central Asian Studies, Australian National University, Canberra, September 18–19.

————. 1998c. "Dead Mountain versus Living Community: The Theban Necropolis as Cultural Landscape." In W.S. Logan, C. Long, and J. Martin, eds. *Proceedings of the Third International Seminar Forum UNESCO: University and Heritage.* 176–82. Melbourne and Geelong: Deakin University.

————. 1999a. "A Living Community." *Al-Ahram Weekly* 439, July 22–28. http://weekly.ahram.org.eg/1999/439/letters.htm (accessed on November 30, 2010.)

————. 1999b. Review of *Stonehenge: Making Space* by Barbara Bender. *Canberra Anthropology* 22 (2): 92–93.

————. 2003a. "Negotiating Life in the City of the Dead: The Political Economy of Tourism, Heritage Management, Academia, and the National Interest in the Theban Necropolis, Luxor, Egypt." Paper presented at the sixth US/ICOMOS International Symposium, "Managing Conflict and Conservation in Historic Cities: Integrating Conservation with Tourism, Development and Politics." Annapolis, Maryland, April 24–26. Washington: US/ICOMOS. Available online at: http://www.scribd.com/doc/38099491/Negotiating-Life-in-the-City-of-the-Dead.

————. 2003b. "Feasts, Fertility and Fear: Qurnawi Spirituality in the Ancient Theban Landscape." Paper presented at the International Workshop on Ancient Thebes, "Sacred Spaces and Their Function through Time." British Museum, London, in conjunction with the Oriental Institute of the University of Chicago and the Department of Near Eastern Studies, Johns Hopkins University, Baltimore, at the British Museum, London, September 15–16.

————. 2004a. Posting on the Theban villagers in the "Export of Antiquities, Collectors and 'Bandits'" discussion thread. Egyptologists' Electronic Forum email discussion list, June 6. See the EEF Archives for May 2004, *Antiquities Export Records* http://www.egyptologyforum.org/archeef/EEFarchives.html (accessed on November 30, 2010.)

————. 2004b. "Making a Living in the City of the Dead: History, Life, and Work at al-Hurubat in the Necropolis of Thebes, al-Qurna, Luxor." PhD diss., Centre for Arab and Islamic Studies. Canberra: Australian National University.

————. 2007. "Feasts, Fertility, and Fear: Qurnawi Spirituality in the Ancient Theban Landscape." In Peter F. Dorman and Betsy M. Bryan, eds. *Sacred Space and Sacred Function in Ancient Thebes*. Occasional Proceedings of the Theban Workshop. Studies in Ancient Oriental Civilization (SAOC), Vol. 61. Chicago: Oriental Institute of the University of Chicago.

————. 2008. "Faked *Antikas* and 'Modern Antiques': The Production and Marketing of Tourist Art in the Theban Necropolis." *Journal of Social Archaeology* 8 (2): 163–89.

Vandorpe, K. 1995. "City of Many a Gate, Harbour for Many a Rebel: Historical and Topographical Outline of Greco-Roman Thebes." In S.P. Vleeming, ed. *Hundred-Gated Thebes: Acts of a Colloquium on Thebes and the Theban Area in the Graeco-Roman Period*. Leiden: Brill.

Van Landuyt, K. 1995. "The Soter Family: Genealogy and Onomastics." In S.P. Vleeming, ed. *Hundred-Gated Thebes: Acts of a Colloquium on Thebes and the Theban Area in the Graeco-Roman Period.* Leiden: Brill.

Vatikiotis, P.J. 1969. *The Modern History of Egypt.* London: Weidenfeld and Nicolson.

Vleeming, S.P., ed. 1995. *Hundred-Gated Thebes: Acts of a Colloquium on Thebes and the Theban Area in the Graeco-Roman Period.* Papyrologica Lugduno-Batava 27. Leiden: Brill.

Walker, Christopher. 1997. "Tourist Bloodbath Deals Blow to Mubarak." *The Times*, November 18.

Walker, Christopher, and Emad Mekay. 1997. "Britons Die in Nile Massacre: Terrorists Open Fire as Tourists Arrive at Valley of the Queens." *The Times*, November 18, 1.

Watson, Peter. 1997. *Sotheby's Inside Story.* London: Bloomsbury.

Waxman, Sharon. 2008. *Loot: The Battle over the Stolen Treasures of the Ancient World.* New York: Times Books, Henry Holt and Company.

Webster, James. 1830. *Travels through the Crimea, Turkey and Egypt; Performed During the Years 1825–1828.* 2 vols. London: Henry Colburn and Richard Bentley.

Weeks, Kent R. 1979a. "Egyptology and History." Editorial introduction to Donald B. Redford's "The Historiography of Ancient Egypt," in Kent R. Weeks, ed. *Egyptology and the Social Sciences.* Cairo: American University in Cairo Press.

———. 1979b. "Egyptology and Anthropology." Editorial introduction to Bruce G. Trigger's "Egypt and the Comparative Study of Early Civilizations." In Kent R. Weeks, ed. *Egyptology and the Social Sciences.* Cairo: American University in Cairo Press.

———. 1979c. "Art, Word, and the Egyptian World View." In Kent R. Weeks, ed. *Egyptology and the Social Sciences.* Cairo: American University in Cairo Press.

———. 1989. *The Lost Tomb.* London: Phoenix.

Weigall, Arthur. 1923. *The Glory of the Pharaohs.* London: Thornton and Butterworth.

Westbrook, Joel, Jason Williams, Robert Gardner, and William Morgan. 1995. *Egypt: Quest for Immortality.* Time-Life Video. Lost Civilisations series. Milsons Point, New South Wales, Australia: Time-Life Video and Television.

Wickett, Eleanor Elizabeth. 1993. "'*For Our Destinies*': The Funerary Laments of Upper Egypt." PhD diss., University of Pennsylvania.

———. 2010. *For the Living and the Dead: The Funerary Laments of Upper Egypt, Ancient and Modern.* Cairo: American University in Cairo Press.

Wilfong, Terry G. 1998. "The Non-Muslim Communities: Christian Communities." In Carl F. Petry, ed. *The Cambridge History of Egypt.* Vol. 1, *Islamic Egypt, 640–1517.* Cambridge: Cambridge University Press.

———. 2002. *Women of Jeme: Lives in a Coptic Town in Late Antique Egypt.* Ann Arbor: University of Michigan Press.

Wilkinson MSS. Wilkinson Manuscripts. The collected personal papers of Sir John Gardner Wilkinson, Department of Special Collections and Western Manuscripts, Bodleian Library, University of Oxford.

Wilkinson, John Gardner. 1835. *Topography of Thebes, and General View of Egypt. Being a Short Account of the Principal Objects Worthy of Notice in the Valley of the Nile, to the Second Cataract and Wadee Samneh, with the Fyoom, Oases, and Eastern Desert, from Sooez to Berenice; with Remarks on the Manners and Customs of the Ancient Egyptians and the Productions of the Country, &c. &c.* London: John Murray.

———. 1843. *Modern Egypt and Thebes: Being a Description of Egypt; Including the Information Required for Travellers in that Country.* London: John Murray.

———. 1847. *A Handbook for Travellers in Egypt.* London: John Murray.

Wilkinson, Richard H. 2003. *The Complete Gods and Goddesses of Ancient Egypt.* Cairo: American University in Cairo Press.

Wilson, John A. 1964. *Signs and Wonders upon Pharaoh: A History of American Egyptology.* Chicago and London: University of Chicago Press.

Winlock, H.E. 1942. *Excavations at Deir El Bahri 1911–1931.* New York: MacMillan Company.

Winlock, H.E., and W.E. Crum. 1926. *The Monastery of Epiphanius at Thebes. Part I: The Archaeological Material; the Literary material.* The Metropolitan Museum of Art Egyptian Expedition. Vol. 3. New York: Metropolitan Museum of Art. Repr. New York: Arno Press, 1973.

Wolf, Eric R. 1982. *Europe and the People without History.* Berkeley: University of California Press.

Zayed, Ahmed. 1998. "Culture and Mediation of Power in an Egyptian Village." In Nicholas Hopkins and Kirsten Westergaard, eds. *Directions of Change in Rural Egypt.* Cairo: American University in Cairo Press.

Index

A

al-'Ababda 51
'Ababda (tribe) 124
'Abd al-Latif 77
'Abd al-Rasul 5–7, 9–10, 27, 50–51,
  105, 141–45, 150–51, 207, 233, 249,
  280, 333, 407n9, 413–14n2, 416n12,
  422n12, 427n17, 441
    Ahmad 5, 141–42, 144
    archetype 7, 9–10, 141, 151
    control over archaeological
      workers 233
    descent 51, 407n9, 413–14n2
    discovery of DB320 Dayr al-
      Bahari Royal Cache 5–6, 9, 27,
      141, 143, 233, 414n2, 416n12
    house 142, 144, 441n30
    Muhammad 5, 141–42, 144, 233,
      427n17
    use of name as marketing
      strategy 249, 280
Abdel Raziq, Mahmud 148
Abed, Abdu-Sittar Ahmad 230,
  426n13
Abt Associated Inc. *See* consultants
Abu Shau Bridge 50, 370
Abu Sufyan 135
Abu Zayd 136
Adams, William 201, 423n13
Adman 135–36
adobe 17

See also earthen architecture
'afrit. See cosmology
Aga Ayat, Mustafa 142, 416n12
agriculture/agricultural 9, 11, 40–41,
  43, 48–50, 57, 83–85, 87–89, 91,
  97–102, 115, 118, 121–22, 131,
  147–49, 161, 164–66, 171–92, 226,
  253, 264, 300, 348, 358, 362, 370,
  421n5, 432–33n3, 434n11, 441n30
    cost-cutting 183–84, 421n5
    crops (modern). *See* crops
    crops as recorded in nineteenth
      century sources 97–99, 101
    differences between al-Qurna and
      al-Ba'irat 49, 101, 118, 121–22,
      179, 253
    farmer Ahmad 174–76, 180–84,
      186–87, 203, 225, 334, 421n5,
      434n11
    farmer Mahmud 185–88, 214, 226
    fertilizer *(nitrokima). See*
      sugarcane
    identity 102, 179
    indirect benefit from tourism 9
    inundation 48, 65, 70, 85, 88–90,
      97, 100, 180, 403n5, 433n3
    labor 173, 176–77, 179, 181–82,
      184–86
    male-female payment ratio
      182–84

collecting agents 82, 105, 219, 220, 412n11

competition and nationalism 55, 104–105, 113

declining availability during nineteenth century 55, 104–105, 113–14, 353

factor in 'pacification' 121

forced labor 112, 126

illicit dealings. *See* illegal antiquities excavations and trade

imitations. *See* art and craft production

impact on relations with al-Ba'irat 118, 122

impact on travelers' language 102

laws. *See* legislation

means of economic resilience 145–49, 353

nineteenth century sales' strategies, secrecy and pricing motivations 107–10, 113, 126

protection by legislation. *See* illegal antiquities excavation and trade: antiquities legislation

protection by jinn and *shaitan*. *See* cosmology

See also fertility practices; guards/ *ghaffir*

anthropology (anthropological, anthropologist) 8–9, 12, 14, 18, 20–21, 31–32, 53, 197, 255, 338, 355–59, 364, 368, 401n10, 402n1, 404n8, 408n4, 428n18, 439n26

cultural anthropology in the USA 31

ethnographic fieldwork. *See* fieldwork

historically informed anthropological political economy 12, 53–57. *See also* Wolf

legitimacy of ethnographic inquiry in the Theban Necropolis 5–11

relationship with Egyptology 7–11, 20–21, 31–32, 292, 338, 348, 404n8, 428n18

relationship with heritage management 349, 401n10, 408n4, 439n26

social anthropology in the UK and Europe 31

Arab conquest 22, 57, 59, 61–62, 135, 407n3, 413n1

Arab hospitality 17

Arab rebellion 69–70, 91, 126, 409n15

Arab tribal ethnic stereotype 21–22, 72–73

'arabiya 2, 164, 186, 335

'arusa 15, 167–68, 188, 254, 286–87, 398

archaeology

archaeological areas considered *terra nullius* 56

archaeological naming conventions 41–42, 45–51

crude excavation techniques during nineteenth century 110–11, 412n11

desertification of surrounding social landscape 6, 33, 348

destruction of post-pharaonic stratigraphy 13, 61, 321, 325, 327, 329, 334, 336–37

English-French nineteenth century competitive relations 55, 104–106, 112–13

excavation concession/permit 127, 223, 233, 337–38, 418n17, 428n18, 439n27

fieldwork practice 224, 230–40, 428–29n19

fieldwork vignettes 29–30

tourist art 9, 55, 247, 250, 252–54, 256, 273, 277, 356, 359
See also alabaster; ceramics: faience; limestone; soapstone; wood
Arthur D. Little. *See* consultants
artists/craftsmen 21, 114, 192, 241, 243–46, 247–87, 356, 359, 363, 389–98, 402n1 430n7–8
Abdelal Ahmad Ghalil 389
Abdu Muhammad Ahmad 266–69, 272, 390
Adham Muhammad Esaman 397
Ahmad al-Harazi 263–66, 271, 344, 392
Ahmad Mahmud Ahmad 397
Azeb Mustaffa Muhammad 393
Hassan Sayyed Muhammad (alias) 272, 344, 391
Jahalan al-Azeb al-Tayyeb Mahmud Hadraby 393, 396
Muhammad Ali Muhammad 260–63, 267, 389, 392
Sayyed Mahmud Ali Abu-Sherifa 269–71, 273, 277, 390, 396, 430n7–8
Sayyed Mahmud Ali al-Matani 395
Tayyeb Muhammad Yusuf 256–260, 275, 391
See also alabaster; ceramics: faience; *ghubuwa*; limestone; soapstone; wood
al-athar 224–33
al-'Asasif 45–46, 48–49, 93, 109, 139, 156, 175, 299–300, 304, 309, 372, 378, 405n3
Ashworth, G.J. 405n10, 438n21
'Atya 49, 86, 135
al-'Atyat 46, 49–50, 130, 132, 135, 198–99, 278, 342, 379, 436n14
Association for the Study of Travel in Egypt and the Near East (ASTENE) 409n10, 436n13

Aswan 76, 266, 269, 281
Aswan High Dam 155, 334, 401n12, 403n5
Australian National University xxviii–xxix
Ayrout, Henry Habib 403n4
al-Azhar 200–201

B
babur 161, 174, 192
Badawi
impact of Luxor Massacre 17–20
income 225–27, 276, 283
informant and research assistant 355–68
mediation by his mother 207–208, 422n12
peddler 211, 276, 283, 422n12, 432n16
SCA employee 224–33
visits to Cairo 18, 211, 226
wedding and divorce 209–10, 226, 308–309
badu. See Bedouin
badu-hadar division 62
al-Ba'irat 48–49, 87, 101, 118, 120–22, 129, 179, 190, 253
al-Bakri 76, 410n19
baksheesh 122, 128–29, 188, 237, 282, 422
Ballas 190
See also ceramics
bangu 285, 430n7
banu hilal 62
baraka 116, 200–201, 294, 296, 301, 324, 433n7
Barur (Baroor) 136
bazaar xviii, 198, 250, 257, 260, 263, 266–67, 269–72, 277–79, 283, 295
Bedouin xviii, 21–22, 62–63, 72–73, 121, 123, 140, 202, 408n8, 413n1
dispersal 63–64, 408n8
settled nomads 86, 120

Dendera 65, 74, 381
Denon, Vivant xxii, 43–44, 77, 81, 84, 86, 89, 91–93, 96–97, 103, 106, 116–17, 119–20, 127, 129, 247, 411–12n7
Desroches-Noblecourt, Christiane 24–25, 27–28, 217, 403–404n5, 404n7
  impact of her 1963 book 25
  portrayal of Qurnawi 23–28
  use of Maspero's photograph 25–26
Detroit Institute of Art 147
Dihya ibn-Musab 59
Diodorus Siculus 76
domestic space 41, 93, 133, 152, 157–69, 339, 371
  cartographic appearance 160, 165, 370–71
  construction methods 156, 158–59, 272
  footprint 41, 157, 160, 165, 370–71, 420n1
  hush 157, 163–66, 168
  in early archaeologists' and travelers' records 93–97
  layout 160–66
  phases of renewal, reconstruction and extension 159–60
  strategic use 165–66
  terms 161–66
  usage and function 160–66
  vernacular storage. *See* mud storage structures
dowlat meia 161
  See also Qurnawi waste disposal
Dra' Abu al-Naga 45–46, 48–50, 59, 85, 89, 91–93, 103–104, 196, 222, 225, 243, 277–78, 362, 370, 372, 375, 379, 406n3, 414n3, 423n3, 439n28, 441n30
Drovetti, Bernardino 90, 104, 112–13
Du Camp, Maxime 410n2

Dziobek, Eberhard 148–49

E
earthen architecture xxv, xxvii, 329, 344, 415n7
  construction methods 156, 158–59, 219, 272
  Hassan Fathy 13, 49, 406n8, 423n3, 435n9, 437n20
  materials and terms 168–69
  mud-brick 41, 101, 156, 164, 435n9
  See also vernacular architecture/vernacular; mud-storage strctures
Eastern Desert 124
economy/economic
  benefits and interests xvii, xxi–xxii, 3, 11, 40, 126, 129, 179, 187, 191, 198, 211, 216, 221, 322, 326, 339, 358, 360, 407n9, 413–14n2, 441n30
  academic inquiry xxi–xxii
  downturns 19, 171, 184, 210, 263, 266, 276, 281, 331, 360–61
  mix of formal and informal economic activity 9, 122, 171
  national political interests xix, 11, 35–36, 56, 97, 138, 149, 187, 221, 322, 331, 333–34, 336–37, 351, 403n3
  perceptions about village economics 6, 10, 20–23, 26, 41–42, 56, 99, 141, 151, 248–51, 353, 356
  tourism 3, 18, 198, 323, 333–34, 339, 356–57
  village economics and plurality of subsistence practices 5–15, 19, 97–98, 101, 139, 141, 145–49, 171–72, 175–76, 179, 223, 238–39, 248–51, 284–85, 339, 353, 357–58, 364, 416n13

education xxxi, 191, 208, 307, 316–17, 360, 366, 384, 433n4, 434n11
Edwards, Amelia 102, 112, 115
Egyptian Cartographic Survey xxiii
Egyptian Museum in Cairo 33, 37, 112, 115, 281, 403n3, 412n13
Egyptologists
  acquiescence with politically motivated heritage agenda xviii, 333, 337–38
  concerns for excavation permits 127, 337–38, 428n18
  language use reflecting British colonial worldview 130, 221–22, 429n1
Egyptologists' Electronic Forum (EEF) 406n4, 436n12
Egyptology
  academic demarcations of fields of study 8, 31, 348
  as classical and literary field of study 31
  dominance over social fieldwork surroundings 6–7, 22–23, 30–33, 47, 56–57, 99, 149, 347–48, 400n8, 425n9
  history 31
  local labor relations 219–46
  relationship with anthropology 7–11, 20–21, 31–32, 292, 338, 348, 404n8, 428n18
  relationship with anthropological archaeology in the USA 31
  relationship with social sciences 28, 31, 338, 404n8
  stereotypical perceptions of Egyptological fieldwork 6
  politicization 36, 333, 338, 402–403n3, 405n10
  west bank naming conventions 41–42, 45–51
  See also archaeology
Eickelman, Dale 53

enclave tourism 37, 331, 333
Engelbach, Reginald 152–53, 156, 165–66, 352, 415n8, 416n14, 419–20n1
  attitudes toward Qurnawi 153, 416n14, 419–20n1
  Commission of Delimitation 165–66
  encroachment 152–155, 353, 416n14, 419n1
    by non-locals 155
  expropriation and eviction 152–56, 353
    unintended consequences 154–56
  Qurnawi not informed about which tombs to be expropriated 152–53
Engineering Systems and Consultants (ESC). See consultants
Enlightenment 44, 64, 79
Esna 59, 68, 124, 257
ethnographic history/historical ethnography 11–12
European consumption of ancient Egypt 73, 79, 405n10

F
Fabian, Johannes 34
al-Fadliya irrigation canal 48–50, 189, 372
faghura 265, 392, 395, 397
faience. *See* ceramics
fake/imitation antiquities xix, 82, 114, 243, 246, 249–50, 254, 265, 271, 275, 279, 344, 353, 357, 360, 362, 431n9–10
  See also art and craft production
Fakhouri, Hani 55, 187, 421
Fakhry, Ahmed 146
feuding 133, 191–92, 199, 341, 410n1
Farouk, King 187, 412n13
Farshut 68, 124–25, 409n13–14
Fathy, Hassan. *See* earthen architecture

honor 22, 194, 202, 216

Hosni, Farouk 401n13

hospital 17, 83, 191, 193, 196, 198–99, 203, 207, 211, 362, 366, 422n12

house. *See* domestic space

Human Genome Diversity Projects 62, 408n6

human rights reports 365

Hurghada 263, 281

al-Hurubat 46, 49–51

hush. See domestic space

I

International Council on Monuments and Sites (ICOMOS) xxiii, xxviii, 337, 438n22, 439n26

illegal antiquities excavation and trade xix, 5–7, 12, 20, 23–24, 28, 41–42, 55, 62, 82, 142–44, 146, 150, 220, 222, 232, 240–46, 249, 251, 273, 278, 280, 312–14, 316, 318, 322, 348, 353, 356

> *antikas* 240–46, 256, 271–72, 279, 285, 431n10

> antiquities legislation 5, 7, 22, 152, 154, 160, 230, 248–49, 256, 323, 348, 371, 415n8, 417n15, 419n20, 431n14, 441n30

> > Law No. 14 of 1912 152, 417n15, 419n20

> > Law No. 117 of 1983 230, 323, 371, 417n15, 431n14, 441n30

> > Presidential Decree 267 of 1981 160, 371

> boundaries between legal and illegal activities 245, 255, 356

> contemporary art used for smuggling antiquities 244–46, 254–55

> damaging extractive techniques 105, 147–49, 151, 231, 240–41, 246, 249, 412n11, 432n14

Egyptologists' views 240–41

export 240, 244, 415n8, 417n15

al-Hurubat versus Dra' Abu al-Naga 243–44

imprisonment 245, 322, 417n14

in-situ specimen 246

makhazin 245–46, 275

middlemen 105, 109–110, 244

> pre-antiquities legislation 105, 109–110

> post-antiquities legislation 244

peddlers 241–44, 249–51, 254, 256, 272, 285, 344

pilfering 29–39, 237, 240, 242–44, 246, 249–50

police action 245, 322, 280–81, 283, 285–86, 322, 417n14, 432n14

Qurna as regional trading center 244

resulting changes in living standard 244–45, 278

sale strategies 244, 249–51, 272, 280

SCA inspectors implicated in illicit antiquities dealings 231–32, 245–46, 275

strategies to disguise increase in wealth 278, 431n14

supervision by SCA inspectors 245, 278

See also inspectors

inspectors 153, 219–46, 334, 336, 419n21, 426n12

> attendance at Noble Tombs 224, 227–28, 426n12

> control over local labor 233–36, 238

> disinterest 224, 231–33, 236, 426n12

> general foothills supervision 146, 245, 278, 318, 323, 426n12

materials 168–69

safat 95, 137, 166–69, 325, 420n2

sanduq 167

suma'/suwama' 167

mulid/mulid of Shaykh 'Abd al-Qurna 2, 116, 211, 213, 289–92, 303

mumiya 75–79, 103, 117–18, 274, 352, 409n17, 410n19–20, 412n9

   See also consumption: patterns

mummy-pits 103, 105, 412n10, 379–80

music/musical instruments/musicians 1–4, 200, 206, 209, 291, 303, 399n3

Muslim cemetery 50, 86–87, 116, 298, 299, 304–305, 351, 380

N

Nag' Kom Lola 49

Nag' Madinat Habu 49, 299

Nag' al-Qatr 49

Nag' al-Ramesseum 50

Nag' al-Rasayla 49, 142, 333, 372, 376–78, 407n9

Nag' al-Sahal al-Sharqi 50, 131

Nagada 190, 410n1

Nagalta 190

naghlu ummiya 317

Nasser, President Gamal Abdel 172, 187

national elections 1995 355

national political and economic interests. *See* economy: national political interests

Nazlat al-Samman 55

Nefertari 230, 260, 389

Newberry, Percy 151, 417–18n17

new communities xviii, 15, 50, 166, 221, 231, 324, 329, 331, 335, 339, 343–45, 350, 356, 370, 372, 380, 436n9

   al-Suyul 50, 200, 208, 235, 319, 323–24, 326, 339–42, 370, 372, 380, 402n13, 435–36n9

   community/outside consultation xviii, 326, 343, 435n8

community fragmentation 326, 339–40, 342, 345

community consultation 1996 leaflet 343, 435n8

homogenization 13, 287, 331, 339–40, 345–46

al-Qubbawi 50, 323, 339, 342, 370, 372, 380, 435–36n9

settlement pattern 339, 342

   See also Qurna al-Gedida

New Qurna. *See* Qurna al-Gedida

Nightingale, Florence 410n2

Nile River xvii, xviii, xxii, 39–40, 48, 65–66, 74, 88, 97, 180, 281, 409n12, 413n14

   hydrography 48

   hydrology 88

   'Qena Bend' 65–66, 75, 124, 409n13

Noble Tombs. *See* Tombs of the Nobles

Norden, Frederick Lewis 74–76, 80, 83–84, 89, 93, 116, 118–22, 124, 128–29, 411n4

Nubia 334, 401n12, 403n5, 411n5, 415n7, 423n13, 435n9

nye 291

O

O'Hanlon, Michael 44

Old Qurna 43, 50, 61, 83, 86–90, 92, 120–21, 123, 135–36, 321, 406n8, 411n6, 439n28

   connections with al-Tarif 86–90, 121

   conveniently situated 88

   destruction 81, 85–86, 88, 90, 123

   permanently deserted 43, 81, 85–86, 88–90, 136

   salvage of usable parts 90

   seasonal migration/habitation 88, 90, 100, 121

   See also Seti I Temple

opium 430n7